LUCY SIEGLE is one of Britain's leading journalists on social and environmental justice. She has written a weekly column on ethical living in the *Observer* since 2004. Exploring labour rights and the plight of workers in the Developing World moved Lucy to take a long, hard look at her own wardrobe and fashion consumerism. She has spent the last five years researching and campaigning for an alternative fashion industry that will replace turbo consumerism with sustainable and equitable style.

Meanwhile she has contributed feature and opinion pieces to publications ranging from *The Times* and the *New Statesman* to *Marie Claire* and *Grazia*, and blogs for the Huffington Post. She launched the *Observer* Ethical Awards, dubbed 'the Green Oscars', in 2005.

In 2011 her collaboration with Livia Firth and Vogue.com took her to the real Oscars as part of ethical fashion initiative the Green Carpet Challenge. A familiar face and voice on UK TV and radio, she has reported and presented on the prime-time BBC 1 programme *The One Show* since 2007. She is Visiting Professor to the University of the Arts, London.

Also by Lucy Siegle

Green Living in the Urban Jungle

TO DIE FOR

IS FASHION WEARING OUT THE WORLD?

LUCY SIEGLE

FOURTH ESTATE • *London*

First published in Great Britain in 2011 by
Fourth Estate
An imprint of HarperCollins*Publishers*
1 London Bridge Street
London SE1 9GF

www.4thestate.co.uk

The right of Lucy Siegle to be identified as the author
of this work has been asserted by her in accordance
with the Copyright, Design and Patents Act 1988

Illustrations by Claire Meharg

A catalogue record for this book is available from the British Library

ISBN 978 0 00 726409 4

Typeset in Minion by Birdy Book Design
Printed by CPI Group (UK) Ltd, Croydon, CR0 4YY

MIX
Paper from
responsible sources
FSC° C007454

FSC is a non-profit international organisation established to promote the
responsible management of the world's forests. Products carrying the FSC
label are independently certified to assure customers that they come
from forests that are managed to meet the social, economic and
ecological needs of present and future generations.

Find out more about HarperCollins and the environment at
www.harpercollins.co.uk/green

Hey Daisy darling
Don't take it all as read
Why don't you ask a few more questions instead?
I know you think that everyone should be paid what they're due
But there are people in this world who don't think like you do
They don't think like you do
And some don't think at all.

KARINE POLWART, 'Daisy',
from the album *Scribbled in Chalk* (2006)

CONTENTS

INTRODUCTION

Every year, around eighty billion garments are produced worldwide. Incredibly, when we buy one of them, we are able to learn very little about where it was made and assembled, and in what conditions. Consumers, retailers, designers and brands have a responsibility to the workers who make our fashion, but we've closed our eyes to a back story of exploitation and dangerous conditions. Every single one of our wardrobes is tainted. Seduced by the alliance of fast fashion with value prices, we've failed to notice that international trade rules and laws have their harshest impact on the most vulnerable in the supply chain. Where once cotton production was based on slavery, today's fast fashion has brought the type of working conditions outlawed in the West at the turn of the twentieth century to every Developing World town with a fabric-processing or sewing facility.

I love fashion. But I want it to excite and inspire me, not to make me really, really angry. I have watched and aided and abetted as the fashion industry and consumers have sunk deeper and deeper into a cycle of exploitation of each other, the planet and the millions of workers who toil on the global assembly line in shocking conditions. But when I took a closer look at the true environmental and social impact of the seemingly innocuous and frippery-filled industry, I came to the conclusion that enough was enough.

For anyone labouring under the misapprehension that their individual decisions are too small and too insignificant to have any influence over the status quo, I want to set you straight. As the global population swells and the amount of natural capital, particularly untouched wilderness, decreases, the planet is under unprecedented pressure. This means that it has never been more important to take wise individual decisions, as well as collective ones. It has never been more critical for us to consume with care and intelligence. It's no secret that the present rates of consumption are unsustainable, and it will come as even less of a surprise that fashion's are wildly out of kilter.

Why give fashion the time of day? Why not dress exclusively in old clothes and charity-shop finds? I've become pretty familiar with the school of thought that regards fashion as unnecessary and corrupt, the deep-green (and dare I say puritanical) doctrine that finds the very notion of fashion distasteful. But it is simply untrue to say that all fashion is superficial, needless and stupid, and to ignore the semiotics of style. The way we dress is fundamental to our self-expression.

But you can see where the distrust of fashion emanates from. We've recently shopped our way through a massive wardrobe upheaval, our buying patterns subverted by multinational businesses with the sole aim of making money for their shareholders. Almost overnight we have become used to consuming fashion with reckless, addicted abandon, buying more clothes than ever before, reversing centuries of fashion heritage, knowledge and understanding in the process. This is a revolution, and a largely unwelcome one. Strangely, given the extent to which we have altered our buying habits, there's a lack of research of this consumerist phenomenon. Which is largely why over the past five years I've taken to carrying out my own unofficial surveys. Wherever I am, and whatever story I'm covering professionally, I usually spot a fashion story. For example, sent to Manchester to do an item on women ruining their feet by wearing high heels, I was more struck by the amount young women on limited incomes were spending on 'it' bags. Our fashion frenzies over the last decade tend to give away far more than just what is or isn't on-trend.

It is a sign of the times that fashion regularly makes newspapers' front pages or business pages, even if indirectly. Today's stories are not just about Kate Moss or the size of Philip Green's yacht (or both); they are about the more prosaic stuff of fashion, such as cotton. Occasionally this leads to some arresting headlines – 'Cotton Bras are Rebounding!' for example – but what it really confirms is that, with the exception of the extractive industries and the food chain, few industries are as connected to the natural world as fashion. At its most simplistic, fashion is dependent on water, on crops such as cotton, and on a whole host of animal species. Yet the fashion industry has barely begun to factor in the consequences of its actions on habitat loss, shrinking biodiversity and climate change.

The good news is that there is a small window of opportunity in which to rescue fashion, the queen of all the creative industries. The rules are beginning to change. Garment workers are fighting back (because so many cannot continue to exist on the wages our wardrobes are willing to pay), and the conscientious consumer has the opportunity to fight alongside them. The huge retailers and brands need your custom, and the government wants you to keep shopping – but it is time to change the terms.

My fear is this: unless we as fashion-lovers and consumers assert ourselves, the industry will take the path of least resistance. The combination of the global recession and the inevitable price rises of major ingredients of the fashion supply chain, such as oil and cotton, will see the big players, the multinational brands and the giant retailers that control the UK high street, become even more ruthless in grabbing their margin. The victims will be the producers, the garment workers, and eventually you and me, as design and quality are sacrificed. I don't want that to happen.

It is a battle: our weakness has become their stock in trade. Meanwhile, their enemy is the intelligent fashion consumer who asks the right questions and buys more carefully. This book is intended to guide you towards becoming that consumer. It takes you beyond the swing tickets and into the heart of contemporary garment production to reveal the truth about materials, production, and the wardrobe lives of our clothes. It also acknowledges the good as well as the bad, and aims to help you forge a fashion future that matches your aesthetic to your ethics. Ultimately, the intention is to reconnect you with the passion and excitement that turned you into a fashion-lover in the first place.

Lucy Siegle, April 2011

1

FAT WARDROBES AND SHRINKING STYLE

How my Fashion Sense and Yours has Lost the Plot

This is not my 'beautiful' wardrobe. Every morning when I wake up I am directly confronted by my fashion history. Mistakes, corrections, good buys, bad buys, comfort buys, drunk buys: they refuse to go away. This is because my 'primary' wardrobe – as distinct from the other two wardrobes I've had to take over in the past ten years to accommodate the growing volume of my clothing collection – is opposite my bed, and the door, like a broken zipper, will no longer pull across to hide the tale of excess. If I squint I can even make out a rather nasty polyester pinafore mini-dress I used to wear in the early 1990s.

Having failed to embrace at least one fashion – the consumerist purchase-and-purge churn of the day – because I'm a bit of a hoarder, you might expect me to be more upbeat about my large collection of clothes. You could argue that my curatorial instincts should have left me with a style treasure trove that I could one day hand on to another generation of fashion lovers. Sadly, it hasn't worked out like that. In the cold light of day many of the micro trends I've 'invested in' – T-shirts with chains, a one-shouldered jump suit, and other designer lookalike items – merge to form a type of sartorial wasteland. However, it is true that my wardrobes (plural) also represent a sort of time capsule: evidence of a revolution in fashion that has changed the way we view and wear clothes forever. They have catalogued the defining macro trends of our generation, and so have a preserved-in-aspic quality about them.

My collection is testament to the extraordinary way we now consume clothes.

The fact that I tend to hang on to many of my clothes might be atypical, but the type, volume and variety in the depths of my cupboards are predictable. Despite the fact that I've spent many years greening up the rest of my life, not to mention urging readers of my newspaper column to try to do the same, for a long time my wardrobe represented a bit of a black hole. I made a few attempts to buy with a keener eye on the ecological fallout – prioritising sustainable fibres, alternative designers and labels that prioritise low environmental footprint or social-justice concepts such as Fairtrade. But I was noticeably still consuming. In fact, I couldn't quite get the hang of not consuming. The truth was, although I might have been more 'green' than most, in that I began to limit my patronage of certain retailers, I was still buying furiously, placing me in a demographic whose spending was increasingly out-of-control. And I don't have to come around to your house and have a look to make a good guess at what you've got in your cupboards, because over the last decade and a half not only have we bought more at increasing speed, but our tastes have become increasingly homogenised.

If your clothing journey follows not only fashion trends but consumer trends, you'll find you have only a small amount of formal wear and a similarly small amount of office wear compared to a decade ago; the whole world appears to have embarked on a permanent Dress Down Friday. Instead, you'll have hangers and shelves and drawers full of home and leisurewear, and there's likely to be evidence that you've bought into some strange new apparel categories such as *luxe* loungewear (a kind of daywear/pyjama hybrid made from a similarly hybrid fabric such as a cashmere blend). The most ubiquitous item is likely to be the T-shirt, along with its close relation the skinny-ribbed vest. You'll also probably find that you've accumulated a number of dresses in the last five years, as we've indulged an obsession with ever more feminine 'flirty' dresses. You'll have more knickers and bras than women at any other time in history. And thanks to the ubiquity of stretch lace and other fancy textile mixes, not only will they be more numerous, but prettier and more sophisticated, now that we've moved on from the tyranny of the thong, more embellished and better adapted to the art of seduction than ever before. The UK market in intimate apparel (the distinctly unsexy trade name for lingerie) had stretched to an amazing £2.8 billion by 2009, which meant that it had grown by 16.1 per cent. For reasons that will become obvious, I'm sticking primarily to women's fashion in these pages, but I will say that if you're male, or have any boys in your family, you'll have found that sportswear will have had a 'profound influence' on their wardrobe. You yourself will almost certainly have more pairs of jeans than you'd ever have thought necessary to own in a lifetime. By 2006 Europe was consuming 391 million pairs of jeans every year. (On this small island we really went for it: in 2007 an incredible three pairs were being sold every second.) I can count nineteen pairs in my wardrobe, of which only four are in what I'd term active service.

You now demand roughly four times the number of clothes you would have in 1980. You will spend at least £625 a year on clothes – but remember that's just the average. And you are getting a lot of bang for your buck (or clothes for your pound). In one year you'll accumulate in the region of twenty-eight kilograms of clothing (again, this is the average) – adding up to an estimated 1.72 million tonnes of brand-new fashion being consumed on an annual basis in the UK. But the really arresting thing is – and I'll keep coming back to this – that almost the same quantity of fashion that you buy you will end up dumping prematurely in the rubbish bin.

Despite your fat wardrobes and hard-to-shut drawers, philosophically speaking you won't be very happy with what you've got. In the way that I think of the shiny leggings (two pairs) that I bought in an effort to emulate the 2009–10 winter season trend, you will often come across pieces in your own cupboards that make you think, 'What on earth possessed me [to buy that]?' We have more clothes than at any other time in history, but have become less and less fulfilled and secure in our purchases, precisely because we have become such passive consumers. We watch, we follow, we pick off the rail – herdlike – and we find ourselves at the cash till.

In moments of clarity I wonder, what am I actually holding on to? If I was being generous, I would say that twenty years of investing in high-street fashion has resulted in a mixed bag. If I was being ungenerous, I'd say it was a shambolic ragbag. There's certainly a jumble of materials –

man-made fibres jostle for space with cotton, and a bit of wool. There's a similar confusion of styles and ideas. Clearly I've invested time, money and emotion in my wardrobe, but after two decades avidly consuming fashion, do I have anything to show for it? I'm sorry to say that the real worth of my wardrobe is probably negligible. To put it bluntly, many garments in my possession are destined for landfill rather than posterity.

FASHION FRENZIES

May 2007 saw the reopening of the former site of a sedate London department store near Oxford Circus. It had been converted into a 70,000-square-foot fashion empire, with seventy-six fitting rooms and eighteen escalators. Though obviously it wasn't the shopfittings that the hordes of female shoppers came to admire that opening day, but the unbelievable prices. For the price of a latte and a panini they could pick up a pair of shoes and a dress that gave more than a nod to pieces by big-name designers.

The extraordinary fashion economics that Primark was able to achieve – bringing hit fashion buys for the lowest prices in living memory – was already enough to generate column inches aplenty, but the opening of the Oxford Circus store was notable for another reason. You would imagine the prices were already low enough, but somehow a rumour circulated among the swollen, near-hysterical and almost exclusively female crowd outside that *everything* was on sale for £1. The scene descended into chaos as desperate consumers battled to get to the front of the crowd. Young women scrambled over each other, pulling hair and collapsing in heaps on the pavement. Mounted police arrived to control the throng, and two would-be shoppers were carried off in ambulances for medical treatment. We'll never know the origin of the everything-for-a-pound rumour, but the ridiculous thing was that if the frantic customers had wandered to another Primark store further down the street they could have picked up exactly the same deals without having to fight to get to the rails.

'Fashions, after all, are only induced epidemics,' George Bernard Shaw pronounced loftily sometime around 1906. True, he wasn't referring directly to the fashion industry – between 1900 and 1938 the market for clothing in the UK was virtually stagnant, so GBS was spared the vision of young ladies staggering under the weight of multiple store bags while trying to manoeuvre the latest overgrown 'it' bag onto public transport. But his observations happen to be unnervingly prescient in the context of present-day fashion, now that we have reached a point at which clothes shopping has more in common with a compulsion than a love or respect for style. 'A demand, however, can be inculcated,' the great bearded playwright continued. 'This is thoroughly understood by fashionable tradesmen, who find no difficulty in persuading their customers to renew articles that are not worn out and to buy things they do not want.' Finally, 'the psychology of fashion becomes a pathology'. George, you would not have liked what our wardrobes have become, but in a way you did warn us.

We weren't listening. The heady mix of celebrity and 'affordable' fashion has been wafting down British high streets. The launch of any line involving both ingredients is almost guaranteed to trigger more scenes of stampeding women and security cordons. 'The arrival of Godot bearing the first Playstation 3 and the formula for world peace could not be more eagerly awaited,' observed columnist Mary Riddell of 'K-Day' in 2007, when Kate Moss appeared briefly in the window of Topshop at Oxford Circus to launch Part I of her eponymous collection (this brand endorsement was worth a reputed £3 million, and raised Topshop's sales by a mammoth 10 per cent).

Despite K-Day being closely followed by L-Day (the launch of singer Lily Allen's range for New Look), I saved myself for C-day, at the hugely successful Swedish retailer Hennes and Mauritz (better known as H&M), when the results of a 'flash collection' from 'designer to the stars' Roberto Cavalli would be revealed to an appreciative public.

By this point H&M was particularly expert at harnessing designers with massive profile and a couture background to produce branded collections of cut-price offerings for mere mortals. It had begun with the launch of a Karl Lagerfeld collection in 2004 that, as revered fashion writer Suzy Menkes put it in the *New York Times*, kicked off 'a media phenomenon, marking a seismic cultural shift and creating lines of eager shoppers in capital cities across the globe'. Of course, this involved a rather different way of operating for some of the couture designers – where they had been making ten to fifty pieces, collaborating with a mainstream label suddenly meant scaling up to runs that were counted in the tens of thousands. Naturally there was a huge trade-off in terms of quality, and some cultural differences to overcome. For example, we learned that Karl Lagerfeld apparently does not think that fat-bottomed girls make the rockin' world go round. He was reputedly dismayed to discover that H&M wished to stock his creations in size 14 and 16, when he had meant them for 'slim, slender people' (welcome to planet fashion). But apart from this embarrassment (H&M quickly apologised), overall these types of superstar designer and high-street-store alliances seemed to keep both parties happy. It is easy to see why. The mainstream retailer got to plug into the public's frenzy for anything with celebrity and luxury cachet, while the A-list designer saw the opportunity to get in front of a huge, mainstream audience. Roberto Cavalli suggested to the press that his H&M collaboration would offer 'a tasting menu of his most appetising signature designs'.

Ultimately, I'm afraid, I failed to feast on much of it. As the doors opened, the burly security guards looked rather nervous – and it was obvious that this was going to be a sell-out. I was quickly enveloped in a scrum of high ponytails and flying elbows as frenzied shoppers pushed, grabbed, swore and ran towards the tills. By the time I got near the remnants of the collection the front of the mob had already gorged itself. Every few minutes a set of courageous shop assistants attempted to restock the area, but as they ripped open boxes and shovelled out more bustiers, macs and Capri pants they were unceremoniously ripped from their hands by shoppers who tore open the thin plastic wrappings themselves. When the crowd moved as one entity across the sales floor to where it had spied, with its single mob eye, another hapless salesgirl attempting to find a way onto the shopfloor from an alternative stockroom door, all that was left behind was a flutter of plastic packaging and a scramble of hangers. Then there were the cold, calculating shoppers gathering up seemingly indiscriminate armfuls of clothes, irrespective of size apparently, and without making eye contact as they marched to the cash desk. These, I learned later, were the eBay buyers. Just a couple of hours later, those who had been unable to make the launch themselves could bid for a piece of diffusion Cavalli at prices that had more in common with his mainline collection than an H&M range.

In an absent-minded way I picked up a zebra-print piece, hoping to look at the label to analyse the fabric content, like the eco-geek I am. 'That is mine!' a young woman screeched, snatching it from me. 'I had that in my hand!' Broadly speaking, I'm a lover not a fighter, and I wasn't committed enough to the project to enter into a catfight. Besides I happen to think shopping and conflict should never go together. The zebra-print bustier slipped from my hands into hers, and I retired from the Cavalli proceedings.

Afterwards I reflected that we were certainly experiencing a new type of fashion-shopping experience. These incidents prompt the question, how did we get to this point, where fashion has more in common with a stampede at a football match than the delicate manners and attention to detail espoused by Coco Chanel? While enthusiastic queues have long been a feature of the January sales, this appeared to be something new: mob shopping. The Primark scuffle was the first such incident involving fashion that I can remember in the UK. In the popular imagination it joined the similarly horrifying spectacle of frenzied consumers, driven mad by the rumour of £50 sofas, battling to get into the opening of a new IKEA superstore in Edmonton, North London, two years previously. It seemed to me to represent a new low, where we lose all critical faculty in a retail space, and move closer to the point where (as eco guru Wendell Berry puts it) we operate in a world in which 'the histories of all products will be lost. The degradation of products and places, producers and consumers is inevitable.'

Berry isn't over-egging the pudding here. The changing fashion landscape has swiftly led to our degradation as consumers. Actually, you can view this less as an anomaly than as a type of natural progression, inevitable given the increasing fetishisation of cheap clothing, as we rapidly learned to prioritise quantity and variety over quality. The trouble was that being punchdrunk with so many store bags and pairs of shoes, we took a while to notice, and even when we did, an easier response than taking a long, hard look at our new, extremely weighty wardrobes was to say, 'Where's the harm?'

SHOPPING JUNKIES

Our ways of buying fashion and our relationship with the garments we own started changing in the mid-1980s. By 2005, academic research was picking up on the salient points. Louise R. Morgan and Grete Birtwistle set up eight consumer focus groups, surveying seventy-one women about their purchasing habits and interviewing 'young fashion consumers', by which they meant eighteen-to-twenty-five-year-olds, in more depth. Nearly all confessed to spending more than they used to, at rates that varied from £20 to £200 a month. This is hardly surprising, but what's really notable is that they had absolutely no plan as to how long they intended to keep any of their purchases for. They also admitted that when 'cheap' fashion tore or became marked or stained, its likely destination was not the washbasket, but the rubbish bin.

The old way of buying clothes, in harmony with one's income and with nature's changing seasons, the way people wore, washed carefully and darned, has absolutely nothing in common with the way we now consume. I should know: I was a fully-paid-up member of the group of avaricious fashion consumers who ensured that spending on womens-wear in Britain rose by a huge 21 per cent in just four years, between 2001 and 2005. I have shoeboxes full of receipts and wardrobes that are full to bursting point to prove my dedication. During the same period prices miraculously dropped by 14 per cent. Instead of buying fewer garments and pocketing the change, we actually bought more, increasing the volume of clothes we welcomed into our homes (often fleetingly) by a third. And don't forget accessories: a quick look at my intertwined hill of shoes, pumps, trainers, wellies (a single pair of wellies is apparently not enough: I have four) and heeled boots – a number of pairs of which are in limbo while I try to find one of the last remaining cobblers – demonstrates that I have bought into the extraordinary global fashion trend for them too: in 2003 total expenditure on footwear in Britain surpassed $50 billion for the first time. We now buy an average of 4.1 items of clothing each a month. Trying to remember what you bought last month is a bit like trying to remember what you ate. You might deny that you bought anything, but you've probably overlooked something

– the vest top you picked up when you were walking past a high-street store, or the cute little pyjama short set you spotted in the concession store at the station.

Yes, I'm complicit, but isn't it comforting that there's always someone who appears to be much, much worse? I breathed one of those rather ungenerous sighs of relief when I interviewed another Lucy, a twenty-one-year-old unemployed graduate, for a TV show. Despite being yet to find a job and carrying a fairly hefty student loan debt, she confessed to spending between £200 and £500 on fashion a month. As she showed me through her wardrobe it was clear that she loved clothes. She planned what she would wear days in advance, she ripped pages from magazines with looks she wanted to emulate – she was serious about fashion. I really admired her sense of style: as a tall, svelte blonde she was a natural clothes horse, but she also knew how to throw a look together. She was one of those people who, reduced to a tiny budget, would almost certainly have had enough style intuition to dress from a car-boot sale and still look great. But she would never take that risk. Her great, expensive downfall in wardrobe terms was that she absolutely refused to wear the same thing twice. With a social life like Lucy's, which centred on frequent visits to the same two or three West End clubs, she needed a lot of different looks. She claimed that her friends would have ostracised her for the crime of repeat showings. Given that A-listers like Kylie Minogue are frequently picked out in magazine fashion *faux pas* columns for wearing the same python shoes more than once, I didn't doubt her.

Hardly a day went by without Lucy adding something new to her wardrobe. About 30 per cent of the rail she showed me was occupied by clothes still with their swing tickets, that she hadn't yet worn. In 2008 Oxfam made a valiant attempt to get buyers like Lucy to donate these unworn but new clothes – a survey for Oxfam and M&S found that one in ten of us admitted to wearing just 10 per cent of our wardrobes, and estimated that there were 2.4 billion garments just hanging there gathering dust. It was the age group just above Lucy, women of twenty-five to thirty-four, who harboured unworn clothes of the most value – reckoned to be an average of £228 each.

Lucy's main aspiration when I met her four years ago was to be a

WAG. There's contention over who coined the epithet – the *Daily Mail* claims it, but *Grazia* magazine certainly popularised it – but it has always been heavily associated with glamour and fashion. I don't know if this is still Lucy's life goal. Perhaps she has even achieved it. In which case her fashion consumption will have graduated to its own Premier League, typified by the fabled Cricket boutique in Liverpool that services the fashion needs of WAGs and soap stars. It stocks a heady mix of labels, from Balenciaga to Marc Jacobs, and has proved an irrepressible fountain of fashion stories, particularly for weekly magazines. When I visited in 2006 I asked the owner, Justine Mills, if negative comments in the style press had any effect – Alex Curran (now Mrs Stephen Gerrard) had, for example, been slated for teaming a canary-yellow Juicy Couture tracksuit with Moon Boots. Yes, there was certainly an effect, she told me: 'After she'd been on every worst-dressed list, we got orders from all over the country.'

THE QUICK DEATH OF SLOW FASHION

It's difficult to remember life before this new model, but that was the time when my style consciousness was really forming. I do recall developing a sort of hunger to dress differently, and a passion for stripy tights and denim cut-offs. And despite the fact that I definitely didn't live in a hub of fashion experimentation during those years – variously I lived in Devon, Derby and Mullingar in the centre of Ireland (you get the picture: these were not style capitals) – I don't remember feeling particularly short-changed or lacking in inspiration. When I think of the 1980s I think almost automatically of *The Clothes Show*. I was a big fan of the original programme, launched in 1986. When it was relaunched in 2006 I watched it still, and appeared in a couple of series when the show broached the subject of ethical fashion. Funnily enough, even though the second run of *The Clothes Show* was screened well into the era when consumers could recreate any look in the blink of an eye for under £20, I never found it as compelling.

Back in the 1980s there was an aspiration to own stylish things, but you usually had to wait, and plan a strategic visit to a limited number of high-street stores – Miss Selfridge, Dorothy Perkins and Tammy Girl, for example. At other times you had to cobble together a look from charity shops, strange independent retailers and markets, or collective fashion spaces showcasing one-off designs or small runs from designer makers. The fabled boutiques of the 1960s and 1970s, Biba and Sex (which incidentally managed to revolutionise design and fashion without having to turn the production model on its head), led to collectives such as Hyper Hyper in South Kensington. (I should be clear here that I'm talking about the real Hyper Hyper, a glorious palace of kooky design that was essentially a market. The equivalent in the North-West was Manchester's Aflex Palace. They were places where new designers with very small collections could sell in central locations. It had absolutely nothing in common with the Hyper Hyper that sprang up in Oxford Street in 2009, filled with synthetic 'value' clothes. So high was the plastic content of most of those garments that you could smell the hydrocarbons as you walked in.)

Another major feature of our wardrobes back then was that a large chunk of our clothes would have been manufactured in Britain, from fibre that was even processed or finished here. From leather stitching and sewing in Somerset to the ancient worsted industry (turning wool yarn into textiles for suiting) in Bradford and Huddersfield, to Coats Viyella producing for M&S in Manchester, 'Made in England' was not a surprising label to see attached to a piece of clothing. Nor did it mean artisanal one-man-band production, as it often does now, when more often than not courageous designer/makers try to give the concept of home-grown fashion some resonance. Until just over a decade ago M&S, something of a UK clothing behemoth, sourced 90 per cent of its own-label clothing in Britain. As you may remember, it was called St Michael, and it was the only clothing that M&S sold. During World War II British clothing production units developed expertise in knocking out uniforms on an assembly line. It wasn't a big stretch to alter this to menswear, and ultimately to the more profitable womenswear. There was always a degree of outsourcing, i.e. sending cut-and-sew work (the actual sewing part of the assembly) to manufacturers abroad, but this tended to be limited to manufacturers in Hong Kong, Taiwan and Korea. In fact it's fair to say that we had built up a rather impressive peacetime army of tailors, machinists, cutters, finishers, colourists, weavers and of course designers. They were served by the sort of infrastructure, of farmers producing sheep for wool, slaughterhouses producing for the leather trade, cobblers, menders and recyclers (who in those days took the more prosaic form of rag-and-bone men), that today's sustainable style warriors can only dream about.

You know how the story goes. In 1981 the British clothing and footwear retail market imported just 29 per cent of all it sold. By 2001 the figure had soared to 90 per cent. Any pretence to style self-sufficiency these shores once had was well and truly kicked into touch.

But the main, overarching distinction between then and now is that back then the fashion industry had built-in air vents to ease the pressure, formalities and systems that dictated the pace of consumption and production. The production model was based on a critical distinction between 'fashion' and 'garments'. At the top of the tree was couture. Its USP was the amount of skilled labour inherent in each piece. The look was in the hands of the designer and creator, and the volume of repeated pieces was limited to tens at the most. Final finishings were typically handmade, and the buyer might not see the finished piece until the very end of the process. This meant that shows could only occur twice a year. The fashion weeks that take place today in New York, London, Paris and Milan (and everywhere else from Copenhagen to Tokyo, Toronto and Beijing) are derivative of these couture seasons.

The next rung down was the ready-to-wear lines – *prêt à porter*. Here the process picked up a little bit of speed, and the designer/maker process became less rarefied. Exclusivity was preserved in the level of design and often by the name of the designer, but the manufacturing process was more industrialised. Pieces were repeated in the hundreds and thousands.

Next came mid-market fashion, highly industrialised and cut from a standard pattern. These items were essentially basic garments with a fashion twist, and they were designed with a shorter lifespan in mind: it was usually envisaged that they would just last the season that ran for half the year – autumn/winter and spring/summer.

And then came the everyday garments: jeans, T-shirts, sweaters – the basic building blocks of a wardrobe.

Today we take it as read that everything we buy will have a direct lineage to the runway. Even wardrobe basics are expected to be infused with the aura of big design and big designers. The distinction between 'garments' and 'fashion' has become ever looser, until now we use those terms interchangeably. In effect, basic garments have become fashion. We expect everything, including knickers, nighties and stuff you wear to the gym to sweat in, to be up-to-the minute and preferably linked to a superstar designer.

So, we buy fast and cheap and in huge quantity. Not only is the global wardrobe heaving, its contents are being discarded and refilled at a spectacular rate. A 1998 study by Dutch academics put the lifespan of the average piece of clothing in a (Dutch) wardrobe at three years and five months, during which it was on the body on a total of forty-four days. Until more up-to-date research is carried out it is difficult to assess today's fashion turnover, but there is unanimous agreement that it has become much, much faster. We know by the rate at which we buy and the amounts we chuck into landfill each year that many pieces can expect to have the lifespan of a mayfly.

Meanwhile, someone like Lucy is locked in a cycle of sustaining a celebrity look on the non-salary of an unemployed graduate. Cricket, with its Prada and Balenciaga, is well out of reach. You might say it is a miracle that Lucy was able to sustain any type of wardrobe growth at all, but she managed, courtesy of another wardrobe miracle: fast fashion.

2

FASTER AND CHEAPER

How Big Fashion has Taken Style to the Brink

By July 2008 Primark's flagship store in Oxford Circus's annual turnover reached £200 million. At Primark prices that's an awful lot of clothes, but not to worry, because in the first ten days of trading this single store sold one million garments. Those lowly prices meant that consumers need not even concern themselves with queuing (or elbowing) their way into fitting rooms to try potential buys on. If they took them home and changed their minds, where was the penalty?

Perhaps that mindset explains why a fashion industry commentator, working for a trade publication, watched in horror as she saw one satisfied customer emerge with six or seven brown paper Primark bags full of clothes. It was raining heavily, and as the young woman proceeded down Oxford Street one of them broke around the handles and folded cotton flopped onto the pavement. Naturally the journalist expected the girl to bend down and collect the brand new clothes, but no. She just walked on. Fashion was apparently so expendable it had turned into litter.

There is little doubt that fashion has become disposable. Researcher Sara Giorgi, looking into what influences consumer change with the goal of finding ways of making our approach more sustainable, has found some breathtaking examples. 'I don't wash socks,' she was informed by one respondent. 'They are too cheap to buy. They are, though! It's dearer to wash them than it is to go and buy them.' I know things have become cheap, but until there's a definitive energy crash I'm not entirely convinced by the economics here. I suspect it has more to do with convenience. The next respondent chips in, 'It's like me. I go on holiday. Go and get like a pack of – underwear, and you just – just throw it away. What are you going to do, bring them back [in your suit]case?'

THE NEW MODEL ARMY

By the millennium the UK's mainstream fashion industry was largely freed from the shackles of actually producing anything. As it cast off manufacturing facilities and disgorged machine operators to the dole queues, it was clear that the British fashion industry was more about the selling of clothes than the making of them. With the exception of a few stubborn outposts, hundreds of years of manufacturing heritage were junked in ten short years, and some extremely high-profile brands, like Burberry, moved their manufacturing abroad. The once brisk trade in home-grown apparel was as dead as a dodo, replaced by a clothing market that relied almost entirely on imports, that was all about shiny shopfronts and the charismatic owners and CEOs behind vast retail empires.

The undisputed king of these was (and arguably remains) Philip Green. Owner of the rather pedestrian high-street staple BHS, Green bought the Arcadia group for £850 million in 2002. It was widely agreed that he had pulled off the bargain of the century: netting Arcadia gave him Topshop, Topman, Wallis, Evans, Miss Selfridge and Dorothy Perkins, and therefore a significant slice of the British high street. But while all of those were much-loved brands, they weren't exactly setting closets on fire. That was about to change.

Within a few months Green was rarely mentioned in the media without the attendant cliché that he possessed the Midas touch. Topshop had achieved something extraordinary. In financial terms it accounted for £1 billion of UK clothing sales by the first half of 2005 alone (bear in mind that the entire clothing market was only worth £7 billion). Green's apparent ability to turn these humdrum stores into cash cows that made the British high street the envy of the world was celebrated by business analysts, the fashion press, and especially consumers. Topshop became a destination point for anybody who was interested in fashion. For us consumers it was a straightforward process. You simply turned to the pages in magazines that prescribed how to 'get the look' from international runways, and popped into your nearest Topshop to find affordable pieces that took their cue from the design trends on the rail. Admittedly the cut, the finish and the fabrics would have given a *modellista* (a handicraft professional working in the luxury industry) a nervous breakdown, but they were immediate and cheap facsimiles.

I wouldn't like to suggest that I was in any way above this. I was as punchdrunk on the formula as everyone else. My allegiance actually pre-dated Green's transformation, as I shopped pretty religiously in Topshop Oxford Circus from 1992 when I arrived in London as a seventeen-year-old university student. I still have a few things from that era: strange Lycra flared leggings and cropped tops – oh dear. My visits began to tail off from early 2000 as I became increasingly worried about Arcadia's sourcing policies and its failure to join the Ethical Trading Initiative (ETI) – at the time of writing, Arcadia is still not a member. There was also the fact that I had begun to feel a bit too old, and instinctively wanted a better cut. By the time I bagged a ticket for the front row at the Topshop show in 2009 I was already researching this book, and the magic bubble had burst for me.

But not, it seemed, for the rest of the style press. At London Fashion Week in February 2009, Topshop's status remained undiminished. By that point, indeed, it had become the most exciting thing about London Fashion Week – a statement that I think would be hotly denied by the British Fashion Council – bolstered by the fact that this spring/summer 2010 season was the sixteenth time Topshop had sponsored NewGen (New Generation, or up-and-coming talent. When you think the alumni of NewGen include Matthew Williamson, Christopher Kane, Erdem, Jonathan Saunders and the late Alexander McQueen, the excitement by association is understandable). Besides, Topshop's mainline show has a reputation for 'delivering'. All of which explained why, even on a Sunday, the great and the good of fashion had faithfully traipsed to a warehouse in Kensington.

Once I had negotiated the many doormen (there was a high security presence, for reasons that were never entirely clear) I too was quickly transported. The Topshop show was every bit the theatrical masterpiece I had been told about. A runway with a surface like silver ice and a backdrop of neon and glitter strips. A bank of photographers at its end assembled in what looked like a precarious vertical pyramid. The legions of fashion editors and stylists, all clad in black, determinedly flooded the place like stormtroopers, albeit ones with purple Moët et Chandon notebooks and outsized leather bags. It went dark. It went very dark. And then we were off: a relentless stream of neon- and glitter-clad teenagers, like glowing tadpoles on the silver runway. Every three or four girls a new motif or accessory was introduced: a clutch bag, a raft of bangles, a scarf. All bang on trend, all fun and uncomplicated. This was fast fashion on the move, and it was deeply seductive. When the audience showed its appreciation with sustained applause it sounded almost grateful. It was a moment of dazzling frippery at a time when the nation was plunging into a dark recession.

I imagine it was even more exciting four years before, when Topshop had its first proper London Fashion Week show, because you can say what you like about this high-street giant, there's no denying it brought some excitement to a rather dull set-up. Much of that 'Midas touch' was actually applied by Jane Shepherdson, who was at the helm of Topshop in 2005, when the flagship Oxford Circus shop's sales exceeded £100 million in a single year in the midst of a consumer downturn, and the chain would sell out of 5,500 sequin vests in half a week.

Shepherdson had a fabled way with style, managing to pick the trends that she knew would be lapped up and getting them instore at just the right time. By 2005 she had twenty years' experience at Topshop, beginning as a buyer who had allegedly earned her sartorial stripes by staking her whole career on a job lot of tank tops that became one of the store's biggest hits.

'A lot of the time these days I actually feel much happier when I go through my existing wardrobe, wearing some of the clothes I've kept for a long time and looking different precisely because I'm not wearing the latest thing,' says the Jane Shepherdson of 2010. 'When you slip into wearing the trend of the hour, maybe that's the easy thing to do.' She laughs. 'Even though of course I'm sitting here in a camel cashmere jumper, which is apparently the trend.' The woman who is credited with engineering Topshop's supreme reign in fast fashion is now head of Whistles, having engineered a management buyout in 2010. She can also frequently be heard expressing sentiments about fashion that have more in common with the ethical fashion movement than the mainstream. For example, she is on record as saying that rich people buying cheap clothes and bragging about it is 'very vulgar', a sentiment with which I wholeheartedly agree. Like me, she appears to have reached saturation point with 'fast fashion'. She's had her fill of insubstantial pieces and the endless churn. 'I know!' she says. 'And I'm in fashion.' 'Jane,' I venture rather timidly, 'do you ever feel like you created the monster?' Her expression is a cross between remorse and bemusement. 'I do get asked this. On one hand it's ludicrous, because I didn't invent fast fashion at all. If I had done, surely I'd be a millionaire by now, and I am definitely not that. Our motives were pretty simple. All we were trying constantly to do was to create the best possible design for the price that we were committed to – one that was affordable to our customer base. We thought at the time, well, we're selling lots of stuff, but let's make stuff that at least has some design integrity and make it interesting and exciting. That's what we did.'

There's no doubt that that simple aspiration to imbue clothes with 'some design integrity' worked. As Shepherdson acknowledges, 'When I joined Topshop a real *fashionista* would not have been seen in it. It wasn't the thing to do. It was a different ethos. You wore designer or you wore high street.' She certainly changed that. It became *de rigueur* to shop on the high street again. 'Every girl admits to shopping at Topshop,' wrote business journalist Nick Mathiason, profiling Shepherdson in the *Observer* in 2005. 'Inevitably you end up creating trends,' Shepherdson says, 'and of course people think they have to have them. It becomes quite hard to pinpoint where it all started.'

Following the indisputable success of Jane Shepherdson's strategy came a raft of retailers who were determined to emulate Topshop's success, and indeed take it further. Fast fashion became an industry standard, and clothes were produced in smaller production batches and at dizzying rates. High-street fashion was on high alert to every trend and consumer whim, defined by the industry as 'quick response'.

Emulating the Topshop magic meant getting the quickest supply chains possible. In industry terms this meant decreasing production times. Staff responsible for buying and sourcing went into overdrive. To compete they needed to react urgently to any change in trend. Every part of the production cycle was squeezed, concertinaed into days and hours rather than weeks. 'Time to market' (the all-important period in which factories sew garments to meet orders and then deliver them to the stores) was halved, then quartered. There was less time to identify future trends and translate them into clothes, as it became commonplace for buyers to fax their Developing World suppliers at all hours of the day and night with tweaks and changes from the UK design team.

A few years ago, a factory supplying a major retailer would have expected to manufacture 40,000 garments across four styles for twenty weeks. Today it will be lucky to get commitment from the retailer to manufacture four styles at five hundred garments per week for just five weeks. The remaining 30,000 will be ordered at the last minute, when the design team has worked out whether the mainstream consumer has been inspired by Taylor Swift, Daisy Lowe, Lindsay Lohan or none of the above.

While Topshop managed to slim its production period from nine to six weeks, H&M cut its lead times from design to rail to just three weeks. In fact, according to the revered fashion journalist Hilary Alexander, it was H&M that launched fashion that was effectively 'disposable', and you don't get faster than that. Even back in 2003 she had reservations: 'I'm not entirely convinced that that is such a good thing,' she said, referring to the fact that some garments were so cheap 'that literally you'd be lucky to get two to three wears out of it, and then you'd chuck it away'. This new money-spinning way of working the rag trade was based on a rather dry notion of 'lean retailing' that subsequently achieved near-doctrinal status in business schools. The new model held everybody's attention – analysts, economists, the press and of course *fashionistas*. After all, if you fitted into the latter category, what was there not to like? For starters, there was a surfeit of choice. Topshop for example would bring in 7,000 lines each season.

If Topshop and H&M were consciously after the youth vote, with cut-for-teen-frame styling and sequined hook-ups with of-the-moment celebrities, they weren't the ones that brought the ultimate revolution. That was left to what seemed like a slightly staider, more grown-up name on the high street: Zara. On the surface Zara represents a conundrum for me. I remember looking at it early on – the Spanish brand owned by Inditex arrived in the UK in 1998, but has been a fixture in its native Spain since 1975 – and thinking it looked like a range for a generic type of European yummy mummy. It wasn't long, however, before I found myself visiting with decreasing gaps in between, despite the fact that I didn't aspire to dress like a Zara woman. It was as if I was being taught to like it.

Legend has it that when the first Zara store opened in Britain, on Regent Street in London, shoppers were a little mystified. The prices seemed high, and I'm told (perhaps apocryphally) that if consumers said they would come back when there was a sale, the assistants would tell them that come sale time the pieces would not be there. In fact, even if the tentative shoppers were to come back next week the pieces wouldn't be there. That was not the Zara way.

The Zara way – the one that broke all previous rules – had several defining characteristics, but number one (and sacrosanct) was that the Spanish retailer manufactured only relatively tiny quantities of each style. This sounds a small deal, but effectively it turned fashion retail on its head. Instead of focusing on quantity, Zara's cadre of around two hundred designers in Spain come up with around 40,000 new designs each year, of which 12,000 are actually produced (that's 5,000 more than Topshop). Years ago, when I worked in a shop as a Saturday girl, we were forever phoning up customers when new deliveries came in (or at least we were supposed to). Not any longer, because in Big Fashion stock replenishments are for wimps. How does this affect the consumer? Well, as a shopper, if you hesitate at the point of purchase you're probably going to miss your chance. This creates a terrible hunger in the consumer, creating what Harvard researchers have referred to as 'a sense of tantalising exclusivity', a pervasive fear that if you pause for thought, the opportunity to bag that affordable version of a catwalk sensation (Zara is known as 'interpreting rather than creating afresh', as retail and fashion analyst Davangshu Dutta sensitively puts it) will be snatched from you forever.

Both Zara's ability to take 'inspiration' from hot catwalk pieces and the hunger engendered by small, fast-changing product lines are in evidence from press coverage around the time Zara opened its largest European store in London, 'a 3,000-square-metre temple to consumption', as journalist and design expert Caroline Roux described it: 'Among the bewildering selection of clothes, I spotted a passable interpretation of a Christian Dior embroidered Afghan on the rails (£95), a Pradaesque brocade waistcoat (£45) and a black wool coat (£65) that was enticingly similar to something by superchic Italian label Costume National (£565). An assistant even pointed me in the direction of what he called "the Anna Sui collection", an up-to-the-minute assortment of patchwork, denim and boho chic (Sui is a veteran New York designer who shows on the catwalk).'

Roux suggested that a reason for Zara's appeal was the short amount of time each line was given to prove itself (absolutely no longer than four weeks). The only way you could be a Zara groupie was to pop in as often as you could manage. Whereas a typical retailer could expect its customers to visit four times a year, Zara could bank on an average of seventeen visits. This explained my frequent sorties, equally frequently resolved by exiting the store with the distinctive blue paper bag. 'The girls in the office know that new stock comes in on Tuesday and Thursday, and off they go,' Julian Vogel, Managing Director of fashion PR company Modus, told Roux. 'It's a guilt-free high.'

'This business is all about reducing response time. In fashion, stock is like food. It goes bad quick,' said former Inditex Chairman José Maria Castellano, who many credit with coming up with the Zara blueprint for blink-and-you-miss-it fashion. The whole point was to take the risk out of fashion for the retailer (as we'll see later, it's arguable that the risk gets pushed down the supply chain, onto those whose lives are already unbearably uncertain). Zara had no truck with discounting 35 to 40 per cent of its merchandise (the normal figure for fashion retailers) because it had ordered skinny jeans in the wrong wash, or a jacket with last week's lapel size. Instead it set up a system that means it only ever discounts around 18 per cent of its products, according to analysts.

Rather than trudging along taking nine to twelve months to decide on a style, using forecasters and analysts to advise on upcoming trends a year in advance, then taking a risk on ordering and choosing colours and fabrics, Zara turned the process on its head. Instead of the usual phalanx of style and colour forecasters poring over industry reports, it set up a relatively large production team at Inditex's Spanish HQ in the distinctly non-fashionable Arteixo-La Coruna, and relied on them to liaise with trendspotters on the ground, constantly emailing and phoning in with suggestions to get a highly reactive consumer-led view of what's hot and what's not. If the hipsters suddenly develop a thing for vampires, or swing away from brogues and Victoriana, the Inditex office will know about it.

The result was that 163 Zara stores across Europe (sixty in the UK) received new fashion pieces twice every week. There were a number of ways by which this was achieved, including some very technical processes. These included buying semi-processed, uncoloured fabric, known as 'greige', that could be finished and dyed at short notice, depending on what hot trends the cool hunters were texting in. There were systems, often enthused over by logistics professionals, of underground tracks that moved finished garments to hundreds of chutes to make sure each store was sent the right packages at the right time. But the big thing Zara did was to produce 50 to 80 per cent (estimates vary) of its lines in Europe, so that it became famous for identifying a trend and having the resulting fashion in store within thirty days. To be that fast requires the heavy use of air freight, and commentators have described the dizzying pace of twice-weekly air shipments with Air France and KLM cargo, as planes from Zaragoza land in Bahrain laden with stock for Inditex stores in the Middle East, fly on to Asia, and return with raw materials and half-finished clothes. In common with other industries that aren't exactly addressing sustainability head on, this is predicated on cheap oil.

Looking at some conventional timespans for getting hold of garments from far-flung production bases, you can see why Zara's model is so attractive to its eager customers. One study of Egyptian exporters of cotton clothing, for example, estimated the time taken to import yarns from India and Pakistan to a storage facility at thirty days. To this had to be added customs clearance, including waiting time (another two weeks), a few days for the preparation of export documents, four hours to pack a container (in recent years clothes containers have increased in length from twenty feet to forty feet, such is the unprecedented demand), and then sailing time (from Alexandria in this case, to New York, where the cargo must again clear customs and then go to a testing laboratory). The result was a yawn-inducing ninety to 120 days, far too long for a trend-based sun dress inspired by a Hollywood actress. By the time it arrived she could be well out of favour.

Even Philip Green doffed his hat to Zara. 'Genius. What the fashion industry is all about,' he said in an interview with *Retail Week* magazine. 'When Madonna gave a series of concerts in Spain,' noted business expert Robin Dymond on his blog Scrum, Agile and Lean Methods, 'teenage girls were wearing at her last performance the outfit she wore for her first concert.' Although I was amazed that looking like Madonna was still a kudos-raising activity for teenagers in Spain, I got the point. He saw another direct translation for an older market: 'When Spain's Crown Prince Felipe and Letizia Ortiz Rocasolano announced their engagement in 2003, the bride-to-be wore a stylish white pant suit. Within a few weeks, hundreds of European women were wearing something similar.'

Other pretenders to the high-street throne got the message. Esprit and Mango tried the same approach: short lead times and multiple seasons, along with reduced delivery times – these could be as little as forty-eight hours. What was definitely out of fashion was holding onto lots of stock, or indeed any stock.

As consumers we rapidly changed our priorities. Long-standing skills of buying clothing, such as assessing for quality or looking at labels, were junked in favour of getting our hands on what was new as we adjusted to the Zara-like thrill of swapping two wardrobe seasons a year (and the delayed gratification of waiting to embrace those two seasons) for upwards of twenty. While the world's mainline Fashion Weeks continue the charade of spring/summer and autumn/winter seasons, in real terms they are now about as relevant to contemporary life as learning Gregorian plainsong.

Zara's policy was what we might call a game-changer. While it won plaudits in the financial press and saw its share price rocket – a share offer to the public in 2001 was over-subscribed twenty-six times, raising 2.1 billion euros – brands such as M&S, with relatively pedestrian stock turns that were at least twenty days slower, and often with lead times of six months, found themselves getting a lot of stick for being plodding and dowdy. Inevitably there were casualties as fashion brands that had long been mainstays of the high street were thrown into a do-or-die situation. Many of these represented the middle market – not too cheap, not too fast, but truly affordable clothing where standards of quality and longevity were still in evidence. Those brands scrambled to try either to up their fashionability (Next, for example, attempted to be clearer about its style and direction), or slashed their prices to try to compete.

In retrospect, the criticism of previously cherished middle-market brands just before the millennium was exceptionally harsh. Laura Ashley, Next and Monsoon were all accused of misreading 'the all-important female fashion market' as they urgently attempted to 'restructure their offer'. M&S famously came in for years of ridicule, not least at the company's own AGMs, which took on a theatrical quality. In 1999 Teresa Vanneck-Surplice, a private shareholder, waved a pair of a rival chain's knickers at then M&S Chairman Brian Baldock. 'Your underwear's got boring!' she said, adding, 'I may be fifty-two but I like my underwear sexy'. To the delight of the assembled media, Vanneck-Surplice proved a similarly dynamic complainant during 2007's AGM, when she told Stuart Rose (by that time Executive Chairman) that she was still unhappy with M&S's offerings, which was why she was dressed head to foot in Primark. ('It won't last', responded Rose with splendid ambiguity.) To varying degrees the crime of the middle market was that it was no longer deemed fashionable. Next to the neon-lit, sequin-strewn running track that fast fashion streaked up and down, the middle market was frankly an embarrassment. So while the Dutch-owned C&A appeared as one of the top ten UK clothing retailers in 1999, just a year later it announced it was closing all of its British stores.

In 2000 you wouldn't have found me mourning the middle market. I was far too busy adding to my collection of jeans and shoes. But now I'm pausing for a brief moment of regret. Yes, it's a case of you-don't-know-what-you've-got-till-it's-gone, but the middle market was, with a great deal of hindsight, the best way to avoid sucking all of the health out of the fashion industry, including a loss of control over the supply chain. It was the most sustainable, mainstream way of ensuring affordable fashion.

OUT OF CONTROL: THE RUNAWAY STYLE TRAIN

I don't want to compound the air of regret, but if only it had stopped there. Fast fashion had its merits – it certainly brought excitement. The jury's out on whether you can have responsible fast fashion (it certainly doesn't sound very sexy), but what if it had stayed true to Jane Shepherdson's original idea, to make better, more fashionable clothes at affordable prices? Naturally there would have been some deficit environmentally – every time you make something there's an impact – but we would have stood a chance of minimising the negative effects.

Inevitably the signs of this revolution – the bulging wardrobes and the women staggering around with multiple store bags – attracted attention in non-*fashionista* circles. By the late 1990s economists and business analysts, alerted by the superleague profits of previously workaday stores, were taking a closer look. What on earth, they wondered, was going on? It was the equivalent of hearing the strains of a prolonged and increasingly wild party until you feel compelled to get out of bed and see the action for yourself. And it was some party: a story of spectacular growth made more captivating to analysts because historically the clothing sector in the UK had always been a bit of a damp squib, but it was now displaying incredible figures. From 1900 to 1938 things were glacially slow, then became even worse with the Second World War, when clothes were subject to rationing. Only from 1975 did the British public finally begin casting off some of its make-do-and-mend attitude to fashion, as the UK market swelled to reach an unprecedented size by 1999. The UK Fashion Report for 1998–99 proclaimed the UK clothing and footwear industry to be worth £26 billion (up from £11.7 billion in 1983). There was more to come. In 2009 it was worth an amazing £46.05 billion, and accounted for 5.3 per cent of all consumer spending.

I call this seismic shift in making, selling and buying fashion the alchemy of fast fashion. Alchemy, the medieval forerunner of chemistry, launched many practitioners on the ultimately fruitless quest to turn base metal into gold. Fast-fashion alchemy has done something similar, turning basic fabrics and a frill-free supply chain into a Balenciaga-alike fashion fix. Just like alchemy, there's an unquantifiable mystical element to this dark art, because the stellar fiscal achievements of fast fashion took place at a time when clothing prices were actually *falling*. This is worth spelling out. We were clearly purchasing a lot of wardrobe fodder. In 1990 we cumulatively spent £23 billion on clothes and shoes – the lion's share, almost £19 billion, on clothes; trends dictated that a large proportion of this will have gone on boot-cut jeans and some on the tyrannical reign of the babydoll dress. We achieved all of this with just 4.5 per cent of our household budget (in the 1960s we spent far less on our wardrobes, but they accounted for 10 per cent of our budget). By 1998 those figures had soared. We were now spending £32.5 billion on clothes and shoes a year, £27.7 billion on clothes alone. But interestingly this still accounted for only 5.7 per cent of our budget. In July 2001 sales of clothing and footwear in the UK were up on the previous year by a huge 12 per cent, the highest annual rate of growth since the mid-1970s.

But in real terms the price of clothes had fallen dramatically (and, I might add, chaotically). This is the point at which the dark side of the fast-fashion alchemy kicks in. Between 1996 and 2000 clothing prices fell each year, and in the epoch-defining year of high sales, 2001, they fell by 6 per cent. The analysts could almost hear a giant balloon deflating. A study by City analyst Mark Hudson from PricewaterhouseCoopers, tracking Next Direct's catalogue between 1995 and 2005, confirms that something very weird happened: prices had actually dropped 40 per cent over that time. In the four years from 2003 to 2007 average prices in retail fashion fell by 10 per cent.

A 1998 study found that between 1982 and 1995 the amount of time a motor-vehicle worker had to put in to earn enough to purchase a suit fell from twenty-five hours to eighteen. Consumers did not require a formula to pinpoint what was happening: we were simply spending less and buying more.

ENTER THE DISCOUNTERS

Fast fashion taught us to prioritise speed. Its influence in most of our wardrobes is undeniable, but it was not the whole story. The real alchemy – turning base fabrics into golden trends that both the consumer and the financial markets went crazy for – only occurred when fast fashion was allied to the lowest price points in history. While the foreign fast-fashion giants – Gap, H&M and Zara – will doubtless have staked some sort of claim in your closet, in 2002 their total market share was still just under 5 per cent. The biggest invasion of planet fashion, with the biggest reverberations, belonged to the so-called 'value' retailers, also known as 'discounters'.

Those leading the charge – Matalan, Peacock's and New Look – were known for their 'aggressive pricing strategies', selling at 30–50 per cent below' the prices of the good old mid-market. But none of them had quite the clout of Primark. Primark originated in Ireland, and growing up there I was familiar with it in its other guise as Penneys, the go-to outlet for school socks and vests. I can safely say I would never have believed that twenty years later it would be earning plaudits in glossy magazines for its military jackets and polkadot dresses. The discount retail chain, whose parent company Associated British Foods provides us with cupboard staples such as Ryvita, Kingsmill and Ovaltine, arrived in the UK in 1974, but it has remained something of an enigma. Little is known about its septuagenarian founder, Arthur Ryan, who stepped down in 2009 after forty years, except that he instilled in the company a belief that all products must make his legendary 12.5 per cent profit margin. According to an article in the Irish newspaper the *Sunday Business Post*, Ryan was supposedly once approached by a factory owner with a product costing £5 that would sell for £10. Ryan reportedly told him he was not interested unless he came back with a product that cost £3 and could be sold for £7: 'I don't care how you go about it – just do it,' he reputedly said. When a journalist from the *Scotsman* tried to verify the story, Primark denied it. 'His view would almost be counter-intuitive,' a former employee told the *Sunday Times* in 2007. 'He would look at a product line that was selling well at £5 and cut the price to £3 because it would sell even more.'

Primark was to the discounters what Zara was to fast-fashion retailers – a trailblazer that showed the profits that could be made, and an organisation to emulate. The opening of its flagship London store in May 2007 was followed by mammoth stores in Manchester and Bristol. The discounters persuaded us to trump all other values with a single myopically focused question: 'But is it really, really cheap?' From then on, that was all the consumer wanted to know.

By 2006 value retailers represented the fastest-growing part of the retail pie: retail analysts Verdict prophesied that by the end of the year, for every £4 spent on fashion, £1 would go to a value retailer. Of course this came true, and just eighteen months later industry bible *Drapers* breathlessly reported that 'Primark has moved a step closer to toppling Marks & Spencer from the top spot in clothing market share, after its volume share leapt to 10.1 per cent.' Who wouldn't want a piece of that? After the high-street retailers adopted this approach, it was only a matter of time before some strange new entrants began to get in on the act.

FROM FROZEN PEAS TO FASHION FIXES: HOW THE SUPERMARKETS GOT IN ON THE ACT

If I hadn't anticipated that my friends and colleagues would one day be fawning over products from a subsidiary of Associated British Food, I was even less prepared for the fashion revolution that would see us throwing in cashmere twinsets on top of frozen peas in our supermarket trolleys. But any market doing obscenely well by leveraging pressure down the supply chain will eventually attract the attention of the British supermarkets. In 2003 Tesco began its quest to take a bigger slice of the non-food retail pie, including fashion. It had secured a licensing deal with the phenomenally successful US global brand-management company Cherokee, that would exclusively supply 'family apparel' – a rather strange, catch-all term – to Tesco. Since clothes attract bigger margins than groceries, it's no surprise that in quick succession three of the Big Four (Tesco, Asda and Sainsburys) entered the fashion arena. By 2005 supermarkets held 19 per cent of the fashion market. In October 2010 Tesco confirmed its intention to become the world's biggest fashion brand, launching its first standalone fashion store (without the frozen peas) for its clothing brand Florence & Fred. It chose to test the waters for this venture into discount fashion in the historic city of Prague.

You can see how it worked. The grocers applied the same ruthless pragmatism to fashion as they had to food, engaging in a series of loss leaders and price wars which changed the landscape of planet fashion beyond recognition. In the great supermarket wars of 2003, when Tesco and Asda were vying to outdo each other with 1,000 products, fashion was key: Asda's George jeans were being sold for £6; tailored women's trousers plummeted from £9 to £7; skirts from £7 to £5; jackets from £14 to £12. If you pause for a minute, does that remotely add up? Granted, a cheap-as-chips jacket will be a fairly straightforward piece, but consider the detail: the buttons, the seams, the pockets, the level of embellishment. If it was at its true price you'd expect it to be made of cardboard. Ditto the Asda wedding dress, launched in November 2007 at £60. The rewards for the multiples (supermarkets) for leaping out of their comfort zone of food and into our wardrobes proved to be huge: Asda's George brand is worth £2 billion a year, making it one of the company's biggest assets. By 2009 Tesco, the undisputed heavyweight of multiple retailing, was making nearly £6,000 a minute, every single day.

PRIMARNI, THE TOAST OF THE *FASHIONISTAS*

The combination of fast and cheap fashion was like catnip to consumers, and we fell completely under its sway. But there wasn't a lot of critical thinking or engagement going on in the style press or the wider media either. In fact the value retailers were aided and abetted in their quest for domination of the UK fashion market by a compliant fashion media that was as titillated by the conflation of fast and cheap as everyone else. The 'wow' prices and directional styling of pieces retailing for £3 to £4 were given reassuring tags, 'Primarni!' and 'Pradamark!' (the latter works less well, I think). They helped to destigmatise fashion pieces that were as cheap as chips. It became rather cool to trot about in worthless, disposable fashion.

A watershed in the British media was the change from the dominance of monthly style titles such as *Marie Claire* and *Glamour* to the weekly style bible *Grazia* in 2005. The emphasis was on refurbishing your look on a weekly rather than a monthly basis, and this tied in perfectly with the emergence of the big value players. Readers could afford to have it all. You could change outfits four times a day, live the wardrobe life of a WAG, pretend you were Lindsay Lohan if you so desired. For a while nothing appeared able to dent the crown of the value players, not even conflicting or troubling undertones. So it did not overly matter that almost at the same time in 2005 that Primark's Arthur Ryan was named 'most influential man in high-street fashion' by fashion industry bible *Drapers*, his retail empire was named 'most unethical retailer on the high street' by *Ethical Consumer* magazine (a publication with fifteen years of experience in grading companies). If it hurt, it didn't show.

Even so, the discounters can get defensive about cheap, cheap fashion, and sometimes consumers get defensive on their behalf. In common with food, where retailers go misty-eyed and tell us about old ladies on pensions now being able to afford ready-made pasta dishes, the same retailers tell us that this is why they have – in the manner of a caped crusader – wrestled down the price of style, democratising the cost of clothes for families on low incomes so that small children can keep warm. The value retailers like to propagate the idea that they are producing 'affordable' clothes for vulnerable consumers who would presumably be reduced to wearing rags if it wasn't for the service Asda, Tesco, Peacocks, Matalan, New Look, Primark *et al.* provide with their commitment to 'family apparel'.

But before we give Terry Leahy, Arthur Ryan and the rest of them good citizen awards, it is worth looking at who has really catapulted these retail gods into millionaires' row. Affordability in fashion is a hot potato of an issue. I see no reason why fashion shouldn't be affordable, but shouldn't the fast-fashion and value retailers drop the Hovis act? The fact is that they moved aggressively into the fashion market, desperate to claim as big a slice as possible of this retail pie, and more often than not their prime audience is not the low-income family but the well-heeled fashion fan.

For starters, it's interesting to see how quickly value retailers move house, shifting into ever more prestigious retail locations. A flagship store plus all the positive press coverage that comes with it attracts a richly profitable clientèle. As one analyst puts it, these factors seem 'to have de-stigmatised discount shopping for the middle-income groups who were [once] the mainstay of the mid-market'. Another expert, writing on Primark's ability not only to hold on to the top retailer spot (in terms of the highest-value share of the clothing market) during the recession-plagued year of 2009 but to increase that share of its market by 18.2 per cent, was in no doubt about which audience the retailer should be thanking: '[Primark] enjoys a relatively young customer base which has been least impacted by the economic downturn because of fewer financial responsibilities.'

Make no mistake, the value retailers are gunning for fashion's most voracious consumers. That includes the 16 per cent of consumers, innovators and early adopters who can be termed 'highly fashion aware': who are not just conscious of trends, but likely to act on them. So it's no surprise that British consumers now buy 40 per cent of our clothes at 'value retailers' with just 17 per cent of our clothing budget. The value retailers are clearly as fashion-conscious as everyone else, going out of their way to attract designers and labels with high-fashion overtones. As I write, Asda is just about to launch its second collection with Barbara Hulanicki, world-famous as the founder of 1960s brand Biba.

You might also discover – and I was alerted to this by an article in the style press – that once a value retailer has its feet under the style table, it might ditch its 'value' dogma altogether. In March 2010, for example, Tesco launched F&F Couture, a sixteen-piece collection. Pieces included a puffball polyester dress at £140. 'F&F signifies a new era for supermarket fashion,' Jan Marchant, Buying Director of Tesco Clothing, said at the launch of the label.

RECESSION CHIC

'Don't worry!' I'm blithely told when I have one of my little turns about levels of consumption and the march of fast, cheap fashion. Ever since the global downturn I have been confidently reassured that the pants and sock discarders, the Primark bargain litterers will change their ways during a recession. By the end of it, they'll be darning their socks in a wholly sustainable manner. To be fair, it did appear that as the economy nosedived in 2008–09 planet fashion began suggesting that there were choices to be made. These may have been small gestures, or pyrrhic victories, but there was some evidence that *fashionistas* were tightening their tiny little belts. 'Gucci or Gas?' asked *Harper's Bazaar*. OK, it was hardly a blueprint for surviving the global downturn, but you get the idea.

Meanwhile, experts predicted that there should be an average rise in womenswear prices by 4.7 per cent between 2008 and 2012. We'll return to this later, but labour costs have increased by 50 per cent in the past four years across provinces in south-eastern China – aka the sewing room of the world. Fast fashion is dependent on cheap fibres, predominantly polyester and cotton – which account for more than 80 per cent of all fibre production worldwide. Both are dogged by sustainability issues. These factors suggest that the fast, cheap party we've been experiencing for over a decade should by rights have started to wind up.

If I had a pound for every time I've been told that the recession would take the heat out of the way we acquire and use fashion, I'd have enough for a *real* aviator jacket. But rumours of the death of fast, cheap fashion have been greatly exaggerated for two main reasons. Firstly, we've adapted to this new style paradigm so enthusiastically that it's difficult to break the habit. Secondly, value fashion offers us the moon on a stick, and anaesthetises us from the real issues in our wardrobe.

In fact the value retailers have never had it so good. They now take a bigger slice of the collective wardrobe than ever before. In January 2009 Primark overtook Asda, Walmart's representative on UK earth, as the biggest low-price clothing retailer. There was more to come. Despite reporting 'challenges' such as cotton and synthetic fabric costs, the value retailer overtook Asda and M&S to reach the coveted top spot of the largest clothing retailer in the UK by volume (i.e. for all clothes sold) by the summer of 2010. In November that year Primark announced that it would be opening six new shops in time for Christmas. Even as times became progressively harder across all sectors, where fashion was concerned the value retailers appeared to have been given a get-out-of-jail-free card. In September 2010, according to the Office for National Statistics, while the rest of the retail trade was in a slump, non-food sales for supermarkets were soaring, and clothing and footwear sales rose by 6.1 per cent by value and 4.8 per cent by volume compared to the same month the year before. In April 2010 Tesco clothing sales had broken through the £1 billion barrier for the first time.

The ascendancy of the value retailers might even be boosted by extra customers in a time of recession, as there will inevitably be some flight downmarket by middle-class consumers. Within hours of the announcement in October 2010 that in future child benefits would be means tested, independent fashion retailers and labels at the pricier end of the market were fearing for their own livelihoods. The connection might not be immediately obvious, but in 2013 benefits to many middle-income families will be cut, and according to independent fashion retailers this money was previously additional disposable income for the household that went on bolstering the wardrobe. 'A middle-class lady [with one child] gets about £80 month in benefits, so in three months she has enough to buy one of my dresses. It's in effect her spending-spree money, and that's who I sell to,' Tanya Sarne, owner and founder of premium womenswear brand Handwritten, told *Drapers*. Let's leave aside the moral rights and wrongs of using taxpayers' money to fund premium-dress buying for a minute, and imagine the likely scenario. If she is too addicted to acquiring new pieces to curtail her fashion buying altogether, Sarne's customer could just take her spending spree down the price chain.

Doubtless, value retailers, from Peacocks and Primark to Tesco and Asda and everything in between, will be hoping that this proves to be the case. At the time of writing even more brands are battling to join the value-retailing fashion fray. Argos, the famous catalogue purveyors of toasters and tents, is reportedly intending 'to stage a land-grab in the fashion market in a challenge to established clothing retailers'. Then there's Japanese fashion chain Uniqlo, that has the fast/cheap alchemy off to a fine art and is currently seeking to 'strengthen its position in the UK market' by planning huge 20–30,000-square-foot stores across London (double the size of its average existing store). It has the rather scary stated intention of becoming 'the biggest global casual-wear company by 2020', according to an interview which Daisuke Hase from Fast Retailing, Uniqlo's parent company, gave to the *Japan Times* in October 2010. He rather laboured the point by adding, 'We call ourselves Fast Retailing. We move things very fast. Please keep an eye on us; we will change the world very quickly.' Yes, Mr Hase, I am watching. And let's not forget a foray from US fashion giant Forever 21, opening any day in Birmingham's Bullring and expecting to do well as, according to its Executive Vice-President, 'Forever 21's fast-fashion concept perfectly suits the European consumer's appetite for trend-led fast fashion at value prices.' No doubt.

Rather than a return to slower fashion, with its natural blowholes and steam vents to ease the many pressures on the system, so far the downturn in global finances seems merely to have consolidated the alliance between ever faster and ever cheaper fashion. This is Big Fashion (its closest relatives being Big Agriculture and Big Pharma – as in pharmaceuticals), where the power of a whole sector becomes concentrated in the hands of a few major players whose primary aim (arguably to the exclusion of all others) is to make money for shareholders.

Unless we do something to break it, we will remain bewitched and in the grip of the alchemy of the cheapest, fastest fashion we've ever known, all the while continuing to squeal with delight, 'How do they get it that cheap?!' It's a question that retailers are understandably loath to answer. When they do provide a response, expect smoke and mirrors and the determined obfuscation of big business that isn't ready to admit a missing ingredient. It's to do, they will say, with purchasing power, efficiency and leverage over the supply chain. Ever hopeful, I decided to ask Big Fashion players again, 'No, really, how *do* you make clothes that cheap?'

So I wrote and asked them. Here's a typical example of my letters.

Dear [Chief Executive of a high-street chain],

A recent trade magazine's review of the high-street stores stated categorically that 'You won't find a cheaper aviator jacket at £25 or military-style coat for £29, while jumpsuits and winter maxi dresses go for £13 and £15 respectively.' The researcher in that case was unable to find any item over £30. My own experiences of several of your outlets tallies with this. I would be very grateful if you could give me the definitive answer to how you are able to offer garments at such a low cost. In short, how do you get them so cheap?

Many thanks

Lucy Siegle

Despite repeated requests, some retailers apparently felt no compulsion to share the secrets of their alchemy, and did not reply. Uniqlo, George (Asda) and Tesco, however, all showed the good grace to do so.

'UNIQLO is a SPA retailer; "Speciality store retailer of Private label Apparel", meaning our activities are fully integrated from manufacture through sales, including material procurement, design, product development, production, distribution, inventory management and final sales,' explained Amy Howarth, head of marketing for Uniqlo UK. 'We control all elements of manufacture, meaning we can pass on the great price to our customer, avoiding the middle man.'

She then outlined the sheer size of Uniqlo, and how its 965 stores in ten different countries globally (as of November 2010) meant that 'we are able to offer customers excellent value based on scale of manufacture and production'. So far so clear, but towards the end of the letter the reasons for Uniqlo's ability to retail at super-low prices become more oblique, and frankly more mysterious: 'Everything UNIQLO does is deeply rooted in our Japanese origin. We always aspire to ensuring the highest excellence in quality, design and technology.' The accompanying sheet explaining Uniqlo's 'Made for All' philosophy gives few actual clues: 'We believe that everyone can benefit from simple, well-designed clothes. Because if all people can look and feel better every day, then maybe the world can be a little better too.' No doubt.

But surely there is an omission here? I saw no reference to the people who actually physically make these garments. From Uniqlo's response, you'd be forgiven for thinking these clothes materialise on the rails by some Japanese design osmosis.

The letter I received from Fiona Lambert, brand director of George (the clothing arm of Asda, which is in turn the UK arm of Walmart), is clear on the central purpose of George clothing: 'George was established by George Davies more than twenty years ago with a simple purpose. He wanted to design and sell clothes that represented Style, Quality and Value. For the past twenty years, we have been working hard to deliver that promise and make fashion affordable for our customers.'

She is quick to correct an apparent assumption: 'It is often wrongly assumed that George's low prices are simply a result of how we source our garments. In fact, it is because of a consistent focus on efficient operations, and margins that are considerably less than those of the high-street fashion retailers. Reducing costs is not achieved by one single measure but instead demands a holistic view and rigorous examination of all of our processes, spanning everything from supplier relationships to reducing the size of swing-tag labels.'

There follows a further explanation of Asda's ability to sell clothes so cheaply: it does not need to spend 'vast amounts of money advertising its George range in order to attract people into its stores'. And as its stores are predominantly based on the outskirts of towns, they enjoy lower rents. Fine. All plausible stuff. But what about the actual making of the clothes?

'The largest cost in a garment is fabric,' Ms Lambert continues. 'We centrally source high volumes of materials including cotton, fabric, buttons and zips to drive cost savings which are then shared with factory owners. In many instances we leverage our scale with Walmart to globally source. We also centrally source all packaging, hangers and swing tags and have even reduced the size of swing tags to cut costs. We have, through our in-store garment hanger recycling process, recycled over 65.5 million hangers to date. The second largest cost is freight. The ways in which we transport our clothing ranges allow us to reduce costs. So, by planning our ranges well in advance, expensive air freight is used only as a last resort.'

Again, all good logistical planning. But it is disconcerting to read, spelled out in black and white, that fabric and freight are the biggest costs of these clothes. Surely we are missing somebody here? There is no reference to the remuneration of the garment workers who actually make them.

Garment workers are not explicitly mentioned in Ms Lambert's letter at all until near the end, where the fact that Asda has 'an ongoing relationship with GTZ', a German NGO working on a pilot productivity scheme focusing on 'worker skills', is highlighted. So, high volumes, intricate planning, and at least three mentions of swing tags, but no reference to garment workers as an entity.

Tesco's response comes from commercial director Richard Jones. 'We work extremely hard to ensure we are more efficient – and more fashionable – than our competitors. We source directly from factories where others go through agents. We leverage our scale and increasing volumes so that suppliers get good-size orders and we get lower unit costs. We employ great staff in the UK and around the world who get to know the suppliers personally, and work out who can offer the best prices with decent technical and working standards. We ensure we give clear specifications so there is little to-ing and fro-ing with suppliers to get the initial design right. Then we have quality and productivity experts regularly visiting factories to ensure efficient production and that there will be few "rejects" among the orders dispatched. We are global leaders in the efficiency (and low carbon) of our transport and logistic systems.'

Mr Jones then introduces the topic of labour rights. He flags up Tesco's 'proud' membership of the Ethical Trading Initiative, and highlights the fact that the company is also working on improving the skills of workers: 'A broader example of our commitment to support improvement is shown in our current work to establish a Skills Academy for the garment sector in Bangladesh, which will help suppliers to both local and international markets improve production efficiency, raise wages for workers and reduce working hours. The challenges of ensuring decent working conditions, of course, face all clothing suppliers,' he acknowledges, before ending with a flourish: 'We're conscious of how valuable the garment sector is to many developing countries' economies and believe strongly that the right thing to do is to face challenges in working conditions head on and help improve them – continuing to provide opportunities for jobs and for economic growth – rather than reduce our trade and see those jobs and the opportunities for growth also reduce.'

3

FASHION CRIMES AND FASHION VICTIMS

A Dispiriting Journey as Fashion's Back Story Unravels

At the risk of sounding jaded, the responses from the retailers are predictable. Overall, the peculiar alchemy of Big Fashion is explained away through the might of their buying power, thriftiness in marketing and advertising (and in some cases design and their avoidance of expensive, flashy offices), their genius at managing stock, and innovations involving swing tags. In the case of major supermarkets, when a price just seems too ridiculously recession-busting to be true – for example, jeans at £6 or T-shirts for £4 – you wonder if there might be another unspoken reason: are these garments being used as 'loss leaders', with the retailer taking a hit on margins, covering the basics of production just to entice a new type of buyer into its stores? After all, supermarkets trade in fashion just as they do in bananas and potatoes. I'm not suggesting that this is outrageous because it's undignified for fashion to be traded as if it were a sack of spuds (although it does make me feel a pang of regret), but because by dropping prices still further and absorbing the hit, the multiples goad everybody else to do the same. Prices that are already deflated spiral ever downwards.

The impact of this spiral is felt thousands of miles away by that human element of the Big Fashion jigsaw which is largely absent in the responses from my value-fashion penfriends and from any mention on the label. A staggering one and a half billion pairs of jeans and other cotton trousers are sewn in Bangladesh every year, while India manufactures over seven billion pieces of over a hundred varieties of Western-style garments annually. By 2002 China, famously a powerhouse of consumer production, was reckoned to be churning out over twenty billion garments every year. (This means that were the global wardrobe divvied up equitably – we know it's not! – every man, woman and child on the planet would have four Chinese items of clothing.) There are now an estimated 250,000 garment-export factories worldwide – as the name suggests, they produce solely for export. In the UK we are hungry recipients of this fashion bounty. According to industry estimates, Britain scoops up half of all the apparel destined for Europe. Does it all arrive by magic?

No, it happens by human endeavour. The Big Fashion engine is powered by an estimated forty million garment workers toiling away, thousands of miles from the teams of buyers and designers in the European HQs. You could call them the Cut-Make-and-Trim army. Cut Make and Trim (CMT) is the point in the fashion chain where – the raw fibre having been spun and made into fabric, and the patterns and trends having been decided – the garments are actually made. According to fashion theory there are 101 stages in the supply chain, the first being 'designer attends fabric show' and the last 'order ready for shipment'. (After that, of course, it still needs to be flown and/or shipped and trucked before it gets put under your nose.) The CMT stages, where the thing is actually made, account for just a tiny part of this whole flow chart: 'only twenty-eight days and nine operations involve actually making the garment'. But these nine stages involve an extraordinary amount of human effort.

Fortunately for the industry, the new fashion model is the poster child of globalisation, and globalisation tends to specialise in sourcing the cheapest (and often the most compliant) labour on the planet. South-East Asia offers much of this labour, which explains why fast fashion's global assembly line snakes its way through countries such as Cambodia, India, Vietnam and Bangladesh, all of which have become increasingly dependent on the garment trade to bolster their GDP. But the conditions created by globalisation do not breed loyalty. In fact you might say that they allow global fashion brands to play the poorest countries in the world with all the fidelity of the average tomcat. In this massive juggernaut of an industry, always on the lookout for the best deal and the quickest turnaround, brands and retailers will source not from a handful of trusted suppliers, but from forty or fifty garment factories. If there are preferential trade tariffs they may look at sourcing from African nations, and occasionally South American. The choice is vast, and if one producer isn't supplying you quickly or cheaply enough, you merely look for a more compliant one.

Not only is the global assembly line long, it can also be brutal. Working conditions are typically very poor, and often dangerous. This leaves our CMT army toiling away in some of the most pitiful conditions in the poorest countries on the planet, in facilities that are most accurately described as sweatshops.

There are several ways to define a sweatshop. The original phrase described a system that outsourced or subcontracted labour. This still holds true, but the term is generally extended, applying to any production facility where the house menu includes long hours, unsafe working conditions and low pay, and where workers are not permitted to join unions or form an organisation to represent their interests. On top of this technical description we can add more imagery, gleaned from reports and exposés over recent years, some of which makes uncomfortable reading and viewing. But nothing like the discomfort of spending most of your waking life in these places. When I think of a sweatshop I also think of oppressive temperatures, perhaps the stench of human sweat, the relentless whirr of machines, overflowing toilets, the whole sorry scene policed by a pacing factory manager, possibly with a baton in his hand.

Although definitions are imprecise, the number of garment workers who can be considered highly vulnerable, the victims of a lax and at times inhumane industry, is disturbingly large. Potentially they stretch into millions. Who are they? It is likely that most of your wardrobe will have been made by women. They dominate the CMT army. They are considered to be more easily pacified, especially as cultures throughout the Developing World dictate that they are less likely to question middlemen or subcontractors over pay and conditions. Women, with their smaller hands, are also preferred for stitching: they are more nimble, and if they are physically slight they may also be more easily intimidated.

In the USA, anti-sweatshop organisations have been unequivocal in drawing connections between the way we consume fashion and the reality of production. 'Over the past fifteen years, powerful US clothing retailers such as Walmart, Lord & Taylor and The Gap have created a global sweatshop crisis,' says a report by Behind the Label.org from January 2001, which goes on to say that in 150 countries around the world over two million people, many of them young women and teenagers, work in garment sweatshops producing for American retailers. Globalisation means that clothes in the UK and across Europe are similarly sourced. We can draw our own conclusions as to how much of our fashion can be attributed to sweated labour.

THE HUMAN FACE OF BIG FASHION

Retailers, manufacturing brands and consumers have all become fantastically adept at divorcing fashion from the fact that it has been made by an army of living, breathing human beings. As consumers we've been completely anaesthetised by the seemingly incredible value of fashion over the last decade. The kick that buying cheap items gives us makes it easy to forget the reality of their production. We tend to make a joke about the fact that deep down we suspect they've been made in loathsome conditions, and sometimes we ignore it altogether. Cue Claudia Winkleman, on a jaunt for *Vanity Fair* at Paris Fashion Week: 'So what about the couture thing – the freakishly expensive skirt that has been hand-sewn? All I'm throwing in is: has anyone here been to Primark? No, really. Their jeans are eight quid, and I reckon a machine sews those seams together in less than thirty seconds.' I can forgive Claudia Winkleman a lot – she is the funniest presenter on TV – and of course she's only trying to show divorced *haute couture* is from reality (more on which later), but uncharitably I'm going to make an example of her. She is not far off the mark with her estimate of thirty seconds for the seams. The forty million garment workers are expected to conform to a standard (known by the industry as the 'virtual factory standard' – more on this later) which generously allows fifteen minutes on the global assembly line for a pair of five-pocket jeans. However, bear in mind that that includes fourteen different pieces of sewing, including 'fly front with zip' and 'leg bottom hems'. She has also omitted to say that a living, breathing human being operates that machine.

The pressure on that living, breathing human being is intense. It is hard to overstate how brutal the assembly line is for the average garment worker. Sixty first-year fashion students at Northumbria University decided to have a go, spending a day in their own sewing room, set up as a simulated version of a typical production line producing T-shirts. From the outset it was deemed impossible for them to achieve the timings expected from garment workers, so our students were allowed 1 minute 55 seconds to sew each sideseam: in a standard factory for export they would be allowed just 48.5 seconds. The film of their efforts, *Been There, Done it – Just Not Sure if I am Entitled to the T-Shirt*, shows them working hard. But every slight slip – a dropped pair of scissors, a pause to re-align the seams – costs them dear. The team of students managed to produce ninety-five T-shirts in seven and a half hours. The daily target in an export factory such as in Bangladesh with the same 'line load' (the same number of machines and the same type of manufacturing conditions) would be nine hundred.

There have been some other notable attempts at conveying the realities of foreign production. The *Blood, Sweat and T-shirts* TV franchise, broadcast on BBC 3 (and extended to Luxuries and Takeaways), has made a good stab at bringing them home to a young audience, the consumers of the future, in the hope that they'll have a more engaged and informed understanding from which to make their purchasing decisions. Other stunts to bring the issue to life have included recreating a sweatshop environment in London and staffing it with celebrities (this didn't make it to transmission, for legal reasons that were never quite clear). Inevitably these programmes adopt a format intended for an audience that, not unreasonably, wants to be entertained. They tend to put either celebrities or teenagers – the most televisually volatile sectors – into uncomfortable positions simulating the reality of production. We watch in part because of the jeopardy. We want to know how long they'll stick out cotton picking or garment sewing. The answer is, usually, not very long.

But ultimately, because you can rightly only traumatise Western celebrities, teenagers and first-year fashion students so far, such programmes don't come close to the true horrors of sweated labour. As far as I can see these guinea pigs aren't exposed to conditions that can include being punched in the face for attending meetings, having their documents and permits taken from them, being denied access to a foetid toilet until their bladders are about to burst, being sexually assaulted or forced to have abortions. And they aren't locked into factories at night that are swept by fires from an electronic fault, and burned alive.

In the end, we, with our comfortable Western lives, simply can't experience the pain of sweated labour. We can be tired, yes, from a day spent hunched over a sewing machine, but we can fall back on basic enshrined principles of human rights, the laws of the land and health and safety. These are all luxuries that the average garment worker on the real global assembly line can only dream of.

A DAY IN THE LIFE OF A GARMENT WORKER

I don't tell Sokny that I've watched television programmes simulating the life of a garment worker. I suspect she'd think I was off my rocker, though possibly she'd be intrigued to know how I had enough leisure time to sit about watching TV. She works with female garment workers in Cambodia, and has offered to introduce me by phone to two women who she thinks will talk. As with so many workers, they live in fear of having their contracts terminated, and as with all garment workers, particularly those with young children, they have practically no time off. To make matters worse (for them), Sokny can only catch them while they are on a short break between shifts (more about these shifts in a second), and they will need to talk on her phone outside the factory. 'If we are spotted,' Sokny tells me, 'they may want to leave quickly.' 'Fine,' I say, feeling a) extremely guilty at putting them in this position, and b) very privileged to get to speak to them at all. I call them from London as agreed, and the women answer from outside a large garment operation in Phnom Penh, known for completing subcontracted orders. This is evidently not a show factory.

For nine long years Yong Li (not her real name), who is thirty, has worked in the garment trade, sewing jeans, T-shirts and other basics. At the moment she thinks they are working on an order just for one factory, but she doesn't know the brand (as Sokny, who translates, explains, she isn't able to tell me which brands she produces for because she doesn't recognise the logos or tags). 'I have lots of feelings about where I work,' she says. 'Lots of bad feelings, really. I feel like we suffer a lot, particularly if we can't meet the targets we are set.' At the moment she has to finish two hundred pieces a day. 'It's really hard to do that, although I think I am a quick worker.' And what's the penalty if she doesn't achieve it? 'It is very bad,' she says. 'This factory has very low standards, and supervisors think nothing of abusing you with very rude words.' But Yong Li's overriding fear is always that her contract will be terminated without notice, leaving her totally penniless.

Ke Ling (again, not her real name), also thirty, has just found a job after months on a blacklist. What did she do to get on the list? 'I joined a union,' she explains quietly, 'but it was very difficult because I have a three-year-old daughter and my husband does not work.' She will shortly begin her next shift at her new factory on the other side of the compound, working from 7 p.m. until 6 o'clock the next morning. Ordinarily I'd call this the night shift, but in her case it's more of a continuation: 'I already worked from seven this morning until 6 p.m.,' she says. 'We have been told we must do this to get the orders finished, because we've just received a big subcontracted order.' For a month's work Ke Ling receives the equivalent of $US92. 'We just don't have enough to eat, and it's very hard because we live in a building behind the factory, but they want rent money every two weeks. If I cannot find it, we will have to leave. That's just how it is.' 'If I want to buy clothes for my own children,' says Yong Li, 'I have to borrow money from anywhere I can.'

I ask how they feel about the future, these Cambodian women who spend day after day sewing clothes for such little money. I'm expecting non-committal answers. Instead I get emotional responses. 'I feel like I cannot cope at all,' says Ke Ling. 'I have no choice. Nobody here wants to work in a garment factory like this. It is too hard, and I cannot work out how to feed my daughter. Sometimes I feel as if I just want to cry, cry and run away. Leave everything behind.' Then, straight away, 'We must leave now as we have to go back to work.' It's a measure of how desperate their situation is that women like this will give up any time to talk to someone they don't know, thousands of miles away. They are constantly hoping against hope that something will change.

RUNNING ON EMPTY

We know that global food prices are under pressure. In developing countries, where 60 to 80 per cent of a family's income goes on food, the stress caused by this is intense. Research suggests that for every 20 per cent increase in food prices, a hundred million more people are pushed into the category of 'the poorest of the poor', living on less than $US1 a day. Having a job in the garment trade doesn't keep you safe. Because clothing companies by and large continue to dodge the issue of paying them anything approaching a living wage (i.e. a wage that is sufficient and regular enough to provide a basic standard of living), garment workers have very little security against debt and disaster. It's no coincidence that hikes in food prices, including staples like flour and rice, have been met with food riots in Asia, notably in Bangladesh and Cambodia. It is even less of a surprise that at the front of many of these riots have been garment workers. As M.K. Shefali, Executive Director of the NGO Nari Uddug Kendra (the Centre for Women's Initiatives), based in Bangladesh, puts it to Labour Behind the Label: 'For an adult living in Dhaka city the minimum nutrition requirement for basic living is 1,805 calories per day. At today's cost of living this means Tk1,400 [just over £12] per person per month for food alone. Many garment workers (particularly female) do not earn this amount, which is severely affecting their health as well as productivity.' Forget the morality of this for a minute: how sustainable is it to run an industry with a starving workforce?

The rag trade demands the type of physical labour that we – or certainly I, as a soft-skinned desk devotee – can only guess at. From ginning cotton in India or Mali, using a scythe to separate the cotton balls, gathering and feeding them into the pipes that suck them into the processing mill, to carrying the bales, to hunching over a machine sewing, checking, rechecking, folding and aligning, the repetitive work in many factories requires workers to stand or sit in one place for seven to eight hours at a time. Meanwhile the lowest, most menial workers crawl on their hands and knees scooping up errant fibre, waste material or cotton balls from underneath machines. They are nimble-fingered human dustpans and brushes, able to fold themselves under the machines as the blades and pipes whirl above their heads. This is dangerous work for tired, malnourished people: the slightest error of judgement can result in a severed finger. It also requires a phenomenal amount of calories. These garment workers have the opposite dilemma to us. We struggle to expend enough calories and to control our consumption – hence our expanding waistlines (and more, bigger clothes). They struggle to acquire enough energy on a 'minimum' wage from low-calorie staples: maize, rice, vegetables and fruit – all of which are subject to the vagaries of global food prices. That's surely the definition of insecurity.

The garment worker is short-changed at every turn, so don't be too soothed by a retailer's promise that it adheres to a minimum wage. Naturally it will be referring to the minimum wage of the host country; and just because the government there has a minimum-wage law, that doesn't mean workers are being paid enough to live on. In the case of Bangladesh, the minimum wage level was set in 1994 at around Tk930, and stubbornly remained unchanged for over a decade. After a series of protests prompted by a swathe of fires in factories it was upped to Tk1,662.50 a month, and then to Tk3,000 in July 2010. This looks like a big increase – until you work out that Tk3,000 is £27. Labour-rights campaigners were certainly not appeased: 'The increase isn't sufficient to support the basic needs of the garment workers and their families, and doesn't cover the huge increase in living costs of the recent years,' said Amin Amirul Haque of the National Garment Workers Federation (NGWF). 'Most of these workers are the sole source of income for their families, and £1 a day is far below what a family of three, four or five need to survive.' It remains one of the lowest minimum wages in the world. We should also remember that just because a minimum wage is recommended by a government wage board, there is absolutely no guarantee that factory owners will observe it.

Incredibly, retailers often manage to duck this issue. Professor Doug Miller, Chair in Ethical Fashion at Northumbria University (a post funded by Inditex, Zara's owner), set his first-year students on the simulated assembly line that we saw earlier. After thirty years working around industrial labour issues and specialising in fashion, he is all too aware that 'the labour cost by and large is embarrassingly low'. He explains that in his experience, retailers tend to avoid the issue of 'CMT costs' in their overall plan of how a line of garments will be produced. Instead of independently ensuring that garment workers receive a wage that might cover their living expenses, and are paid for overtime, the industry euphemistically uses a 'Freight on Board' (FOB) price which covers every cost connected with the garment leaving the factory: fabric, trim, packaging and manufacturing. Very rarely is the labour cost (sometimes called the 'make element') quoted as a separate item.

By bundling everything together and outsourcing all responsibility to the supplier, the retailer distances the brand from the low wage paid to the workers. Meanwhile the buyer negotiates aggressively on the FOB price. An estimated 60 per cent of it is usually accounted for by the fabric. There is not much the supplier can do about the price of cotton or polyester, so the only thing left to squeeze is the wage of the garment worker. The buyer might not have the garment worker at the forefront of his or her mind, but every time he or she squeezes the price there's a huge chance that the worker is the person down the chain who it will impact on. And it's not as if there's much slack in the system. According to Actionaid, out of the £4 Asda charges for a T-shirt, it pays the supplier £1.18.5p, retains £2.80 for itself, and the garment worker receives just 1.5p. Is that a fair slice of the pie? As has been noted, through a partnership with GTZ, a German NGO, Asda is working to increase workers' pay.

RISKY BUSINESS

Risk, in today's fashion scene, means anything that might wind up costing extra. Cardinal sin number one is missing the window on a must-have garment or accessory, so it will have to be discounted. From the outset retailers will place pressure on manufacturers to underbid other suppliers, and as part of the package will demand 'just-in-time delivery', often air freighting to make sure the knits or trousers hit the stores at the precise moment they are in fashion. For most manufacturing facilities that means accommodating every desire of the retailer, or of the agents working on its behalf. If the retailer says 'Jump,' the supplier says, 'How high?'

For the actual garment workers, risk means a very different thing. It doesn't take a genius to work out that ramshackle production facilities with faulty electrical wirings and boilers under pressure, plus piles of inventory and fabric and yarn, add up to a tinderbox. Sweatshops have been associated with fires for generations.

As a sobering reminder of that fact, 2011 is the centenary of the Triangle Shirtwaist factory fire in New York, which killed 146 young female garment workers and remains one of the city's biggest industrial disasters. It was the beginning of the end for New York's sweatshop district (though not sadly for the New York sweatshop), as it proved to be a catalyst for campaign and reform – the birth of the labour rights movement, in fact. The Triangle Shirtwaist disaster is commemorated in a museum and several books, and is recalled on its anniversary each year in news packages, with accounts of panic, grief, burned bodies and piles of charred clothing. Those 146 lives would not have been lost in vain if the fire had heralded the end of dangerous sweatshop production in fashion as a whole. But no. One hundred years on, there are more fires in garment factories than ever before. The danger has merely been outsourced to countries where casualties are reported in numbers rather than by name, and often not at all.

Fires continue to sweep through the rag trade, and are not confined to Asia. Time and time again retrospective inspections (surely the ultimate example of shutting the stable door far too late) reveal the same depressing reality. Young female garment workers without unions to represent them or the confidence to raise safety issues are locked into factories to fulfil Western orders. In 2007 the Argentine government shut down seven hundred illegal textile mills, described as 'clandestine factories', in Buenos Aires. Illegal trade accounted for around $700 million in the Buenos Aires province in 2007. The clandestine trade had been benefiting from thousands of illegal workers from neighbouring Bolivia. In April 2006 the conditions of illegal Bolivian workers trapped in an estimated 1,600 illegal sweatshops were brought sharply into focus when six Bolivians were killed by a fire in an unregulated mill.

In Bangladesh, garment-factory fires cause so many deaths that the country's *Daily Star* newspaper published a helpful list of the most significant, entitled 'Major RMG Fires Since '90'. It runs: '62 killed at KTS Garments, Chittagong 2006; 32 killed at Saraka Garments, Dhaka 1990; 24 killed at Shanghai Apparels, Dhaka 1997; 23 killed at Macro Sweater, Dhaka 2000; 23 killed at Chowdhury Knitwear, Narsingdi 2004; 23 killed at Shan Knitting, Narayanganj 2005; 22 killed at Lusaka Garments, Dhaka 1996; 20 killed at Jahanara Fashion, Narayanganj 1997; 12 killed at Globe Knitting, Dhaka 2000.' The list is sadly not exhaustive. On the morning of 8 August 2001 in Mirpur, a worker on the sixth floor of the building that housed Mico Sweater sounded the alarm after seeing flames from an electric circuit board. The building was home to several different units, and workers from all of them ran down the stairs, only to find the fire escape locked. In the stampede twenty-four were killed, and a hundred injured.

You could easily put together a similar list for many of India's garment districts. I've chosen just one example. In October 2007 eleven workers were killed when a short circuit caused a fire at RR Textiles in Panipat, forty miles north of Delhi. They were reportedly trapped in the main spinning room. Local trade unions claimed that their escape route had been blocked by locked gates. Laws – unchanged since colonial times – penalise such breaches with a fine of around $3: the price of a garment worker's life.

Since visiting Bangladesh and meeting journalists there while researching this book, I have started reading Bangladeshi newspapers online. Frequently there are reports of fires, and impassioned articles asking when they will end. A recent image that I almost wish I had never seen is a photograph accompanying one of these. It shows a dozen young women lying on the floor of a room. They died in a stampede from a fire in a Dhaka garment factory. They look like a collection of china dolls lying next to each other.

They died facilitating fast fashion. It is probably impossible to tally all such workers and to memorialise them. Even for those we do hear about, it's highly unlikely there will be any museums commemorating their lives and untimely deaths, or the contribution they may have made to labour rights. The only tribute we can pay them is to insist that things are done differently in future.

OPPORTUNITY COSTS

'Listen, love,' a middle-aged man said to me on a Sunday-morning TV discussion programme on which the 'sweatshop' issue came up, 'they're glad of the work.' I'm not unfamiliar with this sentiment; I must hear it at least ten times a week. It is second only to the classic 'They're just having their industrial revolution now.' Cheap fast fashion is so often still presented as a wealth-creation scheme for poor brown people that it is frankly a wonder Primark hasn't been given a Social Justice Award. It's not an attractive line of argument. First, there's the crude division between 'us' and 'them'. Second, it just seems too convenient to rebrand our unsustainable, exploitative habits of consumption into a beneficent means of assisting unfortunates in the Developing World.

Garment workers are, after all, individuals with aspirations, just like non-garment workers. For their jobs to offer genuine opportunity would require them to be trained and to have a chance to become better-skilled. The reality isn't like that. Yet again, the pressurised nature of the global assembly line all but rules out the investment, time and training needed for a worker to build a genuine career path.

In fact, when the journalist Akshai Jain took a walk around the garment units of Gurgaon in Delhi in 2010, it seemed that skills in garment production were actually being downgraded. His resulting article centred on the heartrending story of Santosh Kumar Kaushal, who had come to Delhi from Allahabad twenty years before to work as a tailor. Initially he found employment at a small 'fabricator' shop (a thirty-person unit where tailors both live and work) earning enough to lead a modest life because he was paid according to the number of pieces he produced. 'We worked to our own schedules,' he told Jain wistfully. 'The atmosphere was friendly, and newcomers learnt on the job.' But when Jain discovered him in the Nali Wali Gali (the aptly unpromising translation is 'the street by the drain' – an area Jain describes as being 'infamous for its filth'), working in the garment factories of Udyog Vihar, the tailor was an employee rather than a craftsman, and was close to despair because his skills had become virtually useless. The fabricator shop where he had once worked had long shut down as manufacturing shifted to factories. Kaushal described his existence as a robotic stream of monitored productivity. No longer did he work on a single garment from source to completion (a source of professional satisfaction for him as a tailor), but on a production line where, he said, 'An army of thirty to forty workers would work on a single garment. One would do just the hem, the other the zip and the third the collar.' And so on. He also spoke of the lifestyle of himself and his fellow workers, preyed on by ruthless landowners who rented them matchbox-sized fleapit rooms: 'Four to five workers are crammed into a windowless room, for which they pay Rs1,000 [about £14] a month. Their wages are around Rs3,600 [£50] if they are lucky. But the work hours stretch at times to fifteen hours. If they get overtime it's just their average hourly pay.'

Whereas it would take a year on the job to learn to stitch a full piece as a tailor, newcomers to the modern assembly lines were given a two-hour tailoring course that taught them little more than how to sew a straight line. It cost Rs300 (£4.20). To train a checker or a garment inspector was reckoned to cost Rs800 (£11.25). 'The tuition is brutal. [The teacher] Siddiqui paces between the machines shouting at the students, rapping them occasionally on the knuckles. "I need to train them with a stick," he says, loud enough for all the students to hear. "If I train a student in fifteen days I make a profit of Rs100 [£1.40]; if they take a month to learn, I make a loss."' The piece ends with Santosh Kumar Kaushal giving up after twenty years, deciding that the industry has deteriorated to such a point that he really can't take it any more. 'Gurgaon,' he tells Jain, 'is no place for tailors.'

The sprawl of garment factories housing millions of workers on production lines is by no means confined to inner cities. EPZs (export processing zones) are part of the architecture of globalisation. Their use is not confined to the garment industry – medical supplies, toys and computers are also produced in them. But they are a model that lends itself well to the international garment industry. At thousands of square metres, and growing in scale every year, it won't be long before these vast factories and workshops are visible from space in the same way that Fresh Kills Landfill outside New York apparently is. They dominate entire cities, and represent the cornerstone of what we have come to call globalisation. The International Labour Office (ILO) has been monitoring them now for twenty years, and defines them as 'industrial zones with special incentives set up to attract foreign investors, in which imported materials undergo some degree of processing before being (re-)exported again'. They are also often called free trade zones, special economic zones, bonded warehouses, free ports and, in Central America, *maquiladoras*. They are the powerhouses of contemporary high-street fashion, the link between transnational global fashion corporations and some of the poorest workers on earth.

An investigation into just why transnational corporations are attracted to set up shop in these zones isn't really necessary. Multinationals, the brands that you and I know, are kept sweet by EPZs, which anaesthetise them from the shock of doing business in political tinderboxes while ensuring the maximisation of profits through a series of tax and duty breaks. Plonked in an EPZ, a transnational can lead something of a charmed existence. Most are subjected to only 15 per cent corporation tax, and benefit from greater autonomy from the host country, which is useful in places like China. From Hungary to Bangladesh, countries are desperate to attract foreign investment, so all a transnational fashion company needs to do is shop around to get all sorts of concessions. EPZs are everywhere. And you can expect more of them, bigger and better, with bigger and better tax incentives, as they come up to their twenty-year anniversary.

Another big advantage for a multinational company is that it can up and leave without notice. After all, what is there to keep them in a particular EPZ or city when every other developing country is waiting to shower them with tax breaks and preferential access to markets? Depending on the vagaries of international free trade, inter-country hookups and tariff quotas, all sorts of global alliances guarantee countries with access to cheap workers a temporary market in big economies such as the US or Europe. Of course these agreements are as solid as a dust cloud, and as likely to be blown elsewhere. But that's OK: factories can be set up as informally as you like, low-cost workers need no contracts or guarantees, and if preferential rates evaporate, the whole operation can be shut down. Fast fashion doesn't require permanence, which is why it fits today's globalised economy like a glove.

So, for example, Levi Strauss & Co. closed its factory in Manila in July 2008, at a cost of 257 jobs. 'We have examined comprehensively all other options, including cost containment and improving the efficiency and productivity of this plant as first options,' Ramon Martelino, Country Manager of Levi Strauss Philippines, said comfortingly to industry magazine *Clothesource* in March 2008, when the decision was taken. 'Unfortunately,' he continued less comfortingly, 'such measures cannot overcome the significantly lower costs of outsourcing.'

And if you can pick and choose your 'host' country, why not pick and choose a cheap but skilled workforce and bring them with you? In 2007, 832,000 Bangladeshi workers left the country for jobs overseas in the garment trade. This serves as a reminder that most garment workers are migrants. Of these, eight hundred were recruited by agents for four textile factories in Batu Pahat district in Malaysia's Johor state. After just a few weeks, thirty-four of them returned to Bangladesh with claims of horrifying torture and ill-treatment. Among the catalogue of abuses they endured were electric shocks at the hands of the Malaysian immigration police. According to their testimonies they were paid $60 a month in Malaysia, a percentage of which had to go to the recruiting agent, and were not given a proper place to stay. One of the workers told reporters he had paid over $3,000 to an agent in Bangladesh, and was promised a salary of $400 and accommodation. He ended up camping in Kuala Lumpur airport car park.

An extensive *New York Times* investigation exposed the lot of Bangladeshi workers who had been 'supplied' to Jordan, where garment manufacturing was booming thanks to a trade agreement with the US. Jordan was able to produce low-cost garments for some of the biggest fashion retailers on earth. Conditions for the Bangladeshi nationals – this time predominantly men – who had paid between $1,000 and $3,000 to work in Jordan, and were taken to the Paramount Garment factory, near Amman, were described as 'dismal', and indeed they were. Their passports were confiscated on arrival, and they were forced to work from 8 a.m. to one or two in the morning, seven days a week.

Some of these 'guest workers' were placed ten to twenty people in a dormitory, but others had to sleep on the floor in between shifts. When the men objected they were physically assaulted by managers. At 4 p.m. the Jordanian nationals who worked on the production floor left for home. It was clear that the immigrant workforce was being ruthlessly exploited.

'These are the worst conditions I've ever seen,' said Charles Kernaghan, Executive Director of the US National Labor Committee, who travelled to Jordan to investigate Paramount and other garment facilities. 'You have people working forty-eight hours straight. You have workers who were stripped of their passports, who don't have ID cards that allow them to go out on the street. If they're stopped, they can be imprisoned or deported, so they're trapped, often held under conditions of involuntary servitude.'

'Involuntary servitude' sounds a lot like slavery to me.

HOME-MADE OPPRESSION

Looking for something to wear one day, I idly pick out from my wardrobe a garment I can't even remember buying: a black embroidered top with an intricate textured pattern. It strikes me suddenly that I have no idea who made it, where it came from, or in what conditions it was produced. It was cheap – under £20 – and yet I wonder if it was handmade. If so, shouldn't that have made it more expensive? When I hold it up to the light I can see the way the black beads fall not quite symmetrically down each shoulder, delicately sewn in so that they lend the fabric a careful sheen. What sort of machine could do that? Was all this embellishment added by human hands? If so, whose hands were they?

'It's handmade, isn't it?' This is a question I often find myself asking shop assistants, friends and colleagues. How do you know if embellishments have been added by machine or by hand? There are machines that can apply and attach sequins and other decorations in seemingly random patterns that look like handiwork, but they require a considerable capital investment by a garment factory. Ask yourself this: is it likely that the piece you are buying has been sourced from a

£35

Party top. Wash with care – if you can be bothered, with all those sequins. Otherwise, wear once at Christmas, divert straight to charity shop/bin.

Who gave me my sparkle?

You might assume that these sequin discs were added by machine. Wrong. A machine would crease and split them too easily. These are delicate and precious (well, precious for bits of plastic pressed in a Chinese factory). Anyway, who needs machines when there are 30 million women across the world who can do the job in their homes for even less than you'd pay a factory worker? Once the seams are sewn the basic garment leaves the factory and is off to a Middleman, contracted to get the sequins attached. The manager of the factory has been on the phone talking stupidly low prices: 'Take it or leave it'. The Middleman had to take it, as usual. In four days he needs to get these wretched sequins attached to 15,000 garments. Fortunately he knows some fast workers, migrant women from Uttar Pradesh, familiar with Zari embroidery. They can handle a few sequins. More pivotally (for him), they are desperate, which means he can give them as little as Rs15 (21p) per top, possibly even less. So he delivers 100 vests and a box of sequins to the home of Farida, in a notorious Delhi slum, one room with three children – 2, 4 and 12. There's no evidence of a husband, which pleases the Middleman – less chance of hassle over payment. And the 12-year-old is a good sign too, because her mother can get her to work on this as well. But the living conditions aren't ideal, with children and cooking facilities in the same room, and stifling heat. The Middleman shouts at Farida, calls her a dirty pig and tells her she'd better keep these vests in pristine condition. If one becomes damaged or dirty, he warns her, the company will be very angry and won't pay him, which means she won't be paid. And she'd better work faster than she's ever worked before, because the company needs this now. It is a famous company and will not tolerate disgusting work (he doesn't mention its name, as this illiterate woman won't understand that it is a world-famous brand). For extra emphasis he raises his fist to her. 'Not too many sequins, not too few. Just like the example.' She rarely makes eye contact, and says nothing. When he thinks the message has got through he stomps out. He has hundreds of other home workers to see. Farida sets to work straight away. She clears a space, using the plastic wrapping of the vests to line the floor. She tells her children to stay out of the way. She opens the box of sequins. They glitter like silver. She sits hunched over, using a large needle to attach the sequins to the furrows in the fabric. As daylight fades she squints to try to make out where to put the sequins. These things take hours. She calls for her daughter to bring a lamp and an extra pair of hands.

Truth Labels™

production facility that has invested in that scale of equipment? If it's from a fast-fashion label, particularly from the value end, that is highly unlikely. Industry estimates suggest that 20 to 60 per cent of garment production (particularly children's and women's clothing) is produced at home by informal workers. They are most likely to be adding beading, embroidery and general embellishment. In the absence of any clues on the label, by and large we're left guessing.

It's very likely that my top was embellished by human hands. That connects me to the legions of hidden home-workers also operating in some of the poorest regions on earth. In fact for real invisibility it's hard to beat these millions of workers, hunched over, stitching and embroidering the contents of the global wardrobe in their own living spaces in slums where a whole family can live in a single room. They are responsible for sewing, beading and embellishing many thousands of garments every month, the clothes that become everyday stock in our high-street stores. They work as fast as they can and as long and as daylight allows, and then into the night using oil lamps. Some have access to old sewing machines and sporadic electricity, but they must absorb the cost. They are at the bottom of the pile when it comes to rights and remuneration. Such home-workers represent the unseen, isolated, bottom rung of the global fast-fashion industry. They live hand to mouth, presided over by middlemen, tyrannical go-betweens who hand over some of the lowest wages in the garment industry (and that is really saying something). They're proof that gross exploitation doesn't just exist in factory sweatshops. SEWA, or the All India Federation of Self-Employed Women's Associations, battles for rights for these most marginalised workers in the fashion economy. 'The wages paid to home-workers are nowhere near even close to the minimum wage,' organiser Sanjay Kumar, one of the few male faces at SEWA, explained to me, 'and that is a direct result of layers of middlemen.'

Strangely, as I don't often hang out with supermodels, it's the British model Erin O'Connor who crystallised the issue of home-workers for me. I interviewed her in 2010 after she had come back from seeing a SEWA initiative in India. The purpose of her trip was to fact-find and then publicise the lot of home-workers, who just hadn't been on the radar. She went to their houses, saw where and how they worked, and had a go at making some products herself. Admittedly the latter is a standard NGO photo op (I remember pictures of Chris Martin pulling a plough in Mexico on an Oxfam trip to highlight endemic problems in trade tariffs), but it did give her huge respect for their skills. 'I have previously been a very enthusiastic consumer, and I didn't assume the origins of garments enough,' she says. 'The thing is, when you see an article – whether it be a bejewelled pen from Monsoon, or a top in Gap that requires embroidery – you almost don't believe that it is made with a pair of very determined hands, and that it is time-consuming and that each garment in a sense is bespoke, because the way in which they do it – the chalk is their guideline, like a tailor. There's not much to make us aware of women using their hands and their heritage, is there?'

No, there isn't. Instead I think, scanning my wardrobe and flicking through the hangers, looking up close at a bag or a shoe, there is a huge effort to distance us from the people who make our clothes, and their skills. Branding, labelling and trends tend to remove those people's heritage and their history. We'd prefer to believe that our clothes were produced by a fully automated industry.

SMALL HANDS AND THE INEXORABLE SLIDE OF GARMENT PRODUCTION

From unseen workers we turn to what many consider the least acceptable side of a chaotic supply chain, and the one from which companies will do most to dissociate themselves: child labour. Many people's perception of sweatshops will automatically include child workers, based in part on the historical imagery of children toiling in the cotton mills of Lancashire and Yorkshire at the time of the Industrial Revolution.

I was seventeen, and on a trip to northern India with a friend, when our hosts thought it would be interesting for us to visit a small carpet factory. I think they were hoping we'd also buy some carpets. But the only thing I remember is that it was the first time I saw child labour: a small boy propped up at a loom, where he lurched from side to side weaving a carpet, as his feet tried to reach for the pedals. We were told he was eight, but he looked younger, and he was obviously blind. My friend started crying, and we were unceremoniously thrown out, thus failing even to be proper eyewitnesses. We talked about mounting some kind of rescue (this would have been idiotic, obviously), of confronting the carpet factory owner, which I think we tried to do, but he refused to look at us. In the end of course we achieved nothing. This was not an unusual experience in India in the early 1990s, when child labour was not as sensitive an issue as it was to become. I can only say that it's an image that has continued to motivate me.

Child labour in garment production remains *the* emotive issue. How could it not be? The pathos is almost too much to bear. Children have small, nimble fingers, cannot resist violence and intimidation easily, and are bought from desperate parents in rural areas all over the world. Their expendability made them a mainstay of the nascent sports apparel factories that have popped up all over Sialcot in Pakistan in the past twenty years. The major brands are adamant that they have applied so much pressure on the child labour issue that it is in decline in the garment industry. It is true that big brands act very swiftly if they are connected to child labour. When campaigners are able to demonstrate that a brand is using children the news is flashed all over the world by a rapacious media. (This is not always motivated by altruism: there is no denying that brand-slaying is a good story.) In turn this acts like a touchpaper to consumer outrage. There's no ethical story like a child labour story.

Despite the industry's keenness to sort out child labour, it is still rife. In the decade from 1997 to 2007, India gained the ignominious title of the world capital of child labour: it contributes an estimated 20 per cent of the country's gross national product. In effect we are pretty powerless to know whether a child gets home from school and then has to crack on with a needlework project that might make the difference between whether or not the family eats that week. But I don't have to go far to see footage of Indian children doing precisely that: sewing beading onto fashion tops that look rather like the one in my wardrobe. The garment-worker mother was up against a deadline, so the children were expected to pitch in. The five-year-old worked so deftly with a needle that it was clear that this wasn't a rare occurrence by any means. There is no room for sentiment at their end. The supervisor might be a neighbour and possibly a friend (although the one I observed was pretty severe), but he won't allow 'lazy' children to jeopardise an outsource contract: the livelihoods of several hundred villagers rely on a group of five-year-olds pulling their weight with the adults, sitting cross-legged in poor light for four to five hours an evening. Just as the old show-business maxim dictates that the show must go on, these orders must go out.

In December 2007 the journalist Dan McDougall, working with German broadcasting company WDR (Westdeutscher Rundfunk), un-covered ten- and eleven-year-olds working in horrific conditions in the back streets of New Delhi. He met Amitosh, a ten-year-old who along with forty other boys had been sold into the garment trade to men who visited his village in Bihar (a thirty-hour train journey away). His life in a derelict industrial unit was a vision of hell. The corridors flowed with raw sewage from a flooded toilet, food was scarce, and Amitosh and the other boys were forced to work day and night, their tiny needles puncturing the fabric of clothes that could be found on any British high-street rail. Jivaj, a boy from West Bengal who looked about twelve, burst into tears and whispered, 'Last week, we spent four days working from dawn until about one o'clock in the morning the following day. I was so tired I felt sick ... If any of us cried we were hit with a rubber pipe. Some of the boys had oily cloths stuffed in our mouths as punishment.'

As the boys sewed the labels into these unremarkable clothes, it became clear which unremarkable stores they were going to end up in: those of Gap Inc. When this was brought to the company's attention Gap 'admitted the problem, sought to fix it and promised to radically re-examine the working practices of its Indian contractors', according to McDougall. The company's policy and 'rigorous' social audit systems launched in 2004 mean that if it discovers children being used by contractors the contractor must remove the child from the sweatshop, and the child must be provided with access to schooling and a wage.

In 2008 Primark was 'let down' by three Indian factories in Tirupur (soubriquet: T-Shirt City), that apparently contravened the company's 'strict ethical standards' by outsourcing the embroidery of 20,000 pieces to small children (again the story was broken by McDougall, this time with the BBC's *Panorama*). Primark moved swiftly over the allegations about the Tirupur Three (as we'll call the factories in question) that were due to be broadcast and exposed in the *Observer*, pulling out of the factories. This was despite signing up in the previous year to UK trade magazine *Retail Week*'s 'A Source for Good' campaign, which pledged to work with 'failing factories rather than abandon them'. The company was at pains to point out that this unfortunate use of child labour was not in any way connected to the low price of the fashion it sells. This is not a view shared by the whole garment and accessory industry. There are people who have worked extensively on the ground who think that the continued use of child labour and low-priced fashion are indelibly linked. Lawrence Warren, for example, who spent twenty years sourcing shoes for major labels, is very much of the opinion that 'Retailers who sell clothes at particularly low prices tend to use a lot of middlemen and not have much contact with their suppliers.' This, he says, makes the use of child labour more likely, and heightens the odds that it will go undetected.

I'm not saying that globalised companies go out looking for children to employ. In fact they actively try to avoid it. Some even work hard to try to eliminate child labour. Certainly they are very keen to keep their hands free of it. But economic cycles, styles, volume of orders – these are all variables that affect the fast-fashion cycle. Sometimes they're unpredictable. Sometimes not so much. Take Tirupur, for example. According to research this area alone is the source of 40 per cent of all ready-made garment production in India. The garment industry here has increased by twenty-two times since 1985. It is huge. You have to wonder whether part of the attraction is that it is just so cheap. And then you need to ask why that should be. Following the *Panorama* Primark exposé and the local government's and textile exporting associations' subsequent rebuttals and disclaimers, including a statement that there was absolutely no child labour in Tirupur, Indian journalist N. Madhavan went to have a look at the garment district himself. He found plenty of children to talk to, busy working away in the international fashion industry.

It's all very well for governments, manufacturers and retailers to make big noises about getting rid of child labour altogether, but doing it is quite another thing. This is especially true if you refuse to change a system that always wants more for less. It will become even more so as prices climb and buyers continue battling to squeeze that Freight on Board price. That will mean even more pressure on a system that is already at breaking point, even more orders being accepted by suppliers who will subcontract, and even more pressure being applied from European HQs. Any claims about the death of child labour are likely to be premature.

DOLE-CHEAT COUTURE

I imagine that, like me, you're pretty used to the cycle of fashion exposés by now. For every step forward there are a dozen steps back into the type of squalid, clandestine operations you'd have very much hoped would have been consigned to history.

In January 2009 it was once again the turn of Primark to step into the interrogation zone – thanks yet again to Dan McDougall, a prolific thorn in the side of retailers that didn't appear to have control of their supply chains. Hot on the heels of the Tirupur Three example, the company had once again been caught using a contractor that was in turn using illegal immigrants, paid just over half the minimum wage to fulfil knitwear orders. Workers were found in cold and cramped conditions, working twelve-hour days, seven days a week. I still have the Kimball tag details of the pieces they were producing (given to me at the time by Dan): 'petrol-coloured cardigan 80646' and 'black sleeveless atmosphere cardi 81742'. By the time I got down to Primark they'd either sold out of the offending items or removed them from sale. Again, the retailer said it had been badly 'let down' by a supplier. A spokesperson added, 'We are extremely concerned about the very serious allegations made against our supplier TNS Knitwear and against TNS's unauthorised subcontractor, Fashion Waves,' and vowed to launch its own internal investigation. TNS Knitwear denied the allegations. Unfortunately (for Primark), the post-exposé vernacular seems to play better when the subcontractor is thousands of miles away in downtown Dhaka or southern India, not a stone's throw from your flagship store in Manchester.

At TNS Knitwear, Pakistani, Afghan and Indian garment workers were toiling on Primark's bargain fashion for £3 an hour. Since they were paid cash in hand, some were also signing on. The tabloids dubbed this 'dole-cheat couture'. It seemed that, nearly two hundred years after the Industrial Revolution, the British sweatshop had not been consigned to history.

4

TEA, SYMPATHY AND AUDITING

How Superficial Checks and Balances have
Failed to Clean up Fashion

Five men in short-sleeved shirts stand around me. A fan whirrs above my head. I am leaning over a common or garden exercise book, an impromptu visitors' book, clutching a pen and desperately thinking of something neutral to write that cannot later be construed as in any way condoning what I have seen in the factory I have just been shown around. My main aim is for myself and my colleagues, including the Dhaka native who has brought us here as a huge favour on the condition that we don't cause an almighty ruckus, to leave as soon as possible.

My mind is completely blank. 'Write something about your experience and how you have enjoyed the tour of our facilities,' suggests the General Manager of the Epoch Garment Factory, Shantinagar, Dhaka, helpfully. 'Say how we gave you a nice tour.' 'Hmm,' I say, pretending to consider this advice, but thinking that it really depends on your definition of 'nice'. Apart from rather vigorously turning out our handbags to make sure we had no 'surveillance equipment', the many masters of the Epoch Garment Factory have been perfectly accommodating. Our visit was unscheduled, and they were clearly under pressure to finish a giant order; this constituted privileged access.

I am in Bangladesh, the country that produces an increasingly large chunk of the UK wardrobe. By 2006 the Bangladeshi ready-made garment (RMG) industry was thought to be the source of nearly 8 per cent of all the clothes sold into Europe, the USA and Japan. But on this trip, my first, I'm not officially here to analyse the garment trade: I'm the guest of an NGO that is showing me climate-change projects. Bangladesh, already in a hapless geographical position as the biggest rivers in India's north swell, pick up speed and converge within its borders, leaving thousands of people homeless each year through flooding, will in future also have to deal with rising sea levels further threatening its lowest-lying areas. I'm also taking in a national project focusing on women's welfare and eradicating domestic violence – 60 per cent of Bangladeshi women live with daily violent abuse in their own homes. Other NGO workers tell me that following the country's latest round of flooding, which eradicated much livestock, women in the south were being used to pull ploughs. But it isn't long before we come across the garment industry. In my first few hours in Dhaka, meeting women who are for the first time forming groups to resist domestic violence and oppression, I come across dozens of garment workers. Of course, 80 per cent of garment workers in Bangladesh are female.

I met them late at night in a downtown district, on a precious break from their shifts. It was easy to understand what my friends who work for NGOs meant when they said they felt guilty gathering evidence out of hours from garment workers about pay and conditions when these women cannot speak freely at work, and hardly have an abundance of what we in the West know as 'downtime'. Lesson number one for me in Bangladesh was that we should be extraordinarily grateful that these workers sacrifice any of their time to give first-hand testimonies about their working lives. It's a big sacrifice, and one that in itself illustrates just how desperate the majority of workers are to have us understand the truth about garment production, and to help them in their battle against inequality.

I knew I would only get lesson number two by actually experiencing a garment factory in Dhaka. I wanted this to be as authentic an experience as possible, not a carefully monitored tour of a showcase facility that's kept running for the benefit of Western visitors, particularly the leagues of auditors who troop in and out of them ticking boxes on behalf of Western retailers. But I knew that this would be somewhere between highly unlikely and impossible. A contact had phoned me a few days before I left Britain. 'You've got no chance of getting into a garment factory,' she told me. The major NGO fixer, a Dhaka native and activist for change among garment workers, had been imprisoned again on account of his 'campaigning'. This is par for the course in many CMT producing countries: in 2010 three trade union officials working on behalf of garment workers were murdered in Cambodia.

Nevertheless, for four days I am acutely aware that in and around Dhaka there are thousands of whirring machines, operated by the lion's share of the estimated nearly four million women – many of them very young – who have turned Bangladesh into an RMG superpower. This morning, as on all others, they're facing at least a ten-hour stretch hunched over their tables producing low-quality fast-fashion merchandise, much of it destined for the UK. Then, just before we're about to leave Bangladesh we get a lucky break. Ellora, a young woman working for the NGO I am visiting Bangladesh with, has a contact who can get us into a workplace she describes as 'a good factory'. Naturally I don't expect to see anything but a flagship advertisement for globalisation, well ventilated, safety aware, with smiling staff who in all probability will be whistling while they work.

And so we set off in our little bus, heading slowly (all travel in Dhaka is painfully slow) into the centre of town. This surprises me, because I thought bright, shiny new production facilities would be based in the surrounding areas. It is at this point I realise this visit is not going to be to a cosmetically perfect working environment, of the type that would leave an external auditor from a multinational sleeping happily, but to something slightly more haphazard, more real. When the bus finally pulls up, the striking thing is that this is not a purpose-built garment factory.

The most accurate description would be that it looks like an office block. There are thousands of similarly impromptu garment factories dotted around the city. Ostensibly Dhaka is booming. The real-estate price has hit the proverbial roof, and there is constant pressure to provide readymade garments for export. Factories will therefore set up anywhere they can. If no premises can be found, new ones are thrown up in weeks, or new storeys added to existing buildings. This explains how one infamous Bangladesh factory catastrophe took place. In 2002 the owner of the Spectrum factory, built on swampland just outside Dhaka, added five new storeys on top of a four-storey factory. In her book *Clean Clothes*, labour-rights activist Liesbeth Sluiter chillingly makes the link between what happened next and our wardrobes: '1 a.m. of 11 April 2005. To add injustice to injury, they should all have been lying in bed at home, because their shift had officially ended at 6 p.m. the day before. The urgency of meeting orders had prevailed. The accident killed sixty-four workers and injured more than seventy – some for life. They were found between the red children's pullovers the factory had been making for Inditex-Zara, and under the purple-stripe women's tops ordered by the German Bluhm fashion group.'

It's into a similar, seemingly improvised facility that I troop with two friends of mine from the UK, two of our NGO hosts, and a local female communist politician who has worked with local garment factories on the issue of conditions and pay. We are very lucky to get access to any part of Bangladesh's garment trade for export, and she has been instrumental in getting us through the doors today.

The General Manager meets us, his assistant searches our bags for cameras, and we follow him up a narrow stairwell to the sewing floor, where about 250 women, mainly young, in bright saris are hunched over their machines, running pieces of dark denim through them while male supervisors – there look to be one to every fifty or sixty women – in yellow vests stand over them. When I say 'stand over' I am actually shocked at how physically close the supervisors stand, their necks arched so they can watch every single stitch appear from the machines. Incongruously it reminds me of playing netball, in which you're not allowed to touch an opponent with the ball, but as long as your feet are a metre away from her you can crane your face over until you are invading her space. I cannot imagine how it would feel to work under that sort of pressure.

Our hosts are magnanimous. 'You can ask any questions, to anyone! Any one of them!' says the factory-floor manager, waving his hands to include a generous section of the assembly line. But truth be told these girls look terrified, and the pace they are working at, plus the volume of the machines, are not conducive to an exploratory chat. I pick on a poor girl with a bright yellow headscarf. She is momentarily petrified, and stops her machine. 'How old are you?' 'I am nineteen,' she replies. 'How do you find working here?' 'It is good to have a job.' 'What kind of wages do you earn here every week?' 'It is good to have a job.' Clearly I am not going to get anything but the party line under these conditions. One of the friends who are accompanying me is clearly shocked. 'Everyone is so close together,' she says. 'When do they get breaks?' 'I'll show you the cutting floor,' says the factory manager. 'It is nice.'

On the way to the staircase that leads to the cutting floor I notice hundreds of boxes marked for Carrefour, a huge European multiple that after Walmart is the world's second-largest retailer, with an extraordinary 12,500 stores across the world. The boxes are stacked up along the side of the assembly floor, masking the fire regulations and the yellow signs pointing to the exits. But then, given that the staircases are almost completely blocked by more boxes, presumably waiting to be picked up to start their long journey to the stores, the exits might not be all that much use. 'These boxes,' I say, pointing out the bleeding obvious, 'they're blocking the stairs. The fire escape! The fire risk!' My voice is becoming increasingly shrill. As you'll know from the catalogue of fires in the previous chapter, my paranoia is hardly without foundation. The factory manager is unmoved by my persistent heckling, and continues to clatter down the staircase. 'I can show you the cutting floor,' he says brightly. I persist, and to my surprise it is our communist leader of garment workers' rights who fixes me with one of those smiles the subtext of which is clearly 'Stop this nonsense.' 'There will be no fire today,' she says, the smile still in place.

Our host wasn't overstating the comparative merits of the cutting floor. A large, well-air-conditioned space, with computerised, high-definition cutting machines, it is indeed much nicer than the sewing floor. It is also, I notice, exclusively staffed by men. As I learned subsequently, in the RMG trade women predominantly do the basic stitching, which is why it is correctly (if you're going on numbers alone) perceived as a 'women's industry'. But the higher-skilled tasks such as cutting are done by men. It's notable that if technology is upgraded in factories or across the industry, women will be replaced by men.

We end up for tea and biscuits in the factory manager's office, where again we are told we can ask about anything we like – cue more arm-waving. And so I bang on about the boxes and the fire escape again. 'Big order,' he says. 'Huge order!' Yes, I say, but the 500,000-piece order for men's, women's and children's jeans is currently blocking the fire escapes. 'This is not,' he admits, 'a perfect factory. This is just a B-rated factory.' Who has rated it 'B', I ask. 'It is rated B,' he says, and we continue in this vein for thirty minutes. The 'B' rating, I'm finally led to believe, is a Bangladesh trade standard, meaning that the factory is not perfect. Then suddenly the manager turns, his tone becoming increasingly impassioned and accusatory. 'How can I get a good factory when you [in the West] pay so little? It is not possible to be perfect.' I can only agree that what I have seen falls somewhat short of perfection. Which is how I end up writing in the visitors' book in a somewhat shaky hand, 'A very INTERESTING visit. Highly interesting.'

My foray into factory life didn't uncover what might be termed a classic sweatshop environment, but it did bring me face to face with a huge order for a European value chain being made in a supplier facility in which there was clearly a flagrant violation of any self-respecting European retailer's code of conduct. Surely this is something that should have been picked up by the audits that we are assured are carried out on the Developing World suppliers of our clothes. After all, the Carrefour Group has apparently performed 2,067 social audits in seven years, working in Bangladesh with local NGO Karmojibi Nari.

Audits are the checks that are supposed to reassure us that the horrors sketched out in the previous chapter are being consigned to history. Indeed, fleets of inspectors are employed by Western fashion retailers and manufacturers to visit factories and make sure fire escapes are clear and working, children aren't employed, workers have freedom of association and are wearing proper safety equipment when they are carrying out potentially health-ruining activities such as sandblasting our jeans. Go to the website of any of the multifarious brands that make up the fashion jigsaw and you'll be accosted by a Code of Conduct, or Social Responsibility. While some retailers and manufacturers would like us just to take their word for it (I'm loath to do this), most have employed auditors to tick the boxes for them, and happily display their credentials somewhere on their websites, and occasionally and more showily in-store.

This is the sort of practice that allows the British Retail Consortium (the trade association for UK retail, and as such the high priest of shopkeeping and the flogging of all consumer goods, including fashion) to assert at number two in an online section on 'retail myths' – just under the bit about UK retailers not being responsible for binge drinking – that there is no connection between Big Fashion's offerings and backstreet factories. The rebuttal is what I would call unequivocal:

> It's a myth that UK retailers source from exploitative, badly run sweat-shops. That would be unethical and unworkable. For example, China is producing shoes for the world on an unprecedented scale. That requires safe, modern attractive factories, not the backstreets. Standards in fac-tories located in developing countries often surpass those in Europe and America. To provide goods in the quantities, of the quality and to the timescales UK retailers require, they have to … Any factory which can-not compete on this level will simply not be able to meet the standards demanded by BRC members and their customers. Retailers work with the ETI (Ethical Trading Initiative) to ensure that high standards are adhered to. Suppliers are systematically inspected. If they are not able to meet these standards contracts are ended and business is taken elsewhere.

And, broadly speaking, we all want to believe that all supply-chain problems have been attended to. Even I have better things to do than suspiciously check every label and website. We'd like to buy with confi-dence, and I would love to believe the consumerist comfort offered by the BRC, but there is a huge discrepancy here. While audits might be carried out and codes of conduct published, circulated and publicised, it's debatable how much effect they actually have. Some twenty years after the first exposés of sweated labour, and despite teams of auditors and countless reports, we are still flooded by clothes made under the type of miserable conditions we saw in the previous chapter. Critics suggest that this is because the only thing an audit ever taught anybody was how to pull the wool over an auditor's eyes.

A BRIEF HISTORY OF ANTI-SWEATSHOP CAMPAIGNING

The first big modern-day 'sweated labour' stories broke in the early 1990s, beginning with the *Washington Post*'s examination of Levi-Strauss jeans' – at the time (and arguably still) one of the most revered and sought-after brands on the planet – use of prison labour in Chinese jails to make jeans for a few cents each. In what has become the standard practice in mass globalised fashion, they were then marked up by hundreds of times their cost price and sold to worldwide, fashion-hungry consumers.

Few could have imagined how resonant that page-six story would become. While presumably somewhere along the supply chain someone thought they had hit on an ingenious way of producing this all-American classic garment, a significant chunk of the public was appalled. The story touched a nerve in the burgeoning anti-globalisation movement, and chimed with the international NGOs which had already tracked down super brands to child-labour sweatshops in the Far East. Denims were cast in a new light. Over the next eighteen months Nike, The Gap and Reebok were all shown to be in violation of basic human rights, never mind labour laws. One by one the major fashion brands were implicated in troubling sourcing chains that involved allegations of violations and exploitation. Twenty years on, the situation appears little improved. In 2008 alone the international alliance against sweatshops, Sweatfree, inducted six major garment brands into its Sweatshop Hall of Shame: American Eagle, Carrefour, Disney, GUESS, Speedo and Tommy Hilfiger. A number are repeat offenders.

Allegations were made and substantiated by investigative reporters, sometimes in alliance with campaigners on the ground. With every piece of smuggled footage or testimony another discomforting aspect of the international fashion chain was uncovered. One particularly seismic piece of video footage from 1995 shows Charles Kernaghan (an American NGO worker who became known 'the Sweat Detective' for his dogged pursuit of evidence of worker abuse in the garment trade) and his colleagues, who have dressed as business executives in order to gain access to a Central American factory in a free-trade zone producing for major US brands. A fifteen-year-old worker tells them that she is routinely hit and forced to take birth-control pills in front of supervisors – enforced contraception is apparently routine. Afterwards, a fourteen-year-old worker takes the investigators to a dump outside the factory, where the camera zooms in on hundreds of empty blister packs that had held the contraceptive pills prescribed to the entire workforce.

Obtaining stories like this is no mean feat. 'We have lost a number of activists, murdered in the course of their duties. Others have been dragged in chains behind cars and had threats made against their families,' said Bhuwan Ribhu of the New Delhi-based Global March against Child Labour when he was confronted with yet another sweatshop scandal involving a UK high-street giant in 2008. 'A lot of money is at stake here, and life becomes cheap in such a desperate and greed-filled environment. Remember, above all, the money that is creating this desperation comes directly from the wallets of Western consumers.' The onus is entirely on the campaigners to prove allegations of the abuses suffered by desperate workers. The smallest flaw in their investigations inevitably leads to aggressive lawsuits by multinational brands. David and Goliath doesn't quite do this situation justice. Campaigns are run on a shoestring, and investigators put their own lives at risk. Many I know have at the very least been subjected to beatings by the goons who watch out for trouble in sweatshop areas. If cameras are discovered on them they are at huge personal risk.

When a story can be supported by footage, and the painstaking checking of inventories against retailers' codes and lists, there is a receptive mainstream global audience. Fury and disgust at sweatshops has become the stuff of front-page headlines, editorial leaders and television documentaries. The decade up to 2000 was an intense period of allegations by campaigners and NGOs, invariably followed by the corporations trotting out the same excuse: they outsourced their supply line, and therefore they could not be blamed if some unscrupulous Developing World factory owner chose not to follow their code of conduct. Unfortunately, the brands argued, their hands were tied, and while they would love to do something about such unfortunate conditions, it was out of their control.

To a great extent it was this 'Out of our control' defence that stoked the fires of anti-sweatshop campaigners for an entire decade. The Clean Clothes Campaign, No Sweat, Labour Behind the Label and other groups refused to allow the corporations any wriggle room. Millions of consumers worldwide were incensed by the hypocrisy of brands making money hand over fist from aspirational products while the reality of the physical production of the brands was far from the ideals they espoused publicly. By contrast with their slogans like 'Just do it', which were all about freedom, at times the super brands looked at best hypocritical and at worst downright evil – as activist artists realised to their delight, this was an anagram of Levi, which made for some provocative guerrilla campaigning.

Many enlightened consumers found the branded posturing unbearable. Typical of them was the American campaigner Marc Kasky, who found himself unable to stomach any more of Nike's denials of allegations that it profited from sweatshop labour, including the full-page newspaper advertisements the company issued in 1997, such as the following:

> Workers who make Nike products are protected from physical and sexual abuse, they are paid in accordance with applicable local laws and regulations governing wages and hours, they are paid on average double the applicable local minimum wage, they receive a 'living wage', they receive free meals and health care, and their working conditions are in accordance with applicable local laws and regulations regarding occupational health and safety.

Kasky sued Nike on the grounds of false advertising. The case trundled on for a number of years before being rejected by the US Supreme Court in 2003, and the sides eventually settled out of court. In fact, as we'll see, Nike has become one of the more transparent brands, in common with Gap, another company that has had its hands publicly burned.

Meanwhile, a global anti-sweatshop campaign had surged into action. The genie would not be returned to the bottle. The more strategic campaigners didn't just bleat about injustice, they very quickly understood that for the super brands image was everything. They didn't just care about the style of a shoe or the slick direction of an ad campaign, they also held their corporate reputations very dear. And they were not as self-assured and impenetrable as they could appear. For all their posturing about giving us choice and delivering dreams, they were vast corporations set up to deliver profit for shareholders and to maintain their value on the global stock exchanges. But the pesky alliance of investigative reporters and do-gooder campaign groups kept unveiling new stories of enforced labour, criminal wages and physical violence. The backdrop to these ultra-glamorous brands was a horror show of human suffering and exploitation. Shareholders and investors began to get twitchy. The anti-sweatshop movement had found globalisation's Achilles heel: the big brands simply could not afford to lose their corporate reputations.

A GAME OF CAT AND MOUSE

At the end of this book I'll return to campaigning – and what those early campaigners taught us – but mainly this period will be remembered as the era of the boycott. As in, if you didn't like what a brand was doing, you were encouraged to boycott it. And not only were you encouraged not to buy its products, but to write letters, tell all your friends, campaign on campus and stage sit-ins. By the end of the 1990s significant numbers of consumers were starting to boycott brands connected to exploitation.

There is of course a big problem with boycotts, which the brands used in their defence: even the mere threat of one can encourage companies to cut and run. They still had little control over the supply chain – it could be argued that they didn't want any – but each time there was another revelation of sweatshop conditions a CEO would just come out and express disappointment at how the brand had been let down by a subcontractor, and announce that it would now pull out of the offending factory/country. In a giant game of cat and mouse that traversed the poorest economies, mighty corporations abandoned 'bad' factories and took production elsewhere (often to a similarly awful production facility). The effect on local communities was likely to be devastating.

Eventually the big brands changed tack. After years of stonewalling and denying responsibility, a 2003 exposé of Gap's connection to child labour in India prompted the company to issue an extraordinary statement: 'We do have problems in our global supply chain, but we're working to put them right.' For once the brand wasn't just talking about a new marketing campaign, although there did follow a series of star-studded advertisements featuring Missy Elliot, Madonna, Sarah Jessica Parker and Joss Stone. The new buzzword among the biggest brands and retailers was 'transparency'. It was out with the old subterfuge and bucking of responsibility, and in with working with suppliers in a conciliatory fashion while communicating to consumers and media that the brand was trying its best.

Big-fashion names are keen to represent themselves as more sinned against than sinning, and as unwilling partners in the global jaunt to find the most compliant country that can best keep up with cheap, fast fashion. For that reason they have implemented an extensive programme of audits.

In the years since 2003, audits have become big business. In essence, sweatshops spawned an industry to monitor them. Auditing pro-grammes work in so many different ways that frankly as a consumer it can be difficult to know what's going on. Some offer independent approval, others offer to work with a company on self-assessment and then give final assurances. Any brand worth its salt boasts big teams of inspectors: in 2009 Nike boasted eighty in-house employees working on what is termed Corporate Social Responsibility (known by its acronym, CSR), while by 2001 Gap had 115 compliance officers keeping a beady collective eye on 4,000 factories. You won't find many companies that are shy about telling you exactly how many audits they have, and the numbers seem reassuringly large. So, Walmart conducts 16,000 social audits across its supply chain every year, and Carrefour audited 609 factories in 2007. Factories that are found to be slipping or below stan-dard can expect extra scrutiny. Tesco increased the number of 'high-risk' sites audited from 87 per cent in 2008 to 94.7 per cent in 2010.

The fleets of inspectors and social compliance teams borrow their phraseology and zero-tolerance sentiments from the anti-sweatshop campaigners. But although they may sound alike, there are important distinctions. The auditing offices and businesses are, in the main, com-mercial organisations with beating corporate hearts, and have in common with their clients a need to generate and maximise shareholder return.

Most retailers, and certainly the huge agents they use to facilitate production overseas, consider their operation private business, and information about it commercially sensitive. 'It is very difficult to know what to do with some retailers, particularly at the value end of the chain,' admits a contact who works in drafting legislation relating to fashion's supply chain, 'because they are not interested in discussion.' There are only so many cancelled meetings that can be rearranged, only so many approaches that can be made. As all offers to monitor human rights within the fashion industry appear to be voluntary, there is nothing to compel an errant brand to the discussion table.

With such a huge range of audits on offer, there are enormous variations in standards and practices. Some inspectors are trained for weeks, some for hours, and some, alarmingly, not at all. Similarly, levels of abuses and violations vary. Inspectors essentially need eyes in the back of their heads. There are health and safety factors to consider – as we have seen, the characteristics of a badly run or makeshift CMT enterprise can include fire hazards, fumes (sandblasting jeans, for example, produces toxic particulates) in the presence of which masks and goggles should be worn – underage workers, a lack of records and payroll evidence, intimidation and the absence of basic sanitation facilities. Writing down a list of measures that need to be undertaken is easier than actually carrying them out.

Many audits rely on interviews with workers. And many interviewees are likely to be the opposite of forthcoming. In an unusually frank account, 'Confessions of a Sweatshop Inspector', former American inspector T.A. Frank remembers entering a supplier's facility to see a sign reading: 'If you don't work hard today, look hard for work tomorrow'. It is, he concedes, motivation of a kind, but he wonders how open employees working in such an environment are likely to be, and how likely they are to raise problems with an inspector.

Interviews are often tortuous. It is clear that they need to be in private, rather than elements of a staged and accompanied walkabout of the type I was granted at Epoch in Dhaka. But even then inspectors can be at the mercy of a translator, and as interviews are carried out in work time there's always likely to be a manager breathing down the inspector's and the interviewee's necks. 'I don't know' is often the staple response to questions about how many hours a week an employee is expected to work, or whether he or she has freedom of association (one of the tenets of an ethical working policy). Interviewees are coached, proffered for interview (rather than being randomly selected), and in fear of being fired for saying the wrong thing.

Where once brands used the excuse that they had outsourced their production (let's call it the 'Not my problem' defence), they have now adopted a more nuanced strategy. To paraphrase: 'The factories that supply us are fully audited by independent auditors, but on this occasion the auditors failed to spot the particular problem.' The auditors claim they were hoodwinked, and very often this is indeed the case. It is hard to overestimate the level of duplicity to which some factory owners will go in order to trick them: there is evidence in many export zones of entire units being created for an auditor's visit, to give the impression of a perfect production environment. Of course these have extravagantly labelled fire escapes, a generous provision of toilets, charts advising mandatory rest periods, and smiling managers. They are the show houses for the RMG industry, and their purpose is to make Westerners feel that all is well in the fast-fashion bubble, that we can have our cake and eat it. I read of one incident where an auditor was unduly impressed by the 'high quality' toilet paper in a staff lavatory. I say unduly because by the time of the next, unannounced, inspection the toilet paper had gone. As indeed had the toilet itself. Just for show, it wasn't even plumbed in. Other inspectors tell of pushing through a door hidden by boxes to find pregnant employees hiding out on the roof, or a room full of sacks in which child garment makers were hiding.

Even when the subterfuge hasn't been so carefully crafted, auditors are missing things, and sometimes you have to deduce that they are turning a blind eye. Pressures of time and a lack of power mean they don't tend to force the issue if they are told payment records aren't available. One former inspector tells of incompetent or feckless colleagues: one man would habitually dash past obvious serious violations and make straight for the medical kit. On his tick-box form he would make a note that it was devoid of 'eyewash', his only recommendation being that the factory must remedy this as fast as possible. His nickname became 'Eyewash'. Another could clock up five inspections per day thanks to their slapdash nature.

Rather than a cause for concern, this made him the star of his auditing firm. But then, time is money, and there's plenty of money in auditing.

When abuses and violations are uncovered, in many cases the information is kept secret, shared only between the auditor and the client – the multinational that commissioned the audit in the first place.

For obvious reasons, it is very difficult to persuade professionals involved in the auditing industry to talk on the record. Many former auditors and buyers, however, are desperate for things to change, and have been keen to talk off the record. A British buyer/auditor who has worked extensively in China has told me of a big factory that has been on the 'high risk' list for two years, but still the orders keep coming: 'They are the cheapest supplier, and can be relied on to deliver on time. I raised them as a problem several times, but in all honesty although we filed the report, we weren't working towards change. It was a disaster waiting to happen, to be discovered. If the factory was discovered by the press then I guess that the company would have said they had been let down and that we'd flagged it up internally as a problem, but we flagged it up and still used it.' This suggests that major fashion brands are finding problems, but are doing little to resolve them (care and compassion cost money), hoping they don't get found out. If they are, there is a reputation-mending public relations team waiting in the wings. It is cheaper to ride the storm after an exposé than to pre-empt it.

Startlingly few factories appear to be rejected as a result of auditing schemes and voluntary trade initiatives. The system is ill. You might even describe it as rotten. Audits are full of inherent contradictions. Of course workers will not admit in an interview that they work illegal overtime. By and large, all over the world, garment workers are paid by piece rate. This throws up a terrible paradox: a worker in a 'good' factory could end up earning substantially less than one in a non-compliant 'bad' factory that pays no heed to overtime regulations. To combat this, workers and factories need to be paid incentives for conforming to the law. For every extra hour a workers sits hunched over a machine her health suffers, her children are uncared for and her rights are being exploited. Similarly, a small village factory where standards might be broadly described as decent wouldn't have a chance of achieving an 'A' audit rating for one of the big suppliers because it doesn't conform to Big

Fashion's understanding of a modern factory, with its ventilation units and eyewash in the medical cabinet.

It might be thought that I've cherrypicked the worst examples here, to make my point. Actually I was spoilt for choice, because there are so many examples of inadequate audits that border on the farcical. A better system (i.e. one with a cat in hell's chance of uncovering abuses and rectifying them) would, for example, ensure that audits are conducted before a company's first order is placed (this is known as pre-screening), not after, when it has established that this is the cheapest company on planet earth. It would include unannounced inspections, using trained inspectors who know what they are looking for, a confidential and anonymous system for workers to report abuses, and disclosure of the name and address of every factory the business uses. Later in this book, when I look more closely at how seriously the high street is attempting to clean up the fashion chain, I'll flag up some of those companies that are taking a more progressive approach. Suffice to say that there are some unlikely champions.

It should be recognised that the bar for audits has been set pretty low. A worthwhile audit should be able to give proof of pre-screening, and disclose long-term relationships and producers. These are modest requirements.

Just as there are trends in the fashion industry, there are trends in auditing and reporting. In vogue at the time of writing is the use of webcams to reassure consumers that suppliers aren't using children or beating workers. But how reliable is the evidence they provide? The cameras are strategically positioned, and they can't show if workers are entitled to collective bargaining or are receiving a living wage. They leave as many questions unaddressed as they answer.

RUNNING WITH SCISSORS: HOW BUYERS ARE SET UP TO FAIL

It's time to meet the buyers and merchandisers. Without them, Big Fashion wouldn't happen, because it's up to them to make sure that the whims of the design office appear instore on time and on budget. I'm not suggesting that their job is comparable in terms of stress and unbridled misery to that of the garment worker, but the lot of a buyer is not always a happy one. The reality is quite often at odds with the enticing job specs you see in the fashion press. Here's an example:

> As a senior fashion merchandiser or buyer, you'd enjoy the travelling and communications with creatives. You will be directly responsible for ordering products from the apparel manufacturers worldwide, hopping from hotel to hotel and living in several different time zones at once.

As is often the case in life, the reality is more prosaic. Sourcing is a sufficiently complex and financially important activity to warrant whole degree courses these days. There are the finer points of operating in a globalised, free-trade marketplace to be mastered, as well as coping with garment quotas, rising textile prices and a whole selection of sourcing software to rationalise buying practices. The buyer must broker deals between factory owners and huge retailers, driving down prices and putting the pressure on to get competitive advantage on the swamped high street back at home. 'It's a bloody nightmare,' one longstanding freelance buyer tells me, on condition I do not use her name. 'It has become a real mess, driven purely by price. Yes, there are ethical contracts and criteria and stipulations, but it is almost impossible to apply these when you're constantly pressing for bigger volumes to be turned around at breakneck speed. You can't have everything.'

It is no coincidence that one of the most influential industry guides to garment sourcing and costings, by international apparel trade expert David Birnbaum, is titled *Birnbaum's Global Guide to Winning the Great Garment War*. The buyers are the generals in that war. If I haven't made it clear so far, the fashion industry isn't just healthily competitive in a 'Whoever has the best design this season wins' kind of way. It's down and dirty, featuring relentless attrition between brands, retailers, global sourcing agents and factories. As Birnbaum puts it: 'Some buyers, particularly those catering to the low-end mass market, will continue to focus on minimising direct cost … many factories will have to continue to deal with the low-end mass merchandisers for better or for worse.' That is some kind of hellish marriage.

Often I find that the buyers I speak to – who tend in fact to be former buyers who have been able to bear it no longer – are troubled by the role they've had to play in what they perceive as a race to the bottom in the fashion supply chain. Most people, given the chance, are actually quite keen to do the right thing. Unfortunately, buyers are usually so worried by or fixated on driving the price down (it having been instilled in them by management that this is their function) that they never get the opportunity to do the right thing. A former buyer for a large denim brand who now works for a large charity is amazed at how ignorant she was: 'When someone showed me a piece of denim it never even occurred to me to ask anything about its origins. It's difficult for me to believe now, but at the time I just looked at the wash, said whether it was the right colour and then said, "Make it 20 per cent cheaper." ' Having spent a lot of time working on trade policy and its effects on Developing World cotton producers, she now has a very different view of the fashion industry.

Her story is one I hear again and again. Louise – not her real name – used to be a buyer and a box-ticker who frequently went on go-see trips. Although suppliers were warned of her arrival weeks in advance, she says, 'I still saw things that in retrospect I shouldn't have let go. It was obvious that the facility wouldn't be able to cope with the order we were going to put through, and you know that to complete the order the factory owner is just going to subcontract to some hellhole that I haven't checked out. But we're under pressure. Who wants a buyer that can't deliver?'

Louise raises another crucial point, and a clue as to why much enforced overtime and illegal subcontracting takes place. It's the buyer's responsibility to ensure that the order will be delivered – and we're talking huge orders. For a multinational retailer to place an order of 500,000 garments from a factory in Bangladesh or Cambodia these days is commonplace. Increasingly, orders are being placed for units by the million. Two contacts of mine, with many years' experience at the top of the mainstream fashion tree, very nearly fell over when they got access to a Bangladeshi factory deep in an order for *five million* pairs of 'city' shorts for a high-street giant. Five million pairs of one garment in one order! Imagine that. It was the opinion of my contacts that the factory would be pushed to make a tenth that many pairs of shorts in the time allocated. So where on earth would the other 90 per cent be cut, stitched, pressed, labelled and packaged? The answer, unfortunately, is likely to be in several facilities that are less cosmetically convincing. The destination of many huge orders is a subcontractor that has been nowhere near an audit or a check. There should at the very least be some logic behind how a buyer decides whether or not a factory can actually accommodate an order. The factory owner will tell the buyer what capacity his factory has, but of course there will be a tendency to talk this up – in this rabidly competitive industry, everyone wants an order. By using the audit, and possibly making a site visit, the buyer should be able to reconcile the size of the assembly line with the size of the order.

Even if the buyer has done this, the whole system can still come crashing down like a house of cards. 'The estimated amount of time taken to complete a garment has always been a "contested terrain" in the industry, going right to the heart of the twin compliance issues of wages and hours for workers, and to the issue of capacity, efficiency and ultimately profit for management,' says Doug Miller. 'Some factories have achieved 80 per cent efficiency, but some in Cambodia don't rise above 30 per cent.' This means that garment workers, through no fault of their own (their machine, or the pattern cutters, might be slow), will take nearly three times as long to fulfil an order.

This brings us back to the simulated version of the global production line Miller set up for his first-year students at Northumbria University. He believes that an understanding of the rate at which garment workers actually work, and the discrepancy between the estimated and the real time taken to complete a garment (each action is expressed as a Standard Minute Value, or SMV), is fundamental to getting a fair wage and a fair deal for garment workers. His student guinea pigs could achieve less than a tenth of the rate expected of a real garment worker.

While the discrepancy between virtual and real-world production levels aren't that extreme, for millions of garment workers on the real global assembly line the production targets are also out of reach. They are based on a perfect virtual factory where every minute of production is measured as an SMV. These virtual targets have been used to set the piece rates of real-world garment makers in facilities that, as we've seen, are very challenging work environments (I didn't even consider the quality of the sewing machines and needles in such workplaces, but you can imagine that they would often leave a lot to be desired). These are the flawed figures on which even the most competent and judicious buyer makes his or her assumptions. As a source told Miller, unfortunately there isn't a huge amount of evidence to suggest that many sensible calculations are being made in the first place: 'Most companies negotiate using historic data … an example being, you made that shirt for $2, make this one for $1.90. Very little science goes into the negotiation, and certainly 90 per cent of companies that work this way will not give a toss as to what the labour rates are in the factory, as long as the external audits do not put them under the country laws of paying the "minimum wage".'

And don't forget to add other pressures. For instance, that design team in some sunlit European office, ever alert to the changing trends of celebrity aesthetics, might notice that the big thing in high-waisted crop trousers is a brass-button detail on the pocket. Never mind that the order is nearly completed, the supplier must be faxed and ordered to add the button. Each piece must be unwrapped and the button be attached to 10,000 units, which must still be ready for shipping on the agreed date. There is no flex in the system. Big Fashion gets what Big Fashion wants, and all the risk is borne by those who are the most vulnerable, and have the least resources.

In other words, garment workers are being set up to fail, and no audit will spot this. You can be the most nimble-fingered, quick-witted machinist in the world, but if you're in a factory that for various reasons offers only 30 per cent efficiency, it's going to take you three times as long to meet your quota. There is only one way you will make it: overtime, whether you like it or not. Enforced, often unpaid overtime is one of the most contentious issues in the garment trade. Working days are habitually stretched from ten hours to fourteen or fifteen, with workers being locked inside factories at night to finish orders, subjected to intimidation and even violence to make them feel they have no choice but to stay.

A study of one of Bangalore's biggest suppliers examined the conditions in which its 2,000 workers toiled to produce shirts, pyjamas,

T-shirts and trousers for big Western retailers. Rather than local workers, the management preferred to use 'fresh migrants from the villages for reasons best known to them'. This tallies with the internal migration to garment factories that we saw in the previous chapter, and it's not rocket science to suspect that such workers are more compliant and less well organised than an established workforce would be. The staff were compelled to meet their production targets through overtime. A twenty-one-year-old finishing packer, Nagesh, told the researchers: 'In any given month I have to work for four full nights following the day's work. Working until 2.30 a.m. every day.' If an employee refused to work on a Sunday, in a bizarre punishment he or she was forced to stand outside for one hour on Monday, necessitating more overtime to make up the lost time. If a buyer commissioned a social audit, things took on a different air: 'When buyers visit the factory, workers who are known to share their problems with auditors are given out-pass and sent home,' Gowramma, a thirty-year-old tailor, revealed. 'There is a board displayed inside the factory saying "Quality is our Main Priority" and also giving leaves and work timings. But these are put up only when buyers visit.' In addition, safety equipment like masks and gloves was provided for the workers during visits by buyers.

Without identifying the factory involved, the researchers contacted Walmart with their findings, and asked the retail giant what steps it would take to remedy the problems. Walmart declined to provide the information, so the researchers refused to name the factory or to give any details about it, fearing that if they did Walmart might cut and run from a supplier that was clearly falling short of its compliance programme. In June 2009 the factory was shut down in any case, leaving the workers unemployed with no warning.

You could conclude that if a system is this broken, no amount of box-ticking or form-filling is ever going to mend it. No webcam can pick up the fact that a buyer has made a dodgy calculation about how much capacity a factory actually has. Unfortunately, we have attempted to impose a one-size-fits-all solution on an industry that comes in all shapes and sizes. At the beginning of this chapter I asked retailers to be more forthcoming about the equations that allow them to sell fashion at such a low cost. If they failed to mention the army of cut, make and trim workers who are being paid a pittance, there was no allusion either to the more superficial types of audit, increasingly part of the tactics adopted by Big Fashion to ensure that consumers sleep easy at night. I can't be the only one who doesn't find this particularly comforting.

5

IN THE LAP OF LUXURY

How Big-Ticket Accessories Plunged the Wardrobe
Further Into Crisis

As the levees collapsed under the strain, and toxic, rubbish-strewn waters flooded New Orleans, citizens, previously doing the normal things citizens do – TV-watching, cooking, playing with their children – were instead to be found scrambling onto their roofs and desperately waving to helicopters, which unfortunately were more likely to contain TV crews than the emergency services. The images of Hurricane Katrina, beamed all over the world, made us all feel vulnerable. The looting that followed, the thousands of people trapped in abject misery, the lack of federal response, combined to give a horrific snapshot of what the results of climate change might look like. Inevitably you ended up asking yourself, what would I do in those circumstances?

When the emergency response finally began to take effect, several days after the hurricane struck, pragmatic concerns focused on dealing with residents who had become refugees overnight. The poorest and most marginalised (this really meant those on the breadline) were given $2,000 emergency debit cards by the Federal Emergency Management Agency, to enable them to buy essentials. There were conditions: the cards could not be used to purchase alcohol, tobacco or firearms. Not included on the list of forbidden purchases were 'luxury fashion items'.

Within hours, at least two of the cards had been run through the till at the Louis Vuitton concession in Atlanta, Georgia. To the sales assistant's utter astonishment – she was aware of the cards, which had been shown on television by the authorities, who were keen to show they were finally doing the right thing – three women, impoverished victims of a devastating natural disaster, had travelled to the store and asked if it would accept the FEMA debit card. Two had gone ahead and spent $800 each on a handbag. (The assistant's astonishment did not stop her from swiping the cards.)

The media heaped opprobrium upon the Bag Ladies of Katrina – the *New York Daily News* went so far as to brand them 'profiteering ghouls' – and there were tales of other recipients using their cards to buy designer jeans and shoes. The message was unequivocal: society disapproves of you fecklessly using an emergency debit card, intended to provide access to life's essentials, to buy luxury items.

Like the press, you could choose to see the Katrina Bag Ladies as a symbol of our all-consuming (and very passive) addiction to branded luxury. Whether or not we have money or access to credit, we are bombarded every day by suggestions – from peer-group pressure – of how to spend it. Mere days after one of the worst natural disasters ever to hit a Western city, two of its victims were using their emergency relief to buy monogrammed leather 'it' bags.

The opprobrium heaped on these women, however, is a bit rich on a number of levels, not least because they were merely buying into the supposed security offered by 'luxury' products. If you don't have anything – a material insecurity rather increased by having lost your home in a natural disaster – it is conceivable that you'll try to accumulate some stuff you can wear around your neck or carry that would be likely to retain its value. Luxury, as we are often told, is recession-proof, so why couldn't it survive a natural disaster?

CHEAPSKATING

Traditionally, and still today at the very upper echelons of the market, luxury goods are painstakingly constructed in some of Europe's most celebrated workshops and ateliers. The craftsman and seamstress are venerated (*haute couture* translates as 'high sewing' or 'high dress-making'). After one particularly pearl-and-bead-encrusted Chanel show in Paris, the great and the good of fashion, led by Karl Lagerfeld (he of the white ponytail and sunglasses, last seen in these pages in the company of H&M), even paused to pay tribute to '*les petites mains*' (the tiny hands), the highly skilled seamstresses and embellishers who make *haute couture* what it is. 'It took ten embroiderers two weeks to attach the 26,000 pieces of plexiglass to [Stéphane] Rolland's bridal gown, the final model in his collection,' noted fashion writer Lesley Scott. 'Trained for years and often intensely loyal to one fashion house, these women can be spotted backstage putting last touches on a dress with needle and thread, or watching the throng of models and dressers with quiet pride.' Compare and contrast this with the way Big Fashion seems so anxious to skirt over the fact that it also uses women to hand stitch and embellish its clothes. In luxury the handworker is celebrated; in Big Fashion she is an inconvenient truth. Yet these two seemingly polarised links in the style chain form a very unlikely alliance. What is the connection between them?

The connection is 'cheapskating', a style phenomenon. In Britain it appeared on the fashion radar around 2005, when a number of fashion writers and editors began to drop it into their copy. Deidre Fernand referred to it in the *Sunday Times* as 'the art of blending luxury with low-cost items'. 'Fashion sophisticates' need not worry, she advised, because 'Shopping in the value sector no longer holds any stigma.' Sarah Mower, writing in the *Evening Standard*, initially embraced the trend with enthusiasm, 'careering around shops and plunging into areas of supermarkets you'd never thought possible, only to surface, twenty minutes later, five brilliant fashion purchases up, £22 down, and tingling with adrenaline'. 'I was the first to write about the trend,' she recalled in 2007. 'I called it "cheapskating": mixing a modicum of designer stuff with a lot of extremely cheap, fast fashion.'

It was not long before the word peppered just about every trend-based editorial in the land, from glossy magazines to edgy websites. It was the perfect formula for a fashion media that loved the story of fast fashion, but was dependent on the large advertising budgets of luxury conglomerates. Here was a chance for it to have its cake and eat it.

(Metaphorically, of course. Not a lot of literal cake gets eaten in this sector.)

For the consumer this initiated a trend of patronising the fast and value chains and supermarket aisles, cruising bargain-basement fashion that was so cheap it could be bought in bulk, and splurging the money that had been 'saved' on luxury labels. We bought at the extremes – the lowest and sometimes the highest.

THE TYRANNICAL REIGN OF THE 'IT' BAG

For a long while there was no item that was more totemic of cheapskating than the 'it' bag. These ever-larger pieces of monogrammed leather from every high-flying brand and luxury label fuelled a whole new fetishisation of luxury goods that were often mass-produced. In the beginning was a bag called the Birkin. Fashion folklore plots the genesis of this bag to a chance meeting on a plane between Jean-Louis Dumas, the then CEO of the venerable Parisian saddlers Hermès, and the fifth generation of his family to lead the company, and Jane Birkin, muse to Serge Gainsbourg. According to legend, Dumas noticed that Birkin was carrying a scruffy straw bag. She explained that she couldn't find a decent handbag big enough for all her stuff, so Dumas engineered a grey crocodile-skin 'envelope' solution: the Birkin was born. Solutions do not, however, come cheap when it comes to the luxury market: Birkins start at £4,200, and run to £11,000 for a grey croc model. Victoria Beckham reputedly has a collection of a hundred, worth a combined total of £1.5 million.

According to Michael Tonello, author of *Bringing Home the Birkin: My Life in Hot Pursuit of the World's Most Coveted Handbag*, the Birkin's devotees think it is worth every penny. To them the Birkin is not just a bag for putting stuff in (even if that was what Jane Birkin was after), but a status weapon. 'A woman walks into an elevator with a Birkin,' says Tonello, 'I've seen this – and all the other women look at this bag and think, this woman must be a celebrity, who is she? It's an incredible tool.' Tonello travelled the world in order to test the famous nine-month waiting list for the bag that apparently made no exception even for top

American celebrities. He procured one for Oprah, and concluded that the reputed waiting list was seemingly as carefully manufactured as the bag itself.

GENERATION CHEAPSKATE

It is one thing for a celebrity to fork out £11,000 for a handbag, and quite another for an ordinary mortal like you or me to lust after such a luxury object. But remember, cheapskating decreed that if you dressed head to foot in value fashion (save) you could go all-out on one of those status pieces (splurge). It was while making a short film for the BBC in 2007 that I saw just how mainstream this tendency had become. According to various chiropodists and chiropractors, women were endangering the health of their feet and their backs by wearing extra-high heels and carrying huge tote bags (the average weight of even an empty bag had increased to five kilograms, which back-care professionals considered risky). It was my job to stop women and persuade them to let me weigh their handbags, and I was duly set up with a trestle table and a set of scales in Manchester's Arndale Centre. Often it can be quite difficult to get busy people to stop for 'vox pops', but on this occasion I didn't need to persuade anybody. A long line of attractive young women was soon snaking around the shopping centre, and one by one they proffered their handbags for me to weigh and comment on. Forget the weight – although they were heavy! What really startled me was the number of 'it' bags. 'Is this real?' I asked again and again. 'Of course it's real!' they would reply. In just one hour, two Marc Jacobs, a Louis Vuitton and a Chanel passed through my hands, all the latest season's and all purchased a few hundred yards away in Manchester's Harvey Nichols store.

Just how can a student, in an age of tuition fees, afford to spend in the region of £1,000 on a handbag? 'Credit card,' said Gemma, who is in her second year studying international development. 'I did it last year too.' Is it worth it? 'Oh, completely. You feel out of the loop if you haven't got the bag to go with it. To be fair, I'm very good with my clothes. The bag is the only thing that I buy that's that expensive. Everything else is from Primark.'

ALL THAT GLITTERS …

These girls had 'invested' a small fortune in their bags. I wondered if their investment would pay off. Because just as fast fashion has changed mainstream shopping beyond all recognition, at the other end of the scale luxury has undergone a similar metamorphosis. In a world fixated on speed and price, the glorious craftsmanship imbued in a luxury product is no longer necessarily its big selling point. After all, let's face it, 'it' bags aren't in the same league as *haute couture*. The new consumers attracted by them weren't overly concerned about provenance and history. In common with mainstream fashion – and with the exception of Hermès, which has recently introduced a made-in-China brand specifically for the Chinese market – most luxury brands began to shift some of their production overseas, retaining just enough lines in France and Italy to allow their 'made in Europe' claim to retain some integrity. The industry began to focus on efficiency, and huge investment was made in streamlining every one of its processes, from design and production to retailing. This was only made possible by the fact that small, often family-owned luxury companies began obtaining sugar daddies. In other words they were bought out by giant holding companies.

LVMH (Louis Vuitton Moët Hennessy) is the world's largest luxury-goods conglomerate. It is the 'parent' of around sixty sub-companies that each manage a small number of prestigious brands (the Christian Dior group is LVMH's main holding group), and competes with other luxury giants like Gucci (now part of French PPR) and Richemont. Naturally these conglomerates wanted to see a return on their investment, and they wanted it to be quick. They wanted growth and profit at a pace that would have been inconceivable to the old-fashioned, creaky luxury system, which appeared more interested in artistic stature rather than profit. Embracing mass production, the new luxury conglomerates looked to lower-priced secondary labels for growth to keep shareholders happy. One by one, each 'great' designer name rolled out a diffusion range: Giorgio Armani, Donna Karan, Versace and Prada respectively spawned Emporio Armani, DKNY, Versus and Miu Miu – labels designed to ride on the visibility of their high-end parents, and to ring in big sales. The baby lines have lower margins than luxury lines, but higher volume.

Fashion writer Dana Thomas got right inside the mindset and the headquarters of these luxury empires in her book *Deluxe*. Luxury as we know it today, 'New Luxury', is very different from the old world of the luxury houses.

> Corporate tycoons and financiers saw the potential. They bought – or took over – luxury companies from elderly founders or incompetent heirs, turned the houses into brands, and homogenised everything: the stores, the uniforms, the products, even the coffee cups in the meetings. Then they turned their sights on a new target audience: the middle market, that broad socioeconomic demographic … The idea, luxury executives explained, was to 'democratise' luxury, to make luxury 'accessible'. It all sounded so noble. Heck, it sounded almost communist. But it wasn't. It was as capitalist as could be: the goal, plain and simple, was to make as much money as heavenly possible.

'We want to become cheaper,' said Stefano Gabbana of Dolce & Gabbana, furthering Thomas's observations. 'Fashion is for everybody.' With that apparently democratic wish to see every man, woman and child with a crocodile wallet, the industry focused on what it had long referred to as 'entrance products', such as wallets, belts, handbags and shoes, encouraging us to buy into the brand. Before long the entrance products had become the major cash cows.

THE DEMISE OF THE 'IT' BAG, THE ARRIVAL OF THE STATUS SHOE

When Janet Street-Porter opined in January 2008, 'I find the whole thing about paying a lot of money for a handbag obscene. How can you spend that money on a handbag that would feed a family in Africa for a year? You've got to be mentally ill,' I applauded her. And it seemed by 2009 that the it-bag haters could breathe a sigh of relief. 'After its decade in the limelight, the It bag is finally over,' announced Suzy Menkes in the *New York Times*. Given Menkes' status as a world-respected fashion writer, that announcement could be taken as the 'it' bag's obituary.

In some quarters it wasn't just the demise of the totemic symbol of cheapskating that we seemed to be witnessing, but a reassessment of splurge-and-save-style spending as a whole. Some of Britain's top fashion writers had also recanted. 'It is hard to keep on walking past these [value] stores, but I'm determined to do it,' wrote Sarah Mower in the *Daily Telegraph*. 'Style-wise, colour-wise, they do an astonishing job. The sight of the middle classes (I've even seen designers trying stuff on) shopping like crazy has been a social phenomenon. It's skewed our sense of fashion values, and the entire market. As it turns out, in the wrong way. Once you have looked at the charity War on Want's website and its investigation into working conditions in some of the Bangladeshi fashion factories that produce for overseas companies – you cannot ignore this.'

Had the madness ended? Er, no. The luxury conglomerates weren't going to give up. It seemed only a matter of moments before the 'it' prefix was simply transferred to another good old-fashioned staple, the shoe. 'Shoes are out to steal the limelight,' warned Menkes, 'with mighty platforms, carved heels, cages of straps and all sorts of decoration, from feathers to beading.' She was not overstating the aesthetic. Arguably the status shoe began with the Givenchy dominatrix bootie road-tested on several red carpets by the actress Gwyneth Paltrow. Then followed the extreme gladiator sandal, the Ferragamo cage heel, and a spiked-heel platform-balanced strap-frenzy from Yves Saint Laurent. One by one the main fashion houses trotted out audacious, strappy, platformed, studded heels. It was where Spartacus met bling, the message being that you couldn't go too high or have too many tassels or straps. For those who disagreed there was the Louboutin nude heel (with signature red sole), worn as a sort of luxury palate-cleanser in between all the variations of peep-toe bondage boots.

In September 2010 this mass fetishisation of the status shoe was made official with the opening of Selfridges' shoe gallery. At 3,250 square metres, London's new shoe palace deposed Saks Fifth Avenue in New York and Galeries Lafayette in Paris as the world's biggest women's footwear department. With 4,000 shoes on display (and 55,000 pairs in stock) many commentators pointed out that this new shoe department was housed in a space bigger than Tate Modern's Turbine Hall. References to art galleries were peculiarly relevant. Designed by architect of the moment Jamie Fobert, this space wasn't intended just to showcase functional footwear, but to raise the products of 150 brands to the status of precious objects. Shoes were backlit, placed on plinths and shown off as iconic and important pieces – just in the way 'it' bags had once been treated. 'Imagine you are in a gallery,' says Selfridges' Director of Accessories Sebastian Manes on the store's website. 'From the entrance you see a succession of doorways, and at the end a huge window flooding the space with daylight. Your journey begins at the front, with shoes from the best of the high street. Slowly you begin to travel through different galleries until you reach the end – the couture designer gallery, flanked by Chanel and Louboutin, and a vision of Eden – the new suspended garden at Selfridges. Shoe heaven!'

Opening this vision of Eden in the depths of a recession might seem a rather bizarre thing to do. But the luxury conglomerates and the analysts appeared to agree that we would carry on buying. Tory Frame, head of consumer products at consultancy Bain & Company, confirmed to the *Daily Telegraph* that 'In the past couple of years shoes have been the best-performing luxury category, overtaking bags.' By contrast, a Mintel survey in 2008 found that Britain was falling out of love/lust with cheap shoes, projecting the number of pairs bought annually to drop by 7 per cent between 2008 and 2013.

In the *Telegraph* Frame observed that 'As women have been scouring their wardrobes for clothes to wear, or opting to buy a Zara dress over a Gucci one, high-end shoes have become more important than ever in defining a look.' He added, 'Women are buying shoes to lift their spirits.' Cheapskating was alive and in robust health.

And, it transpired, the death of the 'it' bag had been greatly exaggerated too. In early summer 2010 Mulberry posted a 35 per cent lift in sales. The reason? A bag named the 'Alexa', created for television presenter Alexa Chung, was flying out of stores. Despite making five hundred Alexas a week, Mulberry couldn't keep up with demand, and waiting lists were growing.

This, I can only conclude, is the new order of things: shoe-bag-shoe-bag-shoe-bag. Only the odd strike for attention by luxury scarves or headbands might upset this cycle, as the two big cash cows pass the trend baton back and forth between each other. Most commentators now accept that the twice-yearly runway shows unveiling collections from the luxury conglomerates stable are now really no more than brand-promotion exercises. Don't be fooled by the catwalk shows, illuminated by flashbulbs and still given acres of press space: they are merely carefully choreographed window-dressing. As Lisa Armstrong, fashion editor of *The Times*, puts it, 'It has been a truism of the past fifteen years that accessories make the fashion world go round.' In fact it is a truism that appears to be reinforced year on year: at Gucci (owned by PPR), accessories account for 90 per cent of turnover. Luxury isn't about selling clothes, but about flogging the greatest amount of accessories.

A LESS THAN ELEGANT IMPACT

In the rush to 'democratise' their big-ticket products, did the luxury conglomerates lose some control over their supply chains? There is no doubt that a small number of products remain exclusive – Tod's produced just nineteen of its pink crocodile bags – and continue to be produced in ateliers and workshops in time-honoured style. But increasingly the luxury supply chain has aped Big Fashion's compulsion to outsource. Key elements of production have been moved to Eastern Europe and Asia in a quest for lower wage bills. In some cases, these have also been achieved in Western Europe. European production hardly guarantees a sparkling responsibility record and happy workers. The Tuscan textile town Prato now has an estimated army of 25,000 low-wage workers, predominantly from China, making 'luxury' goods. Working conditions can be brutal, as exposed in *Schiavi de Lusso* (Luxury Slaves), an Italian TV documentary, while an investigation by a British tabloid found workers were paid less than half the legal Italian minimum wage.

It has to be said that there hasn't been a great deal of research into luxury's environmental footprint (we will look at this more closely later), or its observance of labour rights. But the findings of the limited number of investigations that have been carried out have been far from glowing. The 2007 WWF report, 'Deeper Luxury', attempted to rate the major luxury brands in terms of sustainability. It gave LVMH a 'C'. This seems pretty unimpressive, until you read that Tod's scored an 'F' (after failing to answer basic questions). That is not a good look. In March 2007 LVMH was expelled from the FTSE 4Good index, which tracks businesses conforming to environmental and social criteria, for supply-chain issues (it has since returned to the fold, re-entering the FTSE 4Good on 23 March 2009). Unions and labour-rights organisations in Europe have found that luxury brands still tend to be paternalistic. The workers come under the control of one figurehead, and unionisation is either heavily discouraged or not permitted. This leaves thousands of workers without protection from labour violations, and puts them in a weak bargaining position.

As a result of her journey into the heart of New Luxury, Dana Thomas concluded that luxury has 'lost its lustre'. This is bad news for anybody who 'invested' heavily in 'it' bags. By watering down their standards and mass marketing their products, the luxury conglomerates may have taken the shine off their wares. The industry seems confused about where to turn – *haute couture*, or mass-produced, heavily-marketed accessories? However, it is not half as befuddled as we are.

CLOSET UPSTARTS

A case in point is provided by my jeans. We've already established that I have a bit of a thing about jeans. Three of my pairs cost over £120 each, with one at over £200. These are my 'luxury' jeans, and in terms of the history of denim, they've accomplished a dramatic social clamber (jeans were famously originally made to be sold cheap to cowboys and gold prospectors, and worn until they dropped off the behinds of that hard-living clientèle). When I wear them I assume I am wearing 'premium denim', but in reality I don't know how superior this denim is. I don't know in which country the cotton was grown or the zipper was sewn in, or how or by whom the 'whiskers' (the stripes of light and shade increasingly found on denim) were added.

Are these social climbers guaranteed a longer lifespan in my wardrobe than my humbler jeans? Possibly not, because there's no doubt that my posh jeans are more trend-led. Truth be told, I'm already tiring of the skinny legs and the diamante pocket detail. The luxury price tag hasn't bought me peace of mind. I'm not sure what it's bought me.

In fact there seems to be no rhyme nor reason as to which pieces move into the price stratosphere courtesy of a fancy label or some rhinestones on the back pocket, and which will be downgraded to become cheap staples. That's why the prices of the items in my wardrobe look as if they could have been thrown out at random in a game-show format. I could hold a garment out at random, and a baying audience could decide whether its price should be higher or lower than the previous one. So cashmere might cost the same as a cinema ticket, while a pair of jeans can be as much as a quarterly electric bill.

WARDROBE ECONOMICS

The wider point, for me, is that cheapskating, with its save-and-splurge logic, is not half as logical as it seems. Similarly, democratised luxury rarely offers the value that it promises. Buying into such polarised positions is symptomatic of large-scale wardrobe malfunction. Not in the Janet-Jackson-breast-out-at-Superbowl sense, but in terms of wardrobe economics. This is a good point at which to talk about spending. Because for real style value, you need to take control.

Later I'll look more closely at what constitutes the Perfect Wardrobe, and whether such a thing is even possible. While I was thinking about it, I Googled it to see if anyone thought they had attained it. Inevitably, many style sites and blogs claim they have found the secret, and I have pored over countless articles that offer the same assurance. This time I wasn't interested in yet more advice on the importance of having a 'great white shirt' and the inevitable LBD (little black dress). What I did come across was a quirky article on 'The Perfect Wardrobe' from an Australian sewing magazine in which the magazine's editor-in-chief Lynn Cook develops a strategy for readers who keep sewing garments for themselves, but still have nothing to wear. They're wasting material, thread and their time. She develops a ten-point plan for identifying what garments are needed from a capsule wardrobe that she calls 'Sewing With a Plan' (SWAP). Among ladies of a certain age with keen sewing skills, it appears that SWAP has become a big hit.

I have a sewing basket, but it's going to take me a while to master the skills I need to put it to good use. However, the thing I noticed about SWAP was the way non-sewers had adopted the idea, turning it into Shopping With a Plan. Budgeting might not be the most alluring concept on the planet, but Shopping With a Plan hinges on having a workable budget, and it strikes me that this is exactly what we need. So few of us now buy fashion with any budget in mind that this contributes to a loss of control over what goes in and out of our wardrobe lives. We buy without regard: when was the last time you assessed the likely lifespan of an item of clothing before you scooped it up? When you analyse our spending patterns, they are interesting. In 2008 the average amount we spent on clothing and footwear went down to a record low of £21.60 a week, representing 4.6 per cent of our total weekly budget. It's worth reiterating that we have been buying more and more clothes for less money, filling up 40 per cent of our wardrobes from value retailers using just 17 per cent of our clothing budget.

What I'm about to say might seem counterintuitive in these cash-strapped times, but the questions to ask are: is our budget big enough, and are we directing that money to the right places? I would suggest that if you are on an average income, the answer on both counts is no. I would even dare to say that you should beef up your budget if at all possible, spending nearer to 6 per cent of your total weekly income in a bid to secure a more socially just wardrobe with far superior staying power. So, out of an average gross annual salary for a thirty-to-thirty-nine-year-old woman (notably it still lags behind a man's) of £22,047 a year, you would spend 6 per cent on your clothes, giving you £1,323 before tax. If you can't break the cycle of buying each week, that will only give you a little over £20 a week.

Slowing down your rate of purchasing to once a month would give you around £100 to play with. Or try thinking of it this way: received wisdom suggests that you wear 20 per cent of your clothes 80 per cent of the time, meaning that most of those weekly fashion fixes aren't pulling their weight. Let's say you are in an addictive cycle of buying two items a week. If you could isolate the 20 per cent of those garments that you really, really want, and are likely to keep wearing, you would change from purchasing 104 items a year to twenty-one. That would give you an average of around £60 per piece to be spent over the year, enough to give you extra options and making you a consumer with more clout.

Of course, it may be that with the other commitments in your life – the mortgage, the bills, the school uniforms – you look at the figure of £1,323 a year before tax and think it's absurdly high. After all, not everyone is in full-time work, or is earning the average salary. I'm not recommending that you blow the family budget on clothes, but I would ask you to look carefully at your current buying patterns, particularly if you've been patronising value retailers, and check that you really are getting value for money. How many quick, cheap buys have ended up unworn on the wardrobe floor, or even thrown in the bin or donated prematurely to charity? How many didn't quite fit or suit, in the cold light of day?

It's high time we restored true value to the national wardrobe, and in my opinion impulsively bought Big Fashion offers the reverse. I want you to spend your hard-earned cash money wisely, not hand it over to the relentless churn of Big Fashion's consume-and-chuck-it cycle.

What does buying higher up the fashion chain actually get you? For example, does the skirt priced between £45 and £65 from a high-street retailer guarantee you a cleaner, more ethical supply chain than the one at under £10 from a value retailer? It's a very good question, and the straight answer is not always, no. As we'll look at in more detail later, the supply chain is so complex, and sourcing patterns so diffuse, that it's difficult to be reassured by price alone. But spending higher up the fashion food chain and entering mid-market territory does do a couple of things.

For starters, a slightly higher but more considered budget gives you more options. You will have more money to spend on the labels and brands that can demonstrate to you that they are working to address issues in the fashion chain that you find unacceptable. This will include some high-street stores, but also independent retailers and labels that prioritise environmental and social justice as well as trend, cut and colour. (I'll come to who these retailers might be, and how to separate the wheat from the chaff, later in this book.)

A second bonus of the slightly higher budget is that it pushes you into a different demographic, helping to bury the myth that the only thing consumers are interested in is low prices. When it comes to Big Fashion, retailers point to their sales figures. If consumers were worried about the conditions in which this merchandise was produced, they argue, would they keep stocking 40 per cent of their wardrobes with it? Ask yourself: are you prepared to keep supporting lower garment prices, no matter what the consequences? Every pound spent in a value-fashion retailer when you can afford to shop elsewhere is a vote cast for a particular way of working the fashion-supply chain. Is that really what you want to support?

6

FASHION'S FOOTPRINT

The Ecological Wreckage Left Behind by Your Wardrobe

The men in white coats have not yet arrived to take me away. But in the autumn of 2010 one does arrive to go through my wardrobe. Phil Patterson is a colour chemist with vast experience of the textile industry. I met him a while back through various eco textile and sustainable fashion conferences, and I've written about the EcoMetric system he has developed in order to help both consumers and the industry build up a picture of the impact our clothes have on the environment. Since devising this standard he has become well-versed in going through people's wardrobes, particularly those of journalists as they attempt to uncover a little of the back story of what lurks in there. But until now I've never offered up my own wardrobe for analysis. I've wimped out because, frankly, I am more than a little worried by the volume of clothes I possess and the danger of being exposed as a prolific and feckless fashion consumer. I am also a little ashamed to reveal that in real terms I have very little knowledge about the materials that actually make up my clothes.

I'm far from alone here. Despite the UK's vast industrial textile heritage, most of us have little or no knowledge about fibres. Presiding over a contemporary wardrobe means bingeing on clothes while periodically opening up a kind of metaphorical hatch to release all the unwanted, end-of-line, last season threads. How much time is there to consider what a garment is made from during the buying process? Our reaction times to clothes have become shorter and shorter. In the scramble to get to the cash desk, frankly, who has time to consider whether something is polyester, viscose, cotton, a cotton blend or real wool? Who knows, and who cares?

Once, this knowledge would have been ingrained in us. It was considered important that consumers knew by sight and feel what a garment was made of. They knew because they cared, and they cared because they were buying for different reasons such as warmth, durability or longevity. Certain fibres, such as cotton, with a high thread count were associated with quality. The practical and the thrift-minded (more numerous then than they are now) were conscious of how a fibre might wash and even darn – pre-fast fashion, the consumer was wary of spending hard-earned cash on garments that weren't up to the rigours of everyday life. Knowing a little about the fibres was part of the toolbox of buying well. It was a consumer right, and manufacturers had to print the main fibre types on the label, along with the care instructions. Of course, that information is still there. One of the few things that is on the label is what fibres the article is primarily made from. But the irony is that the more we could do with taking an interest in this sort of information, the less we actually care. The less inclined we are even to take a peek at that label, in fact. One day curiosity drove me to do my own research into our declining knowledge of the fibres that make up our wardrobes. I stopped a small sample of thirty people outside a shopping centre and asked them a question that seemed relatively easy, if perhaps a little unexpected: 'What are the clothes you're wearing made from?' 'You've got me there,' said one woman in her fifties. 'Cotton, I suppose.' Not a bad guess, since half of all the clothes we buy are made from cotton. We discovered by untucking the neck label that her long-line knitted cardigan was actually acrylic. Only one person was certain about what the shirt on her back was made from. 'Definitely cotton,' she said. And it was.

Reconnecting myself with fibre proves to be surprisingly easy (and more fun than I thought), courtesy of a very small microscope bought from Toys 'R' Us that Phil Patterson hands me. I look down the lens, and can see the actual fibres. Uniform and shimmering for a high-quality cotton; bitty, frazzled edges showing a synthetic. I look at denim, viscose, nylon, Tencel. It's a visceral and immediate way of getting to grips with the fact that every garment represents the end of a process of dyeing, finishing and twisting some sort of yarn. Under the light of the little microscope the natural fibres form smooth, perfect woven patterns, and the synthetics show frayed, plastic edges.

If only it was equally easy to pinpoint which are the 'good' and 'bad' fabrics. I can only imagine what it would be like to casually walk around high-street stores peering through my child's microscope at the clothes on the rails. Possibly it would be a fast-track way to get ejected from a store. But apart from revealing these rather pretty and intricate weaves, it wouldn't really tell me which fibres are to be celebrated and embraced, and which to be given a wide berth. Working out fashion footprints is a complex business. We are consuming more fibre and more clothes than ever before – in the UK we're now up to around fifty-five kilograms of new textiles per man, woman, child, and possibly pet (even my dog has two coats with poppers and Velcro fastenings) per year. The world has never been more hungry for fibre to make fabric. Textile production has doubled over the last thirty years – which means that more arable land that could grow food is needed for cotton, and more fossil fuels for man-made fibres. In 1977 humankind demanded thirty-one million tonnes of fibre to keep it in flares, T-shirts and bedlinen. Let's not mince words: that is an enormous amount. But by 2007 this figure had risen to nearly eighty million tonnes, or eighty billion kilograms. This is the amount that the planet must somehow sustain every year in order to keep us in curtains, blazers and jeggings – mainly the latter two, given that the lion's share of textile production is destined to be made into apparel.

Conveniently, as an industry fashion is expert at overlooking the burden this places on a fragile earth. To get that eighty billion kilograms of fabric into shape takes 1,074 billion kilowatt hours of electricity, for which we need 132 million tonnes of coal and somewhere between six and nine trillion litres of water. Yarn does not magically appear, just as garments do not arrive fully formed. There are thousands of global textile mills, and many are operating on a 24/7 basis, running near to full capacity. The figures that make up the collective footprint for global fashion are nothing short of mind-boggling. Take water for example. In one year a large clothing brand will use an equivalent amount to 43,000

Olympic-sized swimming pools. *Every year!* The textile industry is one of the biggest water consumers in the world, using 3.2 per cent of all the 1,400km^3 of water available to the human race each year.

Add to that hypothetical bill millions of tonnes of coal, the land and waterways lost to pollution from pesticides and from dyeing and finishing fabrics, the land lost to other agricultural production and as a carbon sink by raising sheep and cattle in ever increasing herds, and fashion's footprint starts to look like some form of scorched-earth strategy. And we should also add in the production of all the 'incidentals' that our clothes demand: millions of metres of labels, elastic string and zippers, a billion sets of metal buttons, and the same again in plastic. Imagine all the acid dye baths and the power needed for drying fabric under huge electric lamps, and the millions of tonnes of pumice stone in giant washers needed to get the right fashion effects on leather or denim.

The research suggests that each one of us is indirectly responsible for generating 0.6 kilograms of oil, sixty kilograms of water per kilogram and one kilogram of solid waste per kilogram of fashion that we buy. With our yearly average of fifty-five kilograms of textiles, that makes thirty-three kilograms of oil, 3,300 kilograms of water, and fifty-five kilograms of waste in total – for every one of us.

In order to begin to assess my own wardrobe's footprint I need Phil Patterson's system, and it's one that doesn't pull any punches. The starting position is that there's no such thing as an ecologically blameless fabric. It is more a question of finding the ones that are less bad. Patterson has devised an online calculator he calls EcoMetrics (it is very easy to try it for yourself: http://www.colour-connections.com/EcoMetrics) that scores the clothes in your wardrobe based on the fibres they are made from and how much water, energy and non-renewable resources (namely oil) have been used to create those fibres, and how much pollution the process has produced. As I take clothes from my wardrobe and dump them on a chair, Patterson types in the number of each category, such as 'cotton blouse' or 'polyester trousers', classifying them by the predominant fibre type. (Warning: when you begin to categorise even your most cherished, fashionable clothes in this way they suddenly have all the appeal of the description of the 'thermal lined leisure trouser' you might find in the back of a newspaper supplement. Pieces quickly lose their fashion mystique when you strip away the smoke and mirrors of marketing.) The total impact of each piece is expressed in Environmental Damage Units (EDUs). The more EDUs totted up by your wardrobe, the higher your fashion footprint. To all intents and purposes the EDUs can be thought of as calories, and totting up what's in my wardrobe will reveal its true girth. It's a scary prospect.

'It's not the worst I've seen,' says Patterson as I throw open the door of the first wardrobe. I find this comforting, although he might just be being polite. There's also the small issue that I've decided not to come clean about the oversized hinged laundry basket downstairs, which is currently full to the brim.

FASHION'S OILY SECRET

Taking a closer look, just at the label – never mind through the microscope – is nothing short of revelatory. The pyjamas I thought were natural silk are 100 per cent polyester; the stripey jumper I thought was wool is 48 per cent viscose, 18 per cent polyamide, 2 per cent elastane and 32 per cent katoen (cotton). The label also instructs me to 'Have fun washing!', a request that I'm not sure whether to take at face value or to feel vaguely threatened by. Another knit (again, I assumed it was wool) is 77 per cent viscose and 23 per cent polyester. Lace is predominantly nylon (with some viscose); jeans tend to mix cotton with a tiny bit of polyester- or nylon-based fabric to allow them to stretch. All linings seem to be polyester, and everything seems to have a bit of man-made fibre thrown in: acetates, polyamide, elastane, rayon – all figure in supporting roles to either cotton or polyester, followed in terms of popularity by viscose. Then there's a twisted ball of synthetics in the form of tights, sports leggings, tracksuit pants, tops, pyjamas and underwear. I bring out a party dress, a red number that I always thought was silk (how naïve). The label reveals that it's 76 per cent acetate, 21 per cent polyamide and 3 per cent elastane. Not the glamorous mix I had in mind when I wore it on a few big nights. Nor the fibres I had in mind when I paid £150 for it.

But it's faintly absurd to feel cheated when you find out that a prized item is entirely constructed from synthetics, because that's how fashion is: man-made fibres are a big fashion story, and to be honest we enjoy the uplift, stretch and shaping that they bring to the party. They are split between 'cellulosic', such as viscose, rayon and the acetate of my upscale dress, which are originally made from plants (mainly from wood pulp or cotton), and the true synthetics, such as nylon and polyester, synthesised from chemical mixtures at high temperature in a test tube that are entirely laboratory-made constructs.

Demand for these fibres nearly doubled from 1990 to 2005. It is difficult to overstate how huge they are. By 2006 synthetics accounted for 58 per cent of all fibre demand across the planet. And their price has been in freefall over the past twenty-five years, until now they're as cheap as chips, or even cotton – which explains why 50 per cent of UK clothing is made from cotton, and more than 30 per cent from man-made fibres. In fact it's a wonder that there's anything in my wardrobe that isn't made from cotton or man-made, or a combination of the two.

Eager to offset the quantity of clothes that I appear to own (I've even come clean about the laundry basket), I make sure I parade hangers containing garments made of virtuous eco fibres such as hemp, organic cotton and linen. Although Patterson is in favour of 'durable eco-textiles', going natural doesn't always win me Brownie points, or rather lower my EDUs: in some cases quite the reverse. This is not entirely surprising. In the early 1990s, Patagonia (the ethical clothing manufacturer best known to outdoorsy types) analysed the life cycle of a number of different fabrics. The results were unexpected in many ways. Cotton, traditionally considered a 'natural' fibre, was shown to have a greater environmental impact than synthetic materials such as nylon and polyester. It transpired that the average cotton T-shirt, for example, required five hundred litres of water and forty grams of pesticides to make, plus carcinogenic chemicals used in the finishing process.

A Cambridge University study compared a cotton T-shirt with a viscose blouse, and came up with an 'energy profile' for each. Viscose is an interesting material. It was one of the earliest man-mades to be introduced to the British public, who appear to have lapped it up ever since. The original fibre is made from wood pulp, which occasionally buys it some ecological cachet. This, however, is pretty much mistaken, as those plant beginnings are soon transformed by an arsenal of processing and chemicals. Viscose is then dissolved in a sodium hydroxide solution via a technical process called wet-extrusion, and the liquid polymer is 'regenerated' using sulphuric acid. All in all, extracting the fibre requires a lot of energy. In fact the researchers found that 65 per cent of all the energy used by the viscose blouse (including during its life and probable disposal) was expended in creating the fibre. But here's the strange thing: despite all of this, cotton is so energy inefficient to produce, and so soaked in pesticides, that a) I've devoted an entire chapter to it, and b) viscose still comes out on top. Ultimately the scientists calculated that while it took eleven megajoules of energy to manufacture a viscose blouse, a cotton T-shirt required twenty-four. The story doesn't end with the production of the fibre. We also have to factor in the way we (the consumer) handle the product when it comes into our wardrobe. Again the blouse was found to consume vastly less energy during the washing phase: seven megajoules as opposed to sixty-five for the T-shirt.

Similarly, polyester is usually considered 'the devil's creation' by eco warriors (or even those of a light-green disposition), and with some justification, not least because it will take more than two hundred years to decompose in landfill once discarded. However, in its creation it might have an advantage over 'natural' fibres. Synthesised in a laboratory, polyester dope (it sounds accidentally street) is dyed as the yarn is formed, removing the need to apply the dye later. This might sound inconsequential, but it removes pretty much the entire potentially hazardous and inefficient dyeing process. Which means that while under the EcoMetrics system my black organic cotton top scores twenty-eight EDUs (a non-organic top would have scored thirty-four), a polyester top scores just nineteen. Natural is not always ecologically superior.

I am not, however, about to convert my entire wardrobe to crimplene (a form of polyester). Viscose might be from a 'renewable source', but its creation produces toxic emissions that affect air, water and earth. One of viscose's main ingredients is adipic acid, manufacturing which causes nitrous oxide (a poisonous greenhouse gas) to be emitted. And polyester is of course derived from petrochemicals. Avoiding hydrocarbon (oil) based products is one of the tenets of green living, and it's a good instinct to have. From food to fashion, it has become progressively more difficult to delink the stuff we buy from oil extraction and refinement.

When I unfold a polyester zip-up top from one of the drawers in my bedroom I can almost feel the oil on its shiny surface. According to John C. Ryan and Alan Thein During, authors of *Stuff and its Secrets*, this would have started life as thick, black oil somewhere in the world. It would have been transported to a refinery to be cracked at high temperatures to produce smaller molecules, then to another chemical plant where the polymer would be produced using heavy-metal catalysts such as cadmium acetate. One way to imagine all these processes and chemical ingredients is to focus on the fact that a quarter of the weight of the jacket in my hands would have been lost as air pollution. During the industrial process to make the polyester, nitrogen and sulphur dioxides, hydrocarbons, carbon monoxide and heavy metals which impair breathing, cause lung and heart diseases and suppress the immune system would all have been released into the atmosphere.

What I'm saying is that while polyester and other man-mades might square up well in a cold-hearted life-cycle analysis that pits the relative energy consumption of one fibre against another, their processing is nevertheless extremely polluting, predicated on 1970s habits of oil consumption (when oil use was, if not politically more straightforward, at least without the added environmental pressures we now face. It was also believed to be more plentiful) and an arsenal of toxic chemicals. As the author and sustainable-fashion academic Kate Fletcher puts it: 'Fibre assessments and comparisons have also been used ... to defend a company's products, frequently by shifting the spotlight of environmental impact onto other fibres (usually cotton).' She notes that when the synthetic-fibre giant DuPont published a sort of league table of fibres in the 1990s that purported to take into account the full life cycle of each, 'It concluded that polypropylene is the preferred fibre; followed by nylon; joint third position is held by wool, polyester and acrylic; cotton is in sixth place, and viscose is given the worst environmental loading.' It appears that you can trust your own principles (but not your prejudices). I have no idea about the levels of dioxins, produced thousands of miles away in factories I know next to nothing about, that are poisoning the local air, or about the local populations inhaling nitrogen and sulphur dioxides. But I feel distinctly uncomfortable about helping to create a potentially lethal toxic time bomb.

OUTSOURCING DARK SATANIC MILLS

Despite our textile heritage in this country, knowledge of the process of turning fibre into fashion has evaporated with amazing speed. Most textile mills have been left to crumble, but many have been restored and given a new lease of life as discount shopping centres or museums. As kids my sister and I used to play in the pretty playground of a refurbished Arkwright mill turned heritage centre, the belching chimneys and the infernal clatter of the shutter looms consigned to a distant past.

We tend to assume that fashion has moved into some high-tech zone, with garments produced by magic pollution-free processes. This may give us a false sense of security, because the actual production of fibres – turning fluffy white cotton bolls into fabric, and washing the grease out of wool – often remains the backbreaking, pollution-riddled heavy industry it ever was. It's just that now it takes place thousands of miles away. In over a hundred years the essential processes (and some of the chemicals) used in textile production really haven't changed much. You could take a worker from a Lancashire cotton mill in 1900 and set her to work in a textile-processing factory somewhere in Asia. (You might add cynically that her wages and working practices wouldn't be alien either.)

Certainly I felt as if I had stepped back in time when I visited a ginnery in West Africa. The ginnery is the place where raw cotton is taken for processing straight from the field, the first step on a long, energy-intensive journey to becoming the cloth that we'd recognise. This one was in Mali, Africa's second-largest producer of cotton fibre, after Egypt. In the huge hangar that housed the decrepit equipment, a collection of huge, rattling machines that seemed to have no discernible connection to each other was surrounded by bales of processed cotton ready for export. I couldn't ask questions in the ginnery – it was too noisy, what with the whirring and the clattering. So, apart from the first machine, which obviously separated the stalks and leaves from the picked cotton bolls, the exact process remains a mystery to me. One thing I was sure about was the volume of dust – where fibre goes, so does dust, and it can lead to the respiratory disease byssinosis – shafts of light entering the vast hangar picked up thick clouds of it. Face masks were few and far between.

Those lovely, fluffy cotton bolls must be carded, spun, spooled and warped, slashed (filled with starch to make the fibre smooth for weaving), drawn and woven or knitted into sized cloth (known as grey goods) before being sent to the finishing mill. Then it needs to be kiered (boiled in an alkaline solution to a very high temperature) to remove natural impurities, bleached to be made white, mercerised to give the fabric shine and strength, and to enable it to take dye, then printed or dyed and finally sized again. Add to this another application for waterproofing, with the chemical aluminium acetate or a formula mixed with gelatin and a dispersed wax.

Such processing realities apply to every fibre. In the wool industry, impurities from the original fleece (called grease wool) must be removed by scouring in chemicals and hot detergent. To give an idea of how many impurities there are, for every kilogram of grease wool, less than half that amount of scoured wool is recovered (the impurities become waste). The wool then needs to go through the 'fulling' process (where loosely woven wool from the loom is shrunk into a closely woven cloth), which requires soap mixed with soda ash and a chemical agent. This is followed by carbonising, using hot concentrated acids to convert vegetable matter in the wool into loose particles that are later shaken out by a machine called a duster.

We might miss their presence as huge employers and the way the factories gave regions their identity, but in many ways we should be glad to see the back of fabric's environmental heritage. Remove the sepia-tinted glasses, and we see that it was common practice for these monolithic brick structures to spew out chemicals directly into the air or rivers. As people became more aware of the dangers of pollution, legislation in the developed world would attempt to catch up, for example through the 1972 Federal Water Pollution Control Act in the USA. It would be wrong to give the impression that there are no textiles manufactured in Britain today. We still produce specialist woven and jacquard fabrics, for example, but the production facilities are tightly controlled and regulated. They must remove pollutants before expelling water into rivers, use air filters on their chimneys, and abide by legislation forbidding the use of hundreds of chemicals. Centuries after humankind worked out how to heavily pollute water – our primary life-sustaining resource – we have finally worked out how to clean it up. It is an exact science, and a combination of physical, chemical and biological methods along with careful control (some substances just cannot be removed, such is their toxicity) means that pollution can be minimised. But you need equipment, technology and expensive experts, as well as officials to police compliance and hand out punishments for non-compliance. Who in today's mainstream fashion industry has the time or the money for all that?

It does not take a genius to work out what happened next. As anti-pollution laws are enacted to protect First World inhabitants and resources, the fashion industry, with its penchant for quick and cheap, upped sticks and switched production to parts of the world that, if not unseen, are harder to monitor, and where they also often benefit from less stringent, or non-existent, legal controls. The arm of the pollution enforcers doesn't reach many of the facilities being used by multinational companies. This leads me to conclude that factory owners might elect not to follow a code of conduct handed down by a multinational customer. After all, 90 per cent of waste water in developing countries is discharged into rivers and streams without any treatment.

My suspicions were confirmed when a fashion industry contact from Europe shows me some photos taken on a recent visit to a factory in India that is regularly used to dye large batches of clothing that is on sale up and down the British high street. You and I may well have bought pieces that were dyed there. Looking at the pictures, it was incredible to me that any fashion label that valued its reputation could have anything to do with such a ramshackle operation. 'Dyehouse' is a rather grandiose term for this urban shack, and all around its perimeter were stagnant pools and puddles where chemical-infused waste water had been allowed to gather. Inside was a horror story. The photographs revealed tubs of chemicals with their lids off, and workers shovelling these potentially toxic chemicals into vats using pieces of cloth or cardboard, and even their bare hands. Most of the retailers who are using facilities like this have stringent codes of practice requiring workers to wear masks and gloves, and closed-loop dyehouse systems to minimise pollution. As ever, the gap between best practice and reality could be described as a chasm. According to my contact, just two or three years ago Britain's flagship retailers were pretty strict on dyehouses, and buyers could choose from a list of around two hundred that came up to specification. But the big price squeeze has made that list irrelevant. Today, fabric is sent to the dyeing facilities that quote the lowest price – standards be damned.

Put yourself in the position of a factory owner for a minute. An order comes in from a multinational. It specifies date, colour, design and quantity, and adds that certain environmental controls are expected. The economics of avoiding doing the right thing are far more compelling than those of complying. Since 1999, China has effectively doubled the amount of textiles it processes. On the surface this represents good news for the fickle consumer: even cheaper clothes and even quicker turnaround. As prices plummeted, we certainly weren't paying the price for this extra output. So who was? According to environmentalists, it was Chinese waterways, and the people who rely on them. While one in four of China's 1.3 billion population drinks contaminated water on a daily basis, according to environmental analysts Miller-McCune, only about 10 per cent of dye wastes from fabric dyehouses are recycled (kept in a loop and all the synthetic chemicals removed). It's hardly surprising this figure is so low when treating contaminated water costs 13 cents a tonne upwards.

Belching smokestack chimneys were symbols of the Industrial Revolution. In the Developing World they may have been replaced by far skinnier pipes and vents, but their output is no less prolific. Airborne pollution has a dramatic effect on human health. Normal air is a mixture of gases: 78 per cent nitrogen, 20 per cent oxygen, 1 per cent argon, 0.03 per cent carbon dioxide and some other gases such as theane and krypton. Particulate matter and industrial gases from fibre factories change this mix beyond recognition. Clean air isn't an option for anyone living within ten miles of the average garment factory. Those dark satanic mills have just shifted location.

Naturally, my own wardrobe is complicit. I'm not attracted to the sludge-coloured natural yarns that received wisdom suggests for those with an eco conscience. Like yours, my clothes have all been processed, finished and dyed. The truth is that, without a plethora of toxic processes to choose from, your wardrobe wouldn't be half so visually appealing or work so well. With the exception of some pretty dire 'eco' fabrics, a fabric can't go anywhere until it's finished, least of all into your washing machine or even the open air, where its chemistry will unfold within a matter of minutes, dripping dye all over the pavement. All fabrics need to be stabilised and finished. Coating materials including lubricating oils, plasticisers, paints and water-repellent (that usually means oil-based) chemicals and compound waxes or solvents are all liberally applied. After which the coated fabrics must be 'cured' in massive ovens and under dryers at high temperatures, at which point a garment's energy burden (think of all that electricity) can go through the roof. Also going through the roof and out of the chimney are VOCs, volatile organic compounds. There's a distinctive smell in many textile factories, and it is VOCs. One hundredth the diameter of a human hair, they are easily inhaled, and travel straight to the lungs where they cause respiratory disease, and possibly worse – there are some very specific concerns about carcinogenic VOCs. In the US and across Europe, environmental agencies measure the density of opacity of emissions from industrial units: if the VOCs are too much, the facility will be shut down. Who is monitoring the textile factories that produce today's fibre, and checking that they have the correct filters?

THIS SEASON'S RIVER

There are bad ways of producing garments, and there are less bad ways. An 'expert' dyehouse, for instance, will use just sixty litres of water for every kilogram of cotton dyed, while an inefficient one uses eight hundred litres. By now you'll be becoming familiar with my constant refrain that vital pieces are missing from the fashion jigsaw because we are told so little on the label. The lay person has virtually no chance of knowing whether a good (efficient) or bad (inefficient) dyehouse has been used to colour the piece he or she has bought. Phil Patterson has therefore had to base the figures in his EcoMetric system on his own experience, and to take an average. As he puts it, 'It's easy to get concrete figures from the top end of the industry, but impossible to get them from the foul, polluting, inefficient, irresponsible bottom end.'

Some villages will be only too familiar with dyehouses that fit the latter description. Communities based downstream from a collection of 'bad' dyehouses – the fishermen, housewives and schoolchildren who do not read *Vogue* online or the scoops from the shows – will often know what colour is big for autumn/winter season next year without recourse to a team of Geneva-based colour futurists. They know because the river literally changes colour as a result of the dyehouses' inability or refusal to manage waste water. That is how it was that the impoverished inhabitants of Dongguan in central Guangdong, China, stepped out one morning in 2006 to see that their previously life-sustaining water source, the Mao Zhou river, had turned a deep red, the colour of poisoned blood. Citizens in China being not nearly so passive as Western consumers like to imagine, they complained to the authorities, and government inspectors decided to launch a surprise inspection, according to a report in the *Wall Street Journal*. The pollution was traced to the enormous Fuan Textiles mill, owned by Fountain Set Holdings Ltd of New York. What the inspectors found was shocking: a pipe beneath the factory floor spewing 22,000 tons of contaminated dye water straight into the river every day, with no amelioration and no attempt at decontamination before the waste water met one of China's main water arteries. According to inspectors the dye levels in the discharged water were 19.5 times the legal limit. Dyes containing high levels of organic material don't just stain water, the organic compounds such as starch that coats yarn break down and suck the life out of it. Waterways that were once teeming with fish, plants and crayfish are left as stagnant pools.

The residents of Dongguan were understandably upset. The raft of huge-name global brands found to have been sourcing their fabric from fibre produced at the mill – Nike, Gap, Reebok, Tommy Hilfiger, J.C. Penney, Liz Claiborne, Abercrombie & Fitch and Walmart were all identified by the *Wall Street Journal* – also seemed shocked. 'We certainly don't want to be associated with a company that's polluting the waters,' said a spokesman for Liz Claiborne Inc. Most cited the fact that they were supplied through a third party as the reason they were discovered to be using a polluting mill. Presumably they had no prior knowledge of the endemic water pollution problems that were already commonplace in the area. Nearly 2.5 million people around Guangzhou (the capital of Guangdong) face health risks from contaminated drinking water, and fewer than 2 per cent of Guangdong's cities and towns treat waste water. Only Nike was able to provide evidence that it had attempted to monitor the Fuan plant, by insisting that water samples were sent for laboratory testing, in acordance with the company's code of conduct. But as these tests had failed to pick up pollution problems, one might conclude that it's easy for factories to falsify samples. Walmart sent teams of inspectors after the event, and cancelled all pending orders.

While indigo is the classic colour of jeans, it should emphatically not be the colour of the river you draw your cooking water from, or where your children wash. But in 2009 the Caledon river, which forms part of the border between South Africa and Lesotho, a country disrespectfully though honestly described as 'dirt poor', was dyed an unnerving bright shade of indigo at the point that it passed through the capital, Maseru. Local children began to refer to the Caledon and its tributaries as 'Blue River'. The pollution was linked to the Taiwanese-owned garment factories that in 2008 shipped £500 million-worth of jeans, T-shirts and other garments to Britain and America. The specific source of Blue River's shocking inky transformation was found to be factories run by Nien Hsing and Chinese Garment Manufacturers, a prolific operation that once produced for Gap (after reports of Blue River surfaced in the press Gap deemed Nien Hsing's waste-water issues unacceptable, and withdrew its contracts) and one of the main denim producers in the region.

Tseliso Tsoeu, an environmental expert from an umbrella organisation for Lesotho NGOs, spoke to the British journalist Dan McDougall in August 2009: 'Our laws state that no person shall discharge any poisonous, toxic or chemical substance into our waters. So why is the government allowing our people to bathe in bright-blue water stained with effluent and dyes? The Chinese and Taiwanese have come here and have basically done what they wanted. They make enormous profits from employing black Africans on behalf of respectable Western companies who advertise the highest standards of production, but in reality don't really know what is going on here.' Tsoeu's utter despair is almost palpable, and who can blame him? He represents the communities who are picking up the real cost of Big Fashion, which apparently continues to lower its standards. While I would love to give companies the benefit of the doubt, they must by now be well aware that you get what you pay for in terms of both resources and pollution.

DENIM DISTRESS

A few months ago I was convinced that I had found the greenest possible pair of jeans. They also ticked the style box. Not only were they 100 per cent cotton, they clung where they were supposed to, had good pocket detail and made me look thin. Even the patina of the denim worked, by which I mean it was faded in the right places, which in turn meant that these jeans were on-trend. But my good friend Orsola, a fashion designer, couldn't stop smirking when I strode in. The reason I'd become an unwitting object of hilarity, she pointed out, was the detailing. On the backs of my legs below the knee were creases, faded stripes to simulate aged denim. The only natural way to get those indentations would be to pull your trousers down thousands of times. Orsola wondered why fashion would dictate a patina that suggests that I'd been to the loo thousands of times. 'Why,' she asked, 'is that a look?'

It's a good question. These discoloured stripes are called whiskers. They are added to millions of pairs of jeans by hand, by laser or by a Crinkle machine. Now that I've been made aware of them, I see them everywhere: on the backs of knees, and latterly across the pelvis. As a result of Orsola's tip-off I have become faintly obsessed by the things that are done to jeans in the name of fashion. One Sunday afternoon I found myself watching a series of technical DVDs from a trade show that sells equipment to the denim industry. To a pan-pipe soundtrack a camera slowly circles a Crinkle machine that proffers two rubber legs. A worker wearing a cap rushes up and puts a pair of bog-standard blue denims on the legs, tenderly patting down the pockets and doing up the fly. She carefully pleats the front of the jeans on each side. Then the

Crinklemeister begins its work, as another worker moves in with a laser gun and etches the whiskers into the denim.

One of the more surreal few minutes I have spent is watching a video of a denim solarium. A pair of denim-clad mannequin legs are suspended from a large orange machine and rotated through a series of heat lamps to give the drying indigo the fade that we consumers want. The heat lamps look like the ones stationed outside pubs for smokers, and they are definitely not efficient. Any treatment or extra for jeans that achieves mass-market approval needs to be scaled up millions of times to get us anywhere near the true impact of fashion. In the case of denim that includes vertical brushing machines, and huge drums filled with pumice stone in which the denim is tumbled for an aged cowboy look. An estimated 450 million pairs of jeans are sold each year in the US alone. I ask Levi Strauss & Co., the world's biggest manufacturer, how many jeans they sell annually, but they politely tell me that 'The specific number of jeans we produce in any given year is proprietary information. At a general level, it would be accurate to say that Levi's® jeans reach "hundreds of millions of consumers around the world".

BACK TO BASICS

In Phil Patterson's final analysis, my EDUs are significant enough to render me 'fashionably overweight' – one category below the worst, 'fashionably obese', that would condemn me to total ignominy. I can and will work on this, as I'll discuss later on in this book. But for now the significance of Phil Patterson's visit, and a few hours spent analysing the fibres in my wardrobe and the likely procedures that were responsible for dyeing, finishing and fixing them, is that it has impressed upon me firstly how much energy went into creating each piece, and secondly how much of a debt my wardrobe, and yours, owes the biosphere. There is no such thing as fashion without a footprint.

Increasingly, fashion brands like to present themselves as custodians of the environment, allying themselves to little wildlife initiatives and 'giving something back'. Usually this 'giving' is rather indirect, through special product ranges where a proportion of the money received

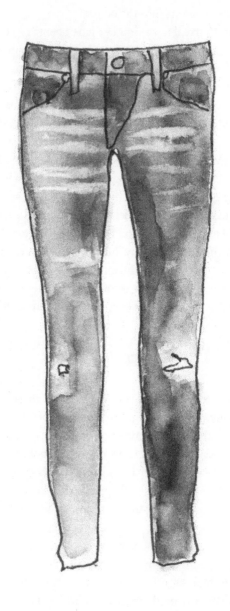

£49

Skinny jeans with on-trend faded patina and 'whiskers'.
One of seven pairs you're statistically likely to buy this year.

What's my poison?

Legend has it that the trend for different washes of jeans that
first came to global prominence in the 1980s was developed by
accident when a forklift truck knocked a container of potassium
permanganate onto a skip of pumice stones and contaminated a
jeans wash. There's a thin line between contamination and pervasive trend in fashion. The legacy of this accident is to be found
in a badly ventilated denim-washing plant in downtown Dhaka,
one of 100 such facilities in the city. A group of young men hold
pneumatic guns that shoot sand removed from the local riverbanks
onto the fabric. They have been told to cover their faces, but no
masks were provided, so they sometimes pull up a cotton bandana
to be worn as a makeshift mask. Just a couple of blasts each side give
the denim that desired worn-out look. But the sand is rich in silica
and is therefore toxic. What our young workers don't know is that
this processs used to be carried out in Turkey, until research there
found that of 145 sandblasters, 83% had respiratory problems and
more than half had developed silicosis. By the time these denim
blasters realise, it could well be too late.

Time to sew these jeans = just 20 minutes
Time to 'distress' them = 60 minutes
Pollution and effect on Bangladeshi workers' health =
unrecorded and incalculable

Truth Labels™

from sales goes to wildlife charities: cue hemp and jute shopping bags with wildflower prints, and T-shirts in organic cotton instructing the population at large to keep its hands off the rainforest. We live in an age where increasingly industry is obliged to take responsibility for the resources it takes and pollutes. I'm not saying things run perfectly: Europe remains the biggest importer of illegal hardwoods, despite schemes designed to stop illegal deforestation. But broadly speaking, whether your business is toilet rolls or garden decking, you are now expected to plant trees or to invest in a sustainable custody chain equivalent to what you've removed. We need to fast forward to a day when fashion brands don't just produce a limited amount of 'eco' tote bags, but are obliged to plant reed beds to clean the waterways outside the dyehouses that turn their fibre dramatic jewel shades for this season's key colours, or dig mulch into cotton fields to replace lost fertility. That's the type of engagement with the biosphere that might mean something.

7

PICKING AT COTTON

How 'the Pig of Botany' Causes Ethical Nightmares

The humble T-shirt is an essential element of life's apparatus. In its own way it has become both a classic (as in the version sported by Marlon Brando in *A Streetcar Named Desire*) and a sartorial nightmare (as in the structure-free garment worn by tourists in Florida and accessorised with a bum bag). In my wardrobe it has many versions: the fitted/skinny T which hugs the body; the retro version with an eighties scooped neck and capped sleeves; countless branded versions and charity T-shirts all collected in the laundry basket of life. In the nineties the humble T-shirt acquired a prolific kid sister: the vest top, again fitted to the body and worn in layers. All of these incarnations now seem to have slid to the back of drawers, where they are breeding, producing more T-shirt offshoots. Meanwhile the drawers in the dressing table are spewing underwear, nightwear and trapped socks so that they can only be opened using brute force. All of this wardrobe filler has something in common – it's made from cotton. Ubiquitous items from the most ubiquitous 'natural' fibre.

For a time it seemed that synthetics had the upper hand, and threatened to squeeze cotton out of our wardrobes. Think of the 1970s, and I guarantee an image of Dralon flares will flash before your eyes. Unsurprisingly our patronage of cotton suffered: world cotton consumption languished during that decade at around 3.15 kilograms per person. But by 2007 it was clear that cotton had wrestled back its share of the market, and people in industrialised nations were consuming cotton with more vigour than ever, at an annual average of 14.2 kilograms each. What had happened in between? Well, we hadn't fallen out of love with synthetic fibres – as you know from the previous chapter, we were consuming those at massive volumes too – but we had found fast fashion, and cotton is an essential ingredient of the fast-fashion story.

Globally speaking, humankind is simply addicted to the stuff. Since 1960, when a comparatively weedy ten million tonnes' worth was grown from the planet's soil, world cotton production has more than doubled, to almost twenty-five million tonnes in 2010. Nor has it ever been so cheap. Topping the cotton-addiction charts is the US, where by 2005 each citizen was getting through seventeen kilograms a year. Asked to choose between cotton or synthetic fibre in a survey by an organisation promoting cotton farmers, 75 per cent of consumers in the UK went for cotton.

It's not hard to see why cotton has become such wardrobe catnip to us consumers. It is cheap, plentiful, easy to live with – in terms of washing, ironing and generally caring for (in fact my iron seems to be permanently set on 'cotton', which is indicative of how much of it goes through my laundry basket) – and does what designers and wearers want it to do, unlike more 'difficult' natural fabrics such as linen. There is nothing new about its appeal. Cotton has been revered by society, pretty much since people first worked out how to turn the rabbit's-tail white fluff of the cotton boll into something altogether more useful. An explosion in cotton production inevitably triggers an explosion in consumerism. Economist Pietra Rivoli, author of *The Travels of a T-Shirt in the Global Economy*, who followed a simple cotton garment through the vagaries of international trade and production, found that that had long been true, unearthing writing from Edward Baines, an eighteenth-century scholar who had no doubt that cotton had everything to do with the birth of a consumer class:

> It is impossible to estimate the advantage to the bulk of the people, from the wonderful cheapness of cotton goods ... The humble classes now have the means of as great neatness, and even gaiety of dress, as the middle and upper classes of the last age. A country-wake in the nineteenth century may display as much finery as a drawing room of the eighteenth.

I can vouch for the fact that it doesn't take long to catch the cotton bug. I have two cotton bolls pinned to a corkboard in my office. One was given to me by an activist who sees the reform of the cotton industry as a lifetime crusade; and one when I went to Mali in 2008 to meet cotton farmers as part of a Fairtrade cotton project. I can't explain exactly why they are there, except that they remind me of the magic of the fact that that fluffy boll grows from a plant, and undergoes so many processes to become so ordinary.

There are fewer magic moments for those who have produced it historically, however. 'By 1834, America became the world's largest cotton exporter – a status it has never relinquished – relying on African slaves to work the fields,' a report by the Fairtrade Foundation, deeply committed to advancing the cause of today's African cotton farmers, reminds us. It's a sad truth that by the time of the Industrial Revolution, when even the sugar and tobacco trades had stopped using slave labour for various reasons, cotton was able to revive it.

Enlightened economists have become obsessed by cotton too. As well as Rivoli, who unpicks the seams of today's international cotton industry with amazing precision, French economist Erik Orsenna has found the cotton trade to be fertile ground for delving into the realities of globalisation:

Cotton is the pig of botany: all of it can be used. So all of it is taken … And so cotton clothes the human race … This is why so many people are concerned with cotton: some hundreds of millions of men and women on all continents. And this is why, for years, I had wanted to make this great journey. Something told me that by following the paths of cotton, from farming to the textile industry by way of biochemistry, from Koutiala (Mali) to Datang (China) by way of Lubbock (Texas), Cuiabá (Mato Grosso), Alexandria, Tashkent and the valley of the Vologne (France, Vosges département), I would understand my planet better.

You can analyse the pig of botany (and, as Orsenna hints, the dark side of globalisation) without embarking physically on quite such an epic journey. Even a glance in the average wardrobe, should you choose to look behind the labels which give little more indication than 'wash at 30°C', is sufficient to make the whole cotton story begin to unravel at alarming speed. Because the fibre most commonly described on labelling as 'pure' is in fact anything but.

Today's army of cotton producers involves an amazing three hundred plus million people, ranging from seed sellers, farmers (about thirty million), pickers, pesticide hawkers, ginners, yarn spinners, knit spinners, warehousers and a huge number of middlemen, merchants and traders. Ninety-nine per cent of this huge army are working in developing countries, near the bottom of the financial reward chain. The ultimate destination of 80 to 90 per cent of this cotton is apparel, and while over ninety countries produce cotton, just six dominate the entire industry, accounting for 85 per cent of global supplies: China, India, the USA, Pakistan, Brazil and Uzbekistan. Each of them has found a way to make its cotton cheaper or more abundant than the other eighty-four producing nations. And the production of cotton is about as far from a fair playing field as you can imagine.

SOAKED IN SUBSIDIES

If I was one of the three-hundred-million-strong cotton army at this point in history, I would definitely want to be a farmer in one of the seventeen states in the USA that make up the American cotton belt. Preferably I'd be in California, where the top 1 per cent of farming subsidy recipients grow mainly cotton. In 2009 alone this top percentile reaped $57 million in subsidies, predominantly for cotton. More specifically, I'd opt to be involved in SJR Farming, California's top recipient of federal farm payouts. In 2009 these cotton farmers received a whopping $2,069,453 in cotton subsidies from the US government. The US-based Environmental Working Group notes (in a report that practically spits with indignation) that this huge amount is by contrast to California's vast harvest of fruit and vegetables, whose producers receive diddly squat in handouts.

The recipients of these subsidies are heavily mechanised cotton farms with many shiny new tractors and farmhouses with white picket fences. Despite the vagaries of the international cotton market and the activities of speculators and traders, their owners can sleep easy at night (their sheets will be of the highest thread count, of course). This is an example of why 'white gold' remains a fitting soubriquet for cotton. Thanks to subsidies, there's big money to be made in the cotton belt. As Rivoli puts it, 'the 2002 Farm Bill went "over the top" for cotton', resulting in a situation where by 2004 a combination of government subsidies guaranteed US cotton farmers a minimum price of 72.24 cents per pound for their cotton at a time when the market price for producers on the rest of the planet was stuck at 38 cents per pound.

As if all these subsidies weren't enough of a boon for US producers, they also enjoy the support of a highly organised trade body, the National Cotton Council of America, that provides 'leadership'; and as you can imagine, it doesn't take a back seat when it comes to lobbying Congress. The US cotton industry is a major employer and therefore a major vote-winner, so you'd have to travel far to find a senator, let alone a president, who is going to question whether it should receive the vast amounts of public money it's become accustomed to. Even so, the National Cotton Council is represented at home and abroad by the Cotton Council International (CCI), which runs a relentless marketing campaign to keep American white gold on top. Its promotional films of cotton production have a Disney quality about them – ruddy-cheeked farmers, those big shiny tractors – and you can almost feel how wholesome and all-American a fibre this is. There's even a theme tune. 'The Fabric of Our Lives', sung by Leona Lewis, has an accompanying video showing Leona stroking home furnishings and running the fashion gauntlet from crisp shirts and blazers to a bejewelled party frock. Cotton is so versatile!

If you couldn't be an American grower, you'd want to be a European one, because they benefit from subsidies too. Call me woefully ignorant, but I hadn't actually realised that Europe produces cotton. There isn't much of it – it represents just 2 per cent of world production – but nevertheless subsidies are received by around 10,000 producers in Spain and 90,000 in Greece.

THE PLIGHT OF THE COTTON 4

Of course, 100,000 subsidised European producers are hardly going to keep our knicker drawers full. Europeans have long looked to Africa to provide a cheap, readily available source of cotton. After the 1850s, when cotton prices rose in India thanks to widespread strikes, 'European powers, desperate to feed their booming garment industries, turned to their African colonies for a cheap alternative'. The GDPs of a number of African countries have become dependent on the export of cotton. And the four pivotal countries – Benin, Burkina Faso, Chad and Mali – are among the poorest on the planet. They are so dependent on cotton (for example, in Burkina Faso 85 per cent of the population farms it) that they are known in trade terms as the Cotton 4, or C-4. These countries produce cotton more cheaply than anywhere else in the world: the cost of cotton production in Burkina Faso is one-third that in the US. Given that the world's appetite for cotton seems insatiable, the Cotton 4 should be cleaning up.

They aren't. The cotton farmers of Benin, Burkina Faso, Chad and Mali remain absolutely poverty-stricken. The American and European subsidies have effectively shut the door in their faces. A recent report by the UK's Fairtrade Foundation, 'The Great Cotton Stitch Up' (the title says it all, really), reveals that in the nine years since the Doha Development Round of international trade talks, which featured countless declarations of support for helping developing countries trade their way out of poverty, $40 billion has been given by the US, the EU, China and India to their own cotton growers. Over half of that has gone directly to US farmers. In a bizarre international trade agreement, Brazil became a recipient of damages from the US after a ruling found that Brazilian cotton farmers had unfairly lost out to those in America. In effect this means that Brazilian cotton farmers also receive a sort of quasi subsidy.

It doesn't take a genius to work out that if taxpayers are stumping up subsidies for developed world cotton farmers, those farmers can sell their cotton at prices below the cost of production (in fact, this complex system of trade tariffs, agreements, prosecutions and counter-prosecutions makes it very difficult to determine what the real cost of cotton is any more). 'It is estimated that the removal of cotton subsidies alone could increase cotton farmers' income by as much as 30 per cent in sub-Saharan Africa,' the British Business Secretary, Vince Cable, said in September 2010. While wealthy American producers receive their shiny tractor subsidies, Developing World cotton farmers carry on in penury.

The market is flooded with subsidised bales of cotton. By 2000 the world cotton price had fallen by a third since 1994. More recently a perceived shortage has led to a price spike, but even taking this into account, cotton has lost more than half of its value since 1995.

It is not hyperbolic to call the collapse of the cotton price a disaster for many communities in the C-4, where it has potentially consigned generations of farmers to absolute poverty. It changed the lives of thousands of people, and the history of many villages and towns. That was brought home to me in 2007, as I sat under a large tree in Djidian, a village in Mali. Terena Keita, the sparkly-eyed chairman of the Cooperatives des Producteurs de Coton de Djidian, implored my fellow visitors from some of the UK's biggest supermarkets to 'buy more cotton. Order more and more.' He was pressing them to buy Djidian's Fairtrade-certified cotton as the village attempted to pick itself up from the great crash in cotton prices of 2002–03. The evidence of that crash was all around us. The statistics of the cotton harvests and the prices paid over the previous decade were jotted down in Keita's notebook, which bore a picture of footballer Thierry Henry. They charted a desperate struggle just to keep the community together and fed. There was an obvious absence of men in their twenties and early thirties. Keita told us that as food grew scarce his own seven sons had begun to leave the area. 'Where are they now?' I asked. 'I'm not sure,' he replied. 'One left for Spain. It is hard to tell if he got there. It is difficult.'

It is not only subsidies that distort the market for the C-4: it seems that big global cotton producers will do almost anything to get their product on the international market at the lowest prices. Even if that involves using state-enforced child labour to pick the annual cotton crop.

AN EDUCATION ... IN COTTON PICKING

Welcome to Uzbekistan, with its apparently rich heritage in white gold. There are even songs to commemorate the glory of picking the annual cotton harvest. Some slightly spooky B-roll footage taken by Dziga Vertov (the great-grandfather of *cinéma verité* and therefore of documentary) in 1929 shows hands plucking at the fluffy cotton heads, images overlaid with a strange, soaring folk song in praise of the noble cotton crop and extolling the virtues of quick picking. It features a refrain reminding pickers, who included children, that their efforts are vital to defeat the foe.

Ninety years later, Uzbekistan's cotton harvest doesn't look very different. During the early 1990s the country abandoned mechanised cotton picking. The authorities had found a cheaper way. They might describe it as a more traditional way. Because come September, if you were to travel to the main cotton regions and take a look at those bent double plucking cotton bolls, you'd find that they are little more than children. The proud Uzbek cotton harvest is picked courtesy of the forced labour of the country's children and young adults.

Filmed and written evidence is sneaked out each year for foreign consumption from under the nose of the Uzbek dictator Islam Karimov. Karimov has ruled here by hook or by crook (his official two terms in office were up in 2007) since 1989, two years before the country gained its independence following the collapse of the Soviet Union. It is difficult to get precise figures, but evidence collated by the Environmental Justice Foundation (EJF), working with a secret network of Uzbek people and journalists, suggests that in 2009 between one and two million children were forced out into Uzbekistan's fields.

Smuggled video evidence shows the harvest in action, small hands grasping at the fluffy white cotton bolls, plucking them from the plants with robotic precision. The speed of work is incredible, but then each child must meet a steep quota (contrary to official Uzbek claims that they take part in the harvest for fun and extra money). The work is backbreaking: if you've ever read John Steinbeck's *The Grapes of Wrath*, a social exposition of the horrors of unmechanised cotton picking, you will have an idea of what these young people endure. Their quota is mandatory.

Karimov, apparently a powerful ally to the West in the war on terror, is also extremely rich. That is hardly surprising: it has been widely reported that the wealth of Uzbekistan's natural resources is siphoned straight into his pockets and those of his henchmen. And a significant chunk of that wealth lies in cotton production. It's estimated that in 2009 alone Uzbek exports of raw cotton, primarily to factories in Asia and to traders, many of them based in Europe, amounted to US$1 billion.

Gulnara (not her real name) is quick-witted, direct and made of discernibly strong stuff. It's difficult now to imagine her picking cotton against her will, but her teenage years were clouded by the inevitability that come the autumn term in her equivalent of Year 11, she would find herself picking cotton. 'I wasn't exactly a lazy teenager,' she says. 'My parents had a farm, so I was used to a degree of manual work. But nothing can prepare you for work in the cotton fields.' Each September, Uzbek students are told to bring a backpack to school, and are loaded onto buses and driven out to the cotton fields. For the next two months their lives are completely disrupted. On basic rations, without any of the amenities that they would usually take for granted, such as washing facilities or electricity, they are housed in sports halls and empty kinder-garten buildings. Each day they are woken at dawn and taken to the cotton fields, where the backbreaking work begins.

It was in 1998, when Gulnara was sixteen, that she was first separated from her family and taken to the fields in the Ulugnor district, nearly two hours' drive from her home in the city. 'I suppose it was such a shock to the system,' she remembers. 'You know it's going to happen on one level. I mean, it happened to my older siblings and my parents too, but somehow it's very difficult to prepare yourself. In other countries young people of this age are getting ready to perhaps go away to college, and that is agonising enough for parents and family, to see them leave, but it is much harder when you know they are going to be put through this very hard manual labour. To make matters worse, there is nothing you can do about it.'

Once in the fields, each student is given a daily quota of cotton to pick. Failure to meet it can mean punishments or fines. 'I was only able to meet my quota once,' Gulnara says of the fifty-four days she worked in the cotton fields during her first period of forced labour. 'After that, physically I wasn't able to pick enough. Just think how light cotton is! Imagine how much you have to pick to meet a sixty-kilo daily target. We used these huge pieces of fabric, like giant handkerchiefs, to put the bolls in. You really can't underestimate how hard that work is unless you've done it. Then they supposedly pay you a rate if you meet the target, but from that thirty to forty kilos' worth is deducted for your food allowance. As the days wear on you get cold, ill, fatigued, and there is less and less cotton available to pick. It became impossible to meet your quota, and then you get fined.'

As Gulnara's father paid for her education, and she wasn't dependent on a state allowance, she figured that there wasn't much the authorities could do about fining her. 'With most students they try to deduct any shortfall from their state allowance. If you protest or rebel too much you will simply be expelled from school. It's harder for them perhaps to expel someone who is paying for their education.'

For fifty-four days her life and those of her friends became a kind of living hell. Twelve years later, she still finds it hard to talk about it: 'I think one of the worst things was the sort of humiliation of having to go to the toilet in the fields, and things like that. It is very difficult for a girl in particular. I don't even really like to admit this now. And the toilet facilities where we stayed – holes in the ground, I wouldn't even describe them as 1 per cent hygienic.' The students had to pay local people to boil vats of hot water for them on wood fires so they could wash their clothes. Every night's meal was the same, 'cheap pasta and maybe a few vegetables. I need to make it clear I am definitely not talking about posh pasta here.' Even so, Gulnara thinks that by comparison to the boys, the girls had it easy: 'The boys were housed downstairs and we heard all the time that their regime was like being in the military and could be very, very brutal. On the first cotton harvest the younger boys are at the mercy of the older boys, and can be very vulnerable.'

Without contact with their families, Gulnara and the other children were presided over by a mixture of teachers, who were encouraged to behave despotically to keep order, and police, who were supposedly protecting the building full of girls for their own safety. 'Although there was a culture of teachers naming and shaming you if you didn't pick enough cotton, and a lot of humiliation and intimidating threats, I don't blame the teachers. I mean, what professional wants to go and supervise children picking the cotton harvest? It's a horrible job. They are under constant pressure from the authorities, and don't forget it means they are away from their families for two months and living in these horrible conditions. In fact, when I was deciding on what I wanted to do after college I knew I wouldn't become a teacher for this reason.'

With so many children away from home, and with only sporadic adult supervision, there is evidence of sexual abuse and fights: in 2009 the EJF reported that a child died after a stabbing. 'You really don't know what will happen to you,' Gulnara says.

Out in the fields from sunrise to sunset, the teenage pickers endure extremes of climate. In September, when they first go out as novice pickers, temperatures rise to 40°C. 'You are perpetually desperate for water,' Gulnara recalls, 'gasping for a drink all the time. But there are no water taps. There was nothing we could do but drink from irrigation channels. They are stagnant, and you can see frogs and snakes, but what else can you do? One thing I will never forget,' she says with a shudder, 'is being attacked by mosquitoes in those fields. I have never known mosquitoes like it.' By the end of the cotton season, when Gulnara and her friends were frantically scratching around for the last bits of cotton, knowing full well that they had no chance of meeting their quotas but every chance of being humiliated and fined, the temperature was freezing and they were chilled to the bone.

One of Gulnara's mementoes from her time as a cotton slave is a digestive disorder. She and her co-pickers and friends wound up with a variety of illnesses, especially kidney problems, attributable to being out in cold, wet cotton fields as the harvest drew to a close, poor nutrition and being held in stressful and unsanitary conditions.

The thing that makes the whole experience bearable to Gulnara is that she was not broken by the cotton harvest. 'I was not an easy student. I rebelled from morning until night,' she says, still with a glint in her eye. Her stint in 1998 involved her organising a protest. Tiring of the constant threat that they would be sent into the fields at night to make up for failing to meet their quotas, she instigated a group of girls to sit in the fields until well after dark, when supervisors had to come and plead with them to go back to their sports hall. 'OK, it didn't change anything, but we made a small point. That was all we could do.' The next year, bussed out to the same fields, Gulnara snapped. Halfway through the harvest she ran away. 'Some teenagers question everything, and I was one of those. The thing that worries me now is that from what I am hearing about the level of oppression in the cotton fields for this next generation, people like me who tend to say what they think and organise rebellions would not be tolerated. I fear for those kids especially. Things have become even stricter, more brutal.' Islam Karimov has little time for dissenters. 'Fraud, Nepotism and Torture Mark Karimov's Reign', according to one headline in the British press.

I have never lived in a dictatorship myself, nor been compelled to work in heavy agricultural industry. My questions are naïve. 'Who gives the orders to make this happen?' I ask. 'Oh, they come from the government,' says Gulnara confidently. 'Nobody on the ground is any doubt as to where the orders come from.' She is backed up by recent reports. There is no such thing in Uzbekistan as an independent cotton farmer. Even chemical fertiliser inputs are controlled. The man who is responsible for the agricultural sector, Prime Minister Shavkat Mirziyaev, reportedly holds conference calls every fifteen days, in which he instructs local government agents and farmers when to seed, weed, apply pesticides and defoliants, and to harvest. In October 2009 Mirziyaev signed a telegraph, later leaked, which amounted to a sinister list of punishments for cotton farmers who hadn't fulfilled their quota. It concluded with the cheerful message that 'In those cases where farms have not complied with contractual obligations, a schedule will be made to levy damages from them. Under the law, their land lease will be revoked.'

Forced labour is of course illegal. The UN's International Labour Organisation Convention 29, banning compulsory labour, was ratified in 1992. In 2008 the Uzbek government was persuaded to sign two ILO conventions, on 'Minimum Age' and 'The Worst Forms of Child Labour', although it concluded that no domestic legislation was necessary. With the possible exception of some members of the US government who view Uzbekistan as a useful strategic base, does anybody believe the Uzbek government's claim to be sorting out the issue, or its blanket refusal to accept that it exists at all?

'This is not the truth,' say two small women who shuffle up to me at the end of a panel discussion about forced labour in the Uzbek cotton harvest at the V&A in November 2008. There is something unnerving about the way they block my way. There are no introductions or 'hellos', but one of them comes close and speaks urgently in a low voice. 'Our people pick cotton for the health and wealth of our nation. It is our culture.' I am taken aback, but tell them that that is going to be a hard sell, given the evidence of conscripted child labour and the level of enforcement. When I look around later they are gone, as mysteriously as they appeared. I assume they were from the Uzbekistan Embassy. I asked Gulnara if she had met any pickers who believed in the inherent beauty of picking cotton for the state's wealth. 'No,' she says with an eyebrow raised, 'although there are some who are brainwashed. Mainly it is about fear.'

In February 2010 the EJF produced a report with the uncompromising title 'Slave Nation: State-Sponsored Forced Child Labour in Uzbekistan's Cotton Fields'. It found that Uzbek cotton production continued to be 'one of the most exploitative enterprises in the world. Two years after the government promised the international community that child labour in cotton production would cease, in the 2009 autumn cotton harvest, forced child labour remained as widespread as ever. In fact, according to many reports, its implementation grew even harsher and more exploitative than in previous years.' There follows page after page of documentary evidence and photographs supporting the claims that children continue to be bussed to the fields. There were reports that school children and college students from eleven of Uzbekistan's thirteen regions had been sent to pick cotton.

I write to an Uzbek journalist, Umida, who now lives in a European capital where she coordinates a campaign to stop the cotton conscription, and who in the past has been arrested and held for periods without trial, charge or representation by the Uzbek authorities. 'In 2009,' she tells me, 'we observed the situation in the cotton fields during the cotton harvest, interviewing forty kids in four different regions. Most of them said that they did not want to be there. It is a better for them to go to school, but there is no option. The government mobilised not only kids but other people who have nothing to do with agricultural sector. For instance, my sister who works in a hospital was forced to pick cotton this year, despite the fact that she has small children.' Umida sends me an open letter from Uzbek civic activists clearly outlining the problems. It is signed by every human rights proponent you can think of, and calls unequivocally for a boycott of Uzbek cotton. 'It is the only thing that will convince the Karimov regime to stop forced child labour,' she insists.

The testimonies of these children are heartbreaking. Many of them suggest that Gulnara got off lightly. 'Every year young children die during forced labour in the Uzbek cotton fields,' said Craig Murray, the former British Ambassador to Uzbekistan and a fierce opponent of the regime, in February 2010. What is utterly extraordinary is the seeming lack of international will to do anything about the situation. Murray continued: 'Yet no government has used available anti-slavery provisions in international trade agreements to ban Uzbek cotton. The EU has never even discussed the matter while, thanks to the influence of Western governments, UNICEF has never made any statement or taken any position on child slavery in Uzbekistan.'

In a later chapter, I'll have a go at assessing who on the British high street has responded constructively to the issue of child labour in the cotton chain. But overall the international cotton market doesn't seem particularly perturbed. The traders and brokers working on behalf of Asian powerhouses of manufacturing need a constant supply of cheap fabric to keep the mills turning and the sewing machines running at full pelt.

Besides, whereas historically Europe has been the biggest market for Uzbek cotton, enabling its routes to market to be tracked, there are many ways of 'laundering' raw cotton. Uzbekistan has a new fan in the form of the Dubai Cotton Centre, a 'strategic initiative of the Government of Dubai', according to its website, and a 'one-stop shop' for textile traders. Its brochure reads like a love letter to Uzbek cotton production. It talks of quality and convenience (Uzbek cotton can be shipped at any time of year), and has a list of special rates and incentives: thirty days' free storage can be provided for Uzbek cotton in Jebel Ali if you buy through the DCC. Storage represents one of the most expensive parts of the supply chain. If traders can solve that, they pretty much have a deal. A helpful map marks out the cotton's route between Uzbekistan and Dubai, then from Dubai to South-East Asian RMG hotspots – China, Bangladesh and Cambodia. There is so much information that you could be convinced that it gives an excellent overview of the cotton scene in Uzbekistan. Except that there is not one mention of the fact that 40 to 45 per cent of this year's Uzbek cotton harvest will be picked by forced child labour.

Raw cotton might just be the beginning of the story, but it feeds the engine of fast fashion, and that engine is relentless and insatiable. Fast fashion doesn't care where or how cotton is produced, it just needs huge quantities of it. And once it arrives and is processed and sewn into a million pairs of knickers or denim jeans, you'd be hard pressed to know anything of its origins. I really don't know how much of my wardrobe has arrived courtesy of the child pickers of eleven Uzbek regions, who sacrificed a sizeable chunk of their education (not to mention their childhood) to provide me with wardrobe filler. Uzbekistan is the world's sixth biggest cotton producer, and the third largest cotton exporter. In 2009 (according to government sources, which must be taken with an almighty dose of salt) it produced 3.4 million tonnes of raw cotton. Its raw export material is cheap and of fabled good quality (because the picking is unmechanised and done by hand, it is said to produce higher-quality cotton bolls for processing).

You have to wonder how much appetite there really is to take a stand on Uzbekistan's cotton conscription. Following the EJF's 2006 'White Gold' report and a spate of international condemnation, in 2007 the international cotton industry decided to hold its annual conference in – er, Uzbekistan. I wasn't invited, but I can only assume that concerns about child labour didn't top the agenda.

THE GREEN REVOLUTION FAILS

Other nations also appear hopelessly attached to cotton. A spinning wheel adorns the Indian flag – growing and producing cotton is a source of national identity. To Gandhi, spun cotton represented the fabric of freedom. He advocated the expression of national loyalty through the spinning of cotton and the wearing of the final product, the *khadi*, the hand-woven Indian garment. It's safe to say he did not have multinational fast fashion in mind.

India's cultural and fiscal commitment to cotton lives on. To say that the fibre is important to the country is an enormous understatement. With over ten million hectares, India has more land devoted to growing cotton than any other country on the planet. It produces an average of thirty million bales of cotton each year (enough to make thirty-six billion T-shirts) and upwards of sixty million Indians are dependent on the cotton chain for their livelihoods. It has even been said that cotton is in the country's DNA. I'm not sure if a country can have DNA, but I suggest that there are now millions of small-scale Indian farmers who wish they'd never heard of the stuff.

Once, the local cotton economy flourished, and farmers could be assured of a price well above the government-set floor price. They were riding high on the promises of the Green Revolution (rather a misnomer, as it transpired). Towards the end of the 1960s, the Green Revolution promised to ensure that the world never ran out of food again, but also extended that promise to other commodities. Its proponents claimed that just as they could increase crop yields for food through industrialised techniques, the same could be done for cotton. And among the main pieces in the Green Revolution's magic set were the agrichemicals liberally applied to the Indian cotton crop. For a while, the Green Revolution appeared to be as good as its word. Two years before I was born, in 1972 a Vidarbhan cotton farmer could meaningfully express the value of his raw cotton crop using gold as a measure. For every quintal (enough for 133 pairs of jeans) he sold, he made enough to buy fifteen grams of gold. Even small-scale farmers bought tractors. Able to think for the first time beyond providing for their families' immediate need to be clothed and fed, they prepared for a lifetime of profitable farming, planning to send their children to school and get their houses fixed. To feed the huge textile industry in Mumbai, a vast cotton monoculture was established in Andhra Pradesh, Karnataka, Madhya Pradesh, Chhattisgarh and Maharashtra. The area became known as the Cotton Bowl. It must have seemed that cotton farmers were living the dream.

But by 1990, in India as well as in the other Developing World nations producing cotton, the good times appeared to have come to an end. In 2002 in Andhra Pradesh, the heart of the Cotton Bowl, 82 per cent of all farm households were recorded to be in debt. By 2005 a farmer would need to sell five quintals of cotton (enough for 665 pairs of jeans) for the same fifteen grams of gold, and a few months later nine quintals (1,197 pairs of jeans' worth). The odds against turning a profit lengthened every year. When journalist and author Dionne Bunsha interviewed members of cotton-dependent communities in Gujarat, she found them despairing. 'A pair of jeans that weighs around five hundred grams sells for 1,500–1,700 rupees in the designer stores, but we get only thirteen rupees for five hundred grams of cotton. Those who are processing get all the profit, not those who produce,' complained one community leader. A group of farmers in the village of Malak Nes expressed themselves more graphically, taking off their *chappals* (the Indian flip-flop/slipper hybrid) and presenting them to Bunsha, saying: 'Our *chappals* have gaping holes and are broken. Can you please send them to Narendra Modi? [a leading Gujarat politician] … We can't even afford a new pair of *chappals*.' Worn-out flip-flops had become a more appropriate way of expressing the value of cotton than precious metal.

PESTICIDE POWER

As far as thankless tasks go, being an Indian cotton farmer now treads near to the very limits of human tolerance. The world cotton crop is disturbingly dependent on agrichemicals. Although globally cotton takes up just over 2 per cent of all available arable land, it soaks up 11 to 12 per cent of all global pesticides. This use is enormous. One third of a pound of chemicals went into producing each of your T-shirts. India is particularly addicted, because cotton yields there are among the lowest in the world. It could be argued that being a cotton farmer in India is one of the most precarious jobs in the fashion chain. The average cotton farm in Punjab yields just 180 kilograms of cotton lint per hectare. By contrast, the average in Pakistan is 1,867 kilograms per hectare, and in China the figure is 3,878. Even if everything goes right, the Indian farmer can only expect a low yield come harvest time. But there are a lot of things that can go wrong with a cotton crop, including a plethora of parasites, among them the notorious bollworm. Small wonder that the Indian cotton farmer relies on pesticides in an effort to keep pests at bay and gain some form of security. While across India cotton covers just 5 per cent of all the land available for cultivation, it accounts for a huge 55 per cent of all pesticides used.

Dirty White Gold (2010), a documentary film by Leah Borromeo, shows the casual and ubiquitous nature of pesticide use in India. The camera zooms in on a corner shop: like millions of others in India it is stacked high with packets. They might be chocolate, or packs of rice or noodles. But as we get closer we see that they are pesticides. Borromeo asks for different brands, and one after another they are slapped down on the counter. The seller seems cheerfully proud of the range he has. 'Do you sell protective clothing?' Borromeo asks. 'Gloves, goggles, anything?' 'No, just agrichemicals,' he says cheerfully.

It is not hard to understand the attraction of pesticides for Indian cotton farmers. Cotton is never low-maintenance when you need it as cheaply and in such huge quantity as consumers apparently do. There are two months between the flowering of the cotton plant and the first opening of its fruit (the fluffy white boll). During that time the crop can be attacked by something in the region of 1,300 serious pests. Cotton insects are the main cause of yield loss, and the bollworm is the most serious of them all. Farmers simply cannot afford to lose a crop and these pressures have made them increasingly dependent on pesticides.

And not just any pesticides, but some of the most hazardous for people and planet that humankind has ever managed to manufacture. Among the roll call of the deadliest chemicals (not just in terms of eliminating pests) in use is Aldicarb, a powerful nerve agent and one of the most toxic pesticides. Exposure to it can cause symptoms including nausea, abdominal cramps, vomiting, hypertension, cardio-respiratory depression, dyspnoea and bronchorrhea, which can lead to pulmonary oedema. To give an idea of how hazardous it is, just one drop absorbed through the skin is enough to kill an adult. Yet, astonishingly, it remains the second most prevalent pesticide in the cotton industry. We can tell it's strong stuff by the fact that in 2003, when almost one million kilos of it were applied to cotton grown in the USA, the result was the contamination of groundwater in sixteen states. In China, which does not have a relatively powerful policing body like America's Environmental Protection Agency, Aldicarb is reportedly applied at between twelve and fifteen kilograms per hectare – at least seventeen times the amount used in the US example. We consumers may never feel the impact of this, but the communities whose soil and water resources are close to cotton-producing areas probably will. While Europe bans hazardous pesticides from its own soil, the First World-registered chemical multinationals that produce them have found a welcoming market in India and West Africa, where government authorities have seemed prepared either to turn a blind eye, or even to make a political case for the use of hazardous chemicals to its own farmers and international observers. And so Endosulfan has been used liberally over the last decade by nine of the top ten cotton producers, despite a report from the Pesticide Action Network suggesting that it is the most important source of fatal poisoning among cotton farmers in West Africa. According to the World Health Organisation, between 20,000 and 40,000 cotton workers die each year from pesticide poisoning. I heard of tragic stories in Mali, where villagers unable to read or to interpret warning signs on empty pesticide containers filled them with water and drank from them, with fatal consequences. Like Endosulfan, Deltamethrin, the other most popular pesticide (applied in forty-three out of eighty-one cotton-producing countries), is a nerve agent. It has global sales of around US$40 million.

DYING FOR COTTON

While NGOs work to get dangerous pesticides on the banned list, parts of the Indian cotton industry appear to be working equally hard to keep using them. As struggling farmers sank deeper and deeper into debt, they attempted to stave off ruin by buying agrichemicals and praying for a good harvest that would somehow allow them to turn a profit.

Many of them hoped in vain, with the result that by 2005 India's Cotton Bowl was being informally renamed the Suicide Belt. There are so many tragic stories that journalists are spoiled for choice when photographing widows and young children with garlanded images of their dead husbands or fathers. Dionne Bunsha's piece for the Indian magazine *Frontline* lingers in the memory, not least for its images of grieving women in Gujarat sitting next to photographs of their dead husbands. Sometimes the photographs are decorated with fairy lights, as in the case of Pahubhai Dakhada, who took his life at the age of thirty-five. The caption tells us that he 'preferred death to a life of debt'. All of the women she speaks to, running their families from the confines of their homes (widows are not permitted outside), have lost their husbands to suicide.

Bunsha and P. Sainath are among the Indian journalists who should be credited with bringing these stories to light before the picture of the widow with the garlanded photo became a magazine cliché. In a series of pieces, Jaideep Hardikar teased out the truth about the lives left behind by these suicides. He found widows and their daughters who had been thrown out of the family home by their in-laws. 'My daughters are as vulnerable to [sexual and physical] exploitation as I am,' one widow, Kavita Kudmethe, told him.

The statistics are simply horrifying. From 1997 to 2008, according to the National Crime Records Bureau of India, there were nearly 200,000 suicides on Indian farms. In 2008 there were 'at least' 16,196 farmers' suicides in India, and while they can't all be attributed to cotton, 10,797, or nearly 70 per cent, took place in the Cotton Bowl: Maharashtra, Andhra Pradesh, Karnataka, Madhya Pradesh and Chhattisgarh. That is surely no coincidence. The sobering fact is that according to many records almost every thirty minutes an Indian farmer commits suicide, and it's highly likely that he will be a cotton farmer. Many of them have made a last, horrifying link between the burden of farming and their hopeless situation: they died by drinking the pesticide they had bought to protect their cotton.

DEPLETED SOILS AND SHRINKING SEAS

How much are we prepared to pay in social and environmental terms for cheap cotton? Certainly some people do well from this exploitation of people and land: the 'textile barons' and cotton traders in Mumbai and other capitals, and the fashion kings of the West whose empires are based on the fastest of fashion. And as consumers snuggled in pyjama sets, or confidently walking out in crisply ironed cotton shirts, we don't do badly ourselves. After all, it's not as if we generally have cotton's environmental impact on our mind.

But there are some truths about white gold that, from an ecological perspective, should be impossible to ignore. Thousands of miles away, the ecological price tag can be immense. The rise of cotton monoculture – vast tracts of arable land converted solely to cotton bushes, with not another plant in sight – has a lot to answer for. Not least because cotton is one of the thirstiest crops on the planet. From 7,000 to 9,000 cubic metres of water are needed to produce one tonne of cotton. By a terrible irony, cotton is increasingly grown in some of the most water scarce areas on earth.

Every cotton product I own has a huge 'embodied water footprint' (taking into account all the water used not just in the growing of the cotton, but in its production. The more complex the production, and the more exacting the finish – a pair of stonewashed denim jeans, for example – the more water will have been used). If you're talking in terms of accounting for water – and some day the world may have to do this – in order to get one kilogram (enough for a pair of jeans) of finished cotton textile, you need 11,000 to 20,000 litres of water, while a shirt weighing 250 grams requires 2,700 litres.

Actually, these kinds of calculations give us only a very superficial idea of the impact of our cotton habit. If you really want to find that out, you need to account for the 'virtual water footprint', adding in all the extra water that has been used in diluting the pollution from growing and processing the cotton, and from combatting the salinisation associated with irrigation. To do this your investigations would need to verge on the forensic. It is difficult enough to find out what country the basic cotton that has been used to make a vest top might have come from, let alone where it was dyed, and whether a closed loop system that minimised pollution and diffused contaminated waste water was used. As a rule of thumb, however, environmental experts say that as much as 20,000 litres of water can be used to produce a single T-shirt. Regular doses of water add salt to the upper soil of irrigated land, causing large-scale salinisation and rendering that patch of earth pretty useless to grow anything else.

But stats are just that: stats. It wasn't until I began looking at pictures of a very peculiar landscape, one that didn't quite make sense, that I really understood what the fallout of cotton pesticides and extensive irrigation could be.

To find a true ecological catastrophe that is directly connected to your sock drawer, we need to go to Central Asia, to an endorheic basin (or, for the less enthusiastic geologists out there, an immense freshwater lake) that at 26,300 square miles was so huge that it was upgraded by name to a 'sea', the Aral Sea. It was the fourth largest inland body of water in the world, and for centuries it was the lifeblood for millions of people in Kazakhstan and Uzbekistan, and throughout the whole of Central Asia.

Nowadays there can be few stranger places on the planet than the Uzbek town of Muynoq. Pictures show a jolly-looking 'Welcome to Muynoq' sign in seaside colours featuring a leaping fish that gives visitors the first clear sign that this was once a big coastal destination. I say *once*, because Muynoq is now a defunct town with boarded-up shops and empty, dilapidated guest houses.

The Aral Sea is conspicuous by its absence. It's not just that the tide is out. The water is now some seventy miles away, and has been in retreat for the past two decades. Where it used to lap against the promenade, now a white and yellow expanse of sandy, dead terrain, punctuated by clumps of weeds, stretches to the horizon and beyond. In places there are glinting dry patches of white dust.

Muynoq's fortunes began to change decades before, when, unknown to the fishermen, the guest-house owners and the visitors to the then-popular spa town, many of whom returned year after year, the Soviet authorities began to divert the waters of the Syr Darya and Amu Darya rivers, which carried fresh water into and stagnant water out of the Aral. Where was the water diverted to, and why? To feed giant cotton plantations throughout Uzbekistan and Kazakhstan. Diverting the rivers cut off the Aral Sea's arteries. By the late 1980s it had lost more than half the volume of its water. Meanwhile, huge quantities of pesticide were being applied to the cotton fields. Desertification – the final stage of environmental catastrophe, feared more than anything by ecologists – was certain. With every year that passed the Aral became more and more full of salt. This irreversible decline threatened to make a biological wasteland out of the formerly lush and fertile landscape. A UN report in 2001 estimated that 46 per cent of Uzbekistan's irrigated land had been damaged by salinisation, representing an increase of 42 per cent since 1995. Fish and other wildlife disappeared. Gone were the carp, bream, pike-perch and sturgeon that sustained 60,000 fishermen and made the region famous. The majority of the region's five hundred species of birds, two hundred species of mammals and one hundred species of fish have now gone. By 1995 the Aral's surface area had decreased by half, three quarters of the volume of its water was gone, and its depth had been reduced by an amazing nineteen metres.

The Aral Sea is dead, and it was killed by cotton. And once a sea dies, the surrounding population is plummeted into a spiral of neglect and decline too. Thirty-five million people who depended on the Aral for fishing, leisure or associated activities lost out as the waters evaporated. Conservative estimates suggest that the lives of five million people have been devastated (not just affected or inconvenienced) by the loss of the Aral, and by living in a saline dustbowl full of the remnants of cotton chemicals. Every year over a hundred million tons of salty dust, containing particulates of agrichemicals and household waste, are whipped up into the air. Respiratory infections are the main cause of death among children, tuberculosis (at its peak there were four hundred cases per 100,000 people in some towns) is endemic and the drinking water contains more than six grams of salt per litre (four times higher than the safe level recommended by the World Health Organisation). Over ten years, mortality rates increased by fifteen times. Life expectancy is down by five to ten years in some areas, and in the region as a whole it now stands at sixty-two for women and fifty-nine for men.

The firms, manufacturers and brands that rapaciously capitalised on cheaper and cheaper cotton did not sanction the destruction of the Aral Sea. They could not have known the impact – including the removal of the water barrier between the mainland and Vozrozhdenya Island, a former USSR weapons-testing site which is contaminated by anthrax – that the means by which that cheap cotton was produced would have.

After many false starts the world, largely in the shape of the World Trade Organisation and the UN, has begun rescue conservation projects to try to save the Aral Sea, although it's debatable what's left to save. Some have been credited with a certain amount of success, and certain species have been reintroduced. You might even see occasional headlines about life seeping back into the Aral, implying that there's life in the old sea yet. But it's seeping, not flowing, and these are specifically controlled small areas. What chance does an ailing population have of replanting and making its land fertile and clean again? Not much in this generation. As the rusting boats on the arid plain that was once a thriving inland sea testify, it is too late. Paradise will not be regained.

COTTON MAKES THE FRONT PAGE

'Cotton is the rag I love to work with,' designer Dr Noki, of the label Noki's House of Sustainability, tells me. 'It's a shame that it has so many skeletons in the closet, because it's a brilliant, brilliant fibre. I absolutely love it.' Dr Noki's sentiments are unusual (not to say progressive). Not only does he acknowledge the dodgy back story of the fibre he is using, but he sets out to reclaim discarded cotton fabric and to reuse it in his collections. His reverence for cotton meanwhile is also unusual. For most of the world it is the ultimate dumb commodity: ubiquitous, cheap and discarded without much thought.

Which is why I almost fainted when I caught sight of my fellow passenger on the tube's copy of the London freesheet *Metro*. Just days before London Fashion Week, 'Soaring Cotton Costs!' was the front-page story, dramatically and unexpectedly displacing the usual Fashion Week fare of size-zero debates and whether *enfant terrible* designers operate in a moral vacuum. All day my phone rang – BBC Breakfast, drive-time shows – with producers wanting my comments on 'the situation with cotton'. The media spotlight is swift and sudden, and for a few hours it shone on the production of 'the pig of botany' – to a point. Devastating floods in Pakistan and a monsoon in India that left the cotton crop soaked when it should have been drying out were fingered as reasons why the cotton price had suddenly shot up. But were we consumers really so concerned about what this meant for producers? Why should anyone care if cotton costs were at a fifteen-year high, and 50 per cent dearer than the year before? Another headline soon made the real consumer catastrophe apparent: 'Cheap Clothing Era to End as Primark Warn Customers Prices will Rise Over Cotton Costs'.

Of course it was the spectre of a global shortage of cheap cotton, and the threat of an end to the age of £2 T-shirts, that really caught the imagination. Not for the first time, I was left wondering whether our retailers were telling the full story here. After all, it would be naïve to think that cheap cotton is the only factor in their ability to sell on-trend pieces for the price of a sandwich. Some analysts have suggested that the rise in VAT to 20 per cent in January 2011 will mean a rise in prices in any case. And then there are those oft-forgotten garment workers. Dominic Eagleton, from the NGO Action Aid, which has frequently campaigned for a better deal for garment workers, notes: 'For years, major retailers have been telling us they want to put prices up to help foreign workers – but don't want to upset customers over here. This statement, though, would suggest that, when it suits companies, they can raise prices after all if they want to.' Sadly, it seems likely that unless we do something about it, rising cotton prices will just encourage retailers to squeeze those poor garment workers even more to maintain their margins.

The price of fibre can only hold the public imagination for so long. In a couple of days fashion coverage and opinion pieces reverted to more familiar territory – London's stance against size-zero models, and Victoria Beckham's banning of them in New York. Cotton receded to the innards of broadsheets, where its price is listed with shares and other commodities. You can monitor your investment as you chomp on a Sunday croissant, completely detached from the actual farmers and producers. And it's for you, the investor, that the cotton market works. One thing is almost certain: the rise in the international cotton price will not translate into a rise in the farm-gate price for the millions of farmers struggling to produce cotton and keep their families afloat. If any financial trickledown does happen, it will be as arduous a process as squeezing blood from a particularly unyielding boulder.

8

WOOLLY THINKING

*The Diamond Fibre Creates a Dustbowl and the
UK Loses its Sheep*

You might imagine that the ecological wreckage that is the depleted Aral Sea would serve as a warning to the garment industry that the wholesale pursuit and production of a fibre in a vulnerable ecosystem is at best unwise and at worst catastrophic. But did fashion learn its lesson? Predictably not. Even as emergency ecology committees convened to try to think of ways to breathe life back into the Aral and halt the desertification of this zone, the next disaster was already beginning, driven by another global trend for one specific fibre. In this case, cashmere.

The trend in October to November 2005 was that of the 'sexy secretary' – a recurring fashion fad (we saw it again in 2010 following the success of the TV series *Mad Men*, for example) that wins no prizes for innovation (or indeed the furtherment of gender equality). But no matter, it essentially translated into a pencil skirt and a roll- or scooped-necked jumper overlaid with a cardigan. Square-framed glasses and Biro positioned suggestively in corner of mouth were optional. This trend went down rather nicely with the mass consumer, especially if the two layers were of a superfine fabric that could deliver, with a Jackie O neatness, the promise of cosy knitted salvation in the run-up to a cold snap. It was a style that evoked the golden age of European knitwear, when Pringle reigned supreme and A-listers like Grace Kelly floated around in twinsets displaying the brand's diamond motif. The trend also evoked the golden age of the golden fleece – soubriquets for cashmere include 'spun gold' and 'angel's wool', while ' the diamond fibre' remains the most persistent. They all describe our unequivocal fondness for its softness. When fans talk about cashmere, it's not long before they start sounding like strange fibre fetishists: 'This is the yarn that, when you touch it, causes time to stand still. Your fingers sink effortlessly into the skein, and you are overcome by a sense of otherworldly perfection. Once you've touched an extraordinary cashmere, you're ruined for anything else' – and that comes from the otherwise rather prosaic *Knittersreview*. Cashmere is almost always talked about in superlatives.

I'm the first to admit that I too am completely under the sway of the cashmere story. It is incredible, exotic and reassuring at the same time. The wonderment begins with the fact that there are just twelve regions in the world that are cold enough and have the right geographical features to sustain true cashmere goat herds. In these true cashmere areas the temperature falls 40 degrees below during winter, so the goats develop a thick, protective guard coat over a downy layer of unbelievably fine hair – known as cashmere. The best goats – and this is by consensus over hundreds of years – come from the mountains of Mongolia, China, India and Iran. Cashmere is not only remarkably rare, it is difficult to harvest properly. The wool from one Merino sheep (a relatively common breed) can make around twenty-four crewnecks. Cashmere, by comparison, requires the hair of three to six goats to make just one similar-sized sweater.

In spite of cashmere's inextricable links with Scotland (the venerable Scottish company Johnstons has, for example, been weaving cashmere there since the mid-nineteenth century), it was not a Scotsman but a Yorkshireman, Joseph Dawson, who in 1871 became the architect of the modern cashmere process. It relied on the most elaborate of trade routes and alliances: Dawson bought oily, raw cashmere direct from Mongolian herdsmen, who had hundreds of years of experience combing it from the bellies of goats. Crucially, this could only happen once a year, when the goats were moulting in the spring. Dawson's contribution was to find a way of mechanically 'de-hairing' (a prosaic name for the process that produces such a sensuous fibre, but still) the greasy cashmere. Attracted by the number of experienced weavers in Scotland, and possibly also by the first, rudimentary, preferential business grants, Dawson set up a mill in Kinross.

It was here that the cashmere-producing process was painstakingly perfected to a twenty-step system which mauled, tugged and manhandled the fibre into submission. In later years, knitting frames were introduced to manufacture the backs and fronts of sweaters, and to attach the cuffs and ribbings that were knitted separately. Hundreds of experienced Scottish knitters, needles tucked behind their ears, would anxiously watch out for dropped stitches, ready to make good any mistake. Finally, after the fibre had been dyed in the wool, carded into a yarn, knitted together and assembled, it was washed in Scottish water to give it its distinctive softness. In fact this latter stage has something of a whiff of marketing myth about it – any water will do, really – and later garments were bundled into washing machines to be 'milled' for thirty minutes until they had the right 'handle', or feel. While it mightn't have been essential to use water from the Teviot River, any connection with Scotland's mother earth helped to weave and enforce a sense of ownership, and it wasn't long before ostentatious 'Made in Scotland' labels were inserted into the garments. What was – and remains – critical for the Scottish production of cashmere, however, was the level of human expertise. So while the production of cashmere garments was ostensibly an industrial process created by Dawson, the brilliance of hundreds of men and women who knew and understood the fibre was invested in each piece.

CASHMERE GOES WILD

Yet suddenly in 2005 the diamond fibre was everywhere. And it was cheap enough to be available to everyone, not just the patrons of expensive knitwear shops. It had to be one of the most seductive mass-fashion propositions ever: if you looked in the right places you could find cashmere garments reduced to the price of something as prosaic as a kettle. During December 2007 M&S sold two cashmere sweaters per minute, helping its total annual cashmere sales to rocket by 400 per cent and upping the store's overall clothing sales by 7.1 per cent, while Tesco sold cashmere knits to half a million Brits in the Christmas period alone.

The style press retained its usual considered scepticism, cool analysis and professional distance. (I am of course joking.) Actually, it went mental for cheap cashmere. A new golden goose had arrived. People have raved about cashmere for hundreds of years, but this time the buzz was about the price and the blanket availability. The press clearly saw the 'democratisation' of this luxury fibre as part of the toolbox of success that supermarkets were employing to stay on top. 'He [Terry Leahy, CEO of Tesco] just makes it so easy, ' eulogised Patience Wheatcroft on the business pages of *The Times*. '… Cashmere sweaters at knockdown prices, best-selling books and videos, perfumes and electrical goods: they were all there to be loaded into the trolley …' Consumers and commentators bought into a sort of cashmere hysteria, and you can understand why: suddenly the wool so expensive and exclusive that the cheapest product cost £300 was available for £30. The final bastion of defence for the European luxury knitters, spinners and makers was faced with a massive operation to supply cheap cashmere to the masses, who proved incredibly hungry for it. Suddenly everyone around me seemed to be consumed by the desire for cashmere knits in every conceivable jewelled colour. 'I can't believe it's so soft. It's from the supermarket!' was a sort of mass refrain.

But why, and how? As you may have guessed, this kind of phenomenon doesn't happen by a simple coincidence of trend and availability. Even as far back as 2001 the disparity between Chinese and Scottish production was beginning to cause a huge downturn in the latter's fortunes. Scotland's 4,000 workers employed in the cashmere industry commanded wages up to thirty-six times higher than their counterparts in mainland China. A trade dispute – although centring on bananas rather than fibre – also rocked the boat in the late 1990s when the World Trade Organisation took umbrage at European importers who, it claimed, favoured West Indian (i.e. from ex-colonies) rather than Central American producers. As the argument intensified, the WTO seemed to retaliate by lifting restrictions (and supposed protectionist barriers) on cashmere imports. This meant that by 2004 foreign producers were at liberty to flood the UK market with cheap cashmere; it was at this time that we had the first glimpses of British retailers adopting a 'Pile them high, sell them cheap' maxim with regard to cashmere.

The removal of the Multi Fibre Arrangement, another trade agreement that had become the subject of global disputes, in 2005 meant that all trade barriers for cashmere (and other fibres) had gone. This seems to have led to the final injection of cash, energy and commitment required by the Chinese knitwear industry, which had been building up an arsenal of knitting machines: by 2007 the town of Dalang (with the self-appointed soubriquet of 'China Famous Knitting Sweater Town') had the capacity to produce an enormous 1.2 billion pieces of knitwear per year. Increasingly these machines were the high-tech, computerised kind that can spin finer fibres. Soon these imported machines, operated by an army of 20,000 workers, were clattering away twenty-four hours a day, seven days a week, spinning raw white cashmere. It's a good bet that the cashmere knits on sale in most UK supermarkets and high-street shops will have arrived courtesy of Erdos, a huge cashmere producer that originated in inner Mongolia and is making good on its mission statement to 'warm the whole world'. Indeed, cashmere has become a nice little earner for China: in the six months to September 2010, exports of the diamond fibre were reckoned to have made China some US$900 million, an increase on the previous year, despite the global downturn.

All of which might add up if cashmere was an abundant natural resource. But it isn't. The global cashmere clip ('clip' being the term expressing amounts of wool) has stabilised at a rather puny 16,000 tonnes (this is equivalent to the amount of carrots exported by New Zealand to Japan each year, so a pretty niche amount). When you consider the fact that Tesco sold three times the amount of cashmere in 2006 as in 2005, and that this continues to grow, you have to wonder where it's all coming from. China now produces 12,000 tonnes, accounting for three quarters of the entire planet's output, most of it brought over the border from neighbouring Mongolia.

THE DESERT THAT PICKED UP THE PRICE TAG

You have to ask questions, as ever, about the true cost of the merciless exploitation of a single fibre. In cashmere's case this point was lost on me until I read a piece by the multi-award-winning journalist Evan Osnos, Beijing Bureau Chief for the *Chicago Tribune* newspaper. 'That

£22 + £14

Supermarket Cashmere Twinset.
100% cashmere.
I appear to be an economic miracle, and the
ultimate sign that luxury is for all.

How am I so seductively soft and cheap?!

Thank China for the fact that you are able to casually toss the diamond fibre into your trolley along with frozen peas and multi-buy chicken breasts. There are now 2,000 cashmere companies in China, that together control 93% of the global cashmere clip. The pressure is on; specifically it's on the fragile ecosystem of the Alashan plains of Mongolia to support an ever-increasing goat herd so we can get this fibre fast and cheap. Not that all of my provenance is quite so exotic. Please don't look at me under a microscope. Yes, my label says 100% cashmere, but tests show that I am technically just 88.3% cashmere. All those pressures and an increased herd and production cycle mean things are getting rough out there. Once the diamond fibre was the silkiest thing imaginable, at just 18.5 microns (a human hair is 60 microns). Today, it's edging towards 26 microns. Besides, 3.2% of my fibre is plain old wool, 6.5% is frankly unidentified and 0.7% is rabbit fur – apologies if you're squeamish about animal fur. There's a cost to democratisation, you know.

Truth Labels™

Low-Priced Cashmere Sweater has a Hidden Cost, stated the headline unequivocally. From time to time you read something that makes a real impact. This was one of those occasions. Osnos's piece convinced me more than ever that we must look urgently at fashion trends that single out and promote a natural resource to an avaricious global public. The connection between the cashmere knitwear boom and the fate of a westerly corner of the Gobi Desert, the Alashan Plateau, was one that very few people had made until Osnos patiently pieced together the source of cashmere and the multifarious ecological and social effects of this knitwear revolution. For the millions of us worldwide who have let cheap cashmere into our wardrobes, this represents an environmental blunder, one linked to ecological destruction 5,000 miles away, and atmospheric pollution that kills around 33,000 people a year. The good fortune of the value and fast fashion retailers in exploiting the cheap cashmere boom is directly connected to the fate of herdsmen in Inner Mongolia.

These indigenous, still partially nomadic herders – directly descended from Genghis Khan's armies – had been given their own animals in 1990, when Mongolia was granted autonomy from China and collective farms, imposed by communism, were abolished. The number of Gobi goats being produced for cashmere soared from 2.4 million to nearly twenty-six million by 2004. Without this rise, the cheap cashmere phenomenon would never have occurred.

Owing to the demand for cashmere, the breeding of goats has grown faster than that of other livestock in the past ten years. Add the fact that it takes a goat four years to produce enough cashmere to make a sweater to our desire for ever-increasing amounts of the stuff, and there is an immediate problem. If there is a way of getting a goat to produce cashmere more quickly, or to double the amount it grows, you can be sure it's being worked on as we speak. So desperate is the industry to provide for its hungry, bargain-responsive consumers, in fact, that Scottish goat semen has already been exported to Kazakhstan in an attempt to boost the quality of the fledgling herds there. We await the results with interest.

Among climate-change concerns such as droughts in Australia, forest fires in California and worries over peak oil, the Plains of Alashan, or the Alashan Plateau, occupying a south-western corner of the Gobi Desert, tend to miss out on air time. This region is remote, and is notable primarily as a missile-testing zone for the Chinese military, which doesn't bode well.

The Alashan features some of the world's largest sand dunes: mega-dunes made of coarse, uniform grains of sand. These allow spaces to be created between them, capable of trapping drops of water, which enables plants to grow. As their roots stabilise the sand, each plant helps to fix the dune, while new dunes roll over the top of it. The new dunes are held in place by the plants underneath, and the vegetation settles on the new top layer. The writer Donovan Webster, who travelled to the Alashan in 2002 for a piece in *National Geographic*, described the megadunes as 'like a bed thick with quilts of Velcro'. It's a clever description, and a clever (but very fragile) ecosystem. Take away one of the elements and the whole thing is in danger of crashing down – or rather, being whipped up by the wind into an almighty sandstorm causing extreme atmospheric pollution.

So while parts of the fashion industry were gleefully rubbing their hands at the prospect of increased access to cheap cashmere, environmentalists were beginning to spot a potential catastrophe. By 2002 scientific estimates suggested that some 950 square miles of the Gobi region alone were turning to desert every year (a 58 per cent increase since the 1950s). According to eyewitness accounts given to Osnos, so many cashmere plants and related industries have opened in the region that water rationing has become the norm in factories.

Apologies for lowering the tone, but the phrase 'camel toe' has long stood for something specific in style terms (if you're not with me, it is the effect produced by a woman wearing trousers so tight that they leave little to the imagination). But on the Alashan Plateau camels' toes help to keep the delicate geological structure of the area intact, allowing the population to minimise their impact on the sands, so that the dunes maintain their structure against all the geophysical odds. The Alashan terrain is perfect for the camel, with its wide, soft hoof. The dunes accommodate only the bare minimum of vegetation, but this more than sufficient for the camels, and their big, soft hooves keep the ground together. Contrast this with the twenty-six million goats now estimated to be ranging across Inner Mongolia (including the Alashan Plains), their small hooves chopping up the ground, coupled with their propensity to eat everything in their sight, and you can begin to understand why cheap cashmere is causing desertification on an unprecedented scale.

Without grass and shrubs to hold the dunes in place, the deserts in Alashan are expanding by nearly four hundred square miles a year. One effect of this is a plume of pollution, made up of the dust that is swept up by the harsh winds that blow across the desert. As this crosses China it is believed to encase the ultra-fine particles thrown out by China's coal-fired power stations and other industries, creating a toxic brew of pollution that is transported along the Trans-Pacific stream, an airborne highway of dust and pollutants. The direct effect of this is increasingly felt in western states of the USA, where, as quoted by Osnos, in 2001 Asian dust accounted for 40 per cent of the worst dust days. This has an impact on American cities struggling to meet strict federal air standards. Pollution, let's remember, has little respect for boundaries. You could extrapolate from this, that in some ways this increased pollution is the result of the means of production of at least 10.5 million sweaters (the amount exported to the US in 2005) coming home to roost.

Dust, desertification, pollution: it doesn't sound good. But might it be a fair price to pay if it means enriching a poor and traditionally rather downtrodden population? It's not an ethical equation we even have to try to balance, because, unsurprisingly, that isn't what has happened. Instead, what is happening on the Alashan Plains constitutes an example of fashion slowly killing its golden goose.

Since the end of communism in Mongolia in the 1990s, wealth and prosperity have begun to be determined among the community solely by 'hoof count'. As social agronomist Jennifer L. Butz told *Newsday*: 'And as a result ... there has been a huge increase in the population of animals. You have desertification. You have a decline in the quality of cashmere.'

We have already seen the effects of the former, but why should we really care about the latter, beyond a rueful regret that our bedsocks may get a little less luxurious in feel? Well, actually, this is key. There are international standards for cashmere fibres (a cynic might say that there seem to be international standards for everything to do with fashion except labour conditions). These specify that they must average 18.5 microns in diameter (a human hair, with an average diameter of sixty microns, looks comparatively rope-like). Recent analysis has showed a coarsening of cashmere. This is thanks to two trends: cross-breeding – a number of farms have begun to breed Mongolian goats with Russian goats in an effort to maintain cashmere yields, although this obviously affects the quality of the wool – and the goats' increasingly poor diet, another effect of desertification.

Experts suggest that this coarsening will be irreversible. In the greater scheme of things, this may not seem terribly significant ('Help! My cashmere isn't as silky as it used to be!' is among the more indulgent complaints of contemporary life), but it matters, because it represents a very odd precedent. Here we have a luxury market reliant on a fibre retaining its silky, alluring attributes, yet market pressure is changing the very nature of that fibre. 'Disaster is going to occur,' predicts Ralph van Gelder, an Australian livestock expert and contributor to the World Bank's rather splendidly named report 'From Goats to Coats'. 'You simply have a disastrous circle. You have an ecological, environmental, technical, economic disastrous circle.'

Mongolian identity is tied up with the grasslands, and the goats of Alashan are being herded in increasingly difficult conditions. When the indigenous cashmere trade goes, then so does Mongolia, according to local folklore. The struggle to keep the cashmere industry alive, pure and the source of a luxury product is inextricably entwined with Mongolia's future as an independent nation. The diamond fibre should – if it had been sustainably managed – have ensured Mongolia's future prosperity and the continuation of its indigenous industry. Instead, China holds all the cards. According to Mr Wang Linxiang, president of Erdos: 'We are providing these countries [i.e. the USA, Turkey, Mexico and others whose textiles associations had the audacity to speak out against China's increasing dominance of the cashmere industry] with the raw materials. Without raw cashmere, they wouldn't have these jobs in the first place. There is really no reason to place more restrictions on us. If they continue to impose restrictions, I'll stop selling to them!' This suggests a contravention of that 'warm the world' mission. At the time of writing, talk of cashmere wars appears to have abated.

SUSTAINABLE LUXURY

Does this mean we should completely surrender any aspiration to own cashmere? Not necessarily. I decided to spend some of my clothing budget last year on some quality cashmere rather than on what I perceive to be any old rubbish. So I acquired three pieces of 'sustainable' cashmere from the American company Stewart + Brown, which has in effect launched its own cashmere-production process. The label works with selected farmers in Mongolia, guaranteeing a fair price for cashmere from a limited number of goats, processed through an ethical chain. This does not, however, come cheap. Real, sustainable cashmere should not – and therein lies the rub. The real deal will set you back at least £200 for a cardigan, and you might find that prohibitive. It's a sad fact of life that it is not a human right to own a cashmere sweater for every day of the week. Instead you might see a cashmere garment as a long-term investment, a piece that you can wash with a lot of care and pack away during the summer months (waging perpetual war against moths), and that you will darn for a decade or more. That's the stance I've taken.

I bought a long cardigan in a loose crochet-style knit with a belt, a dark purple jumper, and an extraordinarily beautiful cardigan in a grey filigree knit with ruffles around the base. It sounds like hyperbole to say they made a miserable winter bearable, but they really did. They provided everything you'd hope for from a diamond fibre: extreme warmth and softness. And – which is something that's been lacking in my wardrobe for a good while – they are clothes that I look forward to wearing as much in the eighteenth month of ownership as I did in the first. In fact, I look for (and invent) opportunities to wear them day after day. When my dog chewed the lapel of one of the cardigans I was distraught until I realised that Stewart + Brown would mend it for me: cashmere holes can nearly always be repaired by weavers. When summer came I felt a little sad to be packing them away, sealed in a cotton bag with some (organic) moth repellant. They are genuinely pieces I want to grow old with, and because they cost over £200 each I will need to keep them in circulation for as much time as possible. It's a bit like installing photovoltaic solar panels on your roof: there's a considerable payback period. Is it worth it? I think so. This is real luxury, and it feels different.

A good cashmere piece will last for twenty to forty years. Scottish cashmere producers have been remanufacturing old cashmere for years. As one cashmere cutter observes, 'It's not unusual at all for someone to send a fifteen-to-twenty-year sweater back to be re-shaped. The yarn essentially holds its shape as long as it's been washed properly, so there's no reason why it can't be repaired or tweaked if the shape's a bit out of fashion.'

This longevity is key. Whatever the wrangling over proportion of cashmere hair, quotas and quality, the core fact is that a limited natural resource cannot be treated by the fashion industry as though it were infinite. Once fast fashion starts dictating overproduction, the fate of a unique and ancient habitat is sealed, and the prognosis may be terrible. As a conscious fashion consumer you can rise above the ubiquity of one material. Besides, who wants to be stuck with one fibre? Spread the love.

THE RISE AND RISE OF MERINO

While the mainstream cashmere industry was 'democratising' its wares, throwing off the luxury coat that had been generations in the making, another industry was busy promoting itself as the fine fibre of choice. This time it wasn't anything as exotic as down combed from the stomachs of goats, but simply wool from sheep. Not bog-standard old wool, you understand, the kind that many consumers associate with itchy school uniforms, but Merino, increasingly pitched as an upscale natural material. According to the rhetoric, Merino is no ordinary fibre. It is silky, soft and eminently sustainable. 'Merino wool: science, art and evolution' says publicity material for Australian Wool Innovation (an organisation funded by growers – as wool producers are called – and dedicated to the marketing of Merino wool) self-importantly. I've certainly succumbed to its appeal. In my wardrobe I have at least ten Merino sweaters. It's easy to become fond of. Fine and superfine Merino herds produce wool that is perfect for today's fashion. A superfine Merino will be about eighteen to twenty-four microns in diameter, so it can compete on that front with cashmere, and it is relatively abundant. To say that wool is important to Australia is something of an understatement: only China has a larger sheep population, and it produces less wool. The Australian flock numbers an almost inconceivable 107 million sheep, and its pastures take up a quarter of Australia's land mass. In 2006–07 it produced 425 million kilos of unprocessed wool, and 88 per cent of it is made up of Merino sheep. New Zealand, another huge wool producer, has also gone for Merino sheep in a big way.

What's more, both the Australian and the New Zealand wool boards and bodies consistently tell me that you'd have to go a long way to find a fibre that is quite as green as Merino. Because not only is it hydrophobic (water-repellent), so it doesn't need to be finished with waterproofing chemicals, but it's 'natural', 'biodegradable' and 'sustainable'. Some research even suggests that, managed properly, sheep herds on grassland can provide much-needed nutrients to the soil, allowing it to function as a carbon sink (i.e. soaking up carbon dioxide and locking it away, as opposed to releasing it into the atmosphere, where as a greenhouse gas it helps to accelerate global warming), and therefore an environmental asset. Perhaps we could knit our way to green utopia. Meanwhile, notes the Australian Wool Foundation combatively, 'No man-made fibre can come close to replicating Merino's naturally occurring combination of attributes.' Although it's always wise to be wary of the term 'natural' applied as a blanket term, the industry has a point. Wool could be judged to have the environmental upper hand over synthetics, starting from the fact that it is not derived from oil, and is therefore renewable. It is 'biodegradable', meaning that despite its durability it will return to the soil (I should stress that this probably won't happen if jumpers get slung in the bin, as landfill is technically oxygen-free, and therefore materials tend to have a hard time biodegrading), unlike synthetics, which probably take hundreds of years to decompose. And according to the industry, few synthetic chemicals are used in Merino production in Australia, where 99 per cent of sheep live outside on 'extensive grassland terrain', which on average works out at two acres per sheep. Clean, green and free-ranging, what's not to like? These days, however, wool represents less than 2 per cent of all fibre consumed (compare and contrast with the stranglehold of synthetics).

But while I think wool has a lot of sustainable merits, I'm sceptical about whether we can change the world just by consuming woolly socks at double speed. Wool is hardly without footprint, even Merino. In 2009 less than 0.1 per cent of the 1.1 million tonnes of the global wool clip was classified as organic. At its most basic, 'organic' means that synthetic pesticides are not used on pastureland or to treat sheep for parasites. The latter is particularly significant, given that the top three insecticides used on sheep in 2005 were all classified as 'slightly to acutely' toxic to humans, 'moderately to highly' toxic to aquatic life, and 'suspect endocrine disruptors'. Studies of UK farms have linked pesticides used in sheepdip to damage to the nervous systems of those workers charged with doing the dipping. There is huge potential for pollution from the many processes involved in transforming grease wool into the lovely fibre you and I would recognise, and similar opportunity for gigantic energy and water usage too.

Then there are the greenhouse gas (GHG) emissions that contribute to global warming. Certain livestock produce a lot of methane through the workings of the rumen (stomach), which is why you see a lot of indelicate cow-farts-cause-global-warming-type headlines. I have it on good authority that livestock belching is a greater problem than farting, but either way, the huge Merino herds contribute to livestock emissions. Even the Australian Wool Foundation concedes, 'Biogenic methane remains a major issue.' According to an Australian academic study, the life-cycle GHG emissions of one kilogram of wool are significantly higher than those of wheat and sheep meat. In other words, wool is more environmentally expensive to produce than either wheat or sheep meat. The study also factored in emissions from fertilisers, pesticides and sheep shearing, not just the enteric methane emissions mentioned above. But the big players are working hard to improve and prove their green credentials. In fact, I'd go so far as to say that they see an opportunity to reduce livestock emissions while still producing huge amounts of wool. So we might, for example, expect wool growers of the future to select a breed of sheep by how little methane it produces, as well as by the quality of fibre and how desirable it is to consumers. The industry seems to promise us that in the not-too-distant future our love of superfine, silky fibre will be entirely consistent with saving the planet.

We will be able to stock our wardrobes with little knits and fine wool pencil skirts with total impunity ...

On balance, I think wool is a good thing, and I plan to include more of it in my wardrobe – but only when I can confirm its sustainable back story. In the meantime, it's worth sounding a note of caution about the planet's ability to sustain massive herds. The story of cashmere and the Alashan Plateau could easily have been about the disappeared *estancias*, the huge sheep farms that once spread across a 1,500-mile stretch of Patagonia. You'll notice the heavy use of the past tense, because the *estancias* that sprung up throughout the 1980s have now all but disappeared. This is not because humankind collectively came to its senses and realised that keeping thousands of sheep in this fragile ecosystem was foolish, but because desertification caused by overgrazing made it impossible to carry on. By 2004, near the town of Perito Moreno in Santa Cruz province, once the heartland of Patagonia's sheep industry, just 3,000 sheep remained from a flock that once numbered 12,000. In recent years there has been a drop in global wool production, led by Australia, whose southern and eastern regions have experienced severe drought. Without water, huge levels of wool production just cannot be supported. Shouldn't this be viewed as an early warning?

HOME-GROWN WOOL: FROM THE DOLDRUMS TO RENAISSANCE

Rather than buying wool from the other side of the world and con- tributing (albeit unwittingly) to environmental stresses there, there is a small group of designers and consumers who ask why we can't produce our own wool, closer to home. This prompts a second question: what on earth happened to our wool industry? You can't fail to have noticed that wool is inextricably entwined with Britain's pastoral and industrial heritage. It might seem a little over the top to use the Woolsack, the seat stuffed full of English wool on which the Speaker has sat in the House of Lords since the fourteenth century, as an example, but it is emblematic of the economic esteem in which wool was once held. And you needn't go back several hundred years to find wool playing an important role.

Until fairly recently Britain had a worsted industry – worsted produces yarn suitable for suiting – that rivalled Italy's. But by 2000, according to an understandably downbeat government business report: 'Italy's exports of woollen and worsted fabrics and men's suits were respectively fifteen and twelve times those of the United Kingdom.'

Of course we still produce wool, just not a great deal of it. In 2009 British Wool sold 29,000 tonnes (it was almost double that in the 1990s), a tiny seventy-fifth of the world's wool clip, despite the fact that on average 16.5 million sheep and lambs are slaughtered in Britain every year. The national clip is sold to the Wool Marketing Board, an entity that has existed since the 1950s, and that acts as a type of middleman. In fact all British wool *must* be sold (by law) to the WMB, which grades it and sells it at auction in Bradford. By popular admission, the industry is on its knees. The price of a fleece has plummeted to such an extent – by 2009 it had bottomed out at just 66p per kilogram (down from 93p in 1997) – that the remaining sheep farmers often face desperate choices. The cost of shearing reached £1.20 per sheep, and farmers were unable to make up the shortfall. Either there was nobody to buy the fleeces, or prices were so low that it simply wasn't worth the farmers' while to transport them. Many resorted to burning them. Globally, farmers complain of miserable wool cheques. In 2010 wool prices in New Zealand, for example, were at their lowest level for fifty years. Back in the UK some farmers are resorting to producing hairless sheep for meat, and forgetting wool altogether.

It's the sort of situation that makes you wonder, 'How did it come to this?' Hopefully, it won't. In early 2010 the industry showed signs that it was ready to claw its way back into our fashion lives in a meaningful way. Prince Charles launched the Wool Campaign with Nicholas Coleridge, chairman of Condé Nast, and there was talk of a new 'green' label for wool, of pushing wool back onto the fashion agenda, getting prices up to a sustainable level. There was a dedicated Wool Week just before September's Fashion Week: Savile Row was grassed over and flocks safely grazed so the press and the British consumer could get to see the magnificent beasts up close.

It's not only the number of sheep that is plummeting, but also the varieties. Native breeds, instead of being seen as a huge resource, seem to be viewed as an irrelevance. Whereas once each region had its own type of sheep, with characteristics developed to withstand particular conditions – such as an extra hardy coat for upland pastures – increasingly, and understandably, farmers now want to farm meaty sheep that will fetch the best price at slaughter. In 2001 the foot and mouth crisis and the ensuing compulsory slaughter threatened to destroy the UK's diversity of sheep breeds. That it survived has everything to do with the Sheep Trust, which developed a genetic sheep bank. But we are not out of the woods. Over a billion sheep are produced worldwide every year, but from a rapidly depleting gene pool. According to the Breeds at Risk Register's watchlist for 2010, three hundred breeds of sheep are classified as 'critically endangered' (i.e. have a breeding population of fewer than 2,000), five hundred are 'endangered', and nine hundred 'vulnerable'.

Why should a *fashionista* care about breeds of sheep? It is more than a shame that we're losing variety – not just because they look pretty in fields, but because a decrease in breed varieties means a decrease in ecological resilience. The UN Food and Agriculture Organisation estimates that somewhere in the world at least one breed of traditional livestock dies out every single week. A species that has taken thousands of years to evolve can be gone in as little as fifty years. And once it is gone, it is gone forever. As the Indian environmental campaigner and economist Vandana Shiva puts it, 'Not until diversity is made the logic of production will there be a chance for sustainability, justice and peace. Cultivating and conserving diversity is no luxury in our times: it is a survival imperative. Uniformity is not nature's way; diversity is nature's way.' That goes for sheep too.

A niche but exciting group of fashion designers and innovators gets this message. They might not be able to take on the might of the Erdos 24/7 knitting operations, but they are leading an unlikely fightback against the demise of British wool in fashion by celebrating, and work-ing with, the qualities of the fibre from rare-breed herds. The brand Izzy Lane was founded by Isobel Davies, who was motivated by her vegetarian principles and by what she saw as the inhumane treatment of sheep in the wool industry. This was allied to her barely concealed fury that the British Isles was abandoning its wool-production heritage. Unconcerned by the reputation for eccentricity that she was bound to attract, she began 'rescuing' rare-breed sheep from auctions, particularly Wensleydales (the distinctive dreadlocked sheep of which only 1,800 breeding ewes remain) and Shetlands (just 3,000 exist across the world). Having built up a flock of abandoned rare-breed sheep – she now has in the region of six hundred – she has also established a really credible fashion line. What's even more striking about the Izzy Lane brand is that its yarn is processed in the UK by the last fifty-one remaining worsted spinners, the last wool dyehouse in the Bradford region, and an ancient mill in Selkirk. Gloriously, when you look through the Izzy Lane catalogue (online at www.izzylane.com) you browse by sheep and fibre type – Wensleydale Shetland, or cashmere from a tiny Scottish herd. I can't think of any other fashion experience where the look book is arranged according to breed.

As resurgences go it's tiny, but I still think it's significant. Izzy Lane has also teamed up with the model and actress Lily Cole (and with Katherine Poulton and Alice Ashby) to form the label North Circular. This brand is whimsical – deliberately so. Given that its orders are knitted by a team of grannies, it could be considered the ultimate antidote to fast fashion (although I'm assured that those expert grannies knit pretty fast). North Circular products have more mainstream appeal than you might think: they were being sold in high-street store Jigsaw for Christmas 2010 – although neither the sheep nor the grannies are going to be able to make products in the hundreds of thousands. A potential deal for Izzy Lane to go mainstream, providing Tesco with a sort of diffusion range, was effectively kiboshed by the Wool Marketing Board, which refused to attach an animal-welfare standard to the product. Its reasoning was that to single out one brand as using wool from a flock with superior animal-welfare management would be unfair to other farmers. You could read this another way: that it was unfair for consumers not to have the opportunity to buy a mainstream woolly sweater that came from an extraordinarily clean and ethical supply chain.

Meanwhile, Tom Podkolinski of the Cornish surfwear brand Finisterre ends his talks to the fashion industry with a slide of a sheep. 'Isn't that a good-looking sheep?' he asks his audience, either bringing the house down or raising eyebrows. It is indeed a handsome sheep. It is also the basis of a whole new fibre supply chain that Podkolinski has invested time and research effort in developing for his brand. When he was told that indigenous British wool wasn't fine enough for the base layers, beanies and socks produced by Finisterre for surfers and wannabe surfers, he refused to believe it, and set off to track down his own golden fleece. The journey may not have been quite as epic as that makes it sounds, but it was certainly a hard slog, and Podkolinski took a good few months to sift through the rubble of the UK wool industry to find a lead. Finally he came across some papers from the Macaulay Land Use Research Institute in Aberdeen, detailing an experiment to cross the Shetland, Britain's finest-woolled breed, with the Saxon Merino, the finest-woolled breed in the world, to create the Bowmont.

At first glance the bespectacled and white-haired Lesley Prior might seem an unlikely ally to a maverick outdoor-apparel brand, but the sheep expert from the rolling hills of Exmoor became the final piece in Finisterre's fibre jigsaw. Podkolinski tracked the remaining Bowmonts to Lesley Prior's farm. There were just thirty left. In the whole world. 'Since the closure of the Macaulay Institute research farm and the slaughter of all their remaining Bowmonts,' she says, 'I have the only provably pure, quality-tested Bowmont flock in the country. Each sheep has a pedigree longer than mine, and can be traced back to the original Shetland/Merino cross.' Over the last three years she has worked with Finisterre to build up the flock from thirty to eighty. By the time you read this, the first products made from British Bowmont should, with any luck, be on the market. True, this represents an infinitesimally small part of the fashion market: eighty sheep are hardly going to be able to compete with antipodean Merino herds of 40,000. But what I love about it is that it's an example of proactive design, where the designer has spent time and energy investigating the supply chain until he found the sustainable solution he was looking for. Compare this to the fashion brands that just fax orders from head office with the number they would like delivered and the date. As a consumer, the Finisterre approach is the one I'm looking for. Even if there are fewer products, I have to wait, and this sustainable wool is blended with another fibre (to make it go further), I want to buy into the whole story and invest in the sheep, not just the jumper.

9

ANIMAL PRINTS

*How Mock-Croc, Faux Fur and Plastic Python got
Trumped by the Real Deal*

Unravel any part of the wool story and it soon becomes apparent that
there is another giant elephant in the room, or in this case the closet:
animal welfare. While most sheep free-range in their huge flocks, another
way of producing ultrafine, deluxe fibre is to keep them in sheds. It is an
extraordinary thing to see footage of thousands of sheep penned into
sheds wearing strange canvas coats in order not to damage the wool.
This produces sharlea, from Saxon Merino sheep which are kept indoors
(although the term sharlea technically refers to the wool rather than
the breed, sheep that produce it are often referred to as sharlea sheep).
And according to campaigners the way they are treated is beyond the
pale. While the animal appears expendable, the fibre is definitely not.
Ultrafine has become an increasingly lucrative part of the wool trade:
according to the RSPCA, ultrafine from sharlea sheep now accounts
for 12 per cent of the Australian wool market. The conditions in which
'battery sheep', as sharlea have become known, are kept are considered
indefensible by many. Naturally, producers resent the implication of
animal cruelty, and deny it completely, claiming that shedded sheep
are treated humanely. Yet again, it is difficult for consumers who might
have an issue with this practice to divine how the fibre they are wearing
has been produced. With the exception of traceability schemes such as
New Zealand's Baacode – get it? – how would you know that the fine

fibre in your suit or jacket was not produced from shedded sheep?

There is a wider question about tolerance. In her 2009 report *Died in the Wool*. Fiona Galbraith of the group Vegetarians International Voice for Animals (more commonly known by its acronym, Viva!) lists a number of animal welfare issues connected with wool production. They include lambs dying of hypothermia or being moved from their mothers too early, and sheep suffering lameness, disease and other horrors such as 'infectious abortions', starvation, premature slaughter, castration and cruel shearing practices. Her solution is as unequivocal as it could be:

Boycott Wool

When purchasing wool, you are supporting the cruel practices of sheep husbandry … A common misconception is that sheep are sheared to improve their welfare. Years of selective breeding have guaranteed that sheep can no longer moult enough fleece for the summer months. This does not mean sheep are sheared with their welfare in mind; they are sheared for the promise of financial return. Once they are unable to provide high quality (and high profit) wool, they will be slaughtered and have their skins removed and processed for wool production. Some people mistakenly believe that wool comes from happy sheep; in fact there is a good chance that the wool you purchase has been stripped from a dead sheep.

Frankly, this ideological position is too extreme for me, and will be for many consumers. For example, while Galbraith worries that 'sheep live their entire lives under human control', I'm not sure I do. All farming requires a degree of human control, and most people do not take the position that this makes farming untenable. However, I do accept that there are humane and inhumane farming practices. This too comes down to a question of tolerance. A practice that a farmer considers necessary might seem barbaric to a non-farming consumer.

Mulesing provides a case in point. If you're not familiar with mulesing, it is an undeniably gruesome practice. Merino sheep, being rather corpulent, with lots of folds of skin – after all, more skin means more wool – have a tendency to suffer from flystrike, which occurs when blowflies lay their eggs, which almost immediately hatch to produce maggots, in these folds of skin, particularly around the back end of the sheep. This causes a particularly horrible parasitic disease which invariably leads to an agonising death. In an effort to counteract this, wool growers in affected regions adopt a seemingly rather rudimentary response, literally chopping part of the backside from the sheep, a technique 'invented' by a sheep farmer called John Mules some eighty years ago. This 'surgical mulesing' is typically performed without any anaesthetic or follow-up care. Campaigners and other appalled bystanders talk of witnessing thousands of sheep staggering through long grass with freshly mutilated rear ends.

So it came as some surprise when I was chatting to a stalwart of the eco and sustainable fashion movement who observed that 'Mulesing is an ethical neurosis,' the implication being that there were far bigger issues to be concerned with in the battle to create a more sustainable fashion industry. But 'surgical mulesing' has captured the attention of global campaign groups, notably PETA (People for the Ethical Treatment of Animals). In turn, activists have galvanised consumers, who have put pressure on UK retailers. While I haven't exactly seen mass demonstrations about mulesing on Saturday afternoons in the West End, the campaign had enough traction to worry the wool industry. In 2004 Australian wool-growers launched a legal campaign to attempt to stop PETA from 'threatening global retailers' over the use of mulesing. In 2007 there was an uneasy truce: PETA came to an agreement with Australia Wool Innovation that it would stop pushing retailers in this way until 31 December 2010, the point by which the Australian industry had agreed to stop all mulesing.

Many large retailers were already speaking out. In 2009 the British Retail Consortium announced: 'Following consultation with the RSPCA (UK), BRC members will, until the end of 2010, seek wool from suppliers who provide flocks with pain relief when mulesing. After this date, they will seek to use suppliers who don't use mulesing – even if pain relief is provided.' M&S made non-mulesed wool a cornerstone of their knitwear operation, and pushed commitment to the 2010 date. Nike, Gap, Liz Claiborne and H&M all 'voiced concern'. Next began sourcing away from Australia to countries where mulesing wasn't so prolific: New Zealand, also a massive player in the wool industry, which produced some 154,000 tonnes of wool in 2008–09, for example, claims to have completely phased out mulesing, which is why its Merino wool is often described as 'ethical' or 'clean'. Attempts at appeasing retailers through supposedly more humane methods such as attaching clips to the sheep's rear end until the skin fell away didn't always wash: Hugo Boss dismissively called this supposed innovation 'clipped mulesing', and promptly added it to the list of things that were deemed unacceptable for the brand.

But by the summer of 2009 it seemed that the Australian industry was backing away from the 31 December 2010 deadline. As I write, that date is only weeks away, and I would stake everything I own on the fact that it ain't gonna happen. But then, the counter argument to the anti-mulesing campaign runs like this: according to the AWI, research shows that mulesing reduces the risk of flystrike to 1 to 3 per cent; without mulesing, it runs at between 40 and 100 per cent. A hobby farmer in Britain, who would ostensibly seem to have little in common with a wool grower with 40,000 sheep in Australia, tells me that she now agrees with mulesing: 'Having seen a couple of my own flock die an agonising death through flystrike in the UK I believe that it is a necessary evil.' For the record, the Australian wool industry might have missed the deadline, but it points out great progress to the press: 'In 2009, 54 per cent of lambs were unmulesed, a significant leap from 5 per cent in 2005.'

FROM CALLOUS TO NEUROTIC

Wherever you decide to buy your next jumper from, there is a truth that should not be ignored: our wardrobes owe a great deal to the animal kingdom. The global apparel, accessories and luxury goods market, which raked in $1,334.1 billion in 2008, is extraordinarily successful in many ways. But we cannot ignore the fact that, as we have seen, it achieves this stellar success thanks to millions of garment workers, millions of crop pickers, dyers, ginners and weavers, millions of hectares of land and millions of litres of water. And millions of animals.

Becoming aware of the animal fibres and products included in your wardrobe is useful before you draw a line as to which species you consider expendable or worthy of exploitation, and which you do not. It's perhaps here that tolerances are most polarised, and sometimes unexpectedly so. I'm no longer surprised when I get letters from vegetarians wondering whether I can sanction their wearing fur when the temperature plummets. On the other hand, I also get emails from the terminally sensitive berating me for failing to acknowledge the death of silkworms.

I'm serious about the worm sensitivity. Silkworms are fed on mulberry leaves, and form a cocoon that is woven into the finished fibre. So far so good. But what vegans and others with an intolerance of any animal exploitation have a hard time stomaching is that during the production process the silkworms are either baked or drowned, in order to prevent the long silk threads of their cocoons from breaking. In this genocide of invertebrates, fifteen silkworms are killed to produce one gram of silk, which means 1,500 are expended for every metre of material.

There is, however, Peace silk, produced by a technique developed in India under the Ahimsa label, whereby the silk is only extracted after the silkworm has emerged unscathed from the cocoon. There are actually some very important attributes to Peace silk: it is often organic, and there is an emphasis on fair trade – production is returned to the historical producers, weaving on hand looms, and those producers are given not just a part in the narrative again, but also a proper share of the money. Arguably, without Peace silk (give or take worm protection) we'd be hard pressed to preserve even the fragments of an ailing indigenous silk trade in India, Bangladesh and Cambodia.

So, all in all, I find Peace silk a good thing. But the well-being of the worms is to me the least of its attractions. On the whole, 'violence' against 'innocent' worms (I borrow the phraseology of the of Peace silk website) is not an affront to me.

CROCODILE TEARS

But while the fate of silkworms leaves me relatively cold, I do find myself exercised about the exploitation of some other species, not just because of animal cruelty issues, but also on conservation grounds. In recent years fashion has made a strange return to materials that last saw their heyday in the 1930s, before pesky innovations such as the Convention on International Trade in Endangered Species (CITES), which came into force in 1973, attempted to set some controls to prevent wild stocks of fauna and flora from being wiped out. At-risk species were formally divided by CITES into appendices denoting levels of endangerment: Appendix I and II classification indicated that a species was threatened with extinction, and acted as a sort of 'hands off' warning to industries that had previously just bagged (literally) an exotic snake and sold its skin to Paris. Appendix III meant that the species was protected in at least one country, and also aimed to control its use in trade.

Take crocodiles. As a generic species, crocodilians can trace their lineage back two hundred million years, as an offshoot of the 'ruling lizards' of the Triassic period. To put it reductively, they are the closest thing we have to a dinosaur: an extraordinary creature that seems entirely out of sync with the contemporary world. But despite their elevated position near the top of the food chain, they are ecologically sensitive, and have been rendered vulnerable by habitat destruction and climatic alterations. Yet they have prevailed. In fact, there's only one thing that has truly brought the crocodilian near to extinction, over two hundred million years. Yes, you guessed it – it's the fashion industry.

This is, however, a historical charge to be levelled at the industry rather than a contemporary one. At least fifteen species of crocodilian have been commercially traded for their skins since the turn of the twentieth century. By the 1920s crocodile had become the byword for luxury. By the 1930s crocodile products were being mass produced, and between 1954 and 1970, two to three million skins were sold each year.

But by 1984 this had been reduced to less than one million. Why? It wasn't because we all fell out of love with crocodile, but because for years the industry had been dependent on 'wild caught' crocodiles, and the hunters were suddenly finding it very difficult to find any crocodiles to catch and kill (or 'harvest', as it is politely termed). In desperation, conservation laws kicked in. In 1973 the wild caiman harvest was banned in Colombia – it was estimated that more than 12.5 million skins had been removed from that country over the previous forty years. In 1975 all living crocodilian species (including alligator and lookalike species) were listed under CITES as a matter of urgency, as some were thought to be on the cusp of extinction. The fashion caravan rolled off in search of other materials – ostrich became popular – and crocodile farming went into decline. But not for long.

An ordinary industry might have left it there and moved on to another raw material, perhaps working on new types of plastic (as the mass market did), or even going for boring old bovine leather. But the luxury fashion industry is a quirky beast, and it could never quite let go of crocodile. I'm going to put my cards on the table here, and say for the record that the 'continuing allure' of crocodile skin is lost on me. I find it basically repellent. But Big Luxury (as we know the conglomerates had become by the 1990s) always knew that the majority did not, that crocodile was so fused in the popular imagination with luxury that it needed to remain a core part of their design strategy. In other words, a luxury fashion brand without crocodile was a bit like a luxury car brand without a sports model.

And so the fashion industry came up with a way of producing crocodile skins that would both appease the conservationists and provide all the skins it figured it needed: crocodile ranches. The system relied on crocodile eggs found in the wild by local harvesters or hunters (so the communities who'd formerly hunted crocodiles still got a small, albeit far smaller, slice of the pie), then hatched in a hatchery, and the crocodiles being raised on a farm until they were ready to be slaughtered. According to a number of conservation surveys, crocodile populations can sustain 'moderate harvests' of eggs from the wild. Better still, this system of rearing crocodiles allowed a lot more control of the product. Rather than relying on hunters to trap enough uniformly sized and skinned beasts, the animals could be reared in a controlled environment. Any that didn't make the grade could be disposed of early. Overall, far less was left to chance, and if there's one thing that suits a multi-billion-pound luxury conglomerate answerable to its shareholders, it's control.

I have to admit that I've never been to a crocodile farm, and I'm not sure that I'd like to. When I look at pictures of them, I experience that slight shuddering sensation that hints at a full-blown phobia. I gingerly scan through the websites of the high-spec producers in Australia. Around a hundred crocodiles lie on the fake bank of a fake oasis – without them, the pool could be the centrepiece of an all-inclusive holiday resort. The very fact that these pictures are available as promotional tools means that these are the farms that encourage a degree of transparency. The Darwin Crocodile farm in Australia's Northern Territory, for example, produces 12,000 to 15,000 skins every year, selling them all to European fashion houses. It aims to produce the crocodile within three years, growing it until its belly width reaches between thirty-five and forty-five centimetres (it's this soft belly area that the upscale handbag brands are interested in). When they are first hatched the crocodiles are put in hatchling pens, where the water is maintained at around 32°C. At one year old they are moved into the yearly pen, and they are then moved to their final pen until 'harvest'. (Pens play a big role in croc farming, not least because segregation prevents fighting. Nobody wants bite marks on her Birkin.) Grading occurs throughout, and crocodiles that are failing to gain size are slaughtered prematurely. According to insiders a true luxury brand will only use the top 2 per cent of skins, and will therefore destroy or reject thousands of skins each month. After the growing comes the processing. I scroll through the website of a South African factory. Men with hairnets and white wellies hang up the bright green carcasses and then skin them to reveal the translucent flesh underneath, which will go for meat. It looks like a horror version of a pie factory. But that's my problem. Processing and skinning crocodiles is just routine business in many parts of the world.

By the 1990s hundreds of crocodile farms had been established worldwide. Uniform skins, of uniform quality, from a known source were now available to luxury conglomerates. Some brands even invested in their own farms. 'It can take three to four crocodiles to make one of our bags, so we are now breeding our own crocodiles on our own farms, mainly in Australia,' Patrick Thomas of Hermès told the Reuters Global Luxury Summit in Paris in 2009, adding, 'The world is not full of crocodiles, except the stock exchange!' which presumably passes for a hilarious joke at a luxury-goods conference. The crocodile was back in business. From the dark days of 1977 (the first year for which CITES has established figures), when an estimated 300,000 skins were supplied to the industry, by 1999 this had risen to 1,205,239 skins being legally exported for the international fashion market. Nearly 900,000 of these were 'farmed'.

Today, twenty-three species of crocodile are covered by CITES, but many have been dropped from the critical list (Appendix I) to Appendix III, meaning their trade is subject to close control, but is not forbidden. This shift acted as a green light to the fashion industry, which shifted crocodile farming up a gear. It moved from ranching (harvesting eggs or hatchlings from the wild and then rearing them in captivity) to carrying out the whole process within a farm environment, so that the finished animals were entirely 'captive-bred'. The captive breeding and farming of crocodiles appears to have provided what many consider to be a sustainable solution. As a luxury conglomerate using crocodile or alligator will tell you every time, should they be so inclined they could trace the leather in a pair of crocodile loafers or a handbag back to a particular farm and even to a particular pen, using the tag number on the crocodile. It's true that this offers a level of traceability that almost no other garment or accessory can offer, but conservation and crocodile experts such as James MacGregor are wary. He warns: 'Conservation principles are reported to be absent from retailing strategies and consumers' buying decisions. Where conservation is considered, judgements are simplistic and favour captive-reared crocodilians, without any distinction between ranched and captive-bred sources.'

So, are captive-bred crocodiles a luxurious sustainable solution? Well, no, because while crocodile farms take the pressure off wild populations in one way, they put it back on in another. Two studies into crocodile farming – one on nascent farms in 1985, and a later one in 2001 – found that countries reliant on captive (or farmed) breeding of crocodiles for export also had poorly monitored, depleted wild crocodile populations. It seems that once a lot of animals are produced in captivity, the wild population can become even more vulnerable. After all, local landowners and farmers are less likely to put up with dangerous wild crocodile populations if they've lost all their commercial value.

Meanwhile, there are concerns over the farms, including their energy and water use, the pollution they produce and their treatment of the crocodiles. In Cambodia, crocodile farmers have switched from feeding their charges fish (too expensive) to water snakes. We're not talking about the harvesting of just a few water snakes, but at least four million a year, the heaviest exploitation of any snake community in the world.

That is the type of quantity that sends an ecosystem into meltdown as the natural balance is irrevocably upturned.

Some environmental economists are even calling for the reintroduction of hunting crocodiles and curbs on farming. 'The crocodilian skin industry, or any industry founded on wild resources, is unwise to turn its back on the wild supply,' warns James MacGregor, who believes that wild harvesting helps to incentivise conservation among local populations. Indeed, what incentive is there for local people when only crocodile farms owned or financed by remote conglomerates are making money? The sustainable solution requires a return to 'moderate harvests' and the restraint that ecological experts have talked about. Will the luxury industry do the right thing? As always, there's another path. Big farms are being set up in some of the poorest countries in the world. In the village of Bhaluka, north of Dhaka in Bangladesh, Mushtaq Ahmed's crocodilian dream is unfolding. His enterprise, Reptiles Farm Ltd, is the first in the country to commercially farm saltwater crocodiles in an impoverished region with eyes firmly on the luxury-goods market. There are two ways of looking at this: to congratulate the young man on his entrepreneurial spirit, or to question whether an impoverished landscape like this has any business producing animals for the luxury market when there is not enough land to grow crops for its own burgeoning population.

There are no plans to stop using crocodilian leather in accessories any time soon. In fact the big luxury houses have plans to scale up production. Capacity is increasing as the emerging markets in China and India are taught (not least through huge marketing campaigns) to value not only the intense craftsmanship of top-end luxury goods, but also the exotic skins they are made from.

The market has also been impressed by the way exotic skins appear to have weathered the recession. Is crocodile insulated from economic downturn? Heng Long, a giant Singapore processor and tannery that supplies crocodile leather to Prada, processes 280,000 skins a year, making it one of the biggest in the world. It plans to double its factory space to 10,000 square metres by 2013. Certainly Heng Long executive Kohn Choon Heong didn't seem to be losing too much sleep over the global downturn: 'The rich always spend money!' he said buoyantly, while the only moaning coming from Hermès in 2009 was that it was facing 'massive over-demand'. Meanwhile, intensive caiman production through farming in Colombia, where a brown caiman hide goes for around US$44, has led to a reprieve from the endangered list and a burgeoning trade in mass-market low-grade crocodilian products such as watch straps, belts and cowboy boots. Zimbabwe company Innscor, which produced a gigantic 64,000 reptiles in 2009 and provides crocodile skins to Hermès and Gucci, meanwhile enjoys a profitable ascent despite being based in a country where crocodiles were once classified as vermin, and where political upheaval is rife.

RETURN OF THE PYTHON

It's not all saltwater crocodiles. The top end of fashion has a whole palette of odd and in my opinion slightly gruesome pelts and skins to choose from: alligators, young bulls, adult bulls, 'baby' lambs (apparently not tautological on planet luxury) such as Astrakhan, 'the fur of newborn or foetal Persian lambs called karakul', buffalo, and various luxury 'kid' goat leathers. But along with crocodile it is snakeskin, and in particular python, that has made the most successful and unexpected comeback into the fashion lexicon. According to the WWF's 2008 'Trade in Wildlife' report, close to fifty million products made from reptiles are now traded each year. By 2007 you could hardly open a magazine without seeing python: Naomi Campbell modelled it for Dolce & Gabbana, Jennifer Lopez and Kylie Minogue stepped out clutching large, shiny python bags and – hold the front page – Sienna Miller was seen in a pair of Devi Kroell python boots. All of which qualified python as A. Major. Trend.

I was initially surprised that some within the luxury industry who did not seem overly worried about crocodile or particularly sensitised to animal rights still baulked at the idea of python. 'The way those animals are treated is categorically disgusting,' the head of one luxury house (which uses no animal skins) told me. As ever, it would be pretty hard to tell much about the process by which python goods are produced from the label. To get an idea of it, you'd have to go somewhere well off the tourist trail, such as the old part of the city of Kano in northern Nigeria, and speak to a skin tanner, such as thirty-five-year-old Ismail Dauda, who has been processing crocodile and python skins from the age of fifteen. You'd be likely to find him stirring an acrid-smelling pit full of a dark mass. This is actually an unappealing brew of potash and soda ash, and python and crocodile skins. If you can deal with the smell long enough to take a breath and ask him what it's like to 'process' 20,000 animals a year in this way, he might tell you (as he told journalist Aminu Abubakar) that the sustainability of his business is a little shaky: 'It is a fact that the volume of supplies has dropped in a decade, which is perhaps an indication the rate of killing is higher than their regeneration rate, but this is a business we can't stop because it is very lucrative,' he says candidly. But how lucrative is it? Well, Ismail receives $4 a square metre for his processed python skin, which makes it even more lucrative for the luxury conglomerates – the python bags I have seen (that were also, incidentally, plumped with Botox) range in price from £1,200 to £5,000.

Most python species are now listed in Appendix III of the CITES. This means that their trade should theoretically be 'controlled'. In other words, certification is needed to sell them to the international market, and they are only to be taken from controlled farmed environments or habitats where their numbers are sustainable, and only in specific quantities. In short, it's no longer legally acceptable to 'harvest' a whole area of pythons to sell commercially. Furthermore, one subspecies of Indian python, *Python molurus molurus*, is listed in CITES Appendix I, which means it is classified as endangered and cannot therefore legally be sold as a handbag, shoe, belt or anything else. All of this certification should engender a huge amount of confidence, and allow me happily to follow the style path set by Minogue, Longoria, Knightley and others.

It doesn't. Dig a little deeper into the snakeskin trade and you begin to wonder how effective these controls actually are. In 1977 India was supplying more than four million snake skins to the international market. The trade was so dynamic that by 1984 the Indian whip snake was becoming rare, and it was duly placed on Appendix III of the CITES register. However, this didn't seem to do much to help: while the formalised trade switched to other snakes, smugglers continued to trap and kill whip snakes. Who's to say the same isn't happening now with pythons and their subspecies? The species look very similar: even experts say it is very difficult to tell a rare snake (Appendix I) from a snake from a controlled and sustainable population. According to *The Endangered Species Handbook*, CITES' categorised listings of python are 'totally ineffectual because of confusion with other subspecies of this snake'.

When they have been thrown into a seething pit – it is hard to view the snake trade without the biblical overtones – it is very difficult to differentiate between one subspecies and another. Take the snakeskin one step back from the acrid pit of the tannery, and you'll find the original animal. Tom Rawstorne gave an account in the *Daily Mail* of a Javanese slaughterhouse, describing 'blood-stained hands [untying] a wriggling sack and [pulling] out a ten-foot long python. The snake is stunned with a blow to the head from the back of a machete and a hose pipe expertly forced between its jaws. Next the water is turned on and the reptile fills up, swelling like a balloon.' After ten minutes a cord is tied around its head to stop the water escaping before the python is 'impaled on a meat hook, a couple of quick incisions follow, and the now-loosened skin is peeled off with a series of brutal tugs – much like a rubber glove from a hand'.

After this description (and there are plenty more horrific such eye-witness accounts) it's difficult to defend python production by playing the humane card. But the industry will still have a go at defending it with a generalised sustainability argument. The pro-python fashion houses point to the fact that in common with crocodiles, python and other snakes are produced in farms, eliminating the need to remove them from the wild. Clifford Warwick, an expert on reptilian health and behaviour who has consulted for animal welfare organisations, doesn't buy it. 'I'd love someone to show me the farms that are raising so many adult snakes a year,' he has said in response to the fact that during 2005 some 350,000 skins and leather products from reticulated pythons (i.e. the type found in South-East Asia) were imported legally into the EU. He maintains that snakes take a long time to mature, and therefore would not be profitable to rear in captivity, and suggests that fashion is continuing to plunder the wild for its python fix: 'We are seeing smaller and smaller snakes caught and hunters having to travel across wider areas; classic signs of a species in decline.'

£1,200

The 'It' Bag

What makes me so fabulous?

You might be wondering what high-tech, gorgeous iridescent fabric I've been hewn from. Are you sitting down? I'm made from the skins of four pythons. I know that sounds quite retro – snakeskins were big in the 1930s, when we weren't so preoccupied with species loss – but unexpectedly I'm back! Yes, pythons might be listed in Appendix III of the Convention on International Trade in Endangered Species, but don't be boring. If anyone asks, my pythons were raised on a special 'farm', not harvested from the wild. The point is that they were 'processed' on a farm, even if that meant forcing hosepipes into their mouths, blowing them up with water to loosen the skin and then impaling them through the head before the skin was ripped off. In case you think that all sounds a bit regressive, the final product represents the appliance of science, the fusion between cosmetic procedures and luxury accessories. You couldn't really get a better symbol of these ties. Frankly, snake skin can look a bit flaky and a bit, well, snakey. So a genius came up with the idea of injecting me with the botulinum toxin, Botox, now the mainstay of the cosmetic treatment industry. If Botox injections are good enough for your foreheads, they're good enough for mere snakes. It keeps my skin plumped up and ever youthful. It would be a damned shame if I went out of fashion.

Truth Labels™

'I really couldn't care less about snakes suffering,' says Annie, a fashion-lover, but clearly not a snake-lover. 'Of all the animals they are dangerous, vile and cause havoc. They are also cold-blooded reptiles, so don't feel pain in the same way. Surely they're the best resource to use.' Annie's view is far from unique. The suffering of snakes – 'Satan's lapdog', if you will – doesn't exactly engage the population at large as much as say cruelty to or habitat destruction of giant pandas or tigers. That's one of the drawbacks of not being a charismatic species: it's hard to get people to care and take action if you're not cuddly enough to make it onto a calendar for species loss.

My question is, who appointed the luxury conglomerates as St Patrick, with powers to drive all the snakes away? While a dangerous animal killed and turned into a handbag panel, watch strap, belt or pair of cowboy boots might represent one less venomous creature, harvesting from natural communities has an undoubted ecological impact. The removal of vast quantities of snakes, primarily pythons, from the wild in Asia for shoes, handbags and clothing has, according to many experts in zoonotic disease, resulted in an infestation of rats. 'I think we have to ask ourselves, what is the value of a python?' said herpetologist Peter Brazaitis, a former animal curator at New York's Central Park Wildlife Center, a decade ago. 'Is it a pair of expensive trousers? Or is it as a means to check exploding rat populations in nations where communicable diseases are rampant?' I would suggest that if you're in the market for a luxury accessory, this question should be at the top of your list.

FUR BOUNCES BACK

However 'right-on' you are, it's easy to forget what lurks in the depths of your own wardrobe. To my surprise, during one of those changeovers of stock from summer to winter, I find two chain belts nestling among my winter woollies – both presents bought from Spitalfields market in East London – that on closer inspection are in fact dainty links of fur. I remember now opening the parcels and assuming they were rabbit, which is presumably why they were stuffed in here, packed away out of sight, out of ethical eyeline. Fur isn't a look I've ever pursued, but what do you do with unwanted fur gifts? It might seem obvious to you that fur should be an ethical no-no, but for those whose tolerances are set differently to those of the average PETA activist, the argument is worth exploring, because once again this territory is fought over with great vigour from both sides.

When I was coming of fashion age, fur was deader than the pelts. You could barely walk down the high street without bumping into a trestle table staffed by junior PETA members who gave up every Saturday afternoon to plead with the general public and show them laminated pictures of dogs in cages and foxes with their feet cut off. It was hard not to take any notice. I was in my second year at university in 1994 when Peter Lindbergh shot the famous 'We'd rather go naked than wear fur' pictures for PETA. The 'we' just happened to be a clutch of supermodels: Naomi, Cindy, Elle, Claudia and Christy. By the end of the 1990s, I couldn't imagine anything more likely to get you the wrong kind of attention than wearing a fur coat. It just was not an attractive proposition.

At that time it seemed inconceivable that such posturing was in itself a trend. But it was. The anti-fur climate of opinion evaporated, and fur and fur farming staged the biggest comeback since Lazarus. In fact it not only rose from the dead, but it got bigger and more set in its ways. I'd even contend that because it carried some ethical ambiguity it became subversive, and found a new, devil-may-care audience. I guess when a fibre is culturally prohibited it tends to become a bit cool – perhaps we should try it with British rare-breed wool!

How did this happen? In 2009 writer Elizabeth Day gave a rundown of celebrities who had been seen lately in animal pelts: 'Keira Knightley recently attended an awards ceremony in a black karakul lambskin coat, and Jennifer Lopez has worn an array of mink and chinchilla at red-carpet events over the years. Madonna, Eva Longoria, Linda Evangelista, Kate Moss and Lindsay Lohan have all worn fur in public.' Interesting how many of these names we also saw rocking that python trend.

It's wrong to heap all the opprobrium on the heads of the supermodels, but it's interesting to acknowledge the actions of the 'rather go naked' alumni. With the exception of Christy Turlington, all the others have recently reneged on that epoch-defining slogan and worn fur. Cindy Crawford became the face of Blackglama, a marketing cooperative for

US mink farmers, and Naomi Campbell promoted the wares of both Blackglama and furrier Dennis Basso. They all seemed to say that they had either been misled or misdefined by that original poster – Campbell even suggested that she'd become alienated from the anti-fur lobby because she was turned off by PETA's militant and aggressive tactics.

The truth is that whenever such a campaign is fronted by a group of cultural mercenaries (and I hate to pour cold water on the cult of the supermodel, but they were just models for hire), longevity is going to be an issue. With the right amount of money on offer, at some stage in the future when these models were nearing the end of their editorial careers it was almost inevitable that they would be coaxed into sable and mink to recant on the world's red carpets and in photo-ops.

THE LURE OF THE PELT

Their lack of fidelity isn't so much the issue for me – I'm more interested in ours. Frankly it shocks me to open a magazine, as I did recently within my own newspaper, and read the type of feature where random people are snapped out and about and asked to explain the essence of their personal style – to see Daisy or Freya (I forget which), twenty-five, stylist, London, wearing a fur coat and opining, 'It's vintage, but someone told me it was monkey!' Did they?! What a hoot! Is Daisy/Freya trying to be confrontational or provocative? Or does she genuinely think it's OK to go about her metropolitan business wrapped up in monkey fur?

You'll rarely hear today's fur wearers admit that they are merely slavishly following fashion. Instead there are a number of determined lines of defence on offer, ranging from the ever pragmatic 'It's a by-product' to the newer 'It's a sustainable fibre.' We'll have a look at those in a moment, but first come two stalwarts: 'It's warm' and 'It's vintage.'

Yes, fur, not surprisingly, has a high Clo-value. You are probably unfamiliar with Clo-values. Corresponding more or less to the R-value of fibreglass, they have been drawn up by researchers in the US and Denmark, and denote the thermal properties and insulation value provided by different articles of clothing. To start at the very beginning, if you were naked your Clo-value would be 0.0. When you put your knickers on you go up to 0.06. A skirt ranges in Clo-value from 0.22 to 0.70, a 'typical indoor winter clothing combination' comes in at 1.0, and a cold-weather parka has a Clo-value of 4.0. As the values are additive, you build up your amount of Clos as you get dressed. I love to think of putting clothes on in this way, in a sort of dress-by-numbers scenario. Even more of a challenge would be to shop in this way, but ultimately I think more people are likely to own multiple Birkin bags than will ever utilise Clo-values to build their wardrobes.

If temperatures are unseasonably high, the output of the fur industry falls. There is no doubt that some consumers buy fur for warmth. A 2006 study from the Hohenstein Institute of Textiles in Germany that pitted coyote and mink ('natural' fur) against *faux* fur found real fur to be more insulating at every temperature. But in a broadly temperate climate like ours, does the extra insurance against windchill really justify the whole of the fur industry?

I understand that the search for warmth and a desire not to see a good dead animal go to waste might steer someone towards Granny's wardrobe in pursuit of vintage. Vintage in general is a thriving, dynamic, globalised business, and fur products are no exception. So my suspicion is that few people actually get fur coats as hand-me-downs: they just say they do, because they really like the aesthetic of old fur, and again it also has that subversive, naughty edge of provocation. But there is a problem with this myth of fur as an heirloom handed from one appreciative, warm owner to the next. Fur begins deteriorating pretty much as soon as the animal takes its last breath. The better the pelt and the more access it has to open air, the longer it will retain the sheen and properties of the animal, but in reality keeping a top-end fur, say a mink, is only marginally less onerous than keeping a team of actual living, breathing mink. 'Home storage, using air conditioning or a cedar closet will not protect your fur from insect damage, drying out, becoming dirty or oxidising which can discolor fur or change its texture,' says the Fur Information Council of America, which suggests that owners store their furs in commercial furriers' vaults, where 'air exchange is carefully regulated with temperatures kept below 50 degrees Fahrenheit and a constant humidity level of 50 per cent. No closet in your home can duplicate these conditions adequately.' This raises the issue of how much energy is expended on storing fur 'properly'. The US Humane Society wryly notes that some analysts suggest 'summer cold storage' is one of the most lucrative aspects of the entire fur trade. It's rather as if Adidas opened a humidity-controlled Big Yellow Storage where it recommended you keep your old-school trainers.

In any event, the 'vintage' fur, left in an attic or mothballed at the back of a wardrobe while it was out of moral fashion for two decades, will probably not have worn very well. Its Clo-value will be significantly reduced. The best place for an old fur coat, you might argue, is in a pet shelter as a dog's bed, or retired to PETA or a similar anti-fur organisation where it can serve as an educational or research aid. You might in fact argue that this is the only noble end for a fur coat.

ETHICAL FUR, FASHION'S OXYMORON

If you didn't buy into the warmth or the vintage argument, it would seem that the case was pretty simple: those in the wrong wore a real fur coat, those in the right wore fake fur. But apparently not, because in the latter part of the noughties the fur industry hit upon a rather ingenious plan: a campaign that would celebrate the undeniable truth that fur comes from animals, and that animals are indeed natural. Conversely, the argument ran, fake/impostor or *faux* fur is a chemical, unnatural, polluting substitute. There were other 'sustainable' arguments too: the fur industry maintained that fur was a cultural right for some communities, that worldwide it sustained both indigenous communities and fur trappers (for the record, the animal welfare campaign group Animal Aid contends that less than 0.25 per cent of the fur trade is carried out by 'truly native people'). The 'evidence' as presented by the fur trade was designed to prove that there was really no bar to fur in fashion, that you could be both ethical and wear or use fur. The Danish 'ethical' label Noir, for example, unrepentantly uses fur in its mainline collection on the grounds that it's a sustainable fibre. 'We work with SAGA Furs who have a very strict CSR policy with regard to animal welfare called O.A. [Origin Assured],' explains Noir creator Peter Ingwersen. But perhaps the sustainable fur campaign at its most audacious is summed up by the Fur Council of Canada's designated website, which emerged in 2009: furisgreen.com. It included a section called 'Eco-Logical', and this highlight:

A New Vision of Fur, for an Eco-Conscious World!

Fur is warmth, comfort and beauty. For many, fur is the ultimate luxury. But using fur also makes sense if we want to protect nature while supporting people and cultures.

Until this determined briefing against *faux* fur, the ambiguity of lookalikey animal pelts lay only in the fact that the really good, clever fake furs helped to promote the increased fashionability and therefore desirability of the real thing. It's because of this that I always felt a bit dodgy wearing a padded jacket I have with a fake fur collar – of the organic cotton variety. Not only might people think it's real, leading me to be covered in red paint, but there's that residual guilt that I'm perpetuating the myth that a wardrobe needs fur in it.

By seizing on the whopping environmental price tag behind fake fur, the pro-fur lobby had come up with a much better strategy. This is hinged on the fact that *faux* fur is predominantly made from nylon – and as discussed earlier, creating adipic acid, the feedstock for nylon, produces nitrous oxide, a greenhouse gas.

So the pollution charge against fake fur has legs. And it has a very oily secret too, given that it takes a gallon of oil to make just three fake-fur coats. Teresa Platt, Executive Director of America's Fur Commission, told journalists: '*Faux* fur jackets do not degrade for at least six hundred years, and may take thousands of years. Yet they are being actively promoted as environmentally friendly by animal rights activists. Between four and eight million jackets are being sold every year, creating a disposal nightmare for years to come.' By contrast, real fur (so the furriers, attendant designers, editors and just general pro-fur enthusiasts would have us believe) is a natural, biodegradable byproduct that lasts eternally (almost), and after satisfying both you and your descendants will return to the earth and provide nutritious fodder for the soil. It is practically footprint-free, apparently. The fur lobby was attempting to out-ethicise the anti-fur movement.

So, given their supposed ecological superiority, why am I not dressed head to toe in chinchilla and sable? Mainly because from where I'm standing the environmental integrity of fur products lacks the, erm, integrity needed to make that argument fly. It is not enough to give us something to think about by exposing the pitfalls in a fake-fur product when the majority of real fur has a huge environmental footprint. For a start, fur is in the main processed with formaldehyde and chromium, two highly polluting, potentially carcinogenic substances. This processing is vital to 'inhibit rot' – the truth about fur is that without this extraordinary degree of intervention, without being messed with and covered in chemicals, it would degrade until it resembled a 'high' piece of meat. It's difficult to explain away this chemical involvement – the standard industry response is to say that it is harmless.

In some areas of Scandinavia and North America, mankind's right to wear fur is guarded as assiduously as the right to bear arms. The fur industry loves to make the link between heroic indigenous trappers and the sustainable pelt hanging in Bergdorf Goodman. The right of native peoples to hunt native animals has partly sustained the international trade in seal fur. You may well have let out an audible gasp here, in a 'Surely-seal-hunting-doesn't-still-happen?' kind of way. But come March the Canadian east-coast seal hunt will head out to kill juvenile harp seals. Since March 2009, seal products have been banned in the EU. This must make a dent, given that Europe was formerly the biggest market. But despite reports that over 70 per cent of Canadians wanted an end to seal hunting, the Canadian government remains unrepentant. In 2010 the parliamentary restaurant began offering seal meat as part of its menu – as defiant a sign as any – and the seal hunt is referred to as the 'sustainable seal hunt'.

Granted, seal fur is an extreme – the images of seal clubbing are so resonant. Even some of the most obstinately pro-fur designers know better than to incorporate seal. But there are other pelts that have also championed the fair-trade-alike argument. When Madonna pitched up in a Prada astrakhan sometime in 2003 she was the latest to fall for the trend for supersoft fur. But she didn't pursue it – rumour had it she got a bollocking from her friend Stella McCartney, whose views on the material could have been predicted. But the appearance of astrakhan did leave a lingering whisper around fashion weeks and showrooms alike of 'How is it so soft?' Animal welfare groups said they had the answer – they claimed that lambs were barbarically ripped from ewes' wombs, gaining astrakhan the horrible soubriquet of 'foetal fur'. Not so, countered the fur industry, which insisted that astrakhan is derived only from stillborn lambs, giving desperate farmers in Central Asia a livelihood after soil erosion had ruled out growing crops. Now, I'm all for giving desperate farmers a lifeline, but one saturated in claims of medieval cruelty for a skin that was in fashion for approximately five minutes? The attempt to cast astrakhan as the Bono of the animal pelt industry fell flat where I was concerned.

Your decision as to whether to allow fur into your wardrobe will eventually come down to stacking the 'pro' arguments (including the idea that it is ethical) alongside the 'cons' and seeing which carry more weight. To do this we need to know the truth about fur, and during the course of my research I had to accept that the true data is extremely restricted. The industry holds the keys to its farms extremely tightly, and it has little time for possible dissenters. But one thing seems clear to me. To cast the international fur industry as a sort of wholesome Davy Crockett arrangement in which trappers harvest local animals to survive, eat the meat and fashion weather-defying garments to last the winter, is wide of the mark.

It's an argument that might have some bottom were animals trapped from the wild. For example, New Zealand has developed a possum-fur industry which proponents argue is legitimate because the country is overrun with possums, which destroy native trees and eat birds' eggs. (For the record, PETA vehemently disagrees.) But more than 85 per cent of fur used globally comes from fur farms. China is the biggest exporter. We've seen elsewhere how China can ramp up fashion production in every other area, and fur is no exception. Take mink. Just a decade ago, it is estimated that China produced about two million mink pelts a year. In 2007 Oslo Fur Auctions – which keeps the most reliable statistics on the fur industry – estimated it to have produced twenty million pelts, more than a third of world output. China had become a fur superpower.

DOWN ON THE (FUR) FARM

What is a fur farm, anyway? The industry version, as presented by the US Fur Commission for example, is homely, humane and logical, if of course you can get around the issue of farming and killing the animals in the first place. So the Fur Commission's description of a typical mink farm in America (black mink pelts accounted for over half of all pelts produced by the US in 2009) is of a family-run business, 'often operated by two or three generations of the same family', with an enlightened, progressive and educated view of the business: 'A young farmer will typically take time out to gain a college or university degree in agriculture, biology or business.' Life down on the farm revolves around the 'natural reproductive cycle of the animals'. The 'kits' (young) are responsibly weaned and vaccinated for disease, and whereas in the wild most young mink don't survive their first year, 'In contrast, a farmer's care ensures that almost all domesticated mink live until the end of the year when they are harvested.' At the time of 'harvest' a mobile euthanasia unit comes to the farm and the animals are 'immediately rendered unconscious and die quickly and humanely'. Providing the mink with 'humane' care is naturally an 'ethical obligation'.

Presumably it was not such an 'ethical obligation' for the farms that have been covertly filmed over the years by various animal rights or humane organisations. It was never my intention here to go on about the cruelty of the fur trade. From YouTube to PETA to the ADI (Animal Defenders International), you don't have to go very far to see a film about fur production. A large body of evidence suggests that 'fur farm' is in fact a rather formal name for a very varied series of establishments. We are awash with horrific images – from foxes chewing their feet off, to cages of dogs being trucked around a Chinese town. It's depressing, but investigation after investigation seems to turn up similar horrors. The first ever report from inside China's fur farms found appalling conditions, including animals being skinned while fully conscious. I'm a relatively tough customer, but in trying to figure out exactly where I stand on this subject, I've regularly been reduced to tears by some of these images. They never lose their resonance. A 2010 report from the ADI suggested that we shouldn't assume things are any different in Europe: footage shows the putrid cages of a variety of foxes across seventy farms in Finland, some of them so disturbed that they expend every fast-twitch fibre throwing themselves at the wire mesh of their small cages. It is a vision of Hades, appalling in its cruelty.

But images of cruelty and campaigns based on animal welfare do not seem to be able to stop the fur industry. Over a thousand tonnes of fur was imported into Britain alone in 2005 as the British Fur Trade Association (BFTA) celebrated the fact that retail sales had risen by nearly a third in just two years. Some industry insiders claim that Britain is one of the fastest-growing markets for fur in the world.

Perhaps you've begun to buy that green pro-fur message. If so, I'm here to tell you to tread very, very carefully. Pollution, a common denominator in the lion's share of industrial farmscapes, is endemic to this process too. The US mink industry alone is made up of around 270 farms producing an average of 10,546 mink a year, enough to make over 80,000 coats. According to PETA the industry adds almost a thousand tons of phosphorus to the environment each year. When washed into watercourses phosphorus can cause algal blooms that starve them of oxygen, leading to the biological death of rivers and lakes. And note that although I'm picking on the US, it's only the planet's fourth biggest mink-killer: China, Denmark and the Netherlands could be producing even more phosphorus.

Then there's the air pollution, which includes dioxins (some of the most harmful molecules to human health) and heavy metals. The Industrial Pollution Projection System, devised in the mid-1990s as a tool to help the World Bank, rates 'fur dressing' as one of the five worst industries for toxic metal pollution to the land, along with the dyeing industry. That's one of the five worst of *all* industries. At various times during the past five years the Chinese government has become so worried about the pollution caused by fur-dyeing factories that it has threatened to impose a punitive levy on fur processing.

But don't stop there: we need to factor in the energy needed to raise and process a pelt – from feeding the animals (fur companies are at pains to point out that creatures such as mink are fed on scraps from slaughterhouses, but these still have to be collected and transported) to running the tanneries, through to transporting the pelts to international auction. But before it gets to auction the freshly killed animal needs to be processed – pelted and dried. 'A pelting plant is not complete without a storeroom in which the temperature can be kept between 10 and 12 degrees C … and the humidity at about 70–80 per cent,' the Danish Fur Breeders' Association's *Manual for Breeders* reliably informs me. That is a seriously energy-intensive process.

Even where fur is still trapped (often considered the more 'sustainable' route), trappers use everything from snowmobiles to planes to check their traps. The whole process and the whole industry are entirely predicated on that great environmental foe, fossil fuel. Given all of this, it's not particularly surprising that longstanding research by Michigan University put the amount of energy needed to produce real fur coats from farm animal skins at twenty times greater than that required for a fake product.

It's hard to avoid the conclusion that if you buy fur – even from the limited amount of fur that has sustainability credentials, such as Origin Assured – you're buying into the whole industry. 'Careful' fur production does not appear to be indicative of the broader picture. It is easy to miss this, however, as fur farms and trappers tend to come under the umbrella of the big associations – SAGA furs, representing Nordic fur auction houses; NAFA, the North American Fur Auctions; and the Fur Council of Canada – all branding, protecting and removing (you might say) the association of fur with the variety of farms and producers that actually feed the auctions. They give the impression that the fur industry is tightly regulated, carefully controlled and extremely organised. Is that really the case?

Or is it that on a global scale there is actually very little control in the fur industry, to the point that consumers don't really know what they are getting. In America, Neiman Marcus is the last word in upscale department-store shopping. Historically it has always had a lively, flourishing and well-stocked fur section. But a proportion of its clientèle obviously has a beating ethical heart, because in common with the rest of the fashion scene, it began to sell *faux* fur. Which is how Neiman Marcus came to be selling a Burberry *faux* fur jacket online. Despite its relatively high price tag of $1,300, it was apparently doing a roaring trade. Perhaps the reason for its success was that it had all the luxurious sheen of a real fur, while its owners could rest assured that it was entirely fake. Except that it was not. Not only was the coat 'misdescribed' as fake fur, but it was actually from one of the furs that makes anti campaigners feel particularly ill – Finn raccoon. According to the campaigning organisation the Humane Society of the United States, Finn raccoon is a bit of a construct. The animal from which the pelt is taken is not a raccoon, but a canine (i.e. a dog) indigenous to East Asia, and pivotal in the resurgence of the worldwide trend in fur.

Nobody knows how much of the fur that is imported to the West is dog fur. Nobody quite wants to believe it happens, and a law prohibiting the importation of cat or dog fur to the UK finally came into effect in 2009. Can we now sleep safely in the knowledge that there is no dog or cat fur that is not attached to a dog or cat on these shores? Given the confusion about what is what, and the tendency to pass off strange furs as 'fox', or even *faux*, who knows? It's telling that the Neiman Marcus *faux pas* was only revealed after the Humane Society of the United States, which has lawsuits pending against Macys and Saks for similar cases, tested the coats itself, an expensive process. Should the buck really stop with the campaigning organisations?

Luckily for the fur industry, it has friends in high places. One of the best must be Anna Wintour, the editor of American *Vogue*. Wintour is an extremely smart cookie, famed for giving style nuanced gravitas. And yet she is rarely seen without a chinchilla fur collar. *The September Issue*, a film that followed the production of one edition of *Vogue*, caught her on camera demanding that more fur be used in one of the main fashion shoots. You have to wonder how much this reflects her personal affection for fur, and how much it is influenced by the commercial realities of producing a doorstop-sized glossy paean to luxury brands in a world of declining advertisers.

The rationale isn't much different from the rest of the fashion industry. 'In 1985, forty-five established catwalk designers were using fur in their ready-to-wear collections. In 2000 this number had increased to four hundred,' Jan Brown, a UK fur trade spokeswoman, was quoted as saying in 2001. The European Union remains the world's biggest consumer of fur, and while fur farming may have been banned in the UK, London is the world centre for buyers. As has already been noted, only Lazarus has staged a bigger bounce-back.

TRIMMING THE ARGUMENT

And here we come to the final pillar of the pro-fur argument: the byproduct defence. I've noticed recently that larger and larger pieces of pelt are being passed off as 'trim' by editors, stylists and designers. It is sold as a byproduct of the 'full fur-coat industry', the leftover remnants, presumably scooped from the furriers' cutting-room floor during assembly, and lovingly fashioned into accessories or added to other products as embellishment. It is passed off as innocuous – you see it around the hoods of parkas, in the lining of gloves (where it bumps up the Clo-value) or around the hem of a Prada dress. It is hard to prove or disprove whether an animal product is a byproduct, made from the waste hide or pelt when the rest of the animal has been used for meat. But fur trim is on shaky ground.

The fur trim industry is so huge that it practically eclipses the full fur-coat industry. Evidence suggests that nearly all foxes raised in fur farms are now turned into trim. In Russia and China the number of animals killed for trim exceeds those killed for full-fur items. According to campaigners such as the Global Action Network, at least one animal dies for each piece of fur trim or fur accessory. It is not such a leap to suggest that fur trim is the primary reason for producing millions of animals, which means it is not a byproduct at all.

Once upon a time in Brighton – that hotbed of right-on living where I lived for a while myself – you would have been alerted to the presence of fur in a shop by all the paint on the window and the protesters chained to the railings. Not any more. The last time I went into a boutique there I found three fur stoles for sale. When I enquired about their provenance I was told they were 'sustainable, because the fur's a byproduct'. There was nothing to certify this was the case.

I want to bring the argument full circle for a minute, and flash back to the chorus of supermodel disapproval feeding into the pervading societal objection to fur, and the time when wearing a dead animal pelt seemed unfashionable and anti-aspirational, shorthand for idiot rather than icon. How did the big fur producers weather this cultural distaste for the best part of a decade? How did the fur industry store its energy and purpose, gather momentum and manage to spring back from effective extinction? Look, and you'll find that fur trim is very much in the frame.

Throughout those troubled times for the industry, warehouses in the major producing zones quietly locked the doors on their stockpiled fur, but never let it go. Instead, the fur industry cleverly began to target the fashion industry from the ground up. It didn't bother to chase after us, the consumers, and convince us we'd got it wrong. Instead it went to fashion colleges and gave perennially struggling fashion students access to a 'versatile', 'luxurious' and free material. It began to offer pelts, named as 'fur trim', to the up-and-coming NewGen designers. Deftly, and with more than a hint of cunning, the fur industry bought a place near the heart of UK fashion, by sponsoring student fashion. And now that it has done that, it is difficult to imagine how we will ever get rid of animal fur from our collective fashion chain.

10

LUST FOR LEATHER

Fashion's Biggest Cash Cow Shows its True Colours

What is it that makes leather such a damned attractive proposition? At the risk of sounding like a fetishist, my first instinct when I get a 'quality' leather bag or shoe in my hand is to inhale deeply and savour the smell. The cooing I can do over a finely turned real leather shoe or boot with that classic, timeless appeal far transcends anything I've ever managed over a baby or puppy, and I can wax lyrical on the weathered patina of a vintage leather satchel for pages. But when you break down leather production, it's one of the grittiest parts of the fashion chain. The physical waste products alone sound like items on Sweeney Todd's shopping list: fleshings, trimmings, split off-cuts, shaving from raw hides.

Then there is the other small matter that I don't eat meat. Yet I have a leather blind spot. To a certain extent I think leather's ubiquity has made it disappear from our moral conscience. Leather shoes, belts and bags are so much a part of our fashion culture that I think many of us have forgotten to think about leather as an animal fibre at all. Millions of so-called vegetarians worldwide continue to wear leather shoes and carry leather bags. Many of them even recline on leather sofas.

Similarly, there are plenty of eco warriors preaching their top tips to leaving a lighter indentation on planet earth while marching about in leather shoes and carrying leather bags. But as well as leather being one of the most prevalent materials in our wardrobe, its production and processing phase is one of the most polluting systems that humankind has managed to come up with. Leather production is widely considered to be one of the ten most harmful industries as far as pollution goes, its impacts, according to ecologists, leading to a deterioration of a wide range of organisms and ecosystems. Leather's ubiquity ensures that it boasts the highest head count (literally so, since cattle are prosaically referred to as 'head') in terms of animals destroyed of any material stream. But its impact is felt way beyond the slaughterhouse.

In common with other fashion fibres and materials, leather has become progressively more 'affordable' for us, the consumers. You used to know where you were with shoes: if you wanted expensive, you bought leather uppers exhibiting varying degrees of craftsmanship which were reflected in the price. If you wanted cheap and with a short lifespan, you went synthetic. But it's no longer true to say that leather is a premium product. It's a theme we've seen develop throughout these pages, but fast fashion works partly by pummelling down the cost of its raw materials. It therefore comes as little surprise that the inexorable rise of fast fashion has coincided with a world deluged by cheap, low-quality leather. Today it is perfectly possible to buy a pair of leather shoes for the price of a DVD. I am not of course talking about the 'status' or 'it' shoe that we met back in Chapter 5 – those are predicated on design and expense – but fast-fashion footwear, which actually includes many bargain basement interpretations of the 'status' shoe. And overall contemporary shoes have the briefest of lifespans, while we are losing capacity and knowledge when it comes to repairing and restoring our footwear.

I'm picking on shoes because I have a lot of them. I count six pairs of in-service boots (distinct from the many pairs I no longer wear, squirrelled away under beds or boxed in cupboards) and eighteen pairs of shoes, mainly heels – two in fabric but the rest in leather, including a vertiginous £400 pair. My trainer count is not as high as it once was: I now have four pairs, two of which are pretty functional. All in all I would say I come in at double the average number of shoes per capita in the UK – the average for women being fourteen pairs.

Then there are the belts, in various thicknesses and colours. I embraced the wasp-waisted look of a few seasons ago with particular vigour, so I've got a number of wide, heavy leather belts, some in matt, some in patent, with a variety of beautiful buckles and fasteners. Some of them are really quite stunning, but from prosaic through to ornamented rose links, all the leather has one thing in common: I have absolutely no idea where it comes from.

Statistically, most of my leather will be bovine (from cows). Cows are the most farmed animal on earth. The international herd now numbers over 1.5 billion; you can make out their bony shoulders from every corner of the planet. But cows do not exactly have an unassuming ecological profile. Cattle farming is, according to a seminal (though often disputed) United Nations report, 'Livestock's Long Shadow', responsible for some 18 per cent of the world's greenhouse gases, and cows currently take up 33 per cent of the world's arable land in terms of the crops grown in order to feed them. The simple cow has been named as one of the top three environmental blights on humankind.

And most of the world's leather goes into shoes. About half of the six to seven million tonnes of hides annually processed by the world's tanneries is destined for shoes. A staggering number are produced every year: in 2006 (the last year for which I have reliable figures) around 14.8 billion pairs of shoes were manufactured globally. Nearly five billion of these had leather uppers.

POISONING THE RIVER OF LIFE

To get behind the numbers, once again we need to follow a long fashion chain. This one snakes 4,500 miles away to the banks of the Ganges (Ganga, as it is known in India) and one of the planet's most overcrowded cities, Kanpur, the most populous city in Utter Pradesh. It's long been an economic hub – in fact it was once given the soubriquet 'the Manchester of the East', but that was before the tanneries came to town in a big way. Despite its industrial heritage, the Manchester of today would not put up with even a fraction of the destruction and chaos that our collective predilection for low-cost leather has caused in Developing World cities like this one.

I have been to the Ganges myself, to the *ghats* (banks) at Varanasi, where the extraordinary mix of *sadhus* (mystical holy men), bathers and traders – a few with dancing serpents and flutes – and the din and the

£75

High-street version of the Status Shoe.
Heavily inspired by the bondage shoe platform
developed by luxury labels for spring/summer 2009,
it features an abundance of real leather straps and detailing.

Who gave this shoe its real-leather status?

Ibrahim spends his days thigh-deep in acrid milky-blue water, stirring animal skins so they absorb the chemicals that have been poured into the pit. Only then will the hair and all the impurities fall away to make a smooth piece of leather. He works at one of 400 tanneries in an Indian town on the banks of the Ganges. One of the worst bits of Ibrahim's job is when the skin fragments into small parts, and he has to fish about in the milky soup to retrieve them. He tries to save the most energetic bits of the job, when he pummels the skin beneath his feet before tossing it into the air, until the boss patrols. But the boss doesn't seem to notice. Perhaps he is pretending Ibrahim doesn't exist, as at 14 he is below the legal work limit. But then, the tannery shouldn't really exist – it has no permit,which means that nobody bothers with goggles and gloves. Ibrahim is Muslim. This was the only job he could get. It is badly paid but he doesn't have an issue working with cow skins as Hindus have, even though the officials who occasionally visit and pretend to close down the tannery always claim that these are 'buffalo' skins. It's best not to wonder where a person might get enough buffalo to provide the 50 skins a day that are limed, pummelled and scrubbed clean in Ibrahim's yard. It's a secret that everone knows: the skins are from common-or-garden cows mass slaughtered in a country where man and cow are supposed to co-exist reverently.

Truth Labels™

scents and the flower petals gave the whole experience a type of romantic intensity. I admit the Ganges didn't look very clean. When our little boat was pushed out into its decidedly murky waters at dawn, we drifted past a dead cow (somewhat marring the 'romantic intensity'), but it was still strewn with flowers, and it all had the flavour of a supremely resonant, authentic Indian experience. I could understand why the Ganges is called the River of Life.

Arguably, however, this was not a very authentic experience at all. I would have got more of the genuine article had I progressed two hundred miles further along the Ganges, to Kanpur, where the city effectively spills out into the river. This is one of the hotspots where the river famous for its mystical ability to regenerate comes unstuck. Where myth is confronted by a pungent, toxic bubbling in the waters and where your nose fills with the unmistakable stench of leather processing.

Rakesh Jaiswal is an environmental politics PhD who has spent over twenty years campaigning to clean up pollution from the tanneries and to control and ameliorate the impact of the international accessories industry on the River of Life. And I don't mean campaigning in an airy-fairy, write-some-letters type of way. He has devoted large tracts of his life to warning that similarly large tracts of the Ganges have become poisoned, and in effect 'dead'. His efforts have been punctuated with important breakthroughs: in 1998 a legal battle with Kanpur's tanneries concluded with the enforced closure of 127 of the worst-polluting offenders. In 2001 he forced the authorities to face up to the fact that in outlying villages chromium poisoning (chromium being a key ingredient in the vast majority of leather processing) was endemic. But this is not a question of 'case closed'. Far from it. So Jaiswal continues to persuade national and foreign journalists to take a walk along the banks of the Ganges at Kanpur, where some four hundred tanneries edge down to the famous river. From the *Wall Street Journal* to *Time* and the *Smithsonian* magazine, the responses are uniformly horrified. 'I had expected to find a less-than-pristine stretch of river in this grimy metropolis of four million people, but I'm not prepared for the sights and smells that greet me,' says Joshua Hammer, writing in the *Smithsonian*. 'Jaiswal stares grimly at the runoff – it's laden with chromium sulfate, used as a leather preservative and associated with cancer of the respiratory tract, skin ulcers and renal failure.' The eyewitness accounts of the journalists are consistent with many of the opinions of the locals attempting to function with this toxic brew. '[Kanpur] is drowning in its own filth,' Ashok Mishra tells a correspondent from the *Wall Street Journal*.

For a mile or more inland, reports tell of pits and pools full of blue and black water, with flakes of oily debris floating on top. Where the water has evaporated it leaves behind a marble pattern of blues and greens, the telltale chemical palette of leather processing – manganese, chromium, sulphur, lead and copper. The dark waters of the Ganges itself look ill, which I guess is what happens when a river is used as an outflow dump for the waste water from around four hundred tanneries (there are an estimated 2,100 tanneries in India as a whole). In 2010 a journalist from *Time* magazine described Jaiswal as being 'worn out' from his battle against tannery pollution. You can understand why. Jaiswal suspects it's just a matter of time before this stretch of the river gives up the ghost entirely. He reckons it is already biologically dead, and that you are more likely to win a million dollars in the lottery than to see a Gangetic dolphin or a turtle. Naturally, all journalistic reports describe the juxtaposition of the Ganges with its dead fish and the *sadhu* wading in to perform his ablutions in the Holy River, the synthetically dark-blue water lapping around his thighs, the implication being that it will take more than prayers to resolve this situation.

TOXIC FOOTPRINTS

Ecologists charged with communicating the issue of an increasingly hostile planet, and toxicologists charged with monitoring an increasing cocktail of synthetic chemicals in our environment, talk in terms of 'toxic loads' (the sum total of the accumulation of chemicals or molecules that are foreign to our biological systems). Well, the toxic load of producing leather in the conditions found in some tanneries in Kanpur is enormous. Naturally, the producers are under the impression that they are being victimised. 'People are making culprits out of the tanneries, only it's not true. Only 2 per cent of total generation of effluent comes from tanneries,' claims Imran Siddiqui, director of Super Tannery Ltd, one of Kanpur's largest, which is located in Jajmau, the oldest district for leather production. Environmentalists such as Rakesh Jaiswal disagree, and say the destructive knock-on effects of the industry are impossible to quantify. As well as the misery of the workers, who are exposed to a devastating combination of toxic substances, there has to be an acknowledgement of the impact on the wider community. In Kanpur, official measures to curtail pollution could politely be described as half-hearted.

But why be polite about this sorry mess? The evidence of serious heavy metal pollution and the way it impacts on Kanpur and other tannery centres from Ethiopia (as the cow population expands, so does the opportunity to become a huge player in the leather market) to Pakistan to Brazil is impossible to ignore. Leather is not just a voracious consumer of cow skins, but also of water. To produce leather you need a practically limitless supply of it, which explains why most of the world's tanneries are situated on the banks of rivers. This moves us into dangerous territory. You may have had the sense in other parts of this book that water, and its lack of availability now and in the future, is something of a preoccupation for me. Commentators predict that future wars will be fought over water rather than oil, and some countries are already getting very nervy about water security. At least one third of the world's population suffers from water shortages, and nations are squaring up to each other over rights to fresh water – see as evidence India and Nepal, and Egypt and Sudan. Millions of impoverished peoples globally do not have ready access to clean, safe water supplies.

Not only does the leather industry have a constant need for fresh water to convert cow skin into 'wet blue' leather (in its raw state, once it has had all the hair and fat removed), but it flushes waste water, filled with the chemicals used in processing, back out into the host river. Evidence suggests that Kanpur processes some sixteen to eighteen million hides a year. Super Tannery alone makes 5,000 pairs of shoes a day for export. That adds up to a lot of water. 'Actually, nobody knows for sure how much waste water they generate,' says Ajay Kanujia, a local chemist in Jajmau, 'but everybody accepts that tanneries produce between twenty to thirty MLD [million litres per day] of waste water.' So far, so frightening, because it is not fair to say that there have been no efforts to install pollution controls at Kanpur. It's just that the efforts are merely a drop in the (possibly polluted) ocean compared to what the city's leather industry really needs. The treatment plant which is supposed to remove the manganese, chromium, sulphur, lead, copper etc. from the water can, by the authorities' own admission, only deal with nine million litres of leather waste water per day. The remaining twenty-one million litres or so are flushed into the Ganges. No wonder Kanpur is rapidly becoming known for hosting the most polluted stretch of the Ganges in its entire 1,500-plus-mile journey through the Indian subcontinent.

The chemical processing of leather creates a massive amount of toxic sludge. Residents tend to know they've been affected by this when their children are born with neurological disorders, and the groundwater, the water they use for drinking, cooking, bathing and watering their crops, turns a mysterious shade of yellow. In fact it's not so mysterious. In Kanpur the leather industry dumps twenty-two tonnes of solid waste, or sludge, out in the beating sun every day. One official told environmental investigators, 'This solid waste contains chromium, a hazardous substance, in good measure: eighteen to twenty-two milligrams per gram.' That means 440 kilograms of chromium gets dumped every day. Over seven years the official treatment plant has dumped about 1,125 tonnes of chromium on Kanpur's soil. Factoring in all the unofficial leather processing in this area through 'illegal' tanneries, the actual total is likely to be a hell of lot more.

This is the soil tilled by subsistence farmers, growing vegetables to feed their children. These are not crops that the local population can take or leave. They provide calories to sustain their lives. Scientists across the globe have monitored with alarm how heavy metals such as chromium are absorbed by vegetables and enter the human food chain. What effects does this have on health? Well, inhaling concentrations of some forms of chromium causes nosebleeds, ulcers and 'holes in the nasal septum'. Higher doses can lead to kidney and liver damage, stomach ulcers, convulsions and even death. Research shows that around 10 per cent of particular types of chromium can remain in the human body for five years, and in the stomach chromium can mutate, causing damage to DNA.

In Noraiakheda, a Kanpur community of 30,000 people, there really is nowhere to run to. Noraiakheda has grown up right on top of a plume of gaseous hexavalent chromium (chromium VI – the substance over which Erin Brockovich went to battle with the Pacific Gas and Electric company in the United States), the heritage of an old leather-processing plant. Heat and wind throw out dust particles, and during the hot summer months methane flares shoot flames into the air. In short, thanks to the leather industry producing shoes mainly for the UK, German and US markets, the soil and the air are poisoned, which means the people are poisoned too.

Of course the leather-processing industry doesn't set out to poison everyone who comes into contact with the production cycle, but it is dependent on chromium, a tanning agent that finishes leather by strengthening it and making it 'fast' – ensuring the colour stays and that it remains water repellent. In fact there are other ways of processing leather, including vegetable tanning, a more traditional process, but it is time-consuming, and therefore expensive. Chrome has become the chemical of choice, despite the fact that it is relatively unstable. While Kanpur tanneries may start out using a basic chrome sulphate (chromium III) to treat their leather, when the waste is dumped outside it reacts with the air and is converted to the potentially toxic chromium VI. 'And in Kanpur,' says one sad campaigner, 'chromium just needs a good rainfall: the soil and groundwater both have got severely contaminated. Chromium goes where the rainwater goes.'

While there are a number of Erin Brockovich-type campaigners within and without the local community – including Rakesh Jaiswal – there is no Hollywood blockbuster on the horizon that might shock us all out of our complacency. Or are we all just too fat and happy on a diet of cheap shoes and handbags? To date there has been just one major campaign about the conditions under which Indian leather is produced. Back in 2000 Pamela Anderson, the go-to *Baywatch* babe for animal-rights issues, narrated a PETA video plugged as the first on-film exposé of the slaughter of cattle in India. It featured graphic and disturbing footage of the transportation of cows, crammed into trucks, some of them attempting to leap out, others collapsing to the floor, and of them being skinned alive in the most distressing conditions imaginable. Since then a lot of similar evidence has emerged which clearly shows an industry that doesn't conform even to minimum expectations of animal welfare. It all makes a similar point: that the Indian leather industry is not only brutal, it goes against the country's constitution: in all but two Indian states it is illegal to butcher cows, which are revered in Hinduism.

For a while the PETA campaign appeared to be having an effect, as major retailers around the world, including our own M&S and Arcadia, agreed to boycott Indian leather. PETA claimed that this cost the Indian leather industry $68 million. The Indian government and the Council for Leather Exports promised to improve transport and slaughter conditions. Has this really happened? Recent video evidence suggests not, and that for Indian abattoirs operating somewhere between blind indifference and official concern, on the margins of legal and illegal, formal and informal, it's business as usual. That is, feeding the demand for millions of cow hides and our desire for the cheapest of products. Britain remains the third largest importer of Indian leather in the world. In 2010 one leading leather technologist said that '75 per cent of all Indian leather could come from illegal sources.'

HELL FOR LEATHER

In any case, if you are an international fashion conglomerate doing a roaring trade in leather ankle boots or bomber jackets, you can always switch countries. Bargain leather production is by no means confined to India. All over the world there are tanneries operating to various codes (none of them internationally standardised), or to no codes at all. The leather industry has become an international pollution time-bomb.

I hate to nominate Bangladesh once again as the axis of fast-fashion evil, but the Hazaribagh region, just outside Dhaka, is becoming as famous a blot on the landscape among environmental campaigners as the poisoned Ganges at Kanpur.

In 2008 UK environmental investigation unit Ecostorm and the *Ecologist* magazine investigated the 'appalling and unreported human and environmental cost of the leather trade in Bangladesh'. The resulting footage and written evidence, under the title 'Hell for Leather', is sobering for a shoe fan like me. In many ways it confirms our worst fears, exposing a litany of toxic chemicals used in the processing of $240 million worth

£120

The high-street aviator jacket.
Shearling (or is it?) and leather (or is it?).

Why am I so popular?

When the real deal, the Burberry aviator, was shown on cat-walks for autumn/winter 2011, the high street let out a collective sigh of relief. Here was something we could really get behind. At £1,895, few people would be able to shell out for the real thing, particularly as it was bound to go out of fashion, but the high street is famously brilliant at bringing the 'essence' of ideas like this to life. If you didn't have an aviator jacket on offer during winter 2011, you might as well shut up shop. This is a mid-range jacket, not like the nasty synthetic offerings from some of the retailers starting at £30. We know consumers like cuddly sheep, so we wouldn't insult them by having real shearling on this collar (shearling isn't like wool, you know, it's sheepskin with the wool attached, so the animal is killed). We are very sensitive to things like that. But this is a high-class product – genuine, buttery soft leather that looks like a dream. In truth that's because of the extensive processing this leather has undergone in one of the hundred-plus tanneries on the banks of the Ganges. Around 300 different chemicals are applied in pits where workers pummel the leather beneath their feet. The industry can barely keep up with the demand for cheap leather – for sofas, boots, skirts and shorts and now these jackets. Thousands of cows are slaughtered – there are varying reports as to how conscious the cow is when it is skinned. Even in this predominantly Hindu community, the treatment of cows doesn't seem to be an emotive issue.

Truth Labels™

of skins which can be traced to the British high street. It also throws interesting light on the role of giant European chemical manufacturers and its unseen impact thousands of miles away on essentially voiceless communities.

By this point you'll be aware that leather needs chemicals as much as it needs water. Trucks full of blue, green and yellow tubs containing chemicals rock up to tanneries almost constantly. The *Ecologist* and Ecostorm investigation found that 20 per cent of the chemicals used in leather processing in Dhaka were from an English-based company, Clariant. Clariant highlighted the fact that each individual chemical complied with European safety regulations, but the investigators pointed out that there was no telling the effects they might have on workers and the environment when they were all mixed together, and if released without proper treatment. And the plants that were observed during the investigation did not have any proper treatment facilities.

All around the world, local communities await their Erin Brockovich moment – their day in court, followed by acknowledgement of the pollution they have suffered. Sometimes they may even think they're getting somewhere. Tellingly, almost every leather-producing country seems to have a tannery 'relocation scheme' in process, with lists of commitments and earnest officials promising that the blight will soon be moved to some rural area with a treatment facility, giving the community a chance to regenerate and to produce a generation without birth defects. The tragedy is that these plans come to nothing. I've tried to keep up to date with various relocation projects in Bangladesh and India, but I've lost count of the number of times they've been postponed, or the deadline for installing safeguards has been extended. I can only imagine the frustration of the people on the ground, forced to live, work, raise a family and grow vegetables amidst the toxic sludge.

The official response is best described as impotent. Back on the outskirts of Kanpur, the Central Pollution Control Board (CPCB) put up signs warning the public against 'hazardous' pollution in the groundwater. The problem, however, is that residents have no other source of water, so what can they do but ignore the signs? Meanwhile there are claims that the money levied to build a proper treatment works has been diverted, while waste water is still on course to the Ganges, and sludge is being dumped on open land. Plans for a common treatment plant were drawn up over fifteen years ago, but chromium levels in the Kanpur stretch of the Ganges today stand at seventy times the recommended maximum.

AMAZONIAN IMPACTS

If I'd turned a blind eye to the suffering and the perpetuation of unfettered pollution in Southern Asia caused by my shoe collection, I was also pretty ignorant of the fact that it could well have had a hand in the destruction of the most important carbon sink we have left, the Amazon rainforest, known as 'the lungs of the earth'. Here, huge ranches corral hundreds of thousands of cattle. They appear to be ever-expanding, pushing out from their boundaries and into the rainforest, turning the landscape from trees to scrubland within weeks. We know this is a bad situation. A fifth of the Amazon rainforest has been lost since 1970, and 65 to 75 per cent of that can be attributed to the growth of cattle ranching. In 2009 the Brazilian government announced its intention to grab a bigger slice of the world beef market, from 30 per cent to 60 per cent, before 2020, even though the scars of expansion in the form of giant zigzags of scrub through the forest are visible from space already.

It's here that I want to return to the 'byproduct' argument. There is no doubt that cattle ranching in the Amazon rainforest is predominantly intended to produce meat for the insatiable global market: Brazil has the world's largest commercial cattle herd at two hundred million beasts, and is the world's largest beef exporter and second largest beef producer. But along with China, it shares the dubious honour of top exporter of tanned leather. To assume that Brazil's leather industry is just some cottage-industry-sized adjunct of its beef industry would be a big mistake. In 2008 Brazil's revenue from beef exports topped $5.1 billion. It was a bumper year. But leather sales weren't too shabby either, raking in $1.9 billion from a mind-boggling 24.8 million cow hides. Leather is no side story.

The growth of the Brazilian cattle industry is the planet's biggest-ever agricultural project. The country's herd grew from 153 million head in 1995–1996 to 205 million in 2004, an increase of more than a third.

By 2006 over 40 per cent of these beasts were accommodated in the Amazon, the equivalent of three cattle for every human inhabitant of the region. In order to shuffle in even more, the 'project' has required cutting further and further into the rainforest, home to indigenous tribes. We need to ask ourselves whether we buy the idea that it would be wasteful not to use all the leather this produces – after all, the cows have already been slaughtered for meat. Or is that just a convenient argument that lets us off the hook?

During the course of the three-year investigation that led to its report 'Slaughtering the Amazon', Greenpeace found evidence that the Brazilian government was 'bankrolling' the destruction of the Amazon through the 'illegal expansion' of the national herd, while simultaneously proclaiming itself committed to its role as custodian of the planet's most crucial carbon sink. Witness the performance Brazil's President Lula da Silva turned in at the otherwise disastrous Copenhagen climate change summit in December 2009:

> Developed countries can no longer avoid sharing in the costs and sacrifices. Brazil believes that developing countries should equally be part of the solution. We have therefore made a significant offer at the negotiating table in COP15: an ambitious proposal to reduce by 2020 national CO_2 emissions by between 36.1 per cent and 38.9 per cent. We have also committed to cutting deforestation in the Amazon by 80 per cent over the same period. This year alone deforestation of the Amazon dropped 45.7 per cent by comparison to 2008, a testament to Brazil's earnestness. These proposed reductions in emissions from deforestation alone will be larger than those offered by many developing countries in Copenhagen. Such glaring disparities will have to be ironed out during negotiations.

Meanwhile, according to Greenpeace's report, the Brazilian government was quietly buying up over $2.5 billion worth of shares in some of the biggest beef and therefore leather processors on earth. Which were the processors that received the lion's share of this investment? Three of the world's largest leather traders – Bertin, JBS and Marfrig. Under investigation the complex global trade web of ranchers, slaughterhouses, processors, finishers, brands and retailers began to unravel (as these things do if you throw enough energy and commitment at them). Greenpeace managed to identify the hundreds of ranches supplying the big leather corporations which were being backed by the Brazilian government. It compared official maps, displaying the supposed boundaries of ranches and the Amazon rainforest, with satellite images. This unearthed a web of deceit, with ranches having illegally annexed huge swathes of rainforest. Greenpeace found that 'significant supplies of cattle come from ranches active in recent and illegal deforestation', as was made clear by satellite imagery which clearly showed telltale circles of hot white ash still smouldering as cattle forlornly made their way across the scrubland.

Staying with a fashion angle (of course), of these Brazilian leather giants it's Bertin that interests me most. As you would expect of a leather company, Bertin is a major exporter to China, where 60 per cent of the world's total shoe output comes from. In fact Brazil is the single largest exporter by value of unfinished leather to China, where it is finished, quickly and cheaply and in Christ knows what conditions. The Greenpeace investigation found Chinese manufacturers, supplied by leather finishers that are direct customers of Bertin, producing trainers for seriously big names such as Nike and Adidas/Reebok. Adidas alone uses fourteen million square metres of leather per year, 85 per cent of it from South America, and almost all processed by just ten supertanneries.

The trail of shame linking the destruction of the Amazon rainforest with fashion quickly led to Italy, which after China is the second largest exporter of leather and leather products. Italy, which appears to be addicted to leather – I see no way of staging an intervention – imports mainly unfinished leather: it still likes to do its own processing, though not necessarily within its own borders. A quarter of this material comes from Brazil. Greenpeace traced regular consignments of leather from Bertin subsidiaries to two leading Italian leather processors, Rino and Gruppo Mastrotto. In turn, company sources for the Italian leather processors confirmed that Boss, Geox, Gucci, Hilfiger, Louis Vuitton and Prada were among Rino Mastrotto's customers. Should these brands get a kicking? We can't prove anything definitively – often you can't – but the statistics and pattern of sourcing suggest that there's a high chance that my leather accessories contributed to the destruction of the Amazonian rainforest.

To add insult to injury, Greenpeace's report also revealed the type of 'slave labour' at the cattle-ranch end of the chain that you'd have thought had vanished with the nineteenth century, with bonded workers kept virtually prisoner and forced to work despite non-payment of wages. And in a number of cases Bertin received supplies of cattle hide ranched on land that had been illegally annexed from its rightful owners, indigenous Indians. I'm sure I don't need to remind anybody that this is not a good look for some of the world's most prestigious fashion brands.

When charges of illegal ranching and slave labour were levelled at them, responses from the companies in question varied. Some stressed that they had 'full traceability' for their supply chains and stipulated that they excluded Amazon products. Greenpeace found that some of these guarantees of 'full traceability' were pretty pathetic, demonstrating 'a woeful ignorance of the true nature of leather processing in Brazil'. For example, one brand had based a claim to a 'clean supply chain' on the fact that it had a statistic for the distance between the biome (where the cattle were raised) and the processing facility. Yes, 'woeful', and possibly something stronger.

As has become the practice among behemoth brands with a reputation to protect, anyone connected to dodgy Brazilian leather distanced themselves with the rapidity of men jumping from a burning ship. Nike changed its sourcing pattern so that it could avoid leather from the Amazon biome altogether. Adidas, Walmart (owner of Asda), Clarks and Timberland introduced a moratorium on buying Amazonian leather until new systems were in place to guarantee a sustainable supply chain, with the latter giving the clean-up act an extra boost by launching something called the 'Earth Keeper Boot', which we'll meet later.

These ambitious new commitments were praised by Greenpeace, but other agencies are less confident. Like the moratorium that followed the outrage over the slaughter of Indian cows, and the one that may one day follow a toxic catastrophe on the shores of the Ganges, who knows how long it will last? As the spotlight shifts to another part of the world and another issue, the bovine headcount keeps growing, ranches push further into pristine rainforest, and the insatiable pressure for bargain leather continues, how long will it be before we walk back into the arms of the Amazonian leather producers?

11

DUMPED, TRASHED AND BURNED

The Disingenuous Afterlife of Discarded Fashion

'Bounced around' doesn't quite do justice to the involuntary physical trajectory I was experiencing in the back of an ancient 4x4 as it hurtled along wide orange dust roads three hours out of Bamako, Mali. There were four of us in the back, and yet it was a bit like being in zero gravity, with each of us being thrown around in our own orbit, unable to bond together to form any resistance. This was hour five of an apparently suspension-free, bottom-numbing journey that accentuated every pot-hole – and there were many. We had spent all day in the cotton fields, followed by a visit to a ginning plant where our official trip to Mali to see the wonder of Fairtrade cotton had come to an end.

I was staring fixedly out of the window, partly to distract myself from one of my fellow travellers, who was partial to singing 'Kumbaya'. As the sky darkened, the view suddenly became compelling. We were approaching a long, winding village that unfurled itself along the road for a good mile or so. The scene was a hive of activity as night folded in, perhaps the local equivalent of rush hour. I could make out the figures of women and small children, pushing goats along, and carrying buckets. But the strangest sight was the men: silhouetted against the skyline they formed tall, gangly shapes, each clad unmistakably in a woman's trenchcoat. Even more surreal than seeing a series of belted trenchcoats in the Mali dustbowl was the fact that all the sleeves were three-quarter length.

I knew the shape and design of this high-street coat – shorter than the classic trench and paler in colour – because I'd bought one of these imperative spring/summer transitional pieces myself, at the behest of the magazines.

FAMILIAR FACES

In the course of a week in West Africa, this was far from my only familiar fashion spot. We spent most of our time in rural villages with cotton farmers. There was a diverse dress code. Women of my age tended to wear traditional garments, lightweight chitenges (wraps of fabric) in coloured prints that would sometimes hold their babies to their backs in a papoose. Older women looked more formal, with high headdresses. But the young women, including teenage girls, all favoured Western dress – hot-pink T-shirts seemed to be a must-have. Denim, for girls and boys, was in evidence everywhere, always with a flared leg.

As for the small boys, it was difficult to gauge what they were wearing, because their pace of life wasn't conducive to any analysis: they flitted about at such speed, or just peeped around corners before zooming off. It was only when the village came together for a midday meeting and presentation to us, the guests, that the formal code decreed that they must come and stand around the edge of the meeting space; furthermore, they had to keep very still and quiet if they were to avoid a clout around the ear from a particularly zealous schoolteacher. At these times I could see that almost every small boy was draped in a nylon football shirt – Arsenal, Manchester United and Real Madrid. I'm no expert, but I know enough to recognise a shirt that I see on a daily basis in my own country. Wherever you turned in that hot, sticky midday meeting you were never far from the familiar names of Beckham or Zidane.

Little did I know then that football shirts are one of the most coveted commodities in Africa today. They are so sought-after, in fact, that recyclers can't keep up with the demand, and many now restrict football shirts to one bale per container in the continuous stream they dispatch from European ports. These containers take thousands of tonnes of our old clothes on a 10,000-mile one-way trip. Ghana, Tanzania, Angola,

Rwanda, Congo, Cameroon – the roll-call of countries eagerly awaiting our second-hand clothes is a register of sub-Saharan Africa. Jeans, shirts, trainers, summer dresses, kids' clothes – our cast-offs are spread across every town and large village. 'At times the whole of Africa seems to be an immense open-air bazaar of Western hand-me-downs,' observed journalist Michael Durham as he followed a £50 blouse, donated in Leicester, on its extraordinary journey to the Zambian city of Chipata. Shrink-wrapped into a forty-five-kilo bale, the blouse was part of a consignment loaded on to a Maersk shipping container in Britain, and taken on what until recently would have seemed an unbelievable voyage for a second-hand garment. The discarded clothes travelled through the Bay of Biscay, across the Mediterranean, through the Suez Canal and down the east coast of Africa, to arrive seven weeks later in the port of Beira in Mozambique, before being trucked to Chipata in Zambia, where they became *salaula* (a term from the Chibemba language that literally translated means 'to select from a pile in the manner of rummaging'. In Uganda, second-hand garment imports are known as *mivumba*).

In the last few decades the fate of 'old' garments has changed beyond recognition. Not very long ago, even within the framework of readymade garment production, our clothes had many lives: they became hand-me-downs, you could resell or swap them, their use was continuously extended by sewing and alteration. It is incredible to me that there's now a younger generation that has never known hand-me-downs. If you think that we must always have chucked out newish clothes just because they weren't on-trend, a fashion historian will quickly disabuse you of that notion. One of the reasons so few period pieces of fashion still exist, and why we have big gaps in our vintage heritage, is that in living memory we used to wear fashion to rags. Quite literally.

We are certainly out of *that* habit. Instead, for the last two decades we have increasingly chosen to export our second-hand clothes, aka 'fashion waste', primarily to Africa. From time to time an African nation will attempt to ban or restrict the influx of Western clothing imports: Uganda, for example, banned imported underwear and nightwear in 2004 on hygiene grounds; South Africa maintains strict restrictions on all second-hand garment imports; and in parts of Nigeria traditional dress is still dominant, aggressively wrestling out cast-off clothes. But in the main, *mivumba* and *salaula* are the way Africa gets itself dressed. Over one-third of all people in sub-Saharan Africa wear second-hand. As Mustaq Rawji, of leading clothes importer Beltexco, put it to a *New York Times* journalist: 'The buying power of the African is so low that it's the only way people can get clothes.' The ports that once dealt in copper, gold and ivory are now largely given over to this part of the rag trade.

It may be useful to try to imagine how we would cope without being able to convert our fashion waste into *mivumba* and *salaula*. Without these convenient dumping grounds, we would very probably be wading through old clothes. British landfills would be overflowing with trainers and trenchcoats (it's bad enough as it is), and charity shops would be even more cluttered than they are now. If you support fast fashion, this trade in your discarded clothes to the Developing World has given you something of a lifeline: an immediate solution to your need for wardrobe space to accommodate the oncoming season. And better still, it has charitable overtones, offering no-strings, fast-fashion redemption. What more could you ask for? Ostensibly, it's where Mother Teresa meets Trinny and Susannah.

SHOP AND TOSS: THE EFFECTS

In any case, who knew that our old clothes are literally destined for Timbuktu? We don't exactly ask many questions when clearing out our wardrobes. Every now and then the consumer dictated to by fast fashion tackles her wardrobe with the assiduity normally reserved for the fridge. But instead of tipping out milk that's past its sell-by date and emptying out the salad drawer, it's clothes that are on the way out as we engage in a desperate bid to stay in control of our ever-increasing wardrobes. During these 'chuck out your chintz' moments we are fixated on clarity, space and order. Our primary goal is to be rid of the sartorial clutter that's crowding our vision of next season. Call this cycle 'shop and toss' or 'consume and chuck', there is no shortage of snappy cultural slogans to describe our fashion detox programme. But what we need to do is ask the question, 'What happens next?'

Increased consumption inevitably means an increased discarding of clothes. Oddly, it seems that nobody ever stopped to think about this as fast fashion was taking off like a jet plane. It has been left to the charity shops to deal with the resultant mayhem.

GOODWILL OR CONVENIENCE?

A while ago I took to lurking in the basements of some charity shops that still did their own preliminary textile sorting, in an effort to find out the extent of dumping. It was also a valuable instruction in what is and isn't of use for charities (it's not always immediately obvious). At first I have to say I found this rather exciting. For anybody who likes clothes, the prospect of tipping out a bag of someone else's garments is filled with possibility. I was, after all, hanging out in the West End, in Oxfam's Drury Lane shop. I knew from a reliable source that Madonna, in those days Mrs Guy Ritchie, used to have some of her cast-offs dropped off here. What might I find? A conical bra? A Galliano coat? In truth I was half hoping there'd be a shop policy that you could put aside the best finds for personal purchase, in a case of finders keepers (there wasn't). More to the point, there was no bag from Madonna while I was there, just a relentless stream of very low-grade, tired clothes – slightly discoloured fabrics (often victims of the wrong wash setting), trousers with broken zippers, droopy jogging pants.

I was unimpressed, but my disappointment quickly gave way to fury. 'What is that?' I asked Biha, the volunteer who ran the in-store textiles sift, pointing – thankfully with a Biro and not my finger – to a yellow-patterned piece of fabric, 'Oh, that,' she replied, without a hint of emotion, 'that's somebody's dirty underwear'. It dawned on me with creeping revulsion that the general public, the consumer – a demographic, remember, of which I am one – appeared to be quite happy to use a charitable organisation as a dump. There was nothing else in that knicker-tainted bag to write home about: no forgotten Dior ballgown, no First World War nurse's uniform, no Zandra Rhodes that could be sold to a curator and would keep the shop in lighting and rent for a few months. Just some vests, a flowery summer dress, and lots of mouldy jumpers. 'How many pairs of dirty knickers do you sift through a day?' I asked Biha. 'A few,' she said, 'like one in five bags. Some bags really just contain dirty things.'

Research by the Salvation Army – one of the UK's biggest charitable clothes recyclers – first alerted me to the fact that 'donations' can be a rather mixed blessing, even when they don't include dirty knickers. The point is that the charitable clothes recycling industry is predicated on quality rather than quantity. This means there is an obvious mismatch when, as consumers, we insist on prioritising quantity over quality. Our discards obviously reflect what we buy, and there is no doubt in the minds of the recyclers and the charities that quality is declining. The sales value of recycled material has fallen by some 71 per cent in real terms over the last fifteen years. At times it can dip lower than the cost of collecting and sorting donated textiles. This is obviously devastating for charities that are dependent for their income on recycling our old clothes.

In research undertaken by the Salvation Army and other partners, 63 per cent of consumers surveyed agreed that clothing had become lighter in weight over the last three years, and 62 per cent said that the lifetime of clothing had become shorter. They weren't imagining it. Charities will testify that even though on the face of it they should be swamped with excellent, hardly-worn clothes, given that new clothing sales volumes in the UK increased by 60 per cent between 1996 and 2006, they are finding it very difficult to make a good profit from the clothes they get. So, swamped? Yes. But lucrative? No. Basic standards in fabrics, trimmings and manufacturing are all perceived to have declined.

When I ask consumers (as I frequently do) what they do with their 'old' clothes – I use the term 'old' with caution – their answers are upbeat and cheerily green: 'I recycle them,' or 'I donate them to a charity.' We have a tendency to overvalue or talk up the items that we give away: people will remark on how they've given up a 'very good skirt' or a 'top quality piece'. They appear to expect to be walking down the street the following Thursday and to see their skirt or jacket occupying pride of place on the central mannequin in the window of their local charity shop. This is highly unlikely: only around 10 per cent of UK donations, the 'cream', will actually be retailed through the shops (these make up the most valuable donations to the charities). Most are likely to be found somewhere on a 10,000-mile journey. We are back to *salaula*.

THE BUSINESS OF JUMBLE

I am always impressed by clothes recycling plants. Again, there's the anticipation of coming across a really good find, but mainly there's the sense of scale. Up and down the country huge hangars housing conveyor belts and piles of clothes work to transform donations from the public into recycled clothes. Because until they come here, those two things are not at all the same. From Wastesavers in Yorkshire (the plant that sorts predominantly for Oxfam) to LMB (formerly Lawrence M. Barry) in the East End of London, these vast, experienced clothes recyclers sort and grade our cast-offs into hundreds of different permutations, baling waste fibre and selling it to markets all around the world. Charities now devolve all their sorting and selling to these operations. You may think that when you donate clothes they are sold in a charity shop, or sent to somewhere in need – perhaps experiencing a famine or in a war zone – given directly as aid. In reality, your contribution is far less direct. The charity is paid for the textiles by weight or bin, and the reprocessors or recyclers then sell them on for profit. If you aren't a friend of globalisation, and feel more Fairtrade than Free Trade, you should think long and hard before you donate your clothes to a charity. Their journey to the second-hand markets of sub-Saharan Africa is inextricably entwined with the march of globalisation.

The recycling plant has its own rhythm. The whirr of the belts and the trundling of crates full of fresh jumble is methodically punctuated by the noise of shoes seized from the shoe belts and hurled by hand up to the next sorting lane. Most of the recyclers working the belts in the UK are from Eastern Europe. They are very skilled. As I struggle to make out the form of a garment gliding towards me on the belt – it looks a bit like a body-warmer, but its stuffing has come out, and it's tangled up in pyjamas – the women stationed on either side of me are deftly separating pure wool from cashmere blends, self-shade synthetics, school shorts – and throwing them in different bins. One thing is abundantly clear: you could not properly sort these clothes without human elbow grease and a sharp, experienced eye for fibre and cut. The fate of second-hand clothes is decided in an instant by the hand of the recycler.

First grade (which makes up that tiny 10 per cent I mentioned) goes into shops. Any vintage or quirky piece is pulled out. Which leaves the lesser grades – some recyclers (i.e. the good ones) sort into hundreds of different grades. Wool used to be sent to Prato in Tuscany, a town with hundreds of years' experience of recycling wool in its enormous, often family-run operations. There it was turned into fibre for suits or – if it was of a lesser quality – shredded fibre to be sandwiched inside car doors. Today it is more likely to end up in landfill.

Out of 300,000 tonnes of garments collected annually in the UK, only 52 per cent is of a high enough grade to be sold on (10 per cent will be used for car-seat filler or wiping rags for industrial machines). This is down from 60 per cent a few years ago, reinforcing the point made by the Salvation Army researchers above. Around 50 per cent will be graded further and baled into *salaula* or *mivumba*. At this point you can't really describe your second-hands clothes as a pure 'donation'. Consumers in sub-Saharan Africa will pay for *salaula* (although many people have suspicions that it has been donated by the West, and object to paying for it) and the quality of the clothing available to them depends largely on the quality of the sorting. 'There are big charities with really lenient sorting techniques,' says Michelle Goggi, the latest in a long family line to run LMB in East London. She sounds genuinely angry. 'This is how the rubbish is dumped on developing nations. You've got completely inappropriate clothing going to somewhere like Uganda. It's just dumping, pure and simple.' Each item of clothing under her watch is checked seven times before being sorted into one of 160 different categories. Every country has its idiosyncrasies. In this strange waste democracy, labels count for very little, except apparently if an item is from Next, which means it has immediate currency in Poland. A pair of Christian Dior trousers does not impress the sorters much – none of the 160 large pigeonholes is for luxury labels. In fact they will be viewed on the same level as a pair of M&S trousers. Only if they have a crease down the front and a turnup will they be elevated to the 'expensive' *salaula* pile. If jeans aren't flares, then forget about them for Africa. If not exactly toast, they are certainly relegated to insulation. This makes me worry about the onslaught of skinny jeans that is surely coming the way of every recycling centre soon, given their dominance in fashion circles over the last five years. But ultimately I find the quality of the sorting at this centre, and the care taken over the specific fashion decrees of different sub-Saharan states, heartening.

SALAULA CONSUMERS

You would hardly call *salaula* wearers powerful consumers – they are among the poorest people on earth. What other access to clothes do you have if you exist on less than a dollar a day? In Kenya a new man's shirt would cost around eight times as much as a Western import sold as *salaula*.

I watch a German documentary (subtitled, I might add) on clothes recycling. A German recycler has trucked a container load of *salaula* to a town in Cameroon called Mada. Local stallholders, hearing the consignment is in, come to check prices, but are clearly far from happy, considering them to be extortionate. It is late in the day before the film crew finds a woman who is willing to buy a bale of *salaula*. As she's not permitted to open the bales, she checks them from every side to see if she can make out any patterns or anything else that will give her an indication of the quality within. She spots a little bit of gingham fabric in a pinky colour, and decides to plump for this bale. This isn't a small decision. The bale costs as much as it would take to feed her family for a month.

Watching her head to the marketplace and slit open the bale in front of an eager crowd, then anxiously paw through the clothes as they fall out and making a nervous calculation about whether she will make her money back or sustain a loss – which would result in her or her children going without food – made me feel ambivalent about *salaula/mivumba*. Here we have unwanted clothes that have been given away, then sold for a song by a charity, but which could bankrupt a Developing World seller with very little capital. She is totally reliant on the quality of the sorting, and places her trust in a recycling plant thousands of miles away. Not all are as scrupulous or as responsible as LMB.

Under the gaze of the camera, the woman does little to hide her disappointment. There is nothing special in here. 'Put my clothes back,' she says to a young man who has scooped up four garments and is holding them proprietorially. She doesn't believe he is a *bona fide* customer. By the end of the day she's sold two dresses. She scoops up the clothes, which she's put on wire hangers, and leads the film crew back to see her house, her husband (who doesn't have a job) and her four boys. It will take her two weeks to sell off the *salaula* bale she bought today, she hopes. She pitches high at first to traders, including a friend who takes *salaula* to the business district, where office workers like to buy *salaula* but don't like to be seen bidding for it in public. As she gets to the remnants of the bale, prices will plummet. She needs to make her money back to pay for the next one.

Since second-hand clothing began to dominate the African market from the mid-1990s, goods from Britain have been the first choice for the many middlemen and traders who depend on *salaula* and *mivumba*. They tend to be fresher and less worn than their counterparts from North America, which has everything to do with the speed at which clothes enter and leave our wardrobes. But the demise in the quality of British donations has by no means gone unnoticed. Broken zippers, discolouration, flimsy clothes that mark and rip easily, leave the subsistence trader with a bag of worthless tat.

These days there's an extra hurdle for *salaula* traders to overcome. Dubai, arguably the most liberal economic zone in the world, is getting in on the act, opening recycling centres in its vast free-trade warehouses. Using low-paid workers, these facilities can sort more quickly and far more cheaply than UK recycling companies. There is also less scrutiny as to how well sorted the bales are. This increases the risk for the *salaula* trader of spending a month's wages on little more than rubbish.

The second-hand clothes trade has turned the international garment marketplace on its head. You don't have to go very far to find supporters. You don't even have to look outside the UK; after all, the recyclers here would not be able to finance their collecting and sorting without the income it brings them. Meanwhile the trade is sold around the world as a happy match of interests. Take this, from British journalist and apparent *salaula* enthusiast Kevin O'Connor: 'For example, in sport, as they stand at the start line, what is a Ugandan runner likely to be wearing? It will be a hotchpotch of gear. The vest may be Adidas, the shorts Nike, the socks Brooks and the spiked shoes Asics. But every item will have one thing in common – it will have had a previous First World owner, who no longer wanted it and discarded it for something new.' Indeed, it's hard to imagine any First World professional athlete in a pick 'n' mix of sporty hand-me-downs, but there's something quite strange about selling the idea of *mivumba* as a charming tale of ingenuity and opportunity.

In truth, these second-hand consumers are not really consumers; there is no choice involved in their decision. The global trade in second-hand clothing is estimated to be worth more than $1 billion each year. It is big, big business for First World countries. One study showed that 16 per cent of all containers on ships bound for Africa were full of used clothes. It's clear that it is simplistic to see these as 'donations' to a grateful African public. Our cast-offs are all these 'consumers' can afford. Meanwhile, First World consumption patterns dictate that second-hand clothes swamp their territory. While *salaula* and *mivumba* are around there is absolutely no chance of sub-Saharan Africa developing its own textile trade. Academic Karen Transberg Hansen, who has followed the complete cycle of *salaula* in Zimbabwe, notes how older, 'respectable' civil servants there remember buying their first suits from the local clothiers, Sories, who cut cloth and tailored to order, a tradition that has been all but drowned in second-hand clothes. Zambians are ambivalent about what *salaula* does and doesn't bring. Hansen quotes the popular columnist and satirist Jowie Mwiinaga, defending imported second-hand clothes when the government mooted the idea of clamping down on them to encourage a home trade in textiles: 'People are upset because the government is trying to force them to wear brand new clothes … some poorly cut things from, say, Deetex [an indigenous textile industry] … when they are perfectly comfortable with the ones the DAPP sells in its second-hand section. We resigned ourselves to leading our second-rate lives in second-hand things a long time ago.'

Would stopping *salaula* really result in a burgeoning indigenous fashion industry springing up across sub-Saharan Africa? And what right does anybody have to stop an industry for the products of which there is clearly a demand, albeit a rather desperate one? Some economists are very clear on the subject. Professor Garth Frazer from the University of Toronto has written that no country has ever achieved a sustainable per capita national income, of a level associated with a developing economy, without also achieving a clothing manufacturing workforce that employs at least 1 per cent of the population; i.e., in order for a country to develop, it must have an indigenous clothes industry. He makes no bones about it: while *mivumba* and *salaula* continue to dominate African wardrobes, that will not happen. Between 1980 and 2000 the African clothing industry declined (as a share of all manufacturing industries) by an average of more than 5 per cent a year.

Have things gone too far? We live in a time when wearers of 'traditional' African fabrics might not realise that these are more likely to have been printed in the Netherlands than by a local company. In Nigeria, the largest producer of textiles in this region, 80,000 jobs in fabric and sewing were lost over the ten years to 2005. The late Neil Kearney, a tireless campaigner for human rights and fair pay in the garment industry who died in 2009, warned as early as 2003 that *salaula* and its regional variations left indigenous fashion industries 'unable to compete. Local industries are collapsing, leaving hundreds of thousands of workers jobless.'

While Africa produces cotton (at huge environmental and social cost, as we saw in Chapter 7), it reaps little of the profits to be made from clothes – which come largely from the design, the making, the selling. For example, West Africa transforms just a tiny 5 per cent of its production in cotton into clothing, while its markets are invaded by cheap garments from Asia and second-hand clothes from Europe. As the President of Mali, Amandou Toumani Touré, puts it, 'Mali is the biggest cotton producer in sub-Saharan Africa but does not produce a single T-shirt.'

Whichever way you look at it, *mivumba* or *salaula* represents the flip side of our fast-fashion pandemic. It's time for charities to be up-front about how the donations well-meaning people make to them work, and the fact that this is a little more indirect than most people think. Shovelling clothes into a charity bin is not the munificent act we might think it is. The whole process undoubtedly works a lot better when clothes are responsibly sorted and selected by knowledgeable recyclers who treat their customers in the Developing World with respect, as opposed to using them as a dumping ground for a lot of rubbish. Roll on the day when recyclers are audited and answerable for their 'donations'.

CRIMINAL CLOTHING WASTE

Despite the fact that our old clothes lose value so quickly in our own eyes that we're just thankful to be rid of them, there's a war going on under our noses. Thanks to *salaula*, ragging and a flourishing price for old textiles, 'donation crimes' are rising sharply. There are almost 18,500 charity shops and textile banks in the UK, offering a place for us to drop off our old clothes. Most textile banks are operated under licence by the big recyclers, and are branded with the name of a charity. Meanwhile, in a long-standing drive to get us to clear out our closets in a constructive, charitable way, many charities or operators acting on their behalf will deliver bags for you to fill up, which they return to collect, saving you the effort of trundling down to the local clothes bank or charity shop. Sadly, a number of these operators have been found to be entirely bogus, commercially motivated rag traders who contribute nothing to the coffers of charities at all, but who simply copy or 'borrow' a charity's logo.

And don't be surprised to spot clothes banks where the lids have been forcibly removed by scaffolding poles, the backs torn off with a grinder, or that have just been demolished by the cutters normally used by firefighters. Thieves are intent on getting hold of our donations. In some instances children are used to crawl in and grab donated clothes – in the worst cases they've been found trapped inside by passers-by. Charities have spent huge amounts of money trying to secure the bins – SATCOL (the Salvation Army trading company) loses the equivalent of £600,000 per year, and on average forty tonnes of textiles each week is stolen from its banks. No wonder it had to spend £250,000 during 2010 in its attempts to keep their donated contents safe.

Now, I'm not expecting you to police clothes bins yourself until collection, but you can help with door-to-door collections. Bogus collectors are not averse to turning up an hour before the official collectors come round and swiping the bags before the charities get so much as a sniff. So hand over your clothes recycling with care. Make sure that the collectors have an official registration number, and check it with the Charity Commission. Ultimately, if your recycling gets into the wrong hands, you're unwittingly contributing to the chaos of textile dumping on the Developing World – these contractors aren't going to sort, and re-sort, to make sure they're providing genuine *salaula*.

A LOAD OF RUBBISH

With all the clamour and competition for our cast-offs, it is frankly amazing that so many of them end up in the rubbish bin. But they do – some two million tonnes of textiles is shovelled into landfill every year. The lion's share of this will be clothes, and there is no more ignoble end for them. When you consider the man hours and the resources that have gone into them, slinging them into black bags and giving them a one-way ticket to landfill is something approaching a tragedy.

This might seem a bit of an operatic response, but I can't tell you how annoyed I get when I see fragments of cardigan, bits of denim and shoes – I see shoes everywhere – rolling about in vast landfills. We're nothing short of addicted to landfill in the UK: the decline of mining left empty holes dotted around the countryside that once seemed the perfect receptacles for our trash. Since then, thinking has moved on. Landfill is considered less as a convenient way of disposing of our redundant consumer goods and more as a seething pit of toxins, sludge and most importantly emissions. Food, computers, building waste: one by one environmentalists and policy writers have started to address the goods that cause the biggest problems, and to try to divert them from landfill. Clothing has only recently been added to the list. And I'm not the only one haunted by the stray shoes (in particular football boots) I see in landfill dumps: oceanographers can trace currents by the trainers caught in the swirl of the Pacific.

In a familiar refrain, we just didn't realise what a problem it was. Who cared if clothes and shoes weren't given a new lease of life? After all, there were plenty more to fill the void. But at some point around 2005, the authorities began taking a keen interest in our wardrobes, and what was being chucked out of them so frenetically. The Department for Environment, Food and Rural Affairs (DEFRA) launched what it rather dryly called 'The Sustainable Clothing Roadmap', in an attempt to assess and then to minimise the impact our fashion habits were having on the environment. Research into landfill revealed that fashion was a startlingly heavy hitter. The nation's penchant for instant 'McFashion', that resulted in over one and a half million tonnes of unwanted clothing dumped in landfill every year, was found to translate into more than three million tonnes of carbon dioxide emissions. It stands to reason, when you think about it, that as wool, leather or cotton break down they emit methane, a greenhouse gas (the one we're always hearing about) twenty-three times more potent than carbon dioxide.

If you discount slogan T-shirts, fashion and politics do not have a very illustrious or convincing allied history. It's always a little cringey when they get together. But the recognition of this part of fashion's environmental footprint suddenly brought politicians to London Fashion Week, giving us the odd spectacle of the then Minister for Sustainability poised awkwardly behind a Philippe Starck Perspex plinth on a catwalk, announcing a plan to minimise fashion's waste.

My favourite foray by politicians into the national wardrobe was a report on waste by Lord Howie of Troon and the Earl of Northesk, both members of the House of Lords' Science and Technology Committee. Their analysis of the fashion industry read at times like a deconstruction of the woodland defecation procedures of bears: '[The] culture of "fast fashion" encourages consumers to dispose of clothes which have only been worn a few times in favour of new, cheap garments which themselves will also go out of fashion and be discarded within a matter of months,' announced the venerable Lords, in tones of shock and awe. I would suggest that they may have less up-to-date wardrobes than the population at large.

BONFIRE OF THE VANITIES

If consumers haven't managed to delink fashion from waste in anywhere near a convincing way, designers carry even more of the blame. After all, it begins during the design process, where waste is effectively designed into the manufacture. On average 15 per cent of fabric is discarded during the cutting process. I realised this when I came across a young designer, Mark Liu, a graduate of the London College of Fashion, who advocates Zero Waste design, cleverly designing and cutting patterns so that no fabric ends up on the sewing-room floor. His system casts a light on the rest of the industry that is far from flattering. Every design house is a lesson in profligate waste: the proof is to be found in the wheelie bins outside their back doors, which are bursting with chiffon petticoats, denim and leather offcuts.

And because no buyer, however organised and slavishly devoted to just-in-time ordering, can avoid hiccups, delays, missed sales opportunities and wrongly dispatched orders, overstocking (surplus stock that just will not shift, however big the 'sale' tag) is rife. In major exporting countries like Bangladesh, and huge transitional free-trade zones like Dubai, there are warehouses full of unloved overstock, just waiting for a sales opportunity. This is less of an option in the more hallowed and protected arena of luxury goods, where brand and reputation is all. Put simply, a luxury or high-end designer brand would rather its mistakes from overproduction and off-trend design simply didn't exist. Discounting must be carefully controlled in order to preserve the brand's expensive integrity. After all, who wants 'it' bags and tailored dresses ending up as *salaula*? There is only one way to 'disappear' mistaken merchandise effectively and thoroughly, and that's burning it. In a distasteful bonfire of the vanities, luxury houses frequently incinerate overstock.

Once in the shops, the waste carousel doesn't stop. Just before Christmas in 2009 Cynthia Magnus, a student at the City University of New York, was walking along 34th Street in Manhattan minding her own business when she came across twenty garbage bags that had been thrown out of a large branch of Swedish retailer H&M. As a thrift-conscious and creatively minded student, when she thought she saw clothing seeping out of one of the bags, she went over to take a closer look. Like many of us, I would imagine, she baulked at the idea of new clothes being chucked out. What she found left her speechless: every bag was stuffed full of new garments and shoes. She described the contents to the *New York Times*: 'warm socks, cute patent leather Mary Jane school shoes – maybe for fourth graders … men's jackets'. She noted that the bags of clothes were just metres away from where homeless people were curling up in shop doorways for the night. But despite the fact that the air was bitter and the bags contained warm clothes, nobody had helped themselves. Each item had been deliberately damaged: the gloves had had their fingers cut off, the jackets had been slashed across the body and the arms with a knife until the 'puffy fibre fill was coming out in big white cotton balls'. Even the insteps of the Mary Jane school shoes had been cut up with scissors to prevent resale. There was no doubt in Magnus's mind that the clothes had been deliberately damaged by the store in a clumsy attempt to protect sales and that ever important entity, 'the brand'.

Magnus said she had previously found trash bags full of T-shirts and trousers dumped on 35th Street by a Walmart contractor. This time 'each piece of clothing had holes punched through it by a machine'. The *New York Times* claimed that unworn clothing was being destroyed 'nightly' by big-name retailers. The story of the callous slinging out of fashion waste metres from the homeless spread like wildfire among consumer groups. In Britain the Radio 4 programme *You and Yours* discovered a branch of Millets that was slashing and binning jackets and sleeping bags. Predictably, retailers responded with vehement denials that this was their policy. The issue of damaged overstock (over-ordered or unsold merchandise), they said, was left to the discretion of store managers. 'We are currently looking into if we can further improve our routines', H&M told just-style.com. 'Going forward, we are re-evaluating what we categorise as damaged garments and we continue to be committed to donating as many of these items as possible to our aid organisation partners.' Walmart told the *New York Times* that it ordinarily donated 'its unworn goods to charities, and would have to investigate why the items found on 35th Street were discarded'.

Going forward, we should probably all re-evaluate the blind eye we've turned to fashion waste. Although the H&M story made the headlines and brought consumers face to face with overstock and waste, they are endemic at every stage of the fashion process, and are found all over the world. Take the 'Blue River' in Lesotho that was described in Chapter 6. Alongside waters running bright blue with chemical dyes, investigative reporters found child rag-pickers deep among thousands of Gap and Levi's labels, buttons and studs, alongside mountains of 'heavily dyed cotton and denim'. In this region dumped denim and other garment refuse from unsecured garment tips has replaced traditional charcoal as cooking fuel. It is certainly more abundant.

The backdrop to this is our own compulsive buying and throwing – something I'm going to crudely characterise as style bulimia. It has been estimated by Oxfam and Yougov that an amazing 2.4 billion pieces of clothing unworn for an entire twelve months (many of them possibly never worn) are squirrelled away in the national wardrobe. This adds up to £10 billion-worth of fashion. It is conceivable that if we were to release this stockpile we would have enough fabric to keep the nation comfortably dressed for a decade. Waste authorities are understandably worried that all these clothes will eventually find their way into the overburdened recycling services (more *salaula*), or worse still, that they will go into the bin. DEFRA has warned that 'Textiles are the fastest-growing sector in terms of household waste.'

So let's not pretend that anybody has a grip on fashion waste. I'm going to charitably describe the current system of 'recycling' via donations as imperfect. The point of recycling is that it should be a closed loop. You purchase a product that will have a useful life after you've finished with it, pass it on, and to close the loop you buy another recycled or refashioned product. All the evidence suggests that you and I need to get into that loop as quickly as possible.

THE PERFECT WARDROBE

Consumers the world over are dismayed and fed up with a fashion industry with links to enslavement, oppression and a cycle of waste and pollution. I know, because I am constantly asked, 'How can I buy differently?' We're a wandering tribe of fashion lovers in search of a wardrobe that will nurture our aesthetics *and* our ethics. After all, how sexy and glamorous does a dress feel when you can only wear it accompanied by a nagging feeling that it might well have perpetuated forced labour and slave wages? Frankly, we deserve better.

And so I've arrived at the point where I officially revoke the fashion industry's get-out-of-jail-free card.

Instead of a wardrobe full of clothes of dubious long-term appeal and uncertain provenance, the antidote will be more fulfilling, more considered, trans-seasonal rather than trend-led, and ultimately full of pieces that reflect our own environmental and social justice values. Finally, pieces will have the potential to be reimagined. This will be everything the average current wardrobe is not. Let's call it the Perfect Wardrobe.

Of course, technically, the Perfect Wardrobe does not exist – all clothes will still have an impact and some type of footprint; none are entirely without blame. But it's a useful shorthand for the new consumerist paradigm we need to imagine and work towards.

I'm not talking overnight change. Chucking out your existing wardrobe and starting afresh would obviously take us right back into the waste nightmare we came across in the previous chapter. Besides, who has the money to start again? Rather, you need to invest some time and energy in thinking about ameliorating the full cost of your existing clothes, and assessing how any new additions will look – and not just in terms of their cut and colour.

Anything you buy new from now on needs to be subjected to greater scrutiny and a keener eye for ethical credentials and possibilities. While a piece might not be perfect in sustainable terms, it must have a level of ethical integrity that you are comfortable with. There are huge benefits to be gained from this simple strategy alone. Compare the way we currently and slavishly pander to high-street fashion with the way the conscientious consumer navigates grocery shopping. The process of filling your trolley with an eye to ecological credentials, provenance and fairness can verge on the forensic. Why is it that we know perfectly well how to buy a Fairtrade banana (in fact two supermarkets, Waitrose and Sainsburys, no longer stock any other type), but not how to buy a pair of sustainable tights? Suddenly the way we buy fashion looks rather primitive.

But every industry has to begin somewhere. Pioneers in organic food remember attending exhibitions for the embryonic wholefood move-ment in the 1970s at which enraptured delegates stood around admiring a loaf of wholemeal bread on a plinth. From this unpromising start, interest in and acceptance of ethical food has soared, and now huge numbers of people 'get' concepts such as traceability and shorter supply chains, expressed through slogans such as 'From field to fork' and 'From plough to plate'. The idea of 'From plough to pants' or 'From test tube to trousers' doesn't yet have a whole lot of traction in the wardrobe. But it does in the Perfect Wardrobe.

12

HIGH-STREET THRILLS AND SPILLS

Matching Your Aesthetics to Your Ethics: Does Big Fashion Deserve Hanger Space in the Perfect Wardrobe?

An air of trepidation exists around the subject of consuming fashion differently. We are all afraid that any awakening will render the high street out of bounds, and few of us can conceive of a wardrobe that works without our patronising the fast-fashion model we're so addicted to. Friends become anxious that I'm going to injunct their clothes collections, fencing off their closets with police tape while forbidding them from setting foot in a high-street store or wearing a recognisable label ever again. But I understand as well as anybody that going cold turkey from mainstream fashion is improbable and impractical for most of us.

Yes, it is pretty difficult to envisage British fashion without the high street. The official definition of the UK fashion industry used to refer only to the designers and the manufacturers who were based here. Today it has been extended to include our coterie of retailers, many of whom eclipse designers in terms of public recognition. How could the term not be stretched to include them? Overall the British fashion industry brings £21 billion a year to the economy, and the retailers are a giant part of this. In fact, fashion retail is responsible for nearly a quarter of all of British retail's contribution to the national GDP. At the risk of stating the bleeding obvious, this means our retailers are not just huge sellers, but are extremely powerful. They are unlikely to disappear from the fashion landscape any time soon, or to be pushed into reform very easily (as any group campaigning for a better fashion industry will tell you). What you must decide is whether or not you want the UK high street to be part of your Perfect Wardrobe, and if you do want it there, how you might chivvy it towards reform.

With your new determination to buy better, how much leeway will you give the high street? How much will you believe its claims to be a work in progress, that brands and retailers are committed to change, and ultimately to doing the right thing for people and planet? The answers to some of these questions will come down to personal tolerance, and some will be based on how much you can learn about a company and how open it is in any direct engagement. But one thing is for sure: even if you're not able to sever the cord with the high street completely, there's no need to be a slavishly devoted pushover.

SEARCHING FOR ITS ETHICAL MOJO: THE UK HIGH STREET

If I had £1 for every time I've been asked some version of the question, 'So which shops can I go into?' I'd have enough money to buy up every 'green', 'eco', 'Fairtrade' or 'planet friendly!' range offered by UK retailers – and there have been quite a few, because the high street has flirted with eco reform. At times it has even appeared to find its ethical groove.

At times, in fact, it's been difficult to navigate your way around a store because of all the sustainable initiatives purporting to 'give something back to the earth', and usually taking a form that could generously be described as very light-green indeed. For every shirtdress or pyjama top you bought, you could almost guarantee that a donation would be made on your behalf to save a dolphin or a tiger cub, or that a tree would be planted as your personal contribution to 'fighting climate change'. Or you'd be given a free jute tote to help you 'save the planet' by avoiding all future need for plastic bags.

There was a certain amount of relief on my part when the big retailers and brands began to dip their toe in sustainable style waters. Suddenly my friends could look me in the eye. 'It's organic and Fairtrade!' they'd say, thrusting a little piece made by ethical label People Tree to be retailed in Topshop under my nose. Or, 'This came with its own sewing kit, so I can keep mending it forever!' (Oasis vintage-look collection). Or, 'I got this Fairtrade in the supermarket' (as M&S, Sainsburys and Tesco competed to place the biggest orders for Fairtrade cotton).

There were some stellar moments, and even a Stella moment. In November 2005 Stella McCartney produced another in the line of H&M's celebrity designer hookups (cue the usual queues round the block and sharp-elbowed scrums, as this collaboration sold out so quickly it even broke H&M's Lagerfeld record). Stella for H&M was pronounced a triumph in the fashion press, and not only did the twelve pieces actually look as if they'd been designed by her rather than merely brushed by the celebrity design wand, they were reputed to be in line with McCartney's deeply held ethical values. Reputedly she made the incorporation of organic cotton a condition of the collaboration. In the final event, only one piece – a T-shirt – was actually made from organic fibre.

That may not seem a very significant point, but a big-name designer insisting on organic cotton in such a mainstream collection set a precedent for the company, and arguably for the high street at large. It also showed that we (i.e. the consumer) had come some way since the early 1990s, when the C&A chain tried to introduce organic cotton into its stores. Proving that every innovation has its time, on that occasion the consumer didn't get it. Apparently we were confused by the 'organic' labelling on clothes, because we associated 'organic' with food, and it was obvious that T-shirts, socks and pants were not edible. I like to think we're a little more sophisticated these days. Because this time the idea did take off.

Even the fashion press got on board. Each time a high-street chain produced so much as a pair of organic cotton socks it received a huge amount of praise and publicity for going 'ethical', which only encouraged them. In 2007 a major consumer survey found that one in four women described herself as an 'ethical shopper' when it came to clothes. The doyenne of the ethical fashion movement, Katharine Hamnett, stunned greenies everywhere when she threw in her lot with Tesco (their long-standing nemesis) to produce a range of T-shirts and jeans with overt eco slogans, made of cotton from the organic supply chain she had spent a decade researching. Meanwhile, Topshop threw down the ethical fashion gauntlet to its rival New Look, with each trying to outdo the other on the numbers of lines in organic cotton. After a two-year self-imposed exile from Topshop I returned to the flagship store in Oxford Circus to track down a summer dress made by a woman's cooperative in Ghana from fabric printed locally and sold during Fairtrade Fortnight. Incidentally, I still wear it.

But perhaps there were already hints that Big Fashion was more interested in applying a sort of green gloss than in a revolution that would reinvent the whole system, turning it into a beautiful, sustainable butterfly.

Remember *that* bag, the one that stole the ethical show in 2007? 'I am not a plastic bag', the super-eco cotton tote announced to the world. Fashioned by handbag designer to the A-list Anya Hindmarch, it was available for £5 for a brief moment at Sainsburys supermarkets in April 2007 (20,000 sold out within one hour). I was as smitten as everyone else. Unfortunately, when I got to the checkout to collect my eco tote, the assistant put it in a plastic bag – suggesting that the message wasn't necessarily getting through. It was subsequently claimed that the eco bag had been manufactured using exploitative cheap labour in China, and the cotton was neither Fairtrade nor organic. 'We never claimed this bag is perfect. We have just tried to use our influence as a maker of luxury goods to make it fashionable not to use plastic bags,' a spokesperson for Anya Hindmarch responded, adding that the company had made no secret of the fact that the bag was made in China. However, I think this episode provides a good lesson about considering the authenticity of fashion pieces surrounded by green hype. As a consumer it's important to question not just the message or the fibre, but the rest of the supply chain. How far does this 'initiative' go? Is it the real deal?

By February 2008 I was aware that commentators were becoming a little wary of environmentally-friendly launches. An H&M summer dress made many of the 'lookout for summer' style pages. It ticked the boxes – pretty, apparently eco (thanks to its organic cotton content) and easily available. 'If this dress were designed differently and made from cotton that had been dyed in different (environmentally friendly) colours, and carried an organic and perhaps a Fairtrade certification, then we would have been excited,' wrote green expert Rikke Bruntse-Dahl. 'The prospect of regular H&M customers buying this dress instead of a non-organic, non-Fairtrade dress is definitely a good thing. Unfortunately H&M has only scratched the surface by acknowledging that clothes can in fact be made from organic cotton.'

The ethical fashion revolution the high street had promised over eighteen heady months ultimately evaporated. Symbolically, the partnership between Katharine Hamnett and Tesco came crashing down to earth when Hamnett terminated the deal in September 2007. 'I was initially really excited about the tie-up because I thought we could increase demand for ethical products,' she told fashion trade magazine *Drapers*. 'But I've come to the conclusion that [Tesco] simply wants to appear ethical, rather than make a full commitment to the range.' Naturally, Tesco rejected this charge that its heart was not really in the 'Choose Love' project. 'She is wrong to question our commitment,' a spokesperson said. But ultimately the love was lost.

GREEN SHOOTS

This was not the end of Big Fashion's foray into ethical waters. We live in an era in which corporations appear to be rethinking their purpose and their strategies. Authors and experts on corporate sustainability Jeffrey Hollender and Bill Breen dubbed this 'the responsibility revolution' in their excellent book of the same name. They chart how the big players have rejected the famous maxim of Nobel Prize-winning economist Milton Friedman, some thirty years ago, that 'The only social responsibility of business is to increase its [shareholder] profits.' Instead, corporations are now heaping large helpings of environmental responsibility onto their plates. More intriguingly still, they are competing with each other to see who can come up with the most spectacular ways of proving that it is the corporation that cares most, that has the most enlightened philosophy. More often than not, the brands and retailers leading this responsibility revolution just happen to be those famous names that fill the globe's wardrobe. Could this be the moment when fast fashion becomes ecologically intelligent?

See as evidence the global Eco Index. This initiative, which brings together two hundred of the world's clothing brands and retailers –

among them the really big ones, including Timberland, Target, Nike and Levi Strauss – has come up with a complex series of tools to analyse the products sold by each company through six life-cycle stages: materials, packaging, product manufacturing and assembly, transport and distribution, use and service, and end of life. True, this type of analysis has been done before in other industries (especially in the food sector), as well as in studies where scientists have worked out all the impacts and emissions associated with an individual garment – we saw some of these studies back in Chapter 6, notably one in which the life-cycle impact of a polyester sportswear top was compared to that of a cotton one – as it travels through its wardrobe life. But it's the scale of the Eco Index that has got people talking, and the fact that the project is 'open source'.

In theory, this is the first time we've seen behemoth retailers and brands sharing this type of information. In theory, all of the information about best practice will be available to other design teams, and all the horrible, wasteful, un-eco practices will one day be designed out. In theory, we'll be able to compare brand with brand, tell which pair of trainers or jeans is the greenest, and pick the one with the lowest emissions and the smallest impact on its inanimate conscience. In theory. At least one commentator has observed that collating all this information from all the different parties, and getting them to agree to tell the consumer who is the best, will be a task akin to 'herding cats'.

But it could happen. And if it did, we'd be able to buy green clothes with a provable low impact from the shelves of a globalised supermarket. But the question is, would we want to? Would their greenness be a good enough reason to give them hanger room in the Perfect Wardrobe?

Some people live for trainers. They keep them unworn in their boxes ('box fresh'), know when the latest new launch from Nike or Adidas is coming out, and queue for days for first editions. I am not one of those people, but I do know that Friday, 25 January 2008 was the day the Nike Air Jordan XX3 was given to a grateful public. I know this because the twenty-third incarnation of the basketball shoe named after Michael Jordan was arguably the greenest trainer the planet had ever seen.

A while before the Air Jordan XX3 was delivered to mankind with all the pomp and circumstance previously reserved for the coronation of the Holy Roman Emperor, Nike had begun to make a serious attempt to tackle its environmental footprint. As always, the best place to start is at the beginning – in this case by defining what that eco footprint was. Well, Nike found that its was extremely large: its massive operation amounted to a supply-chain carbon footprint of 1.36 million tonnes. To give some idea of how large that is, in the same year, 2008, Intel and Sony, both global electronics firms, checked in with footprints of one million and 2.7 million tonnes respectively. Who knew trainers had such biosphere-trashing footprints?

The Air Jordan XX3 was the first card-carrying member of Nike's Green Index sustainability programme. In short, it had undergone the fearsomely complex process of having its every component and each element of its production analysed so the designers could be sure they had made the most ecologically considered choice of rubber, leather, polyester, foam and other materials, and that the production process used the smallest amount of energy and produced the smallest amount of waste and emissions. The waste part is particularly important. Fashion's emissions tend to punch well above the level you might imagine, and the waste in fashion at the design process is also astonishing (we had a glimpse of this in Chapter 11). In 2006 a Nike study discovered that the company spent some $800 million a year on material that never made it into shoes or apparel. Put starkly, over 40 per cent of everything it produced was waste. And all of those wasted materials cost the planet in terms of oil, cotton, chemicals, water and emissions.

Nike isn't stopping at one shoe. Far from it. Having developed varying levels of considered sustainability – from bronze to gold – it has stated that by spring 2011 (around now, if you're reading this book soon after publication) 100 per cent of its footwear will meet at least the bronze standard. It could mean green trainers for all.

And in your new green trainers you need only jog down to Marks & Spencer for some more eco-purchasing opportunities. (It's difficult to overestimate the significance of M&S in the national psyche. When current-affairs broadcaster Jeremy Paxman complained about a design change in his M&S underwear of choice, it made headlines.) M&S has stated an intention to be 'the world's most sustainable major retailer by 2015', and in 2007 it unveiled one hundred social and environmental targets. Naturally, this was no ordinary corporate social responsibility

(CSR) report: it was an M&S corporate social responsibility report. It was called 'Plan A', the subtext being that because we're running out of time to stave off climate change and protect resources, there can be no Plan B. Under Plan A, M&S began to grapple with the often unseen impacts of its product lines, using five categories: climate change, waste, raw materials, fair trade and people. And so the UK's largest clothing retailer (by volume) became the UK's largest retailer of Fairtrade cotton, took a stance on mulesing (see Chapter 9), joined up with Oxfam to encourage consumers to return five million garments for recycling rather than having them end up as landfill, and helped suppliers to set up ten Ethical Model Factories to produce part of its clothing lines.

In April 2008 M&S's Executive Chairman Sir Stuart Rose flew to Sri Lanka to open the world's first 'green' garment factory. The Brandix plant, an eco-retrofitted thirty-year-old factory, now boasted low-energy air conditioning, reduced waste and rainwater recycling. A sister plant producing underwear basked in the virtuousness of its grass roofs and giant solar panels. Even the workers were wearing green, just to reinforce the message.

Initiatives like this are like honey to the bee for the *carbonista fashionista*, the fashion and planet fan who is very much attuned to the spectre of ever-increasing carbon dioxide emissions and to minimising her own personal contribution by investing in products that are low carbon, carbon neutral or even zero carbon. If this is your main focus in your search for the Perfect Wardrobe, you're in luck. New products are arriving on the high street in droves. Taking responsibility for your personal impact is a laudable aim, and is very important, but in my opinion it is too narrow a focus.

As we've seen, a number of extremely influential brands and retailers are very much into greening up and cutting emissions, and make excellent stomping grounds for the new *carbonista*. They're looking all over their supply line for chances to slash emissions. As has been mentioned, many retailers are very proud of their prowess in logistics, and the current vogue is to be a leader in making those logistics super-efficient. (Given that the average garment racks up more passport stamps than a foreign correspondent zigzagging across the globe, often by air freight, there's huge scope for greening this particular part of the fashion chain.)

However, no *carbonista* will want to spend too much time doing extensive carbon calculations, and there are so many variables. You need to know a little of everything: whether the cotton was grown using pesticide (high emissions), whether the cutting machine was powered by biogas (lower emissions than oil), whether the end product was air freighted or shipped ... the list goes on and on. So the *carbonista* wants this information distilled into a handy label, and frankly, who can blame her?

STAMPS OF APPROVAL

I happen to think that we all need more information on our fashion labels. Currently, the average clothing label must take all of two seconds to deconstruct. With the exception of the fibre content (legally mandatory since the 1980s) and some washing instructions, there is rarely much to go by. Retailers are under no legal obligation, for example, to include a garment's country of origin (at the time of writing there's a move afoot in the EU to change this). But what would that mean in any case, given that perhaps eighty people will have been involved in the production of a jumper, thirty-four in a pair of leather shoes and ninety in the production and distribution of a man-made-fibre suit during the 101 stages needed to produce it? These workers could be scattered across the planet: the fibre originating in Africa, being spun in India, assembled in Sri Lanka; the zip coming from China ...

There are all sorts of risks associated with the taciturn, secretive labels we currently have to put up with. To take just one example: incredibly, there is at the time of writing no legal requirement to label fur as real and to name the species. The fur industry points to a voluntary code which it claims its members largely adhere to. But really, is this enough? It's entirely possible that some British consumers are marching around in winter coats and gilets with fur trimmings that they assume are fake but that are in fact real (not least because the economics of the jumbled global closet can make real fur the least expensive option). In the USA a similar situation used to exist, as labelling laws specified that only garments costing over $150 needed to be upfront about whether they were real fur or not. This loophole has since been sewn up by the Obama administration, and all fur sold in the US must now be labelled as such under the Truth in Fur Labeling Act. Where's our legislation?

Ideally, I'd like labels on all clothes that unfurl like a historical scroll to acknowledge that the piece has been on a substantial journey, taking into account the origin of raw materials, ginning, printing and dyeing, finishing, the cut-make-trim actual sewing (CMT), the journey of the zippers, buttons and fasteners, the place where they were attached, the final pressing, the packaging, the trip to the port (or airport), the unpacking at the destination docks, the by-road trip to the centralised distribution centre and the final rush to get it in store. I'd like to know what chemicals have been used in its lifespan and whether they were regulated; and above all I'd like to know that the many hands who brought me this garment had received a fair proportion of the profits, at least a living wage, and for the Environmental Damage Units we saw in Chapter 6 to be printed on the base of swing tickets, along with a carbon footprint. But for now I must be placated by the smattering of green labels that have begun to appear at the discretion of brands.

At least US-based apparel and footwear giant Timberland is making an attempt to satiate my gnawing hunger for information. The labels it has attached to its thirty million (100 per cent recycled post-consumer waste fibre) shoeboxes a year are actually termed Nutritional Labels, as they are modelled on the information required by law on food describing its nutritional content. Timberland has decided to apply some of this to its shoes and boots. A grid on the outside of the box shows the energy used to produce the item, the company's purchase of renewable energy (Timberland boasts that its Californian distribution centre has one of the fifty largest solar panel systems on the planet), the number of hours served by Timberland employees in community service (which I admit is a bit schmaltzy), the percentage of the company's factories assessed against a code of conduct (helpfully expressed as 100 per cent), and the amount of child labour employed in making the product, which is 0 per cent, as you might hope. It also tells you where the shoes or boots were manufactured. And the brand goes one better on its Earthkeepers range, using a Green Index to assess climate impact, phasing out of harmful chemicals and measuring material use.

But some commentators are less than convinced by the Nutritional Label, not least because until the Eco Index comes to fruition and other brands also declare their ecological footprint, we have little to use by way of comparison. We are not at the stage, for example, when I can say which of Adidas, Timberland or Nike is the greenest. 'A laudable first effort – in theory, at least,' says sustainability professional Joel Makower of Timberland's innovations. 'In real life, it's not very helpful. Simply put: there's less going on here than meets the eye.' He adds that the label left him 'feeling hungry'.

Would I allow a pair of Earthkeepers into my Perfect Wardrobe? Yes, I probably would. At this stage in the evolution of green/eco labels they have enough green appeal to get an invite. Let's face it, retailers are testing the concept on us, to see if eco-labels impact on our buying decisions. I'd give them a signal here that I'm a fan.

Now that I've started looking for them, green initiatives appear to be breeding like rabbits. I'm seeing them everywhere. And apparently they don't even need to involve the actual product, but what it arrives in. Puma have got rid of the shoebox altogether, replacing it with a 'clever little bag' designed by super-designer Yves Béhar (known for designing 'some of the new millennium's most coveted objects'). Were I to buy a pair of Nike trainers, I could reduce the amount of cardboard compared to a standard box by 65 per cent. There's no laminated printing or tissue paper! Their shape means they are compact and bijou in shipping and transportation! More of these can be shipped at one time, cutting down on shipments, cutting down on emissions! Does this swing it? Not for me. More style than substance.

Doubtless you will have noticed that all of these initiatives are rather one-note. They are eco rather than ethical (which takes a more holistic view of the supply chain, incorporating social justice). The social justice element is almost entirely missing (with the exception of Marks & Spencer's Plan A, with its Fairtrade cotton obligations and an agreement to ensure a living wage for workers), or at best squished down the list. I don't want to look a gift horse in the mouth. After all, a green piece of fashion is better by and large than a non-green version. And there's no doubt that many of these brands are in a position to research and develop ideas about ecologically intelligent and low-impact clothes faster and more effectively than any other part of the fashion stream. If you have a vacancy in your Perfect Wardrobe for, say, a pair of outdoor boots with a tiny footprint, then you are in luck. But I wouldn't entirely fill my closet with green initiatives, however dynamic the labels.

For starters, the manufacturers may not be entirely altruistic. There is a degree of what we might politely call 'enlightened self-interest' at work here. The fashion sector urgently needs to get its house in order, and the big names aren't stupid. Raw-material costs are rising, and they want to shore up their production bases. To keep millions of sewing machines whirring and cotton separating belts running requires electricity. Generators in the Developing World are costly to run and unpredictable. Frequent shutdowns play havoc with just-in-time order-ing. In this context 'green' factories, using solar panels or focusing on cutting out waste, look less like altruism and more like good business sense. Similarly, reducing waste reduces cost. A win on both counts, maybe, but an initiative that serves the needs of Big Fashion.

It's also a truism that for Big Fashion 'eco' is a far easier prospect than 'ethical'. But easy wins aren't what the quest for a Perfect Wardrobe is about.

FASHION FIXERS

To a great extent our quest throughout this book has been to put the people back into fashion. Ultimately, this is one of the things you want to achieve in your Perfect Wardrobe. Back in Chapter 4, where I was busy being rude about the audit trails behind the majority of fast-fashion retailers, I promised to reveal who in Big Fashion terms offered the most authentic audit trails, and had showed the most progress. The results might be a little unexpected, and not altogether welcome, particularly if you're a seasoned follower of anti-sweatshop campaigning who remem-bers when the two brands in question were regarded as being akin to the personal couturiers of Beelzebub.

Because the best social reports and systems belong to Nike and Gap. Admittedly, it has been a long process, involving much trial and error – after all, these companies have some of the most sprawling, complex supply chains in fashion history. Nike's global supply chain, for instance, numbers 800,000 workers across fifty-two countries. Gap appears to have tackled the problem in stages: in 1992 it developed sourcing guidelines for its suppliers; in 1996 it established a Code of Conduct; and in 2004 it attempted to fling open the gates of transparency by publishing information on most of its factories.

Nike too now publishes a list that it claims lists every factory it uses. Both companies have realised what others have not (or are not willing to pay for): that inspections need to be conducted before an order is placed, not afterwards, when the retailer has established that this is the cheapest company on planet earth (this is known as pre-screening); that they must be unannounced – there is little point in announcing weeks in advance that an inspection will take place; that they need to be carried out by trained inspectors who know what they are looking for; and that there needs to be a confidential and anonymous reporting line for workers. These are the qualities of an audit that stands a chance of working. By all accounts (Nike's work in this area has been enthusiastically examined by academics), Nike and its large CSR team spent a long time trying to unravel supply chain problems, and it wasn't until the company recognised a vital point that it really achieved a breakthrough: it's not just about shifting codes of conducts onto suppliers, it's also about responsibly placing orders so that factories have a fighting chance of completing them. As we've seen time and time again in these pages, minute changes from designers in head office faxed to factories, and scrambles by buyers to pick up on new trends by placing large last-minute orders, lead inevitably to supply-chain disaster.

You might think I've lost my mind, and that by praising the green and social initiatives of these two massive corporations I'm suggesting that the search for the Perfect Wardrobe need extend no further than a trip to Nike Town. Absolutely not. Even these systems are imperfect. However much effort goes into creating an audit trail and system, Big Fashion will always be fighting against itself: it is predicated on a business model that is too vast and too sprawling for the exercise of proper control. So even while a brand is receiving compliments from the industry on its CSR reporting, that same brand could end up in the newspapers, at the heart of a sweated labour scandal, in flagrant violation of its own codes of conduct.

Nike's annual revenue is around $19.5 billion. This might raise the legitimate question as to why it isn't investing even more of its extraordinary wealth in creating a just and equitable supply chain, but that's a matter for you. What is clear is that most other high-street brands cannot compete. They cannot afford the CSR staff, the auditors, the green technologists and the materials scientists. This brings me to the point that when dealing with the smaller high-street brands, the ones that have a few hundred shops across the UK, you shouldn't expect to find ethical badges and marketing campaigns. Sometimes you will have to judge the brand on face value, by its values.

But these brands can be important to the remaining diversity of the high street, and what they lack in global influence they make up for in understanding that 'ethical' applied to fashion isn't just a trend, but a movement that they aspire to be part of. This leads me back to Whistles. We met Jane Shepherdson, the head of the label, in Chapter 2. 'We're not for one minute putting ourselves up as paragons,' she says. 'We really just want to find a way that is acceptable for us. As people in the industry we want to work with suppliers that we personally find acceptable. Our values are living wage for garment workers, as opposed to minimum wage, and we support freedom of association. We aim to get that throughout our supply chain. Then we would be happy.'

Meanwhile Ted Baker, the British retail men and womenswear brand, is trying to formalise its progression towards an ethical supply chain, signing up to the MADE-BY scheme. I think this is a very good thing. You know a garment is certified by this scheme because it wears a distinctive blue button that tells you that the brand (thirty-six are certified at the time of writing) produces its clothes in a 'people- and environment-friendly manner'. In its own words, MADE-BY is 'an umbrella label used by fashion brands to indicate their clothes are okay'. That may sound a little lacking in ambition, but it's a straightforward, pragmatic and honest label that doesn't pretend that everything is perfect. Instead it tells us that we're at the start of a journey, that brands affiliated to MADE-BY cannot guarantee yet that their collections are 100 per cent clean and socially responsible, but they are working towards it, and 'ensure that the door to the production process is wide open'. A track-and-trace system allows you to see where and by whom a garment was manufactured at certain parts of the fashion trail (one day they hope you'll be able to uncover its entire history). In a sense, you are your own auditor.

I first came across this blue button when I was shopping in a sadly now-defunct boutique in Camden Town. I was looking for a summer dress, and I noticed that while it didn't describe itself as ethical, this store had a smattering of 'ethical brands', and had mixed in some organic-fibre pieces. The blue button lets ethical products stand out without needing to be in a designated ethical store, bringing an end to the idea of shoving all the 'good' pieces together in some kind of granola ghetto. I also like the duality of this certification system, the fact that it doesn't rely on purely green criteria.

For the occasions when you do need to be your own auditor, keep an eye out for another label that is about social justice rather than 'green': Fair Wear. It's worth taking a look around the Fair Wear Foundation website. The organisation describes itself as an 'international verification initiative', and is partly founded by the Dutch arm of the Clean Clothes Campaign, the charity campaigning for a better fashion industry. 'There is no single solution for workplace injustice. There are many,' it stresses, and I notice that the FWF is very upfront about problems with brands – one had failed to acknowledge it was using home-workers – and the targets set for correcting issues. There is, however, one problem. I find some very nice small, niche brands signed up to Fair Wear – Nudie Jeans and Odd Molly, which are now sold in some UK independents and in online boutiques – but none of our major high-street friends.

FROM SLACKTIVISM TO ACTIVISM

In the absence of labelling or any other overt information, you'll need to find out as much as you can yourself. Don't be intimidated by the idea of researching before you buy. Not only will it slow down the pace of your clothes buying, it gives you a chance to check out the company's stated commitments and to form an overview of whether it's a brand that has any business in your wardrobe. Be alert to meaningless greenwash. You are looking for strong policies, transparency, openness and a willingness to engage in debate with us, the consumers and wearers.

Typically, a shopper in pursuit of the ethical truth about a fashion brand will be directed to the Ethical Trading Initiative (ETI), which we met back in Chapter 4. This is an alliance of companies, trade unions and voluntary organisations, partly funded by members, which include many of the high street's biggest names. The ETI does not regulate brands or provide a badge to say that a company is clean, rather it works with those that acknowledge that their supply chains could be improved. Any steps a company takes to clean itself up are voluntary. You'll more than likely hear about the ETI in the aftermath of a giant exposé. For example, in November 2010 an investigation by the *Dispatches* documentary strand on Channel 4 found sweatshop conditions in garment production units in Leicester which were producing for BHS, Jane Norman, New Look, Peacocks and C&A. All these brands except Jane Norman were members of the ETI, and therefore signatories of its Base Code, which expressly forbids the conditions revealed by an undercover reporter: these included slave wages of £2.50 an hour and conditions she described as cramped and dangerous, including a fire exit that was apparently locked.

At times like these the ETI is caught between a rock and a hard place, at once needing to admonish the errant member and encourage it to tidy up the mess, and at the same time needing to defend it. On such occasions the ETI can sound like the harangued parent of a troublesome teenager: 'Our Core Business Practices Programme, of which New Look is an active member, is exploring how companies can ease the pressure on suppliers and help them plan their production better, so reducing the incentive to sub-contract. Many are already reporting progress in developing closer relationships with their suppliers that are based on trust and open communication,' read a release issued by the ETI office in the wake of the allegations against one of its members. 'We do not yet have all the answers. But we are committed to working with our members at the cutting edge of ethical trade, to find solutions that will better the lives of the people who make our clothes – whether they are in Bangladesh, Leicester, or anywhere else.'

The ETI's approach might generously be described as measured. Some campaigners are not quite so generous, suggesting that the organisation is too pro big retail to be particularly effective. Certainly it appears uncertain what a company would have to do to get thrown out of or suspended from the ETI. Take Primark, for example. When, as we saw in Chapter 3, it was found employing illegal immigrants on just slightly more than half the minimum wage through a subcontractor in the UK, many people assumed that Primark would be chucked out of the ETI. But the sanctions didn't stretch that far. Primark was asked to remove all of its ETI branding in-store and online for a while, but it stayed in the fold. The ETI reasoned that by working with rather than against the company it could effect real change, and reports remarkable progress since the 'dole-cheat couture' scandal. This stance only confirmed some campaigners in their opinion that the ETI is about as efficacious as a chocolate teapot. (In the wake of the Primark débâcle the ETI has insisted that it has tightened up, and that within the first two years of membership brands must make 'demonstrable progress' in implementing the Base Code, while if existing members are found to be in breach of the code they can be relegated to Foundation status. The ETI has also tightened up its disciplinary procedures so that a company against which allegations have been made can immediately be suspended while an inquiry takes place.)

Part of consuming fashion with your eyes open involves supporting the organisations that keep labour rights abuses on the radar. I would strongly suggest that as a wannabe ethical consumer of fashion you support War on Want (www.waronwant.org), Labour Behind the Label (www.labourbehind the label.org) and No Sweat (nosweat.org.uk), and for an international viewpoint of the global fashion industry and networked campaigns, the Clean Clothes Campaign (www.cleanclothes. org) – we've already met these organisations before. At the very least their websites provide a rich source of information and updates on which retailers need to be leant on. To paraphrase the marketing campaign of a famous lager, the campaigns constructed by these NGOs – sometimes working together, as in the recent case of War on Want, the Clean Clothes Campaign and Labour Behind the Label's joint report 'Taking Liberties: The Story Behind the UK High Street' – can reach the parts others cannot reach.

Labour Behind the Label's 'Let's Clean up Fashion' reports are another useful resource, and I can't recommend them highly enough (downloads are available online). Between 2006 and 2010 LBL produced four of these reports, the last profiling twenty-six major high-street stores and brands, comparing and cross-referencing them to give them an achievement score from 0 to 5. LBL judges respondents (some companies refuse to engage in any discussion, and are duly named and shamed at the beginning of the report) against its commitment to the principle of a Good Living Wage. Freedom of association (where workers are permitted to discuss workplace issues and to get together to bargain collectively with employers, which is particularly useful if, as is so often the case, individuals are subject to intimidation and violence and have no witnesses) is also a central tenet.

LBL has been campaigning for a reasonable living wage (i.e. one that a garment worker could reasonably be expected to live on, as distinct from the 'local minimum wage' or 'national minimum wage', typically set at a level at which he or she would struggle to obtain enough calories to function) since 2006. Since these initial campaigns, the idea of a liveable wage has been refined. You will now see the phrase 'Asia Floor Wage' instead. Rather than waiting for retailers to come to a consensus on what constitutes a living wage (there was a great deal of foot-dragging and disagreement), the Asia Floor Wage is based on the World Bank's Purchasing Power Parity. It is used to work out the wage for a legal working week that allows workers to purchase the same amount of goods and services in their local currency that a US consumer can buy for $475.

In theory this should be a clearer proposition for our high-street friends, but don't expect revolution any time soon. Even the better scorers on Labour Behind the Label's questionnaire have the gall to suggest that they could or would increase wages if only the workers would 'increase productivity'. Yes, our big retailers have the audacity to suggest that if they could iron out the problems in the factories in Cambodia, Bangladesh, Thailand et al., and get the employees in them working a little more efficiently, they would then begin to talk turkey about wage increases. This is a shocking position. For one thing, as we saw from the experiment with Northumbria University students back in Chapter 3, the global assembly line is already running at full pelt. Secondly, this stance reveals the naked truth: that some of our high-street retailers do not appear to believe that a living wage is a human right, despite the fact that it is stipulated under international human rights conventions.

'Let's be clear,' is Labour Behind the Label's unequivocal response, 'wages in the garment industry are not low because of poor productivity. They are low because the structure of the industry creates intense competition between brands and retailers, governments, employers and workers. They are low because governments are failing to protect the poorest members of society through the implementation of labour law. They are low because workers have been prevented from organising and making these demands. These are the root causes of poverty wages and these are the issues that need to be addressed by all concerned with the implementation of a living wage.'

Only when you've built up a full picture of a company, including its stance on Living or Asia Floor Wage, and married it with your own values, should you consider buying a garment. It's about threading together the evidence you have with that from campaign groups to create a picture of what a brand or retailer really represents, and where its priorities lie.

I devote a bit of time to considering whether a new pair of jeans will be allowed in my wardrobe. Levi's, an early nemesis of labour-rights protesters, stresses that it has done a huge amount of work on its CSR, particularly in environmental issues. There is impressive stuff going on here. In 2009 the venerable denim brand reduced its carbon emissions by seven hundred million tonnes, just by changing its transportation routes. It introduced an eco label, 'A Care Tag for Our Planet', that read: 'Wash cold, air dry and donate to Goodwill', linking up with US charity (Goodwill) shops to recycle old jeans. Levi's appeared to be willing to take a moral stance even if it meant abandoning the trend for jeans given an aged look via sandblasting. In September 2010 the company announced 'It's time to ban sandblasting,' reasoning that although 'we've put in place some of the strictest standards and monitoring programs in the industry to ensure that workers who produce our jeans are not subjected to the risks related to silica ... we recognise that there are factories ... that do not apply these same safeguards. And because they don't rigorously enforce proper health and safety standards for sandblasting, they put unsuspecting workers at risk.' At the time of writing Levi's is promising to apply its Water-Less technique, which cuts down on water use in the production cycle (the average pair of jeans undergoes between three and ten washes), to 1.5 million pairs of jeans, saving sixteen million litres of water.

All this sounds highly laudable. But according to Labour Behind the Label's 2009 'Let's Clean up Fashion' report, there is little point in my holding out for Levi's to implement a living wage in its supply chain, as the company has chosen not to respond to questioning on the subject. Thus it scores a big fat zero in the report. Levi Strauss & Co. 'does not accept the principle of a living wage or does not accept responsibility for ensuring that living wages are paid'. I double check with Michael Kobori, the Vice President of Levi Supply Chain Social and Environmental Sustainability, just in case the position of the iconic jeans brand has softened. It hasn't. 'That is not a line of enquiry we're pursuing.' Why is that, I wonder. 'That is not a line of enquiry we're pursuing,' he repeats. Oh, well. Therefore, despite Levi's big ticks for its eco credentials, it is not a brand I will be pursuing (in the sense of letting it into my wardrobe). You may of course feel differently.

THE TALE OF SUKI SEQUIN SHOULDER DRESS REF 923R

If something is unsettling or doesn't stack up, or if information is just missing, then feel free to email the brand and ask directly. It may help you to make a decision. You can also ask in-store, although in my experience you'll get few knowledgeable answers. In an industry where you'd be forgiven for thinking garments arrive on rails via osmosis, you can't expect harried shop staff on a Saturday afternoon to know the provenance of the zipper in a dress you're considering.

Reiss is described by *Time Out* as the 'mid-range label of choice among the discerning *fashionista*', and it has its sights set on the fast-fashion market, reducing its lead times for trend-led items from three months to six weeks. 'Two years ago, I gave my staff a brief to sex up the business, and now the brief is to bring excitement to it too,' said the company's owner and founder David Reiss. Shopping in a Reiss store one day, I pick out a lovely long-sleeved jumper dress. At £120, this piece cannot afford to be a temporary fashion fix. I need it to tick all the boxes of a piece in my Perfect Wardrobe that will stand up to ethical scrutiny and have style longevity. I question the charming assistant as to its provenance, and whether the delicate smattering of sequins is hand-sewn or was put on by machine. 'Oh, they'll be applied by machine,' he says confidently. 'But wouldn't they crinkle? And how would a machine do that?' Hmm, now neither of us is sure. We fail to find any clues on the labels. So the helpful assistant can get on with his job, I jot down the garment reference – 'Suki sequin shoulder dress ref 923r' – and say I'll email head office.

A couple of days later I do just that. I ask of Suki sequin shoulder dress ref 923r:

> Where was it made? Are the sequins hand sewn and if so, by who? Do you pay a living wage and are you a member of the ETI? I'm writing to you because nobody in the store in Covent Garden knew. They did however say a lot of stuff is made in Turkey, but there wasn't any clue on the label. Thanks so much for providing some more information. Best wishes.

A month or so later (see what I mean about slowing down the pace of buying when you approach high-street shopping this way) I receive a reply from Helena, the head of PR.

> Dear Lucy,
>
> Firstly, apologies for the delay in getting in touch. Your enquiry was re-directed to me & I in turn have been liaising with our production team.
>
> In response to your enquiries, please find the answers below:
>
> Where was it made?
>
> The garment was made in China as per the care label. [*Whoops – a label the assistant and I failed to spot*]
>
> Are the sequins hand sewn and if so, by who?
>
> The sequins are hand stitched on to the dress. The manufacturer who made this order confirmed the hand stitching of the sequins was done by a 3rd party who specialise in this type of work.

Do you pay a living wage and are you a member of the ETI?

We are not a member of the ETI, but do visit our manufacturers regularly.

With regards to minimum wage, the manufacturer has confirmed that they exceed the minimum outlined by the Chinese Labour Law (paying salary and workers' insurance). The manufacturer's working conditions meet the guidelines as specified by their government & they are audited annually by their government to ensure they meet the country's requirements. The manufacturer has also confirmed that the 3rd party contractors' wage and working conditions meet the guidelines as specified by their government.

I hope this is helpful.

This was helpful, but I wanted still more clarification. Who, for example, was the anonymous '3rd party', the specialist hand-stitcher. Was it perhaps a home-worker? Again, Helena obligingly responded:

The 3rd party contractor is another facility (not home-worker) and as mentioned on my previous email, like our manufacturer, they are audited annually by their government and the wage and working conditions meet the guidelines as specified by their government.

An annual government audit, a still-mysterious third-party contractor and a wage specified by the government (which as we've seen again and again might not even mean that a grossly inadequate minimum wage was adhered to) made me decide that the Suki shoulder dress ref 923r, however pretty, was not deserving of a spot in my Perfect Wardrobe, and that I should deploy my £120 elsewhere.

After five or six years of toying with ethical fashion, the high street has the capacity to intrigue, very occasionally to delight, but more often than not to disappoint. It could do so much better. In many ways we're still in the early days, gazing at that plinth with the loaf of wholemeal bread on top like those pioneers in the food industry. While we've looked at the best ways to scour the high street for fashion that merits inclusion in the Perfect Wardrobe, and while it's possible to use our knowledge to cherrypick the best, ethical fashion utopia doesn't lie here.

For more than just a light-green makeover you'll need to expand your horizons.

The reason is that there remains at least one stubborn problem with fast fashion. However much it claims that it's trying to do the right thing, and is showing initiative to address its social and environmental footprint, the fact is that the whole structure is built on selling a massive number of units. Stores are getting bigger, and so are their warehouses. We should and can have affordable fashion, and of course we want clothes that are not merely functional but that exhibit design skills and vision. But Big Fashion's aim is to continue to deal with these issues in its own particular way: fast and cheap. And that is an unsustainable combination.

The aim of the high street is to get us to buy stuff, and the unspoken purpose of that stuff is to give us a quick fashion hit, but for it not to hang around for too long. The high street needs us to replace it with a new version as soon as possible. In short, if you're waiting for fast fashion alone to lead to your Perfect Wardrobe, you'll be waiting a long while.

CHANGE YOUR KNICKER DRAWER, SAVE THE WORLD?

Adding Ethical Backbone and Value Through
Wise Fibre Buying

Fibre matters. This is not just because you want to be able to predict how it will wash and which setting the iron should go on, but because the material your clothes are made from accounts for a large proportion of their back story, and therefore their social and environmental footprint. Nowhere does this matter more, in the case of cotton, than in the communities that grow it, whose destiny is entwined with the harvest. But the global cotton trade doesn't really want you to think about that. As we've seen, cotton is traded in global markets as a faceless commodity, without history. That's not to say the industry doesn't have designs on your wardrobe: Big Cotton wants you to increase your spend on conventional cotton, buying more and more every year, stuffing your drawers, cupboards and laundry baskets full of the stuff. It would also prefer if you didn't ask too many questions about its provenance.

Because I'm not very good at obeying such consumerist diktats, I did keep asking questions. For a long time the story of the Uzbek cotton fields and the forced picking haunted me. How could I be sure that my wardrobe wasn't harbouring apparel made from Uzbek cotton, and picked by a conscripted army of children who should have been at school? In 2007 I decided to ask a group of representatives from major retailers, assembled on a makeshift platform at a meeting on making the fashion industry more sustainable, what they were doing. 'Why haven't you taken a stand against Uzbek cotton and refused to allow it in your supply chains?' I squeaked nervously. Then I asked what assurances they could give that Uzbek cotton was not in their garments. Cue withering looks from all of the panellists, apart from the representative of one major retailer who assured me that they would walk away from any deal in which it became obvious cotton was from Uzbekistan. The others (Chatham House rules means I can't divulge who said what) more or less told me to 'get real'. To paraphrase, I was told by the representative of a major supermarket that cotton is sold internationally, and they couldn't waste time working out where it came from – that wasn't how the system worked. Furthermore, it was suggested that it wasn't an important issue. I seethed in silence, and vowed to keep asking.

Actually, I didn't have to. Because by summer 2008 the links between child-picked Uzbek cotton and major high-street names were all too clear to the British public, thanks to a BBC *Newsnight* report that linked Plexus Cotton (a Liverpool company trading in raw cotton, which also incidentally trades in Fairtrade-certified cotton), Uzbek raw cotton and the UK high street. When *Newsnight* told Plexus that child labour was widespread and state-enforced in Uzbekistan, the company responded: 'Plexus Cotton currently sources only a tiny fraction of its total cotton trade through Uzbekistan. We have been categorically assured by the Uzbekistan government that the use of child labour by the Uzbekistan government is prohibited.' The Environmental Justice Foundation (EJF) points out that everybody has been given similar assurances by the Uzbekistan government, but unfortunately they continue to be contradicted by eyewitness accounts on the ground. Then *Newsnight* contacted ready-made-garment manufacturers in Bangladesh. They confirmed that they were using Uzbek-derived cotton, and that it 'may have been used in making clothes sold by [Asda's clothing brand] George'.

But there was to be a more uplifting postscript. Whereas just a few weeks earlier retailers had deemed it impossible (and irrelevant) to act on this issue, now they couldn't revoke their involvement with Uzbek cotton quickly enough. Tesco and Asda implemented track-and-trace monitoring systems for their cotton supply chains, while Walmart joined a boycott of Uzbek cotton. One by one they fell (in a good way). In all, forty international retailers agreed to block Uzbek cotton from their supply chains. As you would imagine, this caused a major hoo-ha, not least in Bangladesh, where ready-made-garment factories with big orders from UK retailers are dependent on cheap Uzbek cotton to get those low, low margins we have become so familiar with. 'If we cannot import from Uzbekistan we have to spend at least six cents more for each pound of cotton to import from US sources, which ultimately will add up to 20 per cent cost for finishing products,' one Bangladeshi manufacturer complained to the Reuters news agency.

The EJF considers that Tesco and Asda's implementation of track-and-trace monitoring systems has proved to be effective. But overall, might this be a pyrrhic victory? According to the Bangladeshi manufacturer who spoke to Reuters, his only option was to buy 'clean' cotton from the US. Just how clean is this cotton? As we have seen, the American cotton industry shuts out African suppliers through a system that involves the trousering of billions of dollars of subsidies.

More directly, we need to ask, if everyone has stopped using Uzbek cotton, then who on earth is still buying it? Before we all start patting ourselves on the back for a problem solved, we had better remember that Uzbekistan remains the planet's third-largest exporter of cotton. Three-quarters of its output goes to China and Bangladesh for ready-made garments. I believe a substantial amount still gets into the average British sock drawer.

You can of course put your trust in the big retailers and hope that they've clawed back control of the supply chain sufficiently to shut out abuses, but equally you can spread your cotton spend. By 'cotton spend' I particularly mean the money that goes on basics – nightwear, simple T-shirts, socks and knickers – the stuff that makes up your underwear drawer. These are not necessarily fashion-forward pieces, although we have been persuaded to consume them as if they were, at an ever-increasing speed of consumption. My strategy is to pay a little more for better quality, and to keep these pieces longer. But above all, I'm giving conventional cotton the elbow in favour of cotton that represents ecological and social opportunity, as opposed to disaster. Cotton, for all its foibles, is not going to disappear overnight like a sock in the washing machine, and there is the pressing fact that globally millions of people depend on it for their livelihoods. Your responsibility in the Perfect

Wardrobe is to buy better cotton. Thankfully, all cotton is not created, or rather grown, equally.

ORGANIC

We've seen how organic cotton has become something of a high-street cliché: note how the top twelve brand and retail organic consumers for 2009 included Nike, Walmart, H&M and Levi's. But although this may make it seem as if the world and his wife are swanning about in his-and-hers organic T-shirts, they aren't. For all the hype, organic cotton still only makes up less than 1 per cent of global cotton. That's a shame, because compared to conventional cotton it has many benefits. The organic production system revolves around maintaining and increasing soil fertility (there are real worries globally that soil fertility is declining). It also reduces the toxicity burden of cotton by forbidding the use of toxic and persistent pesticides and synthetic fertilisers. Instead of monocultures and the use of agrichemicals, organic farmers practise more traditional farming methods such as crop rotation, which fixes nitrogen in the soils. Katharine Hamnett has pioneered the use of organic cotton in the UK supply chain, and is unequivocal about its benefits compared to conventional cotton. 'It delivers a 50 per cent increase in income,' she has said, 'by cutting the cost of inputs by 40 per cent and allowing farmers to access the 20 per cent premium certified organic. It enables farmers to feed and educate their children, dig wells and afford healthcare. It makes agriculture viable.' Hamnett flags up another important part of the ethical jigsaw. As we've already noted in these pages, the cotton price has recently soared, leading some retailers to warn that the days of ultra-cheap clothing have gone. But you would not have to be a cynic to suspect that even if Big Fashion puts its prices up, it is highly unlikely that any of this extra money will reach the cotton growers in the Developing World, who are at the end of a very long chain. The system simply doesn't work that way. So I choose one where a better farmgate price does get to that producer, and that includes some transitional cotton schemes, and cotton that is certified organic, and sports a Fairtrade badge.

As a consumer, it is pretty easy to get hold of organic cotton. There are credible certification standards with labels that are easily recognisable. In fact, of the hundred-plus standards and symbols that can be applied to garments, over half of them must relate to cotton. One of the most common in the UK is the Soil Association symbol, often described as the Rolls-Royce of organic symbols on account of its exacting criteria, and the fact that it includes more rules and regulations than comparable certification schemes. Although perhaps more often associated with artisanally produced cheese, it has been giving its stamp of approval to textiles since 2003. Cotton is represented more than any other material, with 170,000 farmers across twenty-two countries now producing Soil Association cotton. It also has extra criteria: for example, under the SA organic cotton standard you cannot clear primary ecosystems just to grow cotton. But the really notable thing about the Soil Association is that unlike most organic certification schemes, where only the fibre is certified, it can guarantee that the whole production process, including printing, has been carried out in an ecologically benign way that doesn't damage the product's organic credentials.

BETTER COTTON

For any farmer to convert to organic is a long process. We know how susceptible cotton is to pests and disease: remove the pesticides and the farmer needs to employ other methods to keep the pests at bay (perhaps using black ants, or a natural deterrent such as neem). This requires a period of changeover during which pesticides are phased out. Rome wasn't built in a day, and organic cotton fields do not happen overnight – it takes three years for traces of pesticides to disappear from the ground, during which the farmer is not able to access an organic premium. A number of schemes try to ameliorate this. Instead of being left in limbo or forced to sell reduced yields of cotton for the same price as conventional cotton, farmers planning to go organic and working towards that happy day can sell as 'transitional' or 'pre-organic' and attract a premium price. In 2008 Walmart committed to purchasing more than twelve million pounds of transitional cotton, while pre-organic was being championed by Japanese multinational ITOCHU through the Raj Eco Farms in

India. If you see transitional or pre-organic cotton in stores, I would go for it, with the proviso that you've checked that the brand in question has paid a premium. Without the premium prices, you are essentially just buying cotton.

Similarly, other brands are part of the Better Cotton Initiative, which had its first harvests in 2010 in West Africa, Asia and Brazil. Rather than opting for organic or Fairtrade niches, it does pretty much what it says on the tin, and tries to take the sting out of cotton by focusing on low-input techniques for growing, which mainly involves reduced pesticide use. Meanwhile, Cotton Made in Africa is an initiative between German business groups with an interest in cotton (notably the giant OTTO clothing group) and local textile producers in Benin and Burkina Faso which aims to disseminate better knowledge among growers and to scale down pesticide use.

FRANKENPANTS

For many campaigners, one of the most important qualities of certified organic cotton is that it provides a bulwark against the creep of GMOs (genetically modified organisms). It should also be said that there's a school of thought that sees GM cotton as a solution rather than a problem. For its enthusiasts, GM or transgenic fibre represents a silver bullet. It requires less pesticide to be used and promises higher crop yields, which its supporters say is perfect for conditions in places such as Africa and India.

Certainly when GM came calling it found some enthusiastic adopters, particularly in India, where farmers had been driven to distraction by the threat of bollworm ('Bt cotton', engineered by the US agrochemical giant Monsanto, is claimed to control three cotton pests, including bollworm, without needing pesticides) and to desperation by the expense of shelling out for pesticides. And of course there was also the promise of higher yields. So in March 2002 India became the sixteenth nation on the planet to approve a GM crop for commercialisation, rather than just to approve GM crops for trials. Over 80 per cent of India's cotton is now thought to be transgenic. India is not the only country to have been seduced by GM cotton's promises. At the time of writing fifteen million hectares, 43 per cent of the global cotton land, is under GM cotton. Until India got a taste for Bt cotton, China was planting it faster than any nation on earth. So, you may hate the idea of Frankenpants, but it's very likely that at some point this week you'll be wearing them.

Organic lovers will be horrified to think that up to 50 per cent of their cotton clothes are from GM cotton. My main worry is that it's not the godsend these desperate farmers might think.

Studies in India have shown that even in GM cotton fields that showed yields of 60–90 per cent more than their non-GM cousins, gross income per hectare was still low. 'It is easy,' say Ron Herring of Cornell University, 'to imagine a farmer with a medium plot of cotton making less than US$1.50 a day even with the high-yielding and more profitable Bt hybrids. As holding sizes are small [particularly when you compare them to China], and yields low, fluctuations in yield are less tolerable to Indian cotton farmers.' Nobody seems able to agree whether Bt cotton has exacerbated the appalling problem of debt suicide in Indian cotton farmers that we saw earlier. While a Monsanto-sponsored study concluded that Bt cotton reduces farmer dependency on pesticides, others suggest it is no coincidence that the first debt suicides linked to cotton appeared around 1998, when India was tinkering with Bt cotton and five hundred farmers took their own lives. The next year it was six hundred. Suicides do seem to have increased with the march of transgenic crops, but this period has also coincided with the deflation in global cotton prices. A number of experts have come to the conclusion that GM cotton doesn't work as well in India, where small producers have devoted their lives and land to producing cheap cotton, as in the vast monocultures of China. But is anybody going to tell this to the millions of impoverished cotton farmers in India who find the odds increasingly stacked against them? Has the silver bullet been misfired?

FAIR COTTON

Cotton garments in the Perfect Wardrobe need to have less ambiguity, which is why I try to purchase cotton that is not only organic, but also

Fairtrade. It wasn't until 2007, when on the eve of the UK's fourteenth Fairtrade Fortnight I found myself sitting under a huge tree at a village meeting in Djidian, in Mali, that it occurred to me that not all cotton systems were the same, and that there was something I could do as a consumer. I had travelled to meet these farmers to find out how cultivating cotton under the Fairtrade system was working out for them. The men had one big complaint: 'You allow women to grow cotton,' said Mr Keita, one of the older villagers. 'They grow cotton fine, but now they are allowed to talk at the meetings, and they do it all the time.' Mr Keita was clearly aggrieved by this, which represented a massive (and by his reckoning insupportable) departure from tradition. But equality is a non-negotiable part of the Fairtrade agreement. Any villager, male or female, can grow the cotton, and have their say at meetings.

I was taken on a tour of the grain houses that the villagers bought with the first premium they received from Fairtrade sales of their cotton. A grain store may seem a prosaic thing to spend this new income on – later on I saw the local school where subsequent premiums had gone, which was much more the sort of photogenic project I'd expected – but it's also vital. When the cotton price crashed in 2001 the villagers had been forced to sell off their grain supply to US prospectors, as they had nowhere to keep it, only to have to buy it back in instalments at vastly inflated prices. While products made from Fairtrade cotton have become increasingly likely to be featured on fashion pages, the projects the premium funds are often not headline-grabbers. But the premium keeps coming as long as Western retailers and consumers keep interested.

You'll know a T-shirt or pair of knickers is made from Fairtrade cotton because you'll recognise the Fairtrade mark. In fact you'll probably recognise it from other commodities, as it appears on everything from coffee and bananas to footballs. Standards for cotton emerged in 2005, when the Fairtrade Foundation began certifying a small amount of African cotton as a way of supporting Benin, Burkina Faso, Chad and Mali – 'the Cotton 4', which we met in Chapter 7 – after the cotton price had fallen through the floor and they were effectively left destitute. This had to be painstakingly negotiated with producers and government agencies that own state-controlled cotton-processing facilities in West Africa, and the standard was ten years in the making. The Fairtrade stamp only covers seed cotton (before ginning), and is concerned with ensuring that producers receive a fair reward for their work.

Admittedly there are some shortcomings. This label is focused on the fibre. A Fairtrade-marked T-shirt must be made with at least 50 per cent Fairtrade-certified materials (so it can be mixed in with Lycra or equivalent for stretch garments), but 100 per cent of the cotton used in the garment MUST be Fairtrade. But even if you see the familiar Fairtrade logo on the label of a T-shirt or dress, you don't know anything about the dye house, spinning mill or factory that produced it. (There is a social compliance assessment contained in the compact for Fairtrade covering the processing and manufacturing, but it is pretty basic.)

Nevertheless, I returned from Mali committed to Fairtrade cotton, convinced that by converting my knicker drawer I could have some effect. But the fashion industry is fickle. After the initial buzz when retailers, including supermarkets, competed to see who could place the biggest orders for Fairtrade cotton, the novelty appeared to wear off. It wasn't long before I began to see T-shirts wearing the Fairtrade tag at £3, hanging limply on the reject rail.

Having met the farmers who were depending on the continued appeal of Fairtrade, I regarded this as more than just a shame. It made my blood boil. It may sound hypersensitive to get upset about the price of Fairtrade garments being reduced – after all, the premium and the price have already been set and committed to by the retailer. But when I saw this happen, I knew the writing was on the wall. Fairtrade lives or dies by the consumer understanding the way the premium works, and that this quality product has a social dividend. The minute cheap-as-chips pricing destroys that, the whole thing loses its credibility. Sure enough, the big retailers stopped squabbling about who had placed the biggest orders. Perhaps the T-shirts in question, in what can only be described as a dull salmon-pink, weren't fashionable enough in colour or cut, but why make Fairtrade cotton a fashion-led product? In 2009 and 2010 bales of Fairtrade cotton remained sitting on the dock of the bay in West Africa despite an apparent impending global cotton shortage. Cotton was in short supply, but only, it seemed, if it was without the Fairtrade premium.

Fairtrade cotton is not just for Christmas, or for the odd T-shirt when 'giving something back' happens to be in vogue. It works best when supplies are consistent and orders are regular, so that farmers can be guaranteed a sustainable income. In 2010, five years on from the launch of Fairtrade standards for cotton, the Fairtrade Foundation began to reposition it not as an adjunct to fast fashion, but as a quality product. We would be well advised to buy on quality. Cotton expert and label owner Abigail Petit, who works with Agrocel producers in India producing for organic and Fairtrade labels, makes the point that 'A quality cotton garment will contain 500–600g of cotton compared with just 50g for a low-quality T-shirt, where the rest of the fibre is bulked out by chemical dyes and finishes. It is worth paying for quality. You get more cotton for your money, and a product designed to last more than a couple of washes.' Perhaps we should start weighing our clothes before we buy them. But in the Perfect Wardrobe it's about allying a product's quality to its environmental and social justice credentials. In short, paying more for stuff that hasn't trampled over communities and the environment, and keeping it longer. Even the most basic fibres deserve some respect.

MORAL FIBRE

You may also hanker after a more revolutionary approach to fibre, one that breaks the hegemony of cotton and synthetics. A good way to begin this revolution in your wardrobe is to throw open its doors to alternative eco fibres, from peace silk, hemp denim and nettle knits to reclaimed tree bark and custom-commissioned textiles using local techniques and ancient hand-loom skills. Then there are the 'novel' fibres from waste products, some of which sound faintly unhinged: crab shell, salmon skin and even milk fibre. The point is that the profile of these materials should always be provably ecologically balanced and superior to conventional alternatives. Their journey from raw fibre or renewable feedstock to end fabric should use less water and chemicals, and be responsible for fewer emissions and pollutants.

These fibres need more credentials than looking a bit floaty and claiming to be natural. Natural fibres come from a plant or animal source, and in the context of the Perfect Wardrobe they offer some advantages:

they are eventually 100 per cent biodegradable (i.e. in the right context – which does not necessarily include UK landfill – they will rot away after a number of years); they are 'breathable', which is always a bonus with clothing; and they have low-energy requirements during the growing phase. For example, it's been calculated that a tonne of jute fibre needs just 10 per cent of the energy used for the same amount of a synthetic fibre. This makes sense, because jute is mainly cultivated by small-scale farmers, and the main energy input is their labour rather than fossil-fuel-based pesticides.

In the case of many natural fibres (though not all), the raw material comes from the land, and you therefore do not need a laboratory, a patent and millions of dollars in research to cultivate it. Just as responsibly-grown cotton can have a transformative effect on the communities that produce it, other natural fibres can have a very positive impact on the livelihoods of the millions of people who depend on its cultivation and processing. They should be a real boon for the small-scale farmer. Estimates suggest this there are four million small-scale jute farmers in Bangladesh and India, a million silk-industry workers in China, and 120,000 alpaca-herding families in the Andes.

Beware, however, of catch-all terms such as 'natural' or 'eco', un-supported by any coherent story or third-party certification (we can all self-proclaim). Bamboo fabric represents the most cautionary tale of passive acceptance. When it began to appear more regularly in clothing around 2008, it was billed as 'greener than Greenpeace' (to borrow from Jonathan Franzen), and planet eco went nuts for it. It was renewable; apparently carbon neutral thanks to its amazing root structure; fast-growing, so that once harvested a new crop would spring up in next to no time; naturally antibacterial – and so the list went on. It was also everywhere, even making it onto the high street. Unfortunately, too many of us bought in just because we thought it sounded eco. My four pairs of bamboo tights, pair of sleeping shorts, gym leggings, vest top and five pairs of socks are testament to this. But far from the sustainable fibre that was going to oust cotton, what we ended up with was a fibre of uncertain provenance. While bamboo fabric could have originated from a bamboo plant, under the microscope (a proper full-sized one, not my child's version) there was often no evidence that any bamboo cellulose was still in the fibre. It had generally been processed through wet spinning into something that was pretty much indistinguishable from rayon, aka viscose, which also starts out as plant cellulose. You may remember from Chapter 6 that the manufacture of viscose requires an army of toxic chemicals. The view of regulators in the USA and Canada, which between them ordered the relabelling of some 450,000 clothing and textile products from 'bamboo' to the less eco-enticing 'rayon', was that consumers had been stitched up.

However, while I'm annoyed, I don't wish to fling the baby out with the bathwater. Bamboo does have some plus points. It absorbs a large amount of carbon on growth, and it doesn't need to be reseeded, thanks to its root system, which means it could be perfect for communities that need to diversify their cash crop. And it can be processed without recourse to toxic chemicals, if it is pulped mechanically into a linen. This however is an expensive process, and not one conducive to knocking out inexpensive fodder for the global knicker drawer. The truth is that you are really only going to find authentically eco bamboo in higher-end products, which generally come with a higher-end price tag. But, as ever, price shouldn't be your only marker. Contenders for a place in your wardrobe also need to be labelled, in the case of bamboo with an ISO14001 certificate (not the sexiest-sounding certification, this confirms the environmental controls of industrial processes, and should be visible on a brand or retailer's website). And it should have an extra label, usually Skal or Oeko Tex. Attached to clothes, the Skal label actually reads 'EKO', and has developed standards for all natural fibres, including bamboo, linen and hemp. It guarantees that the raw fibre has been produced 'sustainably', and not from some giant mono-culture employing agrichemicals. There are farm visits, social and crop examinations and tissue examinations back at the laboratory.

In my version of the Perfect Wardrobe there's also (limited) room for a subset: regenerated natural fibres. This will have the purists throwing their hands up in horror, as it involves some chemical processing and therefore waste and emissions, although these are heavily controlled by Lenzing, the giant European fibre manufacturer that owns and produces them. Tencel Lyocell is derived from wood pulp (usually eucalyptus), and Modal, a sister fibre, from beechwood. In both cases the raw fibre is dissolved in an Austrian production plant through a chemical process trademarked by Lenzing. While this is hardly a do-gooder fibre like, say, rurally produced jute, it is far less hairy. In fact its proponents compare it to super-fine cotton, and some even claim it has the attributes of silk. It is hardly a planet saver, but its profile is better than those of our two traditional defaults, polyester and cotton, and its versatility and application mean that it gives a garment a feeling of quality that could increase its long-term appeal and therefore its wardrobe life. It's the kind of fibre that can take some of the heat out of buying new garments.

DO I WEAR IT OR SMOKE IT?

Other eco fibres are almost as old as the hills. Take hemp, for example. Its heritage is worthy of quiz-show questions such as: Henry VIII passed an act fining farmers who refused to grow which crop? What 'H' did George Washington and Thomas Jefferson both cultivate? At times humankind has found hemp incredibly useful. Archaeologists in China have found evidence of cultivation from 4,000 years ago. As a fast-growing, low-maintenance crop that can be used in fibre, its stock has been high at various times in the past. But more recently its stock has been low, notably since it became guilty by association with its cousin, cannabis. During the 1930s the US newspaper magnate Randolph Hearst, who had a commercial interest in wood pulp and cotton-seed oil, was particularly keen on churning out 'reefer madness' stories, which ensured that the distinctive hemp leaves fell foul of American public opinion and sealed hemp fibre's reputation as the cloth of ne'er-do-wells. In short, hemp has turned from a leading cash crop that could have been very useful to the global textile industry, to the slacker's toke.

As in the case of other materials, we need to look beyond cultivation. After all, no fibre arrives fully formed: it is pulped, spun and carded into respectability. The question we need to ask is, was this process ecologically sound? Most hemp, for example, hails from China, where it is typically processed using heavy caustic sodas and acid rinses. It may still wind up with a footprint less bad than cotton, but do we just want to be less bad? For a hemp blend to be worthy of a place in the Perfect

Wardrobe, the hemp should be processed using a natural enzyme, or a combination of water and combing.

In fact the default deep-green-granola position is that humankind has little business wreaking ecological chaos with cotton, with its insatiable need for water and pesticides; campaigners have therefore always lobbied for a greater use of hemp in fashion. They talk sensibly about its environmental credentials: it is durable and resilient, does not need agrichemicals as a cultivation crutch, and has long roots which draw on untapped nutrients – all of which mean that hemp flourishes in 'difficult' soil, and can arrest erosion. The problem is that the fashion reach of the deep-green-granola demographic is rather limited, and the hemp-fibred clothing it tends to wear has remained deeply unappealing: think shapeless, baggy trousers and formless, sludge-coloured skirts.

But one reason to be cheerful is that there have been great strides in processing hemp as a fashion textile. It can now be 'cottonised' to remove the natural lignin that binds the fibres, allowing them to be spun and finished on cotton- or wool-processing equipment that has been modified. However, if we're being honest, we should acknowledge that pure hemp garments still have too much of the hairy hippie and too little of the upscale bohemia. The most successful hemp pieces are blended (usually with another natural or eco fibre – silk, organic cotton). That may change, because the hot ticket, the fibre currently being pitched as a rival to cotton, has been developed by Canadian scientists, and is a version of hemp. Using a certified eco-friendly process, it transforms hemp and other flax-based fibres into something that's cotton-like in the way it appears and acts, but has a fraction of the impact of conventional cotton. It's called Crailar, in some circles dubbed super-hemp, and it doesn't have to be blended. Is this where the future lies, in the hands of clever, forward-thinking designers who want to use clever, forward-thinking fabrics, rather than rely yet again on the same old staples?

14

BUYING BETTER CLOTHES

*The Wonderful World of Ethical Fashion, and how
to Unleash Your Sartorial Ingenuity*

If the skulduggery inherent in the Big Fashion system and the slippery background of its wares are getting you down, then 'ethical fashion' promises something different. Here, instead of taciturn labels and seemingly trappist sales staff, you'll find something close to a compulsion to 'fess up to every detail of provenance, manufacture and fibre. From the brands that use the last remaining worsted spinners in the UK, to the trainers whose soles are harvested by wild-rubber tappers in the Amazon, to the ballgown taffeta rescued from the skips outside the sewing rooms of prestige luxury brands, each has a more compelling back story than the one before. This is where you come for fashion with a narrative, clothes that you will variously find described as 'green','eco', 'sustainable', 'ethical', 'local', 'heritage', 'animal-friendly' or 'vegan', from artisanal and/or clean supply chains.

ETHICAL FASHION: WHAT IS IT?

In fact the descriptions and aims of this niche section of the fashion industry can be too diffuse for the liking of some commentators. This from Vanessa Friedman, fashion editor of the *Financial Times*, after attending a Sustainable Fashion conference at Copenhagen 2009 (an offshoot of the UN climate-change conference): 'You can laugh now. Everyone I told at the time did. Not just because I am not a particularly "green" type – though I compost and recycle – but because of the subject itself. "Sustainable fashion?" friends and colleagues would chortle. "What's that?" Good question. And here's the truth: having spent two days in Copenhagen immersed in the concept, having thought about it over the weeks since then, and having canvassed a wide variety of fashion figures, I can honestly answer … no one knows. And the more you try to figure it out, the more confusing it becomes.'

I think this is a valid whinge. There is no denying that there is a certain amount of 'lexicographical fuzziness', as identified by Friedman, in this field. But then, let's remember that mainstream fashion is inclined to bark imperatives: 'Wear pink!' 'Go shorter!' 'Get a hat!' Compared to that, any additional layers can seem complex. As you know, my idea of the Perfect Wardrobe is all about attaining that mix of the green and the socially conscious which I define as 'ethical'. I acknowledge that it is an ugly word, but I haven't got anything better, have you? And my ideal would be that as the principles of sustainability – designing out waste, using virgin resources with the best ecological profile, designing for disassembly – grow in influence and become embedded, they should become the tenets of good design: 'ethical' fashion may not need its own collection of terms at all.

By contrast to fast fashion, ethical fashion production runs are generally very small, and lead times generally much longer. Many smaller designers also make their clothes themselves, or are personally in attendance when they are made. The designer also takes responsibility (a key word) for the supply chain, which is often set up with the producers and handworkers in mind. Yes, the term 'ethical fashion' is broad: it can refer to the fibres used, low-impact production methods, local or heritage production, superior animal-welfare standards, a fairtrade supply route, and indigenous textiles and handicrafts. But a complete ethical brand should be a combination of all parts of the social- and environmental-justice jigsaw (not just something knocked up from organic cotton). It should be a three-dimensional view of an ethical project, not just a flat piece that may convey a tokenistic message (again, the 'I am not a plastic bag' bag pops into my mind). In short, ethical fashion is where the ecological and social impacts are on a level footing with all the usual aesthetic considerations. To my mind it really is no more complicated than that.

And over the last five or six years ethical fashion has become culturally significant. There is a rich scene, and an educated design force who understand that aesthetics and ethics must be merged for the future of fashion, and who are well versed in labour rights. This is underpinned by a drive to educate the next generation of designers and buyers, notably at London College of Fashion's dedicated Centre for Sustainable Design. There are ethical or eco-fashion weeks all over the world – in Paris, Copenhagen, Vancouver, India, Brazil and the green shows of New York's Fashion Week. In London Fashion Week there is Estethica, where the rabbit-warren corridors of Somerset House suddenly open up to reveal a myriad of sustainable designers. Even the winner of season eight of the popular US TV fashion show *Project Runway* (in which fashion designers are pitted against each other, with weekly challenges) in 2010 was the show's only sustainable designer, Gretchen Jones. During heated debate in the final round of judging, both designer Michael Kors and fashion editor Nina Garcia stressed that Jones represented 'the way that fashion is now going'. By 2010 the then director of womenswear for the influential New York store Barneys, Julie Gilhart, was moved to say of ethical fashion, 'It is not a trend, it's a movement.'

I happen to think that the importance of this movement lies in its very difference to mainstream fashion. Fashion needs an opposition that sets markers as to how different standards of ethical production can be achieved. Without this, the fast-fashion chain goes unchallenged, and as we've seen this results in unsustainable levels of pollution, waste and social deprivation.

PUT YOUR MONEY WHERE YOUR WARDROBE IS

In Chapter 5 I attempted to bring budgets back into fashion and had an initial spending review. I concluded that the Perfect Budget, i.e. the one for the Perfect Wardrobe, would go up by about 6 per cent (where possible), and would be allocated more strategically. I want you to swear off the cheapest fashion, to buy fewer things, and to spread your money around. Some consumers might choose to interpret this as a green light to buy very costly luxury items. The theory is that these represent an ethical investment, because they will hold their value and remain in the wardrobe for years to come, offsetting the need for multiple cheap, 'bad' purchases with their attendant footprint. However, this is just a theory, and not a very watertight one at that. As we've seen, luxury labels have embraced a faster, trend-based form of luxury (let's call it 'Fast Luxury'). So, although you might convince yourself that an 'it' bag is a bag for life, in fact it will quickly become outdated, and in a matter of weeks you'll see its successor advertised in a glossy magazine, which I guarantee will take the shine off it. And although luxury brands often position them-selves as the heirs apparent to the sustainable fashion throne, I see very little evidence for that. While they are keen to highlight the traditional parts of their supply chain – the ateliers and the European craftsmen in small bespoke workshops – a large proportion of luxury lines has also been outsourced, and may not be as tightly controlled as you may think. There are skeletons in the luxury closet, and most luxury brands are only at the beginning of their journey towards becoming beacons of green and social justice.

In the Perfect Wardrobe we're looking for solutions that show more commitment and more progress, and that means spending at least part of your budget on fashion that is demonstrably ethical. But a common complaint about ethical fashion is that it is too pricey. This is not always fair. There is a mix of prices among ethical brands, which run the gamut from cotton basics to distinctly fashion-forward pieces that are either one-offs or from very small collections. For an example of the latter you need only go to Estethica at London Fashion Week, where you'll find designers who are pushing the boundaries of what sustainable design stands for. I love seeing these designers, and the ingenuity with which they mix ecological concepts and environmental activism with aesthetics (is it just me, or does 'normal' fashion seem rather hollow by contrast?). For instance, it was at Estethica that I first came across Ada Zanditon, a young British designer who spearheads innovation in ethical fashion. Her geometric cuts, bodycon shapes and kaleidoscopic prints have been singled out by *Vogue* for praise, but she is also a devotee of biomimicry. (To explain this emerging science, it helps to think of a termite mound: to curb climate-changing emissions caused by heating and cooling buildings, architects working with biomimicry observe the way termites regulate the temperatures in their mounds using a complex web of tunnels. Or if you want to build a better solar cell, for example, you follow the structure of a leaf. Eventually, it is argued, this humble approach will lead us to design out waste and toxicity.) As far as I know, Zanditon is the first designer to take inspiration from bio-mimicry for fashion, and she is certainly the first to base a collection on extremophiles (more specifically, bacteria in Arctic ice). But in all honesty, these are themes that are not going to translate into Primark or Peacocks. The prices of this upper echelon of creativity are always going to reflect the extent of design input and originality, and while I'm a big admirer of some of the more innovative eco-couture brands, I own very few pieces that could really be said to fit into that category.

Realistically, most of our ethical purchases will be made down the price scale, below £100, and there is plenty to find here. But you will not find many pieces, however prosaic, hovering around the £10–£20 mark, for the simple reason that this is generally too cheap to guarantee environmental and social justice. Unlike mainstream brands, ethical brands do not externalise the true cost of production by dumping the pressures further down the supply chain. Even if you buy a functional garment, say a pair of pyjamas or a T-shirt, you will end up paying something closer to the authentic cost. This is often described as a 'premium': you pay for fairtrade that goes back to the community that grows the raw fibre for organic cotton. When you think of it, to describe the true cost of a garment as a 'premium', as if it shouldn't really be there, is outrageous. Instead of questioning this 'premium' on the cost of ethical fashion, it would be better to ask mainstream fashion retailers why they've left the true cost of production and fair wages off the price tag.

BUY LIKE A UTILITY

All in all, price (at both extremes) and fashionability are not good markers of whether or not a piece of clothing deserves a place in your

Perfect Wardrobe. Instead, you should be looking to spend on brands and labels that offer more ethical bang for your buck. I've decided not to give you a list in this book of shops and brands that you should go and buy from. For one thing, there are plenty of existing ethical clothing directories and online lists. Not only that, it would have swelled the size of the book to a phone directory. Lastly, since this is what we might call a dynamic part of the fashion sector, new brands appear on virtually a daily basis, and inevitably there are casualties too. So instead I prefer to give you underlying strategies as to the qualities and types of ethical brands you should try to invest in.

This particular strategy is highly unpoetic, but here I go: when deciding where to spend your ethical fashion budget, imagine you're looking for the greenest electricity supplier. I appreciate that that sounds a bit odd, so I'll explain: consumers who want to do the right thing often change to a power supplier that promises to decrease carbon emissions by offering renewable electricity. Because this is now such a popular consumer desire, most companies, even the huge ones that primarily sell power from coal-fired power stations, offer green tariffs. On closer inspection some of their commitments are rather hollow – some actually just sell green energy from a proportion that they are legally obliged to generate for a higher tariff, or fulfil the green part of the arrangement through a series of offsets and carbon trading. This means that the energy company is not really changing what it does at all. So the consumer in search of a real green energy tariff needs to find the trailblazing companies that actually invest in capacity, that actually build wind turbines or solar panels, or both. Similarly, the best ethical fashion brands are the ones that invest in their supply chain and deliver the most benefit throughout it. These are the clothes that do more than just look pretty.

CLOTHES MAKING CHANGE

The Perfect Wardrobe needs more than just light-green ideas, it needs brands that are revolutionary. Those that truly deliver don't just do something for you the consumer by giving you something fashionable to wear that also gives you a righteous glow – they can be a development tool, addressing poverty alleviation or women's rights. We've seen throughout this book that in Big Fashion you don't necessarily reap what you sow. The most important ethical brands are the ones that specifically try to address this imbalance and to ensure that in the future Developing World companies can trade on natural competitive advantage, not just cheap labour.

People Tree, a fairtrade fashion pioneer that has been running since 1995, is the epitome of a fashion brand moving to create change. Its central tenet is to put the Developing World producer at the heart of the system, rather than somewhere at the bottom. As a result, the brand's supply chain is rather fascinating. Its fashion lines are sourced from seventy fairtrade groups in twenty developing countries, with a model that turns conventional fashion production on its head. You'll remember that earlier in the book we saw that designs are sent to RMG factories by the big brands. The workers are there purely to facilitate the RMG part of the global assembly line. Their history, heritage and skill base are largely irrelevant. Any tweaks to designs will similarly be faxed by head office, usually at the last minute. This is definitely not the People Tree way. Instead, its founder Safia Minney takes her cue from the producers. What are their skills? What are the traditional crafts and embellishment techniques in a particular region? How much inventory can they produce? Then she works backwards, presenting the requests of the producers to Western design collaborators. Producers, often highly skilled women embroiders and seamstresses, can be utilising skills that are ignored or industrialised by mainstream fashion. People Tree gives them a lifeline, and a fair slice of the proceeds.

A big part of fairtrade is about increasing access to world markets. So we have lucrative Western markets full of consumers wanting to buy beautiful things, yet the odds are stacked against Developing World producers unless they become part of Big Fashion. Minney recognises this. 'We don't just want mechanised solutions in fashion,' she says, 'because frankly it puts people out of work. India already has ten million underemployed handweavers. But for £100 someone can buy a hand loom and make a fabric with that relatively small capsule investment. So as a label we want to buy the right cotton and then put it on these looms.'

An added ethical bonus, and one that will appeal to the *carbonista* we met earlier, is that if you want low emissions, proponents of low-tech artisanal production say they have the answer: for every hand loom in use, one tonne of CO_2 is saved per year, and if you use organic cotton on the loom, an extra 1.5 tonnes per acre.

Talking of the right cotton, 'It is about investing in capacity, building in your supply line too,' says Minney, highlighting the fact that anybody can buy a bit of organic cotton; it's an entirely different thing for a fashion brand to invest in making sure that the right sort can be grown: 'I can design a range to fit the cotton that they can grow' – in this case long-staple (so called because of its exceptionally long fibre length) irrigated cotton in Gujarat, India. We already know that good ethical companies do not buy anonymous fibres anonymously, but I hadn't quite appreciated how much a brand like People Tree can do. 'We won't simply be led by a merchandiser who looks at planning margins,' Minney says. 'You have a lot of PR departments [for major brands and retailers] talking about philanthropic initiatives or small organic or Fairtrade cotton offers, but that rarely drives the complete procurement or terms of trade with suppliers.' In her case it does. In Gujarat she worked with cotton cooperative Agrocel to bring drip irrigation into a large number of villages, reducing water use by 60 to 70 per cent, an acknowledgement that despite a lot of rainfall in the summer we meet (the 2010 monsoon season dragged on for at least a month after its usual end), this is actually a desert area. 'So through that drip irrigation and the water flow we can increase the staple length of the cotton and produce a much finer fabric like this one' – she tugs on the skirt of the dress she is wearing, a cute floral number with a cotton body, and cotton jersey sleeves and neckline. 'We couldn't have produced this weight of cotton five years ago. It's about commitment to the fibre and its continued success. Without that you cannot innovate. But look, if I was a designer from a mainstream label I might be into this, but my boss certainly wouldn't be. I'd be lucky if I was still in my position eighteen months later.'

It's a good point: only ethical brands will give their employees the time to work with farmers to grow the right type of cotton for the next season, or to track down a specific type of sheep. Then there's the expense. 'Financing the building of a fairtrade supply chain like this means investing 10 per cent of our turnover every year,' says Minney, 'and we've been doing it for fifteen years.' This is clearly not a superficial proposition.

But arguably there would be no point in going to all of this trouble if the lines look like something you might find in a charity catalogue (I'm afraid this has been a criticism of fairly traded garments before, and with good reason). To be frank, any ethical brand worth its salt should recognise that a degree of design and fashionability is also part of the sustainability of the brand. After all, you can't effect change if you can't guarantee orders, and even a well-meaning *fashionista* won't buy an embellished hairy tunic, however ethical it might be. People Tree has notably pursued some big fashion names to produce its collections, such as Gharani Strok and Clements Ribeiro, and more recently it has acquired permission to reproduce vintage Laura Ashley prints.

GO WILD

Sometimes it might take a little trial and error to match the development opportunity with the right fashion product. Bia Saldanha is a case in point. She is an activist whose very specific focus – wild rubber from the Amazon – has led her to fashion. It would be easy to think that everything from the Amazon should be out of bounds, given the horrendous level of deforestation there, but it's also vital that sustainable forest industries are promoted and kept alive. More profit kept in the forest means that both the trees and the community have better prospects, and are less likely to be uprooted in favour of soy or cattle. The Amazon is also the only place in the world where rubber trees grow in a wild state. 'It is a totally different situation from the rubber extracted from huge monoculture plantations, where people often work in really bad conditions and the forests are cleared just to grow rubber trees,' explains Saldanha. 'Native rubber from the Amazon grows among all sorts of other trees. It's a biodiverse, natural habitat. Tapping these trees requires skill, local knowledge and patience.'

You may be asking yourself why, outside of fetish wear, you would need to give wardrobe space to wild rubber. Well, Saldanha, who has dedicated her professional life to exploiting and finding a market for it, and who has even moved her family to the Chico Mendes Reserve deep in the Amazon (named after the hero of the rubber tappers, an ecologist and Saldanha's former mentor who was gunned down in 1998 – this is dangerous work) found that the wild tapped rubber could be used to create a material that looks very like leather. She joined up with luxury brand Hermès, and together they sold thousands of bags, chiefly to Japanese women. There was however an issue. A year or so later the customers began to return the bags, not because there was anything wrong with them; quite the reverse – there was no wear and tear. 'They complained that the leather wasn't wearing in the way that leather did, and the store assistants had to explain that the bags weren't actually leather.' Then, working with a materials scientist to process the rubber in the forest, Saldanha discovered that it could be used to make shoes. At the moment twenty families are sustained through rubber tapping in her local area, which keeps three hundred hectares of rainforest safe. 'I dream of everybody using this product every day,' she tells me wistfully. In 2010 her dream moved a step closer when she struck a deal with ethical trainer brand Veja. Amazonian rubber is now in the soles of every pair of Veja trainers.

I would have been keen for Saldanha to continue to pursue a line of leather-look pieces from wild tapped rubber too. I wouldn't return a bag to the shop because it wasn't actually leather. In fact, I'd buy it specifically because it wasn't. You see, I still find leather a conundrum. I like leather accessories, but are they ethically conscionable?

Admittedly there is much talk in the leather industry about cleaning up its act, and 'eco' leathers using vegetable dye are becoming more common. Pleather ('plastic leather') and other synthetic leathers tend to be given short shrift on account of the fact that they are derived from PVC, but when you factor in the pollution and the energy expended in creating conventional leather, are they so bad? And can the leather industry genuinely cut its footprint? One of the largest high-quality manufacturers, ISA Tan, has reportedly invested in a 'climate-friendly' factory in Vietnam, where the fifty-two megajoules of energy it normally takes to produce one square metre of leather will be cut to thirty-three megajoules. Is this a big enough win? There is also vegetable-tanned leather, which takes the sting out of the usually toxic part of the leather production process – dyeing (often, as we have seen, using chrome, that degrades into chromium, one of the most polluting substances on earth). But the pass notes for vegetable tanning don't blow my socks off from a sustainability point of view. Is it better environmentally? Often it can be, but the whole production process must follow suit: even vegetable-dyed leather needs to be produced in a factory with high environmental protocols. You can't buy vegetable-dyed leather with ecological impunity, because you also need to be sure that the processing facility takes care of its pollution properly.

What I am quite sold on, however, is the idea of buying leather accessories from local, small-scale British leather workers. From John o'Groats to Land's End you will find these leather-working enterprises. Don't be put off by words such as 'artisan', 'leather tooling' and 'workshops' – this is the craft community! Check for leather workers using organic British leather (a byproduct of the meat industry) and tanned using oak dyes: J. & F.J. Baker in Devon is the only remaining oak-barrel tanner in the UK, and it supplies many leather workers. The leather produced here is beautiful, with that intense, rich colour, and it is traceable from animal to belt or phone holder. Naturally these traditional makers don't make high volumes of pieces; that's impossible when you handmake. But increasingly you'll find small pieces in fashion boutiques where the owners understand that there are questions to answer about the provenance of leather. (This *Children of the New Forest* approach is finding traction – I was impressed to see artisan-made organic bangles on the model Laura Bailey's *Vogue* blog for Christmas 2010.)

So my Perfect Wardrobe will still contain animal products, but sourced much more carefully, with an eye on provenance. I want to be sure that these pieces are true byproducts, that the whole animal has been used. Take for example the fact that fourteen million British sheep are slaughtered each year, but just 70,000 raw sheepskins are tanned by the few remaining sheepskin tanneries in the UK. That's a travesty! Why send out to Australia, by way of China, for Ugg boots? Why don't we make our own sheepskin boots?

BUYING THE STORY

It is no coincidence that the pieces in my wardrobe I feel happiest describing or talking about are those that are demonstrably 'ethical'. For starters, there's no need to avoid eye contact and shuffle from foot to foot while I try to fudge the fact that I'm not entirely sure about the provenance of my much-admired handbag or jeans. It's not that I smugly want to show off that I've been virtuous in my shopping, it's that I'm pretty enthusiastic about the item's back story and full of admiration for the ingenuity of its designer. In fact, I enjoy describing the ethical objects in my wardrobe as much as I enjoy wearing and owning them. True, they only constitute about 20 per cent of my wardrobe as it currently stands, but they all have a slightly different emphasis, pinpointing different elements of the ethical-fashion jigsaw.

There is a pair of Terra Plana shoes, for example, 'built' with a pretty dark-green recycled fabric, their components stitched together without solvents, and with a wooden block heel from an FSC (Forestry Stewardship Certified) forest – this design team has been faithful to its vision of a process where waste and toxicity are designed out. It's a point of pride that I can now assemble a few entire 'ethical' outfits. I've introduced a hemp A-line high-waisted skirt from Anatomy, a small bespoke British brand, and wear it with a sustainable silk blouse. I have a bodycon dress from a young label, Goodone, that I can just about get away with on skinnier days. It's artfully constructed from pieces of old sweatshirt, but only I would know that (I also get the benefit of the fleecy lining on the underside in cold weather). There is a dramatic frock-coat-style jacket with military overtones from the high-end Danish sustainable brand Noir. Its tough appearance belies the fact that it's made from the softest organic fibres. But perhaps my favourite is a tweed fitted riding jacket made from British wool especially to my measurements. So not only does it fit like a glove, but it is unique, a spin on a classic country look. I can't think of a time when I won't want to wear it. Again, this is by Anatomy, designed by the label's founder Claire Macauley and constructed in a British textile factory. This is my heirloom piece.

One of the biggest lessons I've learned from ethical designers is how to buy their ingenuity. With ethical fashion you are not necessarily paying just for cut and trend, you are also buying into a vision. In the case of the brand From Somewhere, founded by Italian designer Orsola de Castro, this means understanding her revolutionary approach to waste in fashion, waste that she transforms into whimsical but wearable (and covetable pieces) via upcycling. Upcycling is not just recycling. There are a couple of exceptions, but on the whole you won't find many designers selling themselves as recyclers – unsurprisingly, they are not keen to link their design vision to the activity carried out by the famous litter-pickers the Wombles of Wimbledon Common. Even now, I remember how designers cringed at a sustainable-style catwalk show when the organisers selected the Wombles music. It was not the image they were going for. Recycling is OK if you're working with car parts and paper, but not in fashion. This is not just fashion snobbery, it's also because designers working with reclaimed materials are doing something a little bit different from conventional recycling, which involves shifting molecules and reprocessing a material into a downgraded substance. Whereas recycling as a rule takes material a step down the value chain, upcycling takes pre-worn materials in the opposite direction, adding worth through design. De Castro's pieces are constructed from the waste fabrics from factory floors, and the overstock liberated from the wheelie bins and skips of studios and design houses. True, this isn't any old waste – the scraps tend to include fantastic heavyweight jersey and sublime cashmeres from some of the most famous fashion houses on the planet – but when I wear one of the four pieces of From Somewhere I own, I'm still effectively wearing waste, and that feels pleasingly subversive.

From Somewhere also has the distinction of being one of a handful of sustainable brands to have reached the high street – admittedly many others either do not want to, or their techniques aren't suitable to making at volume. The key to this was uncovering a forgotten source of waste from the mainstream industry: liability stock. For every run of garments – and remember we are talking hundreds of thousands of units – a Big Fashion manufacturer will keep standby stock of the fabric in reserve. So, for a run of basic tops with a cowl-neck detail in grey jersey, thousands of metres of surplus grey jersey fabric will be made (with all the attendant energy and water use) and held in a big warehouse. This is liability stock. If something goes wrong with the main production run, and faults appear afterwards, the RMG manufacturer will scrap those units and call in the liability stock to remake the pieces. In practice this happens rarely, which raises the question: what happens to the bolts of liability fabric (which must number millions of millions of metres)? The answer is that it is kept until it is woefully last-season and therefore has little currency, and then sent to Asian factories, often for shredding or as stuffing for car seats. Orsola de Castro spotted an opportunity, liberating this stock from Tesco's warehouses in Sri Lanka and designing it into a simple tube-form dress. 'I wanted something that could be easily stitched on the production line in the factory, but that used liability stock,' she explained. The resulting Viper dress became Tesco online's best-selling fashion piece. Naturally it is not to everyone's taste – the idea for some of linking with Tesco will always be abhorrent – but it serves to demonstrate that the ingenuity of an ethical fashion designer can unlock the potential of yet another source of waste.

I've chosen to pick up on just a few brands that go this extra distance, but there are many others, and I would recommend that you divert as much of your budget and space in your Perfect Wardrobe as possible to them. There is something rather gratifying about owning a garment or an accessory that has had this much clout. I'm not suggesting that you should saunter around in a smug way, more that there's a warm glow to having bought into something so positive. Ethical brands that seek to do more than just get a range of fashionable clothes into stores at the right time should be shown some love, and fast-tracked into the wardrobe.

BUYING RIGHT

Having found brands that deliver on so many ethical fronts, we need to support them. It is a case of use it or lose it when it comes to ethical fashion. Every time an eco *fashionista* forgets the goal of a Perfect Wardrobe and squanders part of her budget on fast fashion, an ethical brand feels the pain. Because creating and running an ethical label is expensive and precarious. Just ask Edun, the brand that launched in the spring of 2005 with a stated aim to bring fashion production back to parts of Africa racked with poverty. Billed as a 'socially conscious' brand rather than making any specific eco or ethical claims, it had a number of things going for it. First, genuine style cachet. The design director was Rogan Gregory, who made his name designing the 1969-cut jean for Gap in the early 1990s, followed by his own range of top-end jeans and his label, Loomstate, in 2004. With Edun he now offered the same high-fashion, high-quality range of denim, alongside summer dresses, embroidered jackets, halternecked tops – all pieces that you actively wanted to wear and to own but which had been manufactured either from African or Indian fabrics along a transparent supply chain. Initially the bulk of the range was made in Portugal, which carved out a strong niche as the preferred manufacturing base in the early stages of the ethical fashion movement. Portugal was easy to monitor, known for good working conditions, and had convenient transport connections to the UK. Ultimately, however, Edun dreamed of manufacturing in Africa, as a way of delivering real social equity. Specifically in Lesotho, which had suffered when fashion brands that used to manufacture there had largely cut and run after preferential trade quotas ended.

I have to admit I found Edun's styling a breath of fresh air in the nascent ethical fashion scene, and my wardrobe is testament to that: my Edun haul comprises two summer vests with pretty detail, a long purple shirt or dress (never quite been brave enough to try it as a dress) and two pairs of jeans.

But there was another significant thing in Edun's favour: its two directors just happened to be Ali Hewson and her husband Bono. Bono's involvement suggested that the brand's ideas could be taken to people who had never heard of Lesotho. In fact Edun was very much an extension of Bono's famous 'trade not aid' take on spreading social and fiscal equity to Africa. 'How can you be the spokesman for a generation if you've got nothing to say other than "Help!"?' he wondered as far back as 1986. Empowerment was a key part of their thinking. 'People are reading the labels on clothes,' said Ali Hewson. Rogan Gregory visited the factories in Africa, teaching workers how to sew sophisticated garments, so that they wouldn't be making T-shirts for the rest of their lives. But it wouldn't be easy, as writer Craig McLean put it in a profile of the brand: 'Despite the clout of the world's biggest rock star, it wasn't enough to make Edun the trailblazing profitable, ethical, desirable fashion brand Hewson wanted it to be. In 2007, the three shareholders had to pour money into the company, and in 2008, Edun parted company with Gregory. The company slipped off the fashion radar.'

It was, however, to rise again. In May 2009 Edun attracted another backer with celebrity (and fiscal) muscle when luxury conglomerate LVMH became a 49 per cent shareholder. Edun was back, although it is still hard to tell exactly in what form. I'm going to be watching with huge interest to see what impact this luxurious alliance will have on the brand's plans for reviving Africa's fashion fortunes. But it has to be said that as Edun's first collection is released around the time this book is published, most of the press attention it gets will revolve around its aesthetic. Will it or won't it be a fashion hit?

BUY SLOWER

This is disappointing. After all, the whole point of this alternative fashion movement, by turns charming and frustrating, is that it is different to the mainstream, and not just a carbon copy of Big Fashion. It is distinct in its priorities, its outlook and often its pace.

Slow fashion is something to be celebrated. As with 'organic' materials, there's a culinary parallel. You may have heard of the Slow Food movement. It was founded by Italian journalist Carlo Petrini in 1989 as a rebuttal to fast food, following the opening of a McDonald's on Rome's historic Piazza di Spagna. Petrini feared that his culture was being rapidly annexed by multinational corporations. This wasn't necessarily an original observation – even back in 1989 – but Petrini's response was. He launched the Slow movement, with the aim of 'rediscover[ing] the flavours of regional cooking and banish[ing] the degrading effects of fast food'. Paradoxically, the Slow movement gathered a lot of pace. It now covers activism, education and consumption. In an age when there are 1.6 billion mobile-phone users on the planet, and the top ten fast-food chains have 100,000 outlets across the globe – and, as author Carl Honoré tells us, even Mozart sonatas are on a sort of cultural fast-forward: he found that his favourite used to take twenty-two minutes, but that most orchestras now get through it in fourteen – people seemed attracted to the Slow idea as something that could restore a degree of sanity.

Buying into this idea means planning your Perfect Wardrobe well in advance. As I was once queen of the impulse buy, I am hardly practised at this, so it was with some trepidation that I decided to experiment. In May 2010 I spent £70 on a summer dress called 'Coco' from a brand called Choolips that works with batikers and tailors in Ghana, despite the fact that I would have to wait two months to receive it. I can't think of anything more different from the fast-fashion experience. I'm sure that if I'd told my friends I was waiting two months for a summer dress they would have thought I was crazy. But there were upsides, not least the fact that I felt part of the making process, and was kept up to date with every part of my dress's journey: 'This afternoon we will place an order with our batiker, Juliana Mustapha in Cape Coast. She will receive moneys for all the raw materials she will need to get the job done ... plain white cotton, dyes, wax and her workers. She will allocate a production time for your yards for next week. Next week your fabric will be printed and we will give you all the details on how that works when the time comes.' 'Today we have calculated how many yards of white cotton we need to print for you. We will print 3.5 yards.' And so it continued until Juliana and co. had finished, and my dress was put on a single shipment with all Choolips summer orders and dispatched from West Africa. When it arrived on 21 July I was delighted to see it. It was a dark blue, with a yellow batik pattern and ties at the back instead of buttons. I kept turning it over in my hands to see how it had been made. I felt as if I knew this dress, and everything about it. It was one of the strangest, but most pleasing, fashion experiences I've ever had.

TOO GREEN TO BE BEAUTIFUL?

I doubt, however, that the fashion pages of the glossy magazines would be quite so charmed, because the pervading worry continues to be whether ethical brands are 'fashionable enough'. They are regularly dismissed by the style media as not being quite up there, as not having shaken off that granola, knitted-tofu vibe quite enough. Yes, rather than asking itself how it can be more ethical, fashion-at-large asks why ethical can't be more 'fashion'. Naturally this neurosis transfers to us, the consumers, and feeds our fear that should we depart from Big Fashion and its dictatorial grip of trends we will end up looking ridiculous.

Well, perhaps a little jaded by the constant implication that ethical labels couldn't cut the mustard, some friends and I, bonded by an interest in sustainable style, decided to road-test ethical fashion. The 'team' was made up of me; Livia Firth, a film producer and eco campaigner; sourcing expert Jocelyn Whipple; and the designer Orsola de Castro (whom we met above). Our test, we decided, would up the ante. Greener fashion is often given an outing in front of a sympathetic audience – say at siloed ethical shows at international fashion weeks. We thought we'd display it on one of the most scrutinised and demanding platforms known to fashion: the international red carpet. And so, as the nominations for the 2010 Golden Globes were announced we launched the Green Carpet Challenge, which would be covered in a blog on Vogue.com that would run for the awards season.

Clearly we could not just muscle our way onto the red carpets of the international awards season, however determined we were to showcase some ethical fashion designers. But we had an insider. Our Green Carpet Challenge hinged on the fact that Livia is married to actor Colin Firth, who was nominated for a clutch of Best Actor awards for turning in an astonishing performance in Tom Ford's *A Single Man*. (Little did we know that the following year he would follow it up with an equally spellbinding performance in *The King's Speech*, so we were able to run two Green Carpet Challenges back to back in 2010 and 2011.)

'I don't want to sound ungrateful about the red-carpet stuff,' says Livia, with characteristic frankness. 'Of course, it's all very good fun and glamorous, and how great to be able to be with your partner when his work is honoured at all these events. But I did approach the situation with a degree of trepidation. Because I'm not, frankly, someone who spends a lot of time thinking about what I'm wearing or will be wearing in a week's time. The scrutiny of the awards season is daunting. But then I realised I could use it as an opportunity to promote something I'm really passionate about: sustainable style and ethical fashion'. But

Livia wasn't going to compromise on style, even if there was substance. I remember that while we were researching the world of eco couture we both shuddered when we came across an 'ethical' gown fashioned from recycled Tetrapak cartons and worn by a concert pianist. We were looking for something far less literal. 'Remember, I'm a forty-year-old mother of two, not a young actress,' Livia warned. 'I don't want to show any flesh, and nothing that makes me stick out like a sore thumb.'

Depending on where you stand, the international film awards represent either an exciting and glamorous distraction from the real world, or a vacuous and irrelevant sideshow. Luckily, for me it's more the former. But whichever, the red carpets – the Golden Globes (incidentally, the longest red carpet), the Screen Actors Guild awards, the BAFTAs, and of course the most heavily scrutinised (and therefore perhaps the most sadistic) red carpet, leading up to Los Angeles' Kodak Theatre for the Oscars – capture the attention of the world's fashion media. That represents an opportunity, but also a certain amount of risk: those who make what is perceived to be a poor choice in their red-carpet outfit are pilloried for years after, forever cropping up on the 'What was she wearing?' pages of glossy magazines. See as evidence the Marjan Pejoski swan dress Björk wore for the Oscars in 2001.

So we began with the safe entry point for alternative fashion – vintage (see below for more thoughts on this default position): Livia wore a beautiful repurposed wedding gown for the Golden Globes. After that we graduated to new designers (in the context of the red carpet) working exclusively with ethical fashion concepts and new materials, from Peace silk to milk fibre. We developed a roll call of designers in the US and Europe that we could depend upon to supply high-end gowns with compelling back stories and watertight credentials.

Over three months, covering ten big events and many smaller ones, we did the whole thing ethically. My heart was in my mouth sometimes as I sat up into the small hours on my sofa at home to catch a glimpse of the dress live on TV. It was bizarre to be so wrapped up in a dress on the other side of the world. There were some near-disasters: always against the clock, we failed to leave enough time to get a tricky milk fibre fabric altered, and Livia injured her leg halfway through, consigning herself to flat shoes and a series of frantic hem reworkings.

But overall the results were stunning, and received widespread acclaim. On a couple of occasions the dresses made the front page of many a paper without anybody apparently even twigging that they were sustainable, or that that was the whole point. The quality, shape, cut and flow of the dresses made us wonder, why was this such a rarity?

Year II, and with renewed confidence Livia took to the 2011 Golden Globe carpet wearing a gown that was perhaps more ostentatiously hippie. Made by Tennessee designer Jeff Garner, of the Prophetik label, the gown, in Tussah Peace silk and hemp, was uncompromisingly romantic, and had been dyed using a traditional low-tech indigo technique – in fact the designer even grows his own indigo plants on his own farm. To the outsider this might have looked as if we were taking a Luddite approach to the glossiest of awards ceremonies, but we really liked the fact that Garner's purpose was more than just getting a non-toxic colour. He is also trying to revive the idea of a relationship between dyes and culture. 'The chemical process of indigo dyeing was only unravelled in the 1870s,' he explains, 'opening the way for chemical substitutes and destroying the Indian indigo economy. It actually had a profound effect on the movement for independence in India. By 1914 just 4 per cent of the total world production still came from plants.' This is not the sort of back story that often troubles spreads in *OK!* magazine.

Of course, it was obvious from the start that a little experiment like this wasn't going to change the fashion landscape. The Green Carpet Challenge was purely an exercise intended to create a debate and to test the notion that ethical design somehow wasn't up to scratch. But what we hadn't anticipated was just how grateful and keen the designers we met were to be involved. Where I had imagined having to plead to borrow a dress, they were bending over backwards to be included. One designer who works with sustainable silks and fabrics, and who wishes to remain nameless, threw some light on this. The international red carpets are strangely conservative, actresses rarely deviating from big-name designers, preferably with a couture background, and big sparkly jewels. Therein lies the rub. While there are fine ethical designers with top-level skills who are well able to produce a piece with the necessary level of cut-and-finished polish (you don't want any below-par couturier skills exposed under the flashbulbs), they are priced out of the equation. One European eco-couture designer described to me how she got extremely close: 'I talked for months with a young, very beautiful actress who was very much of the moment and nominated for a clutch of awards. She was also enthused by fashion with more of a meaning, and so we worked together to design a dress for one of the major Hollywood award red carpets. It was just hours before that she received a phone call from the representative of a very big brand. They had obviously realised that this could well be her year, and that the press was lapping up her look. The big brand offered her $150,000 to wear their dress on the red carpet that night, and devastatingly for me, after months of work, she took the cash.'

The ultimate prize in the movie business is of course the Oscar, and when Colin won the Best Actor award at the 83rd Academy Awards in February 2011, I felt a little as if the Green Carpet Challenge was getting one too. Livia wore a dress by London designer Gary Harvey. A former creative director of Levi Strauss, Harvey only began designing when he needed a dramatic piece for a jeans shoot and ended up using forty-two pairs of Levi's 501s to create a dress. He became the king of re-use. Previous pieces have been made from eighteen Burberry macs, twenty-eight army jackets, and thirty copies of the *Financial Times*.

For Livia's Oscar dress Harvey used eleven dresses garnered from vintage, thrift and charity stores in south-east London that dated from the era of *The King's Speech*. The result was an unashamedly romantic tonal gown in pink, blush and beige, the shape of which was pulled together by a complex piece of corsetry and engineering (I'll vouch for the complexity, as I did it up!). I loved it, and so in the main did the fashion commentators. They praised the romantic nature of the gown, and the fact that in a safe year for Oscar looks, it pushed a number of alternative fashion buttons. Yes, we made it onto a couple of worst-dressed lists too. That was what I had always dreaded in the past, but in the event even that didn't smart too keenly. Perhaps the ethical nature of the experiment tempered the journalists' scorn, because they seemed to add us to their lists with regret. I went back and had a look at Björk's swan moment. In hindsight, I found it quite beautiful.

THE VINTAGE CONUNDRUM

I hope ethical designers and the industry as a whole get the message from the Green Carpet Challenge that they are deserving of a bigger platform. For the non-designers, I hope it gives them the idea that even if you don't have a reason to buy a ball gown, you can push your commitment to ethical fashion beyond just buying vintage. Because despite this abundance of creativity, this effort, this energy, the default response when you suggest to a consumer that she should buy ethically is often the line, 'Well, I do buy some vintage.'

I find this disappointing. The theory might be sound: you're buying up pre-loved clothes, both saving them and avoiding the squandering of resources on new garments. And I don't think it's hyperbolic to say that those who are deeply into fashion get the idea of precious fabrics, the value of impeccable construction, the beauty of good materials and the time and attention needed to really curate their clothes properly. All of these are fantastic messages and techniques, and if we all adopted them in our wardrobes, we'd be well on the way to becoming enlightened consumers of fashion.

And vintage is attractive. For one thing, it doesn't confine you to a limited season, but liberates you to choose from decades of design. If you're really lucky, and if you've got the budget (this is no naïve thrift industry any more, and the big pieces attract big prices), you can acquire really high-quality items. I'm not what you might call a vintage nut. I don't dress rockabilly or coordinate my fridge and my wall clock with my netted petticoats. But I can spend many an hour in a vintage clothes shop, just gawping at the way they used to make things. I am completely seduced by the weights and drapes of old fabrics, the sublime stitching techniques and all the little touches – the tiny weights sewn into a hem to make sure a skirt falls in the right way, for example.

My problem with vintage pitched as the green solution is that this is a cosy position, and not quite the cure-all that it's sometimes made out to be. Although it is often held up as a virtuous economy, buying vintage actually means buying into a substantial industry. There are of course lots of different grades of vintage, ranging from the nostalgia pieces that flit in and out of fashion (on a visit to Wastesaver's Oxfam plant I snapped up a seventies Adidas tennis skirt before it was put online by the 'vintage' team there) to the serious, historically significant items that represent a part of fashion history. The industry has a wide network of spotters, auction houses, dealers and exporters. In common with mainstream fashion there are warehouses and outlets for low-grade vintage. It is carefully sorted and traded, increasingly online, where there is a huge trade in the more workaday pieces on auction websites, notably eBay. It is graded from 'mint' (in perfect condition) or 'near-mint' through to the prosaically 'wearable'.

As with all such terms, these can be open to interpretation (and dispute) – but then, the term 'vintage' is open to interpretation too. Let's briefly return to the red carpet. Arguably, since Julia Roberts collected her Best Actress Oscar in 2001 for *Erin Brockovich* wearing a stunning mono-chrome pre-loved gown by Valentino, 'Vintage' has become the stock answer to the 'Who are you wearing?' red-carpet question. Actually Julia's gown was only from 1992, making it a grand total of nine years old at the time she took to the stage of the Kodak Theatre. I'll forgive this, because it was a beautifully made piece, and deserved a high-profile outing; but I can't help noticing that vintage is getting younger and younger. Press releases from younger luxury conglomerates during the awards season often alert me to the fact that an A-lister is wearing a vintage piece of theirs from just five years ago. For goodness' sake, that's not vintage, that's an actress wearing something twice! The distinction is important.

But my main issue with vintage is that it represents a missed oppor-tunity. You could set your sights higher up the ethical agenda, and invest in a piece of ethical fashion that has a myriad of benefits through the supply chain instead. Describing 'vintage' as 'ethical' lacks some imagination. After all, you probably wouldn't describe yourself as a green homeowner because you ate off an antique kitchen table. In addition to the vintage furniture, at the very least you'd need to lay down a bit of insulation in the loft, install some solar panels for hot water, and invest in a composter. I feel similarly about the wardrobe. You can't truthfully describe your wardrobe as ethical just because it contains vintage. Vintage is fine as a mix-and-match option, but it won't cut it as the predominant ethical feature of your closet.

NEW THRIFT

But the good thing about looking for vintage is that it keeps us rummaging and looking for alternative outlets in charity shops, and that's a very good thing. There is a distinction between second-hand and vintage, and the market reflects that. It would, for example, be a really good idea to use some of your clothes budget over the next twelve months for plain old second-hand. This is the part of the market that is out of the clutches of the large vintage dealers, and can be a good earner for charities. If we could get a flourishing market in pre-worn basics – shirts, T-shirts, jumpers, etc.: the non-show-stopper items that normally get overlooked – it would be a really good way of kick-starting a more equitable and sustainable fashion cycle.

We've seen from our visit to recycling sorting facilities for textiles that there's the capacity to sort good quality pre-worn basics; we just need the widespread market to go with it. In cold, hard environmental calculations there would be a big bonus if everyone in the UK was to buy one reclaimed woollen garment this year. It would save about 370 million gallons of water (the average British reservoir holds about three hundred million gallons) and 480 tonnes of chemical dyestuffs. Furthermore, even after allowing for collection, sorting and transportation, charity-shop basics retail at lower prices than those offered by value retailers. Pre-worn offers a sustainable buy without the hefty price tag.

Then there are the schemes that I would describe as thrift plus. At the top of this tree is TRAID, Textile Recycling for Aid and International Development. Its distinctive lime-green bins are found across the UK, and it has shops in London and Bristol. What marks TRAID out from the normal thrift store is that it has its own label, TRAID REMADE, that it retails through its stores alongside second-hand clothes. Pieces with potential for alteration and customisation are plucked from the conveyor belt and TRAID's design team give them a quirky makeover (this appears to be targeted particularly at the teenage consumer). The proceeds of TRAID REMADE and the shops go to fund overseas fashion projects that are geared to improving the lot of producers. For example, TRAID is one of the main funding streams for SEWA, the

Self-Employed Women's Association, that runs the Rajiv and Nagar Embroidery Centres in India. These are places where home-workers can go for support and training, and are situated next to the two principal slum districts producing informally for the garment industry in Delhi. According to Sanjay Kumar, who helps to run the project, SEWA's home-worker scheme 'has increased our home-workers' wages by nearly 100 per cent, and enabled a lot of Muslim women to come out of their homes to a SEWA centre to collect their work and meet. Then they engage with other ideas like microfinance or education for their children. This business model doesn't just increase their income but their mobility.' So here's another opportunity for your wardrobe to support a type of fashion with far-reaching aspirations.

TRAID's work is further proof that there is an alternative to just buying clothes that are 'less bad'. It is possible to source clothes that reverse the invidious fashion cycles we've encountered – the supply-chain catastrophes that serve up wanton pollution and trample on any notion of the rights of garment workers. Instead, ventures like this actively promote fashion as a source of poverty alleviation, an equitable system in which skills are valued and rewarded, and waste becomes a resource once again. These constructive supply chains produce clothes that I truly aspire to own.

15

HOW NOT TO BUY

Jumping from the Fashion Treadmill Without Swearing off Style

The Perfect Wardrobe cannot be solely about acquiring new clothes, even those with a tiny ecological footprint and hewn from a dynamic biodegradable fibre. The Perfect Wardrobe is also a regulated wardrobe, where what you don't buy is as important as what you do. This isn't necessarily as crazy as it sounds. Because while I often wish for different clothes, or more fashionable ones, or even that the ones I own made me look better, seldom do I wish for more of them. As we've established, I have quite a few. As we've also established, you probably do too.

Just before the launch of London Fashion Week in February 2010, Dame Vivienne Westwood went even further than this. Speaking on BBC London radio and, according to *Vogue*, wearing her 'environmentalist's hat' (metaphorical, one presumes, though who knows?), she pleaded that shoppers should stop buying clothes unless they really had to, and impose a moratorium on any new purchases for six months. 'We all have a part to play, and if you engage with life, you will get a new set of values, get off the consumer treadmill and start to think, and it is these great thinkers who will rescue the planet,' she declared. I like the cut of her jib, although her noble sentiments might have been slightly undermined by the fact that the story ran with a link at the bottom publicising her new collection (perhaps just for inspiration, not for purchase). But her 'stop shopping' pronouncement days before Fashion Week didn't go down too well elsewhere. 'This morning I almost choked on my cornflakes when one of our great British designers, Vivienne Westwood, popped up … telling the public to stop shopping for clothes to help save the planet,' wrote Jessica Brown of fashion-industry magazine *Drapers*, pointing out that although climate change etc. was obviously important, there was the fragility of the economy to consider before the fragility of the earth.

But why should you and I feel an obligation to prop up an unsustainable economy through frenzied fashion-buying? Especially as, if we can delink fashion and personal style from actual consumption, not only will we have smaller credit card bills and room to swing a cat in the national wardrobe, but we could end up with a much more workable and satisfying aesthetic. We'd be better global citizens who were also better dressed.

The key to this is to think of the Perfect Wardrobe in terms of a collection that needs to be curated. This reinforces the idea that each piece is important, wanted, and needs to be preserved and treasured to the end of its useful life. Curating your clothes is another bulwark against filling your closet with impulse-bought fashion junk. And it is not just about selecting new pieces, but about how you treat the clothes you already own. It begins with how you look after them.

ALL IN THE WASH

The industry response to the large footprint of the national wardrobe, and to cries about cleaning up fashion, has been rather literal: it has focused on the way we consumers wash our clothes. One of the most successful consumer-focused environmental initiatives is considered to be Ariel's 'Turn to 30' campaign. From the multinational Procter & Gamble, the campaign was intended to get the British public washing their clothes with Ariel at thirty degrees, as a long-term change in behaviour that would help to cut their greenhouse gas emissions. It might not sound particularly revolutionary, but there's logic to it. For starters, we in the UK tend to wash our clothes at a far higher temperature than people do in other countries. The result is that we expend more energy heating water to a higher temperature, and therefore produce more global-warming emissions (this could be a legacy of being told for years that it was only socially acceptable for housewives to produce laundry in which whites were whiter than white). Predictably, there was an advertising campaign featuring a supermodel (in this case Helena Christensen) sensibly setting the dial of her washing machine to thirty degrees. The campaign was showered with awards for invoking behavioural change on a big scale.

In terms of making our wardrobes more sustainable, the 'Turn to 30' campaign could be shown to have had some effect. And it suited Big Fashion, as it suggested that the most important element in the carbon burden of the whole life cycle of a garment – from the time the cotton seed is grown or the polyester synthesised from cracked hydro-carbons, right through to the time we decide it's ready for the bin – comes not from pesticides being sprayed on crops, or the fabric being transported halfway around the world to get a zip sewn in, but from you and me washing it at the wrong temperature. Yes, according to this type of analysis, that is the single most important factor when you're trying to work out which bit of the fashion jigsaw causes the most carbon emissions. Therefore it stands to reason that anything you can do to lessen the energy impact through your laundry habits represents a bonus to planet earth.

'Wash Low, Spin Fast, Tumble Less – Cut up to 40 per cent of the energy bill racked up when doing laundry by changing washing and drying habits', advised M&S, following suit. It said 70 per cent of its clothes could be effectively washed at thirty degrees, adding that if you wanted to go a bit darker green you could extend the reasoning to your tumble dryer. Again, there's merit in heeding this advice. Nearly 70,000 tonnes of CO_2 are churned out by tumble dryers across the UK each year, the equivalent to the amount emitted by over 20,000 return flights from London to New York each week. In a year, one tumble dryer can produce around 254 kilograms of CO_2. Drying washing on a line famously produces zero CO_2 and saves you around £60 per year. When the industry described cleaning up the impact of our fashion habits this way, it seemed so simple.

Too simple? Yes, I'm afraid so. While I appreciate that transferring all the responsibility onto us, the put-upon consumer, helps to absolve manufacturers, retailers and even detergent manufacturers from parts of the ethical equation, the 'Turn to 30' focus doesn't take into account the other ecological issues around fashion production. For example, the dyeing of fabric results in seventy different toxic chemicals being released into the world's waterways, and is responsible for 17 to 20 per cent of worldwide water pollution. Nor does it address the gigantic levels of water use we've witnessed, not to mention the working conditions of the people who have made the clothes you are bunging in the drum. Turning the temperature of your wash down will not remove these ethical stains. So, while I'm all in favour of a green laundry strategy, turning to thirty is about the lightest-green thing you can do. It's a start, but nothing else.

Often we prefer to devolve responsibility to the local dry cleaner. This is where we tend to send the high-end, respected members of our wardrobe. But dry cleaning is not an exact science: I was on hand to comfort a friend when she collected her yellow Trussardi knitted piece, bought in a fashion sale and ruined in the local dry cleaners. And of course there's always the opportunity for items to get lost or forgotten. 'It makes me livid to think about the clothes I've lost at the dry cleaners,' the late, great stylist and fashion muse Isabella Blow told me once while I was interviewing her. She totted up an inventory of missing pieces: 'I've got tops but not bottoms, or bottoms without tops. Absolutely maddening.'

Admittedly, I have handed over garments before now with so much neuroticism I may as well have been handing over a newborn puppy. 'Are you absolutely sure that you can clean this OK? It's really, really important that this doesn't get damaged.' To their eternal credit, the dry cleaners always take the time to make reassuring noises and pacify me. But when I began a new round of questions – 'What sort of process do you use? Is it green?' – they weren't half as reassuring.

Because the real damage from dry cleaning is not to clothes, but to the environment and to occupational health. True, it is at least a less explosive process now than it was at the beginning. In the 1850s, when the French dyeworks owner Jean-Baptiste Jolly began using kerosene as a solvent to clean tablecloths and industrial clothes covered in oil, there was a high probability that the whole enterprise could go up in flames. But by the 1930s laundries had discovered 'perc' (perchloroethylene), and they never looked back. Perc is a liquid the colour and consistency of apple juice. It is thrown in with your most precious garments in those oversized washing machines they use in dry cleaners ('dry' cleaning is a slight misnomer), and removes stains and dirt without causing shrinkage or dyes to bleed. At the end of the wash cycle it should be captured and used again. After a few days of accumulating dirt it turns into a thick black liquid with the viscosity of oil. Perc also gives dry-cleaned items that 'clean' smell. What you are actually smelling is chlorinated hydrocarbons mixed with solvents and their VOCs – volatile organic compounds.

In the 1980s perc was found to be both neurotoxic and carcinogenic. Dry cleaners using it have to operate under licence. If your dry cleaner still uses perc – and most do – when you get home, take off the horrible film wrapping (given the flimsiness of this material and the chemical contact it has undergone, I'm afraid I can't think of any other destination for it than landfill), and leave the clothes outside for twenty to thirty minutes to avoid VOCs polluting your home – contemporary indoor air quality is notoriously bad as it is, what with hermetically sealed windows, MDF furniture and 'innovations' such as plug-in air fresheners (I dislike these almost as much as dry-cleaning bags).

You might also spare a thought for the occupational risks endured over the last century by dry cleaners. Perc has been connected to increased incidence of certain types of leukaemia and tumours. Not all that surprisingly, the concentration of perc in the air around dry cleaners has also been observed to be higher than normal, exposing the general population to its effects.

Fortunately, recourse to perc is not the only way of cleaning diva clothes. A few more progressive dry cleaners are bringing in perc-free dry cleaning, and I suggest looking out one of these. Johnsons, for example, the UK's biggest dry-cleaning chain, has been trumpeting 150 GreenEarth cleaners across the country. This process replaces the dastardly perc with liquid silicone, derived from sand. There's also talk of dry-cleaning machines that use CO_2 to blast clothes clean (without emitting it, so don't worry on a climate-change score). These, however, cost hundreds of thousands of pounds. It is thought that perc cleaning will be phased out completely by 2020. Why the delay in ridding us of such a pernicious pollutant? I suspect it comes down to expense. Until that happy day, pick your dry cleaners responsibly and ask yourself first, does this really need a whole clean? We don't make enough use of fresh air. Leave a garment outside in a gentle breeze for half an hour and it will freshen up nicely.

WARDROBE MANAGEMENT

Cleaning aside, we need to pay some attention to another prosaic part of the wardrobe equation: mending. I'm sad to report that we're coming perilously close to losing skilled menders across the fashionscape. This is hardly surprising, when you consider that they've spent the last two decades twiddling their thumbs as clothes and accessories were slung out rather than brought to them. We spend less than 3 per cent of our fashion budget on mending. That's nothing. Probably less than we spend on hairbands. I'm all in favour of upping this to a higher level: I'm now trying to allocate 10 per cent of my overall fashion budget to what I'm going to drily term 'wardrobe management'. In the long run, it's money well spent.

One of the barriers to changing the fashion cycle is that if we take the current pattern as a given, our garments will always have the lifespan of a mayfly. That's problematic. A particular casualty has been the small industries in the UK that repair and service garments and accessories. This is sad, not only for the businesses that go under, but also because it's a vicious cycle: the more of them disappear, the less inclined we are to think that we can give our clothes another lease of life. I had lived in Brighton for several months before I ventured into a basement shop on my street called Clever with Leather. Its name seemed to suggest a sedition and edginess that I wasn't entirely comfortable with, so I was relieved to find it was a quite straightforward leather-repair outfit staffed by a genuine craftsman who had spent years making and fixing accessories 'properly', as he put it. After tutting for a while about the inferior quality of the buckle on a particularly expensive leather belt I had bought, he set to work making more holes (I had bought a bigger size by mistake) and making a loop holder so that I could wear it without the excess inches flapping about. In a few minutes he turned something that was cluttering up a drawer into a main accessory in my wardrobe that gave many pieces a new lease of life. The price for this? Just £5.

When it comes to the remaining repair and fixing population in the UK, it's a case of use it or lose it. Even those that are left have often scaled down the variety of products they can mend in the face of our extraordinary consumer apathy. Among the most familiar emails sent to my newspaper column are those from readers who want to resole their trainers (usually the fashion type, rather than running shoes). After one particularly trainer-heavy postbag I contacted all the shoe menders I could find. The responses were interesting. A change in manufacturing procedures towards mass production has meant that in many designs the sole units are now injection moulded rather than made from sheet soling that can be replaced when the original has worn out. But a number of the cobblers I contacted through the Society of Master Shoe Repairers (such a thing still exists) said that they had been willing to repair trainers, but had been thwarted by us, the consumers, and our lack of enthusiasm. Among them was David, who had even invested in a 'special cup press with individual sizes, tested for the correct solution and the full range of thru soles to match', only to find that fickle consumers would rather just buy a new pair. Most said they were able to repair a limited number of treads and colour patterns – so you should save any remaining tread and try all your local shoe menders before you think, 'Cobblers to this', and a buy a new pair.

We also need to stand up for existing systems. When Pringle closed its factory in Scotland in the summer of 2008, it was the end of the 'cashmere reconditioning service' that seemed to cause the biggest stink. This repair service had long been a fixture of the Pringle top-end buy – cashmere knits costing over £250 could be fixed for free, extending their life in spite of the inevitable moths, pilling and damage that befall a diva fibre. The service was reinstated through another Scottish factory due to popular demand.

UNCLOGGING YOUR WARDROBE

All these steps merely represent the basics – many are measures that your granny would have undertaken without even thinking about them. Cleaning, caring and mending seem like nothing more than good manners when you think about the endeavour that has gone into constructing even the most simple of pieces. There needs to be more to curating the Perfect Wardrobe than this. It is also about imagination and innovation.

After a decade of unprecedented consumption and chucking out, there is probably enough fabric in circulation to keep us all clothed for the next decade. Just think of the two million tonnes that goes to UK landfill each year, and of those pieces locked in closets that will never be worn. This represents an extraordinary inventory of possibility. Indeed, if only we could get the fashion circulatory system going more efficiently, we might never need to buy new again!

And, as one person's fashion mistake is nearly always another's style gold, there's potentially huge mileage in developing a fashion culture that's not just about straightforward retail transactions, but about getting access to each other's wardrobes, mistakes and all. This is what clothes swaps represent. The genesis of formal clothes swapping (informal swapping has probably always happened in a quiet way) appears to date back to the mid-1990s, when Suzanne Agasi, the founder of Clothing Swap in the USA, laid down some ground rules (these are important) and hosted events that would raise money for charities, but also seemed to champion a new understanding of a form of 'green glamour' that would stand outside retail. It was pitched as 'clothes you would lend to a friend' – presumably one you like. The rules stressed that clothes swapping was not about providing a dumping ground for trashed clothes. Swappable items must be clean (freshly laundered) and in very good condition. Most fell into one of three categories: new clothes (with tags), nearly new clothes (worn only once or twice), and 'gently' used clothes, which could be worn, but must still be in very good condition. The recession and the much touted drift-to-thrift has resulted in a spate of clothes swapping internationally, especially in the UK, where it has moved from fringe activity to mainstream event. You can also find clothes swaps branded, in the rather Sloaney-pony vernacular, as 'swishes' (the infinitive 'to swap' becomes 'to swish').

I have to admit that I was a bit wary at my first clothes swap. It was a well-organised affair in Covent Garden, sponsored by a major credit card company, Visa, with the entry fee going to charity. You were given points for the clothes you dropped off, dependent on label/brand, quality etc., which were then put on a credit card from which you could spend as you chose. Having forced myself to be generous – in all honesty, I don't find sharing my clothes particularly easy – giving up some worn-once brogues (I'd managed to buy the wrong size), a few pretty dresses that I didn't feel fitted my style any more, and a neat Hilfiger blazer that was too tight across the shoulders, I accumulated plenty of points. I picked up a couple of skirts: nothing special, but perfectly serviceable wardrobe additions, and looked around at the ever-diminishing rails. It was late in the day, and I was about to leave when my friend pointed to a lonely pair of shoes on a shelf from which everything else had gone. I felt instant chemistry. Size 6, vintage, British-made in fir green with a heel painted racing green. Certainly they're not to everyone's taste, but I immediately loved them. Three years on, they are still among the things in my wardrobe I wear most. They are just the right height, well balanced and beautifully proportioned. To use a design cliché, they don't make them like that any more. Since then I've been a clothes swap supporter, if only because my first outing provided me with such an unexpected fashion fix.

There are swapping/swishing aficionados and obsessives who can spend hours telling you about the special pieces that have boosted their wardrobes. Equally, there are plenty of people who've found swapping a little lacklustre. I think this is because effective clothes swaps require a generosity of a spirit (there are all sorts of other voluntary rules connected with clothes-swapping etiquette) that has hitherto been missing from our wardrobe lives. Firstly, to get a really good swap going, you need to give up items that have value. Good labels and quality design are the lifeblood of a clothes swap, but even if you don't actively want to wear them, it can be a wrench to give quality clothes up. Nobody wants to sacrifice a piece that they could easily have sold on eBay to a swap, only to find that there's nothing there of similar value or appeal. Clothes swapping requires us to open up our wardrobes and to think more generously.

TRANSUMING FASHION

Swapping clothes represents a useful first rung on the ladder to a transumer wardrobe. I can only apologise that it's such an ugly word. But in my defence, it describes a highly sustainable strategy. You'll have noticed by now that there's no shortage of academics engaged in the struggle to find ways of taking the heat out of consumerism in general. Their findings are clear: if only we were less fixated on owning stuff, we could manage our other desires, such as upgrading products, or possessing fashionable pieces with less of an environmental impact. One of the more credible ideas to limit the consumer churn is to focus on selling services, rather than products. This has been trialled, particularly in the Netherlands, with white goods such as washing machines. The concept is easy. Instead of owning a machine, you merely lease it. The company makes its money out of servicing and lease fees, rather than the short-term cash it makes by merely flogging it to you. There are so many things we buy that we rarely use. Number one on the list has to be power tools. A weekend DIY mission will probably just last that weekend, but the drill and all its parts will clutter up your cupboard for years. This is not a statistic that the global $23.4 billion power-tool industry is likely to share, but the average power drill is used for just four minutes a year – a slothful work rate by anybody's standards. So it makes sense as a consumer to join a tool-sharing scheme, or even to start one. This would make you a transumer, someone who rather than being burdened by actually owning a product, merely hires or leases it while it is useful and desirable, ready to relinquish it when a newer updated model comes along.

Imagine being a fashion transumer. For a monthly rate, you could access clothes and accessory libraries. When the 'it' bag you were using had lost its new appeal, you'd hand it back and replace it with another that captured your imagination. You wouldn't have to worry about having a fickle fashion gaze. I've often thought that in the West we lack a truly versatile garment like the sari. The sari's appeal is in its fabric and embellishment, not its cut. Increasingly, it has become subject to the vagaries of fashion: of course there are trends for colours, fabric and embroidery. But its shape alters as you do. It accommodates pregnancies, weight loss, weight gain – the whole series of shifts that we can expect to go through. Many women resent having to fork out for a maternity wardrobe that they don't plan to use again any time soon, which is why a maternity-clothes library from which you can hire outfits for your full term is a really strong idea. On a distinctly less practical level, you can also sign up to a handbag library. In the US, Bag, Borrow or Steal is regarded as the pre-eminent luxury rental service. Different levels of membership give you access to different levels of bag – if you care about the latest design you will pay more to be able to lease those accessories regarded as the seasonal 'must have'. Dress agencies that hired evening wear used to be relatively common – One Night Stand in London has been running for over two decades. Libraries and leasing fashion work on the assumption that we all have different levels of taste – not everybody needs or wants to be kitted out in the offerings of this week's *Grazia* – and different points at which we buy into trends. They don't necessarily attempt to curb our enthusiasm for fashionable clothes and accessories (which will upset green puritans), but they do work on minimising the effects.

Sadly, I'm not in a position to offer you any personal experience of the library idea. By the time I decided to sign up to a UK bag library, it appeared to have closed down, suggesting that there's some way to go before the British consumer gets to grips with the idea of leasing fashion. But what I can do is to seek out fashion projects that take a similarly innovative approach to ironing out the problems endemic in our wardrobe. So, while I appreciate that the term 'community fashion' might not sound hugely promising, when I discovered the Antiform fashion project in Leeds, I felt I'd stumbled upon something important.

Here was a local fashion system that was doing what I had tried to imagine. I've long thought that there must be so many garments swilling around just in my postcode that everyone in the area could quite happily fuel their wardrobes from local offcuts. Well, Antiform takes waste from the Hyde Park area of Leeds and co-designs and produces with the local community, including a local Asian Women's Group whose members have particular skills, from embroidery to crochet, to embellish stock pieces. And once you've bought an Antiform piece you can bring it back for repair or customising, or swap it for another piece at a monthly exchange forum. 'There is no end of life for this product, because it can be continually upgraded, adapted, shared or swapped through the various workshops, events and services we run,' says Lizzie Harrison, who devised the project during her MA at the Centre for Sustainable Design. 'We want customers to move from being a passive consumer to an active user of fashion.'

ARE YOU READY FOR STYLE SELF-SUFFICIENCY?

The most active form of participating in the Perfect Wardrobe is to make your own clothes. How far you take the idea of being your own designer/ stylist and even maker depends on your capabilities, your patience and how much time you have. This is not a craft book – goodness knows, I'm not qualified to write such a thing, given that my last meaningful brush with a needle and thread was when I made a tea cosy circa year seven, and even that didn't show huge promise. And I have heard some sartorial scare stories from those who have attempted to fashion their own wardrobes. One friend tells ruefully about the time her eco-warrior husband decided to make an ethical jumper. He sourced organic wool from Orkney island sheep that eat mostly seaweed, spun it, made dye from home-grown woad and dyed the skeins varying shades of blue. 'If you add up the labour, I think that jumper cost in the region of £2,000,' she noted drily.

So, to paraphrase that famous slogan, I'd rather go naked than wear woad-dyed hemp. But, unexpectedly, somewhere along the road from the high street to the Perfect Wardrobe I have become inspired by do-it-yourself fashion. In his book *Through the Eye of the Needle*, John-Paul Flintoff describes his quest to produce his own clothes, having realised that there's a good chance his threads have been fashioned in a sweatshop. It's a valiant and very funny effort, often played for laughs – as when he experiments with nettle or scratchy wool pants.

Complete wardrobe self-sufficiency may be a fascinating idea, but in practice it's somewhere between extremely difficult and impossible. If you were to follow it to the letter, you'd need to grow your own fibre. Cotton is clearly out, which leaves eco fibres such as hemp or nettle. Having witnessed the frustrations of a farmer friend trying to grow hemp way out in westerly Wales, I know that's not easy – although I note that the environmental charity Bioregional successfully produced textile fibre from British hemp, and Katharine Hamnett made it into a jacket.

While John-Paul Flintoff's wife is so embarrassed by some of his home-made clothes that she won't let him wear them in public, others turned out acceptably well. At a talk I watch him demonstrate how to take an oversized old shirt and sew it to make a smart fitted garment. It takes him a matter of minutes. A highly respected menswear designer who is also there marvels at the home-made hemp jeans run up on a pedal-powered Singer sewing machine. Meanwhile, I've fallen in love with the self-made collection at diy-couture.com, and have become intrigued by the opportunities to buy eco fabrics by the metre for my own projects from websites such as offsetwarehouse.com, which can supply materials from wool herringbone to hemp denim, and source4style.com, an American site with some original, purpose-developed fairtrade prints. So much so that I have recently signed up for a short course in south London run by an outfit known as ohsewbrixton.co.uk that promises to teach me to thread the spool of a sewing machine and make garments with the emphasis on wearability. (One of the courses is promisingly entitled 'How to make trousers that fit'.)

I am not alone in this urge. In 2008 Argos reported that sales of sewing machines were up by 50 per cent on the previous year. Lest that be written off as some sort of blip, in April of the same year venerable retailer John Lewis boasted sewing machine sales up by 46 per cent from the previous year, and a run on haberdashery from dress-making scissors to buttons (up by 36 per cent year on year). Fashion colleges had to lay on more courses in customisation, recycling charity-shop finds, basic pattern-cutting and even customising vintage. Organic-cotton retailer Gossypium launched a kit dress, anticipating a revival of the seventies craze for kit fashion – patterns and fabric for novice sewers. But this time around the instructions could be found on YouTube.

It has become commonplace to see *fashionistas* on the tube pull out their knitting needles and balls of wool and while away the vagaries of the Northern Line's timetable with knit one purl one. I've lost count of the number of trendy knitting groups that have popped up. Tellingly, all this energy hasn't gone in a typical craft direction, which I will offensively describe as knitted cats and pincushions. It has loftier aims, including channelling some of the power back into our own hands – hands that vary in dexterity.

I haven't picked up my knitting needles for some time. In the mid-1980s I briefly attended a primary school that had presumably signed up to a curious educational experiment (or perhaps my teachers were just curriculum mavericks), because the bulk of each day was dedicated to learning spinning, knitting and calligraphy. I was not, it has to be said, very talented at the latter – I would have made a terrible monk – but I took to the spinning and knitting well, and surprised my parents by bringing home balls of natural wool spun by my own small hands. When I say my parents were surprised, they were actually more horrified, particularly Dad, who was of the opinion that school should be about acquiring some basic skills in maths and English. A more conventional primary school was sought out, and my knitting career came to an abrupt end. Now I wonder if that wasn't a mistake. Perhaps spinning and knitting were the two most important skills I never learned. In many ways knitting is the perfect cornerstone for the burgeoning ethical fashion movement. Not only does wool last for a long time, but the art and effort involved in making a garment mean that longevity is designed into it. In an age when business analysts have shown that many high-street fashion manufacturers assume that an item will be worn just a handful of times, home-knitted pieces will be worn on hundreds of occasions.

But the real win for knitters is the way they are able to control the fibre. They now have a chance literally to knit sustainability into their garments. Of course high-volume, badly produced, cheap knitting wool is everywhere, but increasingly there are some extremely sustainable yarns. Not only are knitters their own producers, but they are actually interested (some almost pathologically so) in the processes their fibre has undergone and how it will perform. I've moaned about how far removed we have become from clothes – not understanding labels or knowing what fibres our threads are made from – but knitters are the antithesis of this. They buy with the performance and the foibles of the yarn in mind, and are alert to all its characteristics.

The good news is that yarn manufacturers appear to be falling over themselves to cash in on our enthusiasm for a more 'natural' alternative. Recent additions by major yarn manufacturers include the O-Wool range from Vermont Organic Fibre in the US; Lion Brand's Nature's Choice range; and eco lines from the thirty-year-old British yarn company Rowan, under the Purelife label, including an organic wool, a naturally dyed range and a naturally dyed organic cotton. There's Blue Sky Alpaca's skinny organic (natural-coloured) and skinny dyed organic cotton, which is dyed with lower-impact dyes. Similarly, Sublime organic cotton (englishyarns.co.uk) is grown organically without pesticides through a BioRe cotton project, and is 'gently dyed using environmental products'. There are what we might call 'transitional' yarns, that have some eco merits – low-impact production, or from sustainable herds, or using alternative fibres – but cannot lay claim to being organic, such as Sirdar Eco Wool. Merino wool yarns are from sheep that haven't been mulesed. And conforming to green stereotype it is possible to knit tofu, or at least its byproduct, soy silk.

In fact there are all kinds of displacement fibres, free of animal dependency (or exploitation) or any hydrocarbon (oil) input, including soy and hemp yarns, alongside 'the first vegetable cashmere'. Lenpur is a cellulose (plant) fibre made from tree bark that's not at all scratchy, and indeed rather luxurious. Then there are pineapple, flax and milk yarns containing 30 per cent milk protein or even kelp.

Knitting is not the only option. There are many skills that can help the imaginative to pimp their wardrobes. On TV I've seen signs of limited customisation – the ubiquitous Gok Wan of the *How to Look Good Naked* franchise helps contributors (normal people) to 'customise' their high-street buys with ribbons, beads and all kinds of baubles. That's fine, but altering a high-street piece doesn't represent the full scope of customisation. More effective is going back into your existing wardrobe. Once you know how to embroider or customise, you can re-imagine some of the pieces already in there. Not knowing how to embroider, I came across a design student who was marketing the idea of an embroidery tattoo on clothes that had lost their sparkle. I handed her a pair of my organic cotton jeans in a dark denim, and she embroidered a little heart on the back pocket. It's pretty, and perked the jeans up no end. They went from a wardrobe staple that was frequently overlooked to a garment that I actively looked forward to wearing. Granted, it's a small transition, but it moved that pair of jeans up the wardrobe pecking order and away from the bin. That is definitely a move in the right direction, given that the average household chucks twenty-six pieces of wearable clothes into landfill each year – a statistic the Perfect Wardrobe must distance itself from.

THE NEW STYLE ICONS

Curating an ethical wardrobe is not just a question of supplanting bad habits with a set of 'good rules'. Free of the constraints of endless consumption, you can have a wardrobe that is more sustainable, more valuable, more enduring and more you. Of course, no covetable wardrobe is accomplished overnight. It takes time to experiment, source and research an aesthetic that fits. Who hasn't gone out at some point and bought a head-to-toe look from one store that supposedly guaranteed fashionability and peer respect, only to find that it ended up a damp squib? But still the head-to-toe 'get the look' look, often an 'affordable' version of a catwalk trend, remains our default position.

I have found that once this security blanket was removed, I was driven into the arms of alternative style icons that I would previously have thought too out-there or edgy to be part of my fashion life. I was wrong. By transferring part of my budget towards paying for the creativity and design skill in a piece, rather than just purchasing a prescribed look, I rediscovered some of the excitement I was looking for.

My brush with Junky Styling was to be a defining point. For fifteen years this brand and label has been pushing its own aesthetic envelope in London's Brick Lane. Its founders Kerry Seager and Annika Saunders began by re-tailoring the 'good' suits of City boys, tweaking them to bring them not just back into fashion, but into the vanguard of tailoring trends. Then, over time, they began offering wardrobe detoxes: they would rifle through, pick out garments with fabric potential but whose fleeting style relevance had gone, and rework them into clothes that were trans-seasonal and timeless. The label produces twice-yearly collections for London Fashion Week, and has even had a concession in Topshop. So by the time I dropped off a bag of my 'old' garments with the less than precise instruction to make me a 'piece', I was buying into well-crafted experience and form.

Two days later I picked up a made-to-measure cocktail dress with a cummerbund and bolero. It was one of the big fashion moments in my life. The dress is sleek and sophisticated. It does not scream 'I am sustainable!' It is like an intricate jigsaw in which my first suit – a two-piece blazer and skirt from Whistles in a sober black with skinny red pinstripe – has been reworked into three separate items. The whole thing is exquisitely panelled and put together. On closer inspection a panel at the base at the back of the dress had formerly been a sleeve. It retains one of its neat black buttons.

Don't worry, when I wear my Junky dress I don't go around boring everyone with its narrative. I don't need to, because it sells itself. It is a piece with genuine charisma, and it receives more compliments than anything I have ever owned.

At the beginning of this book you found me throwing my toys. Affronted by the way the clothes industry was damaging my personal style and my perception of fashion, I kicked against the multifarious abuses inherent in today's systems, and encouraged you to do the same. And I think we should continue this campaign until every single horror of the contemporary supply chain has been ironed out. But becoming an opponent of mainstream fashion is not just about the fight – it represents a chance to reconnect with what drew you to fashion in the first place, which I'm guessing had nothing to do with the enslavement of Asian women or one-size-fits-all jeggings. Like my ex-suit, now re-imagined and re-stitched into an intensely charismatic new piece, the Perfect Wardrobe offers a chance to re-imagine the way I dress, and to recreate the joy I first found in clothes. I could never go back.

ACKNOWLEDGEMENTS

Just as with every piece in the wardrobe, there are numerous hands and brains behind this book, too. I am indebted to all the garment workers, buyers, designers, recyclers, academics and shoppers who have spared precious time to educate me. Thank you to everyone who has worked so hard to prove ethical fashion as a movement rather than a trend, particularly my own 'crew', Livia Firth, Jocelyn Whipple and Orsola de Castro. An equally large number of people have cajoled me to this book's finishing line. I would not have got here without Araminta Whitley, Louise Haines and the wonderful Celia Hayley, who has put up with me since I was fourteen (and I am no less annoying now). Thanks also to all the champions of ethical consumerism and social and environmental justice who consistently ask the right questions. And to Bill and Claire Meharg and Ben Siegle, the best champions of all.

Lyrics from 'Daisy' by Karine Polwart are reproduced by kind permission of Bay Songs Limited.

NOTES

Chapter 1: Fat Wardrobes and Shrinking Style

3 '£2.8 billion': Lingerie Market Report 2010, from Research and Markets, quoted in Toby Walne, 'King of Cups', *Daily Mail*, 28 August 2010

3 '391 million pairs of jeans': 'The EU Market for Denim Jeans', *Outerwear*, CBI, October 2007

3 'three pairs': 'Jeans Market Goes from Rags to Riches', Mintel Oxygen Reports, June 2007

3 'four times the amount': 'Apparel Supply/ Demand in the United Kingdom: What Happens Next?', Textrends.org, Xavier Research, updated October 2008

3 'at least £625': J. Allwood, Laursen Soren Ellebaek, Cecilia Malvido de Rodriguez, Nancy M.P. Bocken, *Well Dressed?* (University of Cambridge Institute for Manufacturing, 2006)

3 'twenty-eight kilograms': Ibid.

3 '1.72 million tonnes': Ibid.

3 'almost the same quantity': Ibid.

4 'the former site': In old UK retail language (pre-Primark), the site was considered too far west of Selfridge's to be successful. C&A and Allders had both tried there and failed.

4 '70,000-square-foot': Lyn White, 'Primark Sets Oxford Street Alight', *Inside Retailing*, 5 May 2007

4 'a rumour circulated': 'The Battle of Primark: 3000 Customers Force Their Way into New Store', *Daily Mail*, 5 April 2007

4 'Fashions, after all': Actually,GBS's ire here was directed not at the nascent fashion industry, but at the medical establishment – the subject of his plays *The Doctor's Dilemma, Getting Married* and the *Shewing-Up of Blanco Posnet.*

5 'virtually stagnant': Richard M. Jones and Steven G. Hayes, 'The Economic Determinants of Clothing Consumption in the UK', *Journal of Fashion Marketing and Management*, Vol. 6, No. 4, December 2002, pp.326–39

5 'a reputed £3 million': L. Dishman, 'Kate Moss & Topshop Split: Why Breaking Up Isn't Hard to Do', CBS news website, http://www.bnet.com/ blog/publishing-style/kate-moss-and-topshop-split-why-breaking-up-isn't-hard-to-do/682, 31 August 2010. In 2010, ahead of her fourteenth collection for Topshop, it was announced that this would be Moss's last. 'Everyone was quite surprised it lasted so long', fashion-business lecturer David Shaw remarked to the BBC. 'Topshop is notorious for quick change. It brings in brands and loses brands...Celebrity brands tend to have a product life-cycle, and where they go well, they go very well.' He suggested that customers may have had a little 'fatigue' with the designs. http://www.bbc.co.uk/news/business-11128953, updated 30 August 2010.

5 'Lily Allen's range': In fact, in 2010 Lily Allen showed that perhaps her true sartorial heart lay in a different direction from fast, value fashion when she launched a vintage shop, Lucy in Disguise

5 'a media phenomenon': Suzy Menkes, *New York Times*, Style section, 21 September 2008

6 'slim, slender people': 'Lagerfeld's H&M Insult', Vogue.com, 29 November 2004

6 'a tasting menu': Well, that's what he told *The Times*. N. Copping, 'A Preview of Roberto Cavalli's H&M Collection', *The Times*, 29 October 2007

7 'the histories of': Occasionally I show a flicker of hippiness. Wendell Berry is a US agrarian philosopher, poet and defender of environmental justice. He shouldn't be confused with those who want to save the world through yoga, as he is generally spot-on.

8 'its likely destination': Louise R. Morgan and Grete Birtwistle, 'An Investigation of Young Fashion Consumers' Disposal Habits', *International Journal of Consumer Studies*, Vol. 33, Issue 2 , March 2009, pp.190–8

8 'a huge 21 per cent': Allwood et al., op. cit.

8 'by a third': Ibid.

8 '4.1 items': Oakdene Hollins Ltd, Salvation Army Trading Company Ltd, Nonwovens Innovation & Research Institute Ltd, 'Recycling of Low Grade Clothing, Waste', September 2006

9 'an average of £228': M&S & Oxfam Clothes Exchange press release, 'Home is Where the Hoard is', YouGov, sent to author by Halpern PR, 28 May 2008

10 'After she'd been': Lucy Siegle, 'They've Gotta Have it', *Observer*, 5 November 2006

11 'Hong Kong, Taiwan and Korea': P. Gibbon, 'At the Cutting Edge: UK Clothing Retailers and Global Sourcing', Working Paper sub series on Globalisation and Economic Restructuring in Africa, No. xiv, Centre for Development Research, Copenhagen, August 2001

12 'just 29 per cent': R. Winterton, 'Restructuring of the UK Clothing Industry', *Management Research News*, Vol. 13, Issue 6, 1993, pp.25–6

12 '90 per cent': Richard M. Jones, *The Apparel Industry* (Blackwell, 2nd edn 2006), p.117

13 'A 1998 study': D.E. Uitdenbogerd, N.M. Brouwer and J.P. Groot-Marcus, 'Domestic Energy-Saving Potentials for Food and Textiles: An Empirical Study', Wageningen Agricultural University, 1998

Chapter 2: Faster and Cheaper

15 '£200 million': Laura Weir, 'Primark Oxford Street Flagship Takes £200m', Drapers, 9 July 2008

15 'one million garments': Dan McDougall, 'Primark in Storm Over Conditions at UK Supplier', *Observer*, 11 January 2009

15 'I don't wash socks': S. Giorgi, 'Influencing Consumer Behaviour Around Clothing' (Brook Lyndhurst, 2010). Presented at the annual RITE Group International Conference, London, 6 October 2010.

16 'ten short years': Jones and Hayes, op. cit.

16 'like Burberry': The Burberry factory in Treorchy, Wales, was closed in 2009, and the company's decision to leave its Welsh workforce on the scrapheap was met with opprobrium and celebrity noise: Ioan Gruffudd and Prince Charles made for a stellar remote picket line, and the chairman was summoned before a Welsh Affairs Select Committee ('Burberry Bosses to be Quizzed Over Factory Closure, *Retail Week*, 2 January 2007). The memory of this decision to cut and run appeared to be short-lived. An apparently revitalised Burberry was the darling of the fashion magazines just a few months later, when sales were revealed to be up by 7 per cent ('Burberry Ramps up Investment After Profits Soar', *Retail Week*, 26 May 2010).

16 'almost entirely on imports': Jones and Hayes, op. cit.

16 'vast retail empires': Power had begun to be concentrated in the hands of a limited number of retailers. In 1951, 60 per cent of all clothing sales in the UK were accounted for by retailers with fewer than ten outlets (tiny by today's standards); by 1994 sales of clothing in such stores had fallen to just 28 per cent. Lynn Oxborrow, *Beyond Needles and Thread: Emerging Changes in the UK Apparel Supply Chain*, www.hctar/org/pages/pub.html, June 2000

16 '£850 million': 'Green with Envy', Just-style. com, 9 October 2002

18 'exceeded £100 million': Nick Mathiason, 'Britain's Top Shopaholic', *Observer*, 9 October 2005

18 'a job lot of tank tops': Ibid.

19 'very vulgar': Liz Hoggard, 'Jane Shepherdson Now Aims to Turn Around Whistles After Parting Company with Topshop', *Scotsman*, 5 February 2008

19 'I know!': Author interview, October 2010

20 'I'm not entirely': 'Store Wars: Fast Fashion', BBC TV, 19 February 2003

20 '7,000 lines': Mathiason, op. cit. Academics have also made the point that there was just much more to choose from, and that this was another calling card of the fast-fashion phenomenon: 'Survey findings from the Harvard Center for Textile and Apparel Research indicate that the average number of products offered for sale by manufacturers has increased. UK companies, in general, have identified a comparable increase in product proliferation between 1991 and 1995, with not only the total number of products offered having increased, but also an increase in both the number of new products added to the range and the number dropped. The responses overall, therefore, indicate an increased fluidity within the product range.' Oxborrow, op. cit.

21 'two hundred designers': Kasra Ferdows, Michael Lewis, José A.D. Machuca, 'Zara's Secret for Fast Fashion', Harvard Business School, 21 February 2005

21 '12,000 are actually': Devangshu Dutta, 'Retail @ the Speed of Fashion', *Third Eyesight*, October 2002

21 'tantalising exclusivity': Ferdows et al., op. cit.

22 'seventeen visits': *The Money Programme*, op. cit.

22 'The girls in the office': Caroline Roux, 'The Reign of Spain', *Guardian*, 28 October 2002

22 '35 to 40 per cent': Dutta, op. cit.

22 '18 per cent': Ibid.

23 'within thirty days': Ibid.

23 'One study': Devlin and Yee (2005), quoted in H.K. Nordas, E. Pinali and M. Geloso Grosso, 'Logistics and Time as a Trade Barrier', OECD Trade Policy Working Papers, No. 35, 2006

24 'ninety to 120 days': Ibid.

24 'Genius': Reported in Amy Shields, 'Zara Power', *Retail Week*, 14 August 2008

24 'Crown Prince Felipe': Robin Dymond, Scum, Agile and Lean Methods blog, 24 October 2007

24 'forty-eight hours': GS1 Germany & WP7 Partners (partly funded by the European Commission), 'Supply Chain Management in the European Textile Industry: Problem Analysis and Expected EPC/RFID Benefits', 11 July 2007

24 '2.1 billion euros': Dutta, op. cit.

25 'twenty days slower': Gibbon, op. cit.

25 'Your underwear's': D. Kuo, 'Great Reasons to Attend an AGM', *Investing Strategy*, 5 July 2006

25 'It won't last': James Hall, 'M&S AGM: Sir Stuart Rose Faces the Shareholders', *Daily Telegraph*, 9 July 2008

26 'subject to rationing': Along with so many deprivations that my grandmother's generation suffered during the war, I had difficulty comprehending how unconcerned she was about getting married in a dress that was already in her wardrobe. This would have undoubtedly sent a modern-day bride into apoplectic meltdown. 'I didn't have any coupons left,' she explained calmly. She looks lovely in the photos, but imagine any of us experiencing a fashion denial like that today. (According to *You and Your Wedding* magazine, the average cost of a wedding dress in 2008 was £997.)

26 '£26 billion': 'Research and Markets', Clothing and Footwear Industry Market Review 2010 Report, 16 August 2010

27 'fell by 6 per cent': Jones and Hayes, op. cit.

27 'from twenty-five': This rather clichéd measurement using the archetypal 'working man' is from 'The Purchasing Power of Working Time' (IMF, 1998), and is a bit old-fashioned: A) Where are all the car workers now? B) In this era of dress-down Friday all week long, he probably wouldn't even want a suit, and C) Thanks to value fashion he'd probably only need to work for thirty minutes now in any case.

28 'just under 5 per cent': Deutsche Bank UK market analysis, 2002

28 'aggressive pricing strategies': Gibbon, op. cit.

28 'Arthur Ryan': Zoe Wood, 'Primark's Chief Executive Steps Down After 40 Years', *Guardian*, 11 September 2009

28 'I don't care': Ian Kehoe, 'The Very Private Ryan', *Sunday Business Post*, 8 January 2006

28 'When a journalist': Alice Wyllie, 'Does the Devil Wear Primark?', *Scotsman*, 9 August 2007

28 'His view would': Jenny Davey, 'Primark Oldie's Golden Touch', *Sunday Times*, 22 April 2007

29 'Verdict prophesied': '£1 in Every £4 is Now Spent on "Cheap" Chic from Primark',

http://www.dailymail.co.uk/news/article-413351/1-4-spent-cheap-chic-Primark. html#ixzz13Bx77c65, updated 30 October 2006

29 'Primark has moved': 'Primark Closes on M&S Share', Drapers, http://www.drapersonline. com/news/2008/03/primark_closes_on_ms_ market_share.htm, 28 March 2008

29 'Cherokee': 'Tesco Takes on Next with Cherokee Deal', *Independent Business*, 10 May 2002

30 'outdo each other': Richard Fletcher, 'Tesco and Asda Launch New Price War', *Daily Telegraph*, 5 June 2003

30 '£6,000 a minute': Charlie Gall, 'Tesco Reveal Record Profits Despite the Recession', *Daily Record*, 22 April 2009

31 'to have de-stigmatised': Gibbon, op. cit.

32 '[Primark] enjoys': Verdict Research, 'UK Value Clothing Retailers 2009'. This report examines the top-ten value-clothing retailers, providing key operating statistics, clothing and value clothing market share data and individual retailer outlooks. It analyses the key issues that value-clothing retailers face, both now and in the future, and includes forecasts for sector growth in 2010.

32 'highly fashion aware': Morgan and Birtwistle, op. cit.

32 '40 per cent': Wyllie, op. cit.

32 'Asda is just about': The revival of the Biba brand in October 2010 for Asda resulted in a war of words in the trade titles between Hulanicki and House of Fraser, which had another licensed Biba line with no connection to Hulanicki (the original owner). Hulanicki insisted that Biba was always supposed to be cheap, and that this was one of the ways House of Fraser had got it wrong and Asda had got it right. However, some evidence from suppliers – particularly silk suppliers – to the original label suggests that Biba was in fact an expensive label.

32 'F&F signifies': 'Profiling the Value Retailers', *Women's Wear Daily*, 20 August 2010

33 'Primark overtook Asda': James Hall, 'Primark Overtakes Asda as Biggest Low-Price Clothing Retailer', *Daily Telegraph*, 20 January 2009

33 'largest clothing retailer': Kantar Worlpanel fashion data reported in Suzanne Bearne, 'Primark Gears up for UK Growth', *Retail Week*, 1 November 2010

33 'sales rose by 6.1 per cent': Suzanne Bearne, 'Non-Food Retail Sales Rise in September', *Retail Week*, 21 October 2010

33 'the £1 billion barrier': J. Ayling, 'Tesco Clothing Sales Reach £1bn', Just-style.com, 20 April 2010

34 'A middle-class lady': K. Rushton and A. Bodhani, 'Child Benefit Cuts Threaten Indie Sales', *Drapers*, 15 October 2010

34 'a land-grab': L. Weir and G. Macdonald, 'Argos

Poised for Return to the Clothing Market', *Retail Week*, 22 October 2010

34 'strengthen its position': 'Uniqlo Looks for Large London Store Sites', *Retail Week*, 22 October 2010

34 'the biggest global': Paul McInnes, 'Fast Fashion is on a Roll', *Japan Times*, 8 October 2010

35 'Forever 21's fast-fashion concept': Nicola Harrison, 'Forever 21 to Make UK Debut in November', *Drapers* online, 30 September 2010

Chapter 3: Fashion Crimes and Fashion Victims

39 'jeans at £6': Richard Fletcher, 'Tesco & Asda launch new price war', *Daily Telegraph*, 5 June 2003

39 'any mention on the label': At the time of writing a harmonised EU system that would make it mandatory for clothes in the EU to carry 'country of origin' labels has been approved by the European Parliament but not yet by the EU Council of Ministers. Critics pointed out that even if it were introduced a manufacturer could still put a 'Made in Italy' label on a pair of shoes the sole of which was produced in Albania, and the uppers in India, as long as the shoe was mechanically assembled on Italian soil.

39 'one and a half billion pairs': 'Bangladesh: Investors Set up First Metal Button Facility', Just-style.com, 9 March 2010

40 'over seven billion pieces': Suhasini Singh, 'Richer Bosses, Poorer Workers: Bangalore's Garment Industry', Cividep-India, July 2009

40 'four Chinese items': T.M. Bruce Hines, *Fashion Marketing: Contemporary Issues* (Butterworth-Heinemann, new edn 2007), p.6

40 'half of all the apparel': Ibid.

40 'an estimated forty million': J. Hurley and D. Miller, 'The Changing Face of the Global Garment Industry', in A. Hale and J. Wills (eds), *Threads of Labour: Garment Industry Supply Chains from the Workers' Perspective* (Blackwell, 2005)

40 '101 stages': J. Merk, 'Birnbaum's Global Guide to Winning the Great Garment War: A Critical Review', paper written for the seminar on 'Pricing in the Global Garment Industry', presented 20–21 February 2003

40 'only twenty-eight days': D. Birnbaum, *Birnbaum's Global Guide to Winning the Great Garment War* (Third Horizon Press, Hong Kong, 2000)

42 'Over the past fifteen years': 'US Retailers: Responsible for the Global Sweatshop Crisis?', http://www.behindthelabel.org/pdf/Retailindus.pdf, January 2001

42 'So what about': 'Claudia Does Paris', *Vanity Fair*, November 2010

46 'Research suggests': J. Caldwell, 'Food Price Crisis: 101 Causes and Solutions to the Crisis', Center for American Progress, 1 May 2008

46 'For an adult': http://www.labourbehindthelabel.org/join/item/523-how-low-can-you-go?-support-minimimum-wage-increase-in-bangladesh

47 'it was upped': 'RMG Workers' Minimum Wage will Now be Tk 3,000 (Bangladesh)', Fibre2Fashion.com, 28 July 2010

48 'the labour cost': Author interview, October 2010

48 'An estimated 60 per cent': Merk, op. cit.

48 'According to Actionaid': 'Asda: Poverty Guaranteed', Actionaid report, July 2010

49 'Triangle Shirtwaist factory': Miriam Ching yoon Louie, *Sweatshop Warriors* (Scotch End Press, 2001)

49 'from neighbouring Bolivia': 'Argentina: Government Crackdown on Illegal Textile Mills', Just-style.com, 3 January 2008

50 'a helpful list': 'Major RMG Fires Since '90', *Daily Star* (Bangladesh), 27 February 2010

50 '24 were killed': 'Update on Bangladesh Garment Factory Fire that Killed 24', Clean Clothes Campaign internet update, 29 October 2001

50 'a fire at RR Textiles': 'Panipat Factories Told to Get Registered', *Express India*, 8 January 2008

51 'Akshai Jain': Akshai Jain, 'These Garment Factories Don't Need Tailors', *Wall Street Journal* online, Livemint, June 2010

54 'We have examined': 'Levi Strauss to Close Manila plant', Just-style.com, 12 March 2008

54 'he had paid over $3,000': 'Sufferings of Bangladeshi Workers', Migrants forum website, 18 September 2007

54 '*New York Times* investigation': S. Greenhouse and M. Barbaro, 'An Ugly Side of Free Trade: Sweatshops in Jordan', *New York Times*, 3 May 2006

58 'Industry estimates': 'About the Informal Economy', Wiego.org

61 'outsourcing the embroidery': Dan McDougall, 'The Hidden Face of Primark Fashion', *Observer*, 22 June 2008

62 'According to research': Debabrata Mondal, 'The Ready-Made Garment Industry: Global Chain of Imperialist Exploitation', *Marxist Theoretical Journal* (Kolkata)

62 'N. Madhavan': N. Madhavan, 'Tirupur's Nemesis', *Business Today*, August 2008

63 'thanks yet again': Dan McDougall, 'Primark in Storm Over Conditions at UK Supplier', *Observer*, 11 January 2009

Chapter 4: Tea, Sympathy and Auditing

65 'nearly 8 per cent': 'Everyone Knows How to Source – Or Do They?' Just-style.com, 28 April 2006

66 '60 per cent of Bangladeshi women':

Wecanendvaw.org (We Can End Violence Against Women secretariat website)

66 '80 per cent of garment workers': 'Bangladesh Garment Workers: A Cut Above the Rest', ilo. org (video)

68 '1 a.m. of 11 April 2005': L. Sluiter, *Clean Clothes: A Global Movement to End Sweatshops* (Pluto Press, Asia, 2009), p.49

69 '12,500 stores': 'World's Second Largest Retailer Migrates to Hypercom Integrated Payment Solution', http://www.rfid-ready. com/201002082914/worlds-second-largest-retailer-migrates-to-hypercom-integrated-payment-solution.html, 8 February 2010

69 'women will be replaced': Singh, op. cit.

70 '2,067 social audits': 'At a Glance', Carrefour. com, 2008

71 'It's a myth': At some point in October or November 2010, the BRC's online section on ethical trade/low-paid labour was subtly altered. The sentence 'If they are not able to meet these standards, contracts are ended and business is taken elsewhere' appears to have been removed. I have used the version that was in evidence for at least two years up to that time.

72 'use of prison labour': Rhys Owen Jenkins, *Corporate Responsibility and Labour Rights* (Earthscan, 2002)

73 'empty blister packs': Kitty Krupat, 'From War Zone to Free Trade Zone: A History of the National Labor Committee', *No Sweat* (Verso, 1999), p.51

73 'A lot of money': Dan McDougall, 'Embroidered T-Shirt, Price: £4. Cost: Misery', BBC online news, 2008

74 'Workers who make': S. Joseph, *A New Front: The Nike Case, Corporations and Transnational Human Rights Litigation* (Hart Publishing, 2004)

75 'consumers were starting': There are many contemporary surveys that describe this: see A. Fung, D. O'Rourke and C. Sabel, *Can we Put an End to Sweatshops?* (Beacon Press, Boston, 2001), p.15

76 'audits have become': Jill Louise Esbenshade, *Monitoring Sweatshops* (Temple University Press, 2004)

76 'eighty in-house employees': J. Hollender and B. Breen, *The Responsibility Revolution: How the Next Generation of Businesses Will Win* (Jossey Bass, 2010)

76 '609 factories': M. Hearson, 'Cashing In', Clean Clothes Campaign

76 'Tesco increased': L. Morrell, 'Ethical Trading: The Moral Maze', *Retail Week*, 24 September 2010

77 'If you don't work': T.A. Frank, 'Confessions of a Sweatshop Inspector', *Washington Monthly*, April 2008

78 'One former inspector': Joshua Samuel Brown, 'Confessions of a Sweatshop Inspector', www. monitor.net/monitor, 1 September 2001

83 'The estimated amount': Doug Miller, 'Towards Sustainable Labour Costing in the Global Apparel Industry: Some Evidence from UK Fashion Retail', October 2010

84 'Most companies negotiate': Ibid.

85 'When buyers visit': Singh, op. cit.

Chapter 5: In the Lap of Luxury

87 'emergency debit cards': '$2000 Debit Cards for Katrina Victims: Families at Astrodome are to Get them Today', Associated Press, 9 August 2005

87 'Within hours': Reports of FEMA cards used to buy luxury goods are recorded in the Congressional Record, Vol. 151, Pt 15, 20803, 21 September 2005

88 '$800 each': T. Ravistack, 'Gulf Coast Residents Told to Use Aid for Recovery Only', *Washington Times*, 30 September 2005

88 'profiteering ghouls': As reported by K. Howley, 'Vuitton Values, Culture and Reviews', ProQuest, Vol. 39, Issue 10, 1 March 2008

89 'It took ten embroiderers': S. Hardach, '"Tiny Hands" Let Paris Haute Couture Sparkle', Reuters, 26 January 2010

89 'Shopping in the value sector': A. Hodson, 'Fashionistas are Going Cheap', *Guardian*, 20 July 2005

89 'careering around shops': Sarah Mower, 'Chic to be a Cheapskate', *Evening Standard*, 20 May 2005

89 'I was the first': Sarah Mower, 'Clothes are Fun – Take Them Seriously', *Daily Telegraph*, 10 January 2007

90 'According to legend': Obituary of Jean Louis Dumas, *Daily Telegraph*, 3 May 2010

90 '£11,000 for a grey croc model': William Shaw, 'Who Spends £11,000 on a Handbag?' *Observer*, 28 October 2001

90 'Victoria Beckham': T. Abraham, 'Bag Lady: Victoria Beckham's 100-Strong Birkin Bag Collection that's Worth £1.5m', *Daily Mail*, 20 May 2009

90 'Michael Tonello': M. Tonello, *Bringing Home the Birkin: My Life in Hot Pursuit of the World's Most Coveted Handbag* (HarperCollins, 2008)

90 'A woman walks into': K. Wexler, '"Birkin Man" Made his Fortune Chasing the Elusive Hermès Bag', *Miami Herald*, 30 April 2008

92 'the world's largest': A. Mull, 'LVMH Now Owns Over 17.1% of Hermès', The Purse Blog, 28 October, 2010, http://www.purseblog.com/louis-vuitton/lvmh-now-owns-17-of-hermes.html

92 'around sixty sub-companies': Bloomberg http://bx.businessweek.com/lvmh-group/news/

92 'the Christian Dior group': P. Olsun, 'Sharon

Stone's Own Bad Karma', Forbes.com, 29 May 2008

92 'part of French PPR': 'Out of Africa', *The Economist*, 26 November 2009

93 'Corporate tycoons': D. Thomas, *Deluxe* (Allen Lane, 2007), p.9

93 'We want to become': C. Passariello, 'Some Fashion Houses Bolster Lower-Priced Lines', post-gazette.com, 25 September 2006

93 'I find the whole thing': V. Kennedy, 'Your Life: Janet Street-Porter', *Daily Mirror*, 28 January 2008

93 'After its decade': Suzy Menkes, 'The It Bag is Over. Cue the Hit Shoe', *New York Times*, 2 February 2009

94 'Style-wise, colour-wise': Mower, 'Clothes are Fun', op. cit.

94 'Shoes are out to': Menkes, 'The It Bag is Over', op. cit.

94 'the world's biggest': J. Prynn, 'Shoe Heaven', *Evening Standard*, 23 September 2010

95 'Imagine you are in': http://www.selfridges. com/en/StaticPage/SG-Explore/

95 'In the past couple': N. West, 'Shoes, the Musical: The Shoe Must go on', *Daily Telegraph*, 19 August 2010

95 'drop by 7 per cent': Liz Jones, 'Death of the Cheap Shoe', *Daily Mail*, 14 February 2008

95 'a 35 per cent lift': R. Urwin, 'Mulberry Sales Growth in the Bag as Shares Soar', *Evening Standard*, 17 June 2010

96 '90 per cent of turnover': L. Armstrong, 'Gucci's Golden Girl: The Woman Who Makes it Cool', *The Times*, 1 April 2009

96 'just nineteen': Ronald D. Micham and M. Edward Mazze, *The Affluent Consumer: Marketing and Setting the Luxury Lifestyle* (Praeger Publishers, Westport, Conneticut, 2006)

96 '25,000 low-wage workers': Adam Lee-Potter, 'Designer Labels' Sweatshop Scandal', *Sunday Mirror*, 2 December, 2007

96 '*Schiavi de Lusso*': Broadcast by RAI-Tre, 2 December 2007

96 'an investigation by': Lee-Potter, op. cit.

97 'The 2007 WWF report': J. Bendell and A. Kleanthous, 'Deeper Luxury', November 2007

97 'In March 2007': C. Jones, 'The Significance of SRI', *Interactive Investor*, www.iii.co.uk, 13 August 2008

97 'This leaves thousands': Author interviews

99 'SWAP': Lynn Cook, 'Sewing with a Plan', *Stitches*, Vol. 5, No. 2, 2003

99 '£21.60 a week': ONS statistics for family spending and average annual income are expressed as gross. I have used the mean rather than the median. Sources: mean pay for women aged 30–39 from 'Average Annual Pay (Gross) for Employee Jobs in the UK in 2009', ONS, 2009 Annual Survey of Hours and Earnings, http://www.statistics.gov.uk/

StatBase/Product.asp?vlnk=15313. Average family spending from ONS, 2008 Family Spending, http://www.statistics.gov.uk/ statbase/product.asp?vlnk=361

99 '40 per cent', TNS Worldpanel, *Fashion Focus*, Issue 29, 2006

99 'received wisdom suggests': Stylists, style and *feng shui* blogs quote this constantly, but I'm unsure if it has been thoroughly analysed. It is more a sort of universal truth. The provenance seems to be the Italian philosopher Vilfredo Pareto's 80/20 rule, formed when he found that 80 per cent of the land in Italy was owned by just 20 per cent of the people.

Chapter 6: Fashion's Footprint

105 'fifty-five kilograms': Allwood et al., op. cit.

105 'nearly eighty million tonnes': Oerlikon textile report, 'The Fiber Year 2008', Figure 1

105 '1,074 billion kilowatt hours': J. Rupp, 'Ecology and Economy in Textile Finishing', *Textile World*, December 2008

106 'uses 3.2 per cent': L.M. Shinde, 'Pollution and its Control in Textile Industry', Fibre2Fashion. com, accessed 31 March 2010

106 'the research suggests': Allwood et al., op. cit.

108 'Demand for these fibres': Ibid.

108 '58 per cent of all fibre demand': M. Burke, 'Green Couture: Synthetic Fibres are Back in Fashion After an Ecological Makeover', www. chemistryworld.org, March 2008

108 'five hundred litres of water': Commonthreads Recycling Programme, Patagonia company history

109 'more than two hundred years': Sass Brown, *Eco Fashion* (Laurence King Publishing, London, 2010), p.164

110 'thick, black oil': John C. Ryan and A.T. Durning, *Stuff and its Secrets*, extracted in *New Internationalist*, October 1997

110 'Fibre assessments': K. Fletcher, *Sustainable Fashion and Textiles: Design Journeys* (Earthscan, London, 2008), p.15

111 'Africa's second-largest': A. Baier, 'Organic Cotton Projects in Africa', Pestizid Aktions-Netzwerk eV, http://www.pan-germany.org/ download/africaprojects.pdf, 30 January 2007

113 '90 per cent of waste water': 'World Resources 2000–2001', UNDP, UNEP, World Bank and the World Resources Institute, pp.25–6

114 'one in four': C. Wood, 'Can China Turn Cotton Green?', *Miller-McCune* magazine, 14 December 2009

114 '13 cents a tonne': J. Spencer, 'China Pays Steep Price as Textile Exports Boom', *Wall Street Journal*, 22 August 2007

115 'just sixty litres': Author interview

116 'a surprise inspection': Spencer, op. cit.

117 'fewer than 2 per cent': Linda Hwang, 'Water Management in China's Textile and Apparel

Factories', Business for Social Responsibility, April 2008

117 'Walmart sent teams': Spencer, op. cit.

117 '£500 million': D. McDougall, 'African Dream Turns Sour for Orphan Army', *Sunday Times*, 2 August 2009

117 'Our laws state': Ibid.

119 'The specific number': Author interview

Chapter 7: Picking at Cotton

123 'Ubiquitous items': 'Cotton accounts for 85 per cent of all natural fibres', 'Commodity Fact Sheet: Cotton', WWF, August 2009

123 '3.15 kilograms': 'The Great Cotton Stitch Up', Fairtrade Foundation report, preview copy supplied to author October 2010, authors unnamed

124 '14.2 kilograms each': Alejandro Plastina, 'Cotton Consumption Rebounds but Cotton's Market Share Falls', *Cotton Bangladesh*, 2005

124 'seventeen kilograms': 'The World Cotton Overview', Retail Cotton Consumption report, International Trade Centre, Chapter 1

124 '75 per cent': CCI and Cotton incorporated's Global Lifestyle Monitor and Cotton Incorporated's Lifestyle Monitor Survey

124 'It is impossible': Pietra Rivoli, *The Travels of a T-Shirt in the Global Economy* (John Wiley & Sons Inc., 2005), p.10

125 'By 1834': 'The Great Cotton Stitch Up', op. cit.

125 'Cotton is the pig': Erik Orsenna, *Journey to the Lands of Cotton: A Brief Manual of Globalisation* (Fayard, 2006)

126 'three hundred plus million': Eliza Anyangue, 'My Sustainable T-Shirt', Pesticide Action Network UK report

126 'about thirty million': Graham Burden, 'Somebody Knows Where Your Cotton Comes From', Environmental Justice Foundation, Tesco Clothing & Home, 2009

126 '80 to 90 per cent': Ibid.; CCI and Cotton Incorporated's Global Lifestyle Monitor and Cotton Incorporated's Lifestyle Monitor Survey

126 'just six': 'The Great Cotton Stitch Up', op. cit.

126 '$2,069,453 in cotton subsidies': Ibid.

126 'in a report': Kari Hamerschlag, 'Farm Subsidies in California: Skewed Priorities and Gross Inequities', Environmental Working Group, www.ewg.org

127 'over the top': Rivoli, op. cit., p.53

127 'just 2 per cent': 'The Great Cotton Stitch Up', op. cit.

128 'European producers': Ibid.

128 'in Burkina Faso': M. Helling, S. Beaulier and J. Hall, 'High Cotton: Why the United States Should no Longer Provide Agricultural Subsidies to Cotton Farmers', Beloit College, June 2008

128 'the cost of cotton production': Olvera and McGill quoted in ibid.

129 'It is estimated': Vince Cable, Summit Speech, Economist Emerging Markets 2010, Department for Business, Innovation and Skills, 15 September 2010

129 'fallen by a third': Geneva and Wardha bureaux, 'The Great Unravelling', *Economist*, 18 January 2007

129 'lost more than half': 'The Great Cotton Stitch Up', op. cit.

130 'During the early 1990s': Environmental Justice Foundation, 'Slave Nation' report, 22 February 2010

130 'Filmed and written': Environmental Justice Foundation, 'White Gold' (2006), 'Still in the Fields' (2009) and 'Slave Nation' (2010)

131 'US$1 billion': Environmental Justice Foundation, 'Still in the Fields' (2009)

134 'Fraud, Nepotism': N. Walsh, *Guardian*, 14 May 2005

134 'In those cases': 'Cotton Harvest in Uzbekistan 2009: A Chronicle of Forced Child Labour', http://www.hr-uzbekistan.info/index.php?option=com_content&view=article&id=605%3Acotton261009&catid=1%3Alatest-news&Itemid=48

136 'Craig Murray': http://www.craigmurray.org.uk/archives/2010/02/child_slavery_i.html

138 'over ten million hectares': World Cotton: FAPRI Agricultural Outlook, Food and Agricultural Research Unit, www.fapri.iastate.edu, 1 October 2010

138 'thirty million bales': Krishnan Mohan, 'Cotton Acreage up: Output May Touch 35 Million Bales', *Business Standard*, 13 July 2010

138 'sixty million Indians': R.B. India, V.R. Barwale, Usha Zehr Gadwal and Brent Zehr, 'Prospects for Bt Cotton Technology in Maharashtra Hybrid Seed Company, India', *AgBio Forum*, Vol. 7, Nos 1 & 2, Article 4, 2004

138 'fifteen grams of gold': P. Sainath, 'The Dull Days of White Gold', *India Together*, 8 April 2009. Author's calculations: 0.75g raw cotton per pair of jeans (http://chandrashekharasandprints.wordpress.com/tag/sweatshops/);1 quintal = 2.6792 maunds; 1 maund = 37.3242 kilos; therefore 1 quintal = 99.9 kilos

138 'To feed the huge': D. Saunders, 'Dream Farms Turning into Nightmares', *Globe and Mail* (Canada), 7 July 2007

139 '82 per cent': P. Sainath, 'The Largest Wave of Suicides in History', http://www.counterpunch.org/sainath02122009.html, 12 February 2009

139 'five quintals': Sainath, 'The Dull Days of White Gold', op. cit.

139 'Our *chappals* have': D. Bunsha, 'Farmers are Dying in Gujurat', *Frontline*, Vol. 24, Issue 11, 2–15 June 2007

139 '11 to 12 per cent': 'Living Waters: Conserving the Source of Life', WWF report, http://assets.

panda.org/downloads/wwfbookletthirstycrops. pdf, October 2003
139 'One third of a pound': M. Mulcahy, 'Organic Cotton: Growing Need and Supply', *Co-operative Grocer*, November–December 2000
139 '180 kilograms': Ron Herring, 'Is There a Case for Growing Cotton in India?', Department of Government and DGN, Cornell University, for the workshop 'Indian Cotton: Biology and Utility, Meanings and Histories', Cornell Unversity, 29–30April 2005
139 '1,867 kilograms': http://www.pakistan.com/ english/news/newsDetail.php?newsid=13086
140 '55 per cent': Sainath, 'The Dull Days of White Gold', op. cit.
140 '1,300 serious pests': http://unctad.org/ infocomm/anglais/cotton/crop.htm
140 'the second most prevalent' [and following statistics]: Environmental Justice Foundation and Pesticide Action Network, 'The Deadly Chemicals in Cotton'
141 'the most important source': L. Glin, J. Kuiseu, A. Thiam, D.S. Vodouhe, S. Ferrigno and B. Dinham, 'Living with Poison: Problems of Endosulfan in West African Cotton Growing Systems', Pesticide Action Network UK, 2006
141 'around US$40 million': 'The Deadly Chemicals in Cotton', op. cit.
142 'Dionne Bunsha's piece': Bunsha, op. cit.
142 'My daughters are': J. Hardikar, 'Farm Suicides Turn Children into Farmers', IPs News, 10 June 2009
142 'nearly 200,000 suicides': Data compiled by the National Crime Records Bureau; report by K. Nagaraj, 'Farmers' Suicides in India: Magnitude, Trends and Spatial Patterns', 2008
142 'nearly 70 per cent': P. Sainath, 'Nearly 2 Lakh Farm Suicides Since 1997', *India Together*, 25 January 2010
143 'From 7,000': 'Beginning to Turn the Synthetic Ship', http://www.greensteps.org/ stepone/wickers.htm
143 '2,700 litres': http://www.i-sis.org.uk/ farmersSuicidesBtCottonIndia.htm
144 'large-scale salinisation': Wolfgang Sachs and Timan Santarius, *Fair Future* (Wuppertal Institute, 2007)
145 'A UN report': Sabrina Tavernise, 'A Legacy of Salt Corrodes Uzbek Landscape', *International Herald Tribune*, 17 June 2008
145 'The majority of the region's': 'The Aral Sea', http://www.africanwater.org/aral.htm, May–June 2003
145 'Thirty-five million people': 'Ecosystems and Human Well-Being: Current State and Trends – Findings of the Condition and Trends Working Group', Millennium Ecosystem Assessment Series, 14 December 2005
145 'Conservative estimates': 'The Aral Sea', op. cit.
145 'over a hundred million tons': 'Environmental

State of the Aral Sea Basin', http://enrin.grida. no/htmls/aralsoe/aralsea/english/arsea/arsea. htm
145 'four hundred cases': P. Hveem, 'The Aral Sea Disappears While Tuberculosis Climbs', Médecins sans Frontières, 19 March 2003
145 'Life expectancy': 'The Aral Sea', op. cit.
146 'Soaring Cotton Costs': 'Cheap Clothes Era to End as Primark Warn Customers Prices will Rise Over Cotton Costs', *Metro*, 13 September 2010
147 'a fifteen-year high': Ibid.
147 'London's stance': V. Groskop, 'London Fashion Week Women Storm Catwalk to End Tyranny of Size Zero', *Guardian*, 19 September 2010
147 'Victoria Beckham': 'Skinny Victoria Beckham Bans Size Zero Models in New York Fashion Week Show', *Daily Mail*, 13 September 2010

Chapter 8: Woolly Thinking

150 'This is the yarn': http://www.knitters review.com/article_yarn.asp?article=/review/ product/080110_a.asp
150 'three to six goats': S. Reilly, 'The Golden Hair of the Goat', *Europe* Magazine (Delegation of the European Commission), 28 May 2001
151 'two cashmere sweaters per minute': L. Jones, 'How M&S Cashed in on Cashmere', *Daily Mail*, 11 January 2007
151 'while Tesco sold': S. Poulter, 'Oganic Food and Pink Tool Boxes Star Performers for Tesco', *Daily Mail*, 16 January, 2007
152 'He [Terry Leahy': Patience Wheatcroft, *The Times*, 18 January 2006
152 'thirty-six times higher': P. Kelbie, 'Scots Hire Korean Star to Save their Cashmere from the Chinese', *Independent*, 12 November 2001
153 '1.2 billion pieces': http://www.dgtoday.com. cn/Economic04.htm
153 'courtesy of Erdos': Access Asia Ltd, 'Made in China – China's Leading Brands', February 2002
153 'US$900 million': Fibre2fashion Report online, October 2010
153 '16,000 tonnes': Jiang Jingjing, 'Cashmere Environment Needs Better Balance', *China Daily*, 19 April 2005
153 'Evan Osnos': E. Osnos, 'That Low-Priced Cashmere Sweater has a Hidden Cost', *Chicago Tribune*, 28 December, 2006
156 'from 2.4 million': Ibid.
156 'it takes a goat four years': Evelyn Iritani, 'Cashmere House, Owner of the Tse Label, is Helping China Evolve from a Supplier of the Downy Raw Material to a Producer of Haute Couture', *Los Angeles Times*, 28 May 2006
157 'Donovan Webster': D. Webster, 'Alashan Plateau – China's Unknown Gobi', *National Geographic*, January 2002

157 'a 58 per cent increase': Ibid.
158 'nearly four hundred square miles': Osnos, op. cit.
158 '10.5 million sweaters': Ibid.
158 'Jennifer L. Butz': Edward A. Gargen, 'Not so Cozy Competition: Cross-Breeding Thrust Mongolia's Cashmere Industry into a State of Crisis', *Newsday* (New York), 27 August 2000
159 '18.5 microns': M. Safley, 'The Wool Industry Faces a Prickly Question', article for the Northwest Alpaca Association, 2003–05
159 'You simply have': Gargan, op. cit.
159 'We are providing': 'Cashmere, Environment Need Better Balancing', *China Daily*, 19 April 2005
161 'about eighteen': B. Lyons, representing the Australian Wool Foundation at the UN FAO, Proceedings of the Symposium for Natural Fibres, Rome 2009
162 'No man-made fibre': Ibid.
163 'less than 0.1 per cent': *Raw Material 2*, Novotex inhouse magazine, 2008
163 '1.1 million tonnes': Oerlikon, *The Fiber Year 2009–2010: A World Survey on the Textile and Nonwoven Industry*, Issue 10, May 2010
163 'the top three insecticides': Pesticide Action Network North Amercia. http://pesticideinfor. org, archived October 2005
163 'Studies of': A.D. Pilkington et al., 'An Epidemiological Study of the Relations Between Exposure to Organophosphate Pesticides and Indices of Chronic Peripheral Neuropathy and Neuropsychological Abnormalities in Sheep Farmers and Dippers', *Occupational and Environmental Medicine*, November 2001
163 'Biogenic methane remains': Lyons, op. cit.
163 'Australian academic study': W.K. Biswas et al., 'Global Warming Contributions from Wheat, Sheep Meat and Wool Production in Victoria, Australia – a Life Cycle Assessment', *Journal of Cleaner Production*, Vol. 18, Issue 14, September 2010, pp.1386–92
164 'the disappeared *estancias*': S. Worrall, 'Land of the Living Wind', *National Geographic*, January 2004
164 'severe drought': Oerlikon, *The Fiber Year 2009–2010*, op. cit.
165 'government business report': N. Owen and A. Cannon Jones, 'A Comparative Study of the British and Italian Textile and Clothing Industries', DTI Economics Paper No. 2, April 2003
165 '29,000 tonnes': The Campaign for Wool, Key Statistics. The same source puts world production at 2.2 million tonnes.
165 'it was almost double': L. Prior, Devonfibres. com blog
165 '16.5 million sheep and lambs': F. Galbraith, *Died in the Wool*, Viva report, 2009, available online or in print

165 '66p per kilogram': M. Wardrop, 'Prince of Wales Leading Wool Fashion Comeback', *Daily Telegraph*, 25 January 2010
165 'The cost of shearing': The Campaign for Wool, Key Statistics, prepared for the author by Mission Media
165 'wool prices in New Zealand': Wardrop, op. cit.
165 'Wool Week': L. Milligan, 'Woollen Plans', Vogue.com, 25 June 2010
166 'Over a billion sheep': Galbraith, op. cit.
166 'at least one breed': L.A. Thrupp, 'Linking Biodiversity and Agriculture: Challenges and Opportunities for Sustainable Food Security', World Resources Institute, http://www.wri.org/wri/sustag/lba-home.html (1998)
167 'North Circular products': 'Purls of Wisdom', *Daily Mail*, 15 November 2010
167 'the Wool Marketing Board': 'Izzy Lane in Uproar', daisygreenmagazine.co.uk, 19 August 2009

Chapter 9: Animal Prints

169 '12 per cent': http://kb.rspca.org.au/What-are-the-animal-welfare-issues-with-individual-shedding-of-sheep_114.html
170 'Boycott Wool': Galbraith, op. cit.
171 'PETA came to an agreement': 'Australian Wool Wins Historic Agreement with PETA on Mulesing', *Business Wire*, June 2007
171 'Following consultation': 'Fashion Shops Could Boycott Australian Wool', *Daily Telegraph*, 10 August 2009
171 'M&S made': C. Davies, 'Fashion Chains Threaten Australian Wool Boycott', *Guardian*, 9 August 2009
172 '154,000 tonnes': New Zealand Wool and Textiles industry report, August 2010
172 'Hugo Boss': http://group.hugoboss.com/en/196.htm
172 'by the summer of 2009': D. Gray, 'Mulesing Deadline Abandoned', *Age* (Melbourne), 28 July 2009
172 'between 40 and 100': Davies, op. cit.
172 'In 2009, 54 per cent': 'Wool Growers Under Fire Again', *Sydney Morning Herald*, 23 November 2010
172 '$1,334.1 billion': Consumer Goods: Global Industries Guide report, Datamonitor, March 2009, p.114
173 'fifteen silkworms': 'Silk Saris Take the Ahimsa Mantle', *Deccan Chronicle*, 18 July 2010
174 'Triassic period': 'Crocodilian Biology', Crocodilian Specialist Group, World Conservation Union, IUCN-SSC, http://www.iucncsg.org/ph1/modules/Home/aboutus.html
174 'two to three million skins': J. MacGregor, 'The Call of the Wild', TRAFFIC International Report No. 12, July 2006
176 '12,000 to 15,000 skins': S. Tedmanson,

'Hermès Breeds Own Crocodiles in Australia for Luxury Handbags', *The Times*, 12 June 2009

176 'Patrick Thomas': D. Jones, 'Hermès Breeds Own Crocs to Meet Bag Demand', Reuters, 8 June 2009

176 'Nearly 900,000': MacGregor, op. cit.

177 'James MacGregor': Ibid.

177 'at least four million a year': V. Fitzherbert, 'Cambodia's Snake Slaughter', *Geographical*, 1 January 2007

178 'Mushtaq Ahmed': 'Bangladeshi Businessman Takes Bite at Croc Market', Reuters/ITN, 27 August 2009

178 '280,000 skins a year': M. Lee, 'Prada Crocodile-Skin Supplier Sees Growth Despite Downturn', Reuters Singapore, 20 October 2008

179 'massive over-demand': *Crocodile Specialist Newsletter*, Vol. 28, No. 2, April–June 2009, IUCN, Species Survival Commission

179 'a burgeoning trade': MacGregor, op. cit.

179 'Zimbabwe company Innscor': 'Innscor to List Crocodile Unit', *Market News Zimbabwe*, 5 October 2010

179 'the fur of newborn': K. DiCamillo, 'Un-treehugger: Astrakhan Fur', Treehugger.com, 16 August 2005

179 'Trade in Wildlife': 'Crocodile Farming Booms in Zambia', Africanloft.com, 28 September 2008

180 'It is a fact': A. Abubakar, 'Skin Demand Threatens Nigeria Crocs', AFP agency, 12 May 2009

180 'more than four million': 'Scaly Fashion: An Upsurge in the Trend in Reptile Skins', Wildlife Protection Society of India, online doc 27022004, 27 February 2004

180 'It was duly placed': G. Nilsson, *The Endangered Species Handbook* (Animal Welfare Institute, revised edn 2005)

181 'Tom Rawstorne': T. Rawstorne, 'Pythons Skinned and Left to Die: The Shocking Reality Behind Fashion's New Obsession', *Daily Mail*, 20 September 2007

181 'reticulated pythons': P. Barkham, 'The Question: How Cruel is Snakeskin?', *Guardian*, 3 October 2007

184 'Peter Brazaitis': Nilsson, op. cit.

185 'We'd rather go naked': E. Day, 'Would You Rather go Naked? Not any Longer', *Observer*, 22 November 2009

186 'she was turned off': Milligan, op. cit.

186 'Clo-Values': Bruel and Kjaer, 'Technical Review of Thermal Comfort', No. 2, 1982

187 'A 2006 study': S. Mecheels, Bekleidungsphysiologisches Institut Hohenstein e.V., Test Report No. 06.4.5679, 2006

187 'Home storage': Fur Information Council of America, 'Why do I need to put my fur in cold storage, isn't my closet good enough?', http://

www.fur.org/faqs.cfm, accessed October 2010

188 'The US Humane Society': 'Toxic Fur: The Impacts of Fur Production on the Environment and the Risks to Human Health', The Humane Society of the United States, 29 January 2009

188 'Animal Aid contends': 'The Fur Trade', Animal Aid, http://secure.wsa.u-net.com/www.animalaid.org.uk/education/fur.pdf

188 'Peter Ingwersen': S. Pledger, 'Noir', *Glass* online magazine, 21 July 2009

189 'Teresa Platt': S. Reid, 'Should you be Faking it?' *Daily Mail*, 22 November 2004

190 'over 70 per cent': 'Europe's View of Canadian Seal Hunts', IFAW survey, Ipsos-Mori, 15 June 2003

190 'sustainable seal hunt': 'Seal of Approval', *Economist*, 11 March 2010

191 'more than 85 per cent': 'What Impact has Activism had on the Fur Industry?', 'Earthtalk', *Scientific American*, 15 June 2009

191 'Oslo Fur Auctions': S. Ward, Communications Director, US Mink, 'State of the Industry 2007', FCUSA (revised 21 June 2008)

192 'often operated by': 'Mink Farming in the USA', Fur Commission US, http://www.furcommission.com/farming/index.html

192 'The first ever report': Hsieh-Yi, Yi-Chiao, Yu Fu, M. Rissi and Dr B. Maas, 'Fun Fur?', Care for the Wild, January 2005

192 'A 2010 report': 'Bloody Harvest: The Real Cost of Fur', Animal Defenders Institute, 2010

193 'Some industry insiders': J. Kerswell, 'Fashion Crimes: The Cruelty of the Fur Industry', Viva! report, 2009

193 'around 270 farms': Ward, op. cit.

193 'one of the five worst': 'Toxic Fur', op. cit.

194 'A pelting plant is': Ibid.

194 'Neiman Marcus': 'Neiman Marcus Once Sold Animal Fur as "Faux Fur"',The Humane Society of the US, 10 November 2009

195 'Jan Brown': K. Fraser and S. Eyden, 'Betrayal of the Fur Turncoats', *Daily Express*, 8 December 2001

196 'the number of animals killed': Sandy Parker 'The Facts About Fur Trim', http://www.infu,rmation.com/pdf/hsus01.pdf, Humane Society of the US, 4 September 2000

196 'at least one animal': Global Action Network, http://www.gan.ca/campaigns/fur+trade/factsheets/the+problem+with+fur+trim.en.html

Chapter 10: Lust for Leather

200 'according to ecologists': K.R. Beg and S. Ali, 'Microtox Toxicity Assay for the Sediment Quality Assessment of Ganga River', *American Journal of Environmental Sciences*, October 2008

200 'the average for women': http://www.

homeworkersww.org.uk/what-we-do/
campaigns/footwear-factsheet
201 'over 1.5 billion': International Erosion
Control Association
201 '33 per cent': Henning Steinfeld et al.,
*Livestock's Long Shadow: Environmental
Issues and Options*, Food and Agriculture
Organisation of the United Nations (Rome,
2006)
201 '14.8 billion pairs': China Consulting,
Research and Markets Ltd, China shoes market
report, April 2008
204 '127 of the worst-polluting': J. Thottam, 'How
India's Success is Killing its Holy River', *Time*,
19 July 2010
204 'In 2001 he forced': P.P. Narain, 'Kanpur's
Tanneries Earn it Title of the Worst Polluter
of Ganga', *Wall Street Journal* online livemint.
com, 26 September 2008
204 'Joshua Hammer': J. Hammer, 'A Prayer for
the Ganges', *Smithsonian* magazine, November
2007
205 'Ashok Mishra': Narain, op. cit.
205 '2,100 tanneries': 'Indian Leather Hub
Targeted in Ganges Clean-Up', *Independent*, 9
March 2010
205 'worn out': Thottam, op. cit.
205 'Imran Siddiqui': Yasmeen Mohiuddin,
'Indians keep faith with Ganges dips despite
pollution crisis', http://www.dailytimes.com.pk/
default.asp?page=2010%5C01%5C25%5Csto
ry_25-1-2010_pg20_10, 25 January 2010
206 'At least one third': 'Water: Critical Shortages
Ahead', World Resources Institute, 1999
206 '5,000 pairs of shoes': Thottam, op. cit.
207 'Ajay Kanujia': Mohiuddin, op. cit.
207 'This solid waste': S. Sharma, 'Kanpur:
Chromium Disaster', Clean Ganga Campaign,
June 2003
207 'Research shows': 'Reflections on Hexavalent
Chromium: Health Hazards of an Industrial
Heavyweight', *Environmental Health
Perspectives*, Vol. 108, No. 9, September 2000
208 'methane flares': http://www.
blacksmithinstitute.org/files/FileUpload/files/
PCRs/PCR_Kanpur_11-16-09.pdf
208 'relatively unstable': 'Chromium', Committee
on Biological Effects of Atmospheric
Pollutants, National Research Council, 1974
208 'While Kanpur': Sharma, op. cit.
208 'Pamela Anderson': 'Actor Calls on Designers
to Shed their Skins', PETA India press release,
http://www.petaindia.com/200pam.html, 17
February 2000
209 'For a while': S. Srivastava, 'PETA "Skins"
India's Leather Workers', BBC News, 23 August
2001
209 '$68 million': 'PETA India Relaunches
International Campaign to Boycott Indian
Leather', PETA press office, 3 July 2006

209 '75 per cent': S. Shaheen, A. Hranandani, R.
Miller McCall, 'India's Holy Cash Cow', *New
Internationalist*, July 2010
209 'Hell for Leather': J. Wickens, 'Hell for
Leather', *Ecologist* and Ecostorm, 1 June 2008
212 'Central Pollution Control Board': Sharma,
op. cit.
213 'A fifth of the Amazon rainforest': http://www.
worldchanging.com/archives/010300.html
213 'from 30 per cent': M. McCarthy, 'Rainforest
Razed so Cattle can Graze', *Independent*, 31
January 2009
213 'the world's largest': R. Orihuela, 'Where's the
Beef?' *Bloomberg*, 23 September 2010
213 'two hundred million beasts': 'Brazil's Cattle
Herd in the Amazon', Reuters, 31 May 2009
213 '$1.9 billion': 'Slaughtering the Amazon, Part
Two: How Brazil is "Laundering" Amazon
Leather to Global Brands', Greenpeace USA, 1
June 2009
213 'from 153 million': http://www.fao.org/ag/
AGP/AGPC/doc/Newpub/landers/chap2.pdf
214 'Developed countries can': Luiz Inácio Lula da
Silva, 'Time for Housecleaning in Copenhagen',
Brazilian Government Sustainable
Development website, http://cop15brasil.gov.
br/en-US/?page=noticias/op-ed-lula-cop15,
2009
215 'second largest exporter': K. Abdul Sattar
Khan, Assistant Director, Council for Leather
Export, 'Fair Report' MICAM Shoe Event, 4–7
March 2000
216 'Nike changed': 'Nike Won't Use Leather from
Amazon', Associated Press, 23 June 2009
216 'Adidas, Walmart': 'Adidas, Clarks, Nike and
Timberland Agree Moratorium on Illegal
Amazon Leather', *Daily Telegraph*, 4 August
2009

Chapter 11: Dumped, Trashed and Burned

219 'At times the whole': M. Durham, 'Clothes
Line', *Guardian*, 25 February 2004
219 'In Uganda': X. Rice, 'Uganda Spurns Charity
Clothing', *The Times*, 2 November 2004
219 'Uganda, for example': Ibid.
219 'in parts of Nigeria': K. Tranberg Hansen,
Salaula: *The World of Second-Hand Clothing
and Zambia* (University of Chicago Press,
2000)
220 'Over one-third': S. Baden and C. Barber,
'The Impact of the Second-Hand Clothing
Trade on Developing Countries', Oxfam report,
September 2005
220 'The buying power': J. Brooke, 'International
Report: Used US Clothing a Best Seller in
Africa', *New York Times*, 16 February 1987
222 '71 per cent in real terms': N. Morley, S.
Slater, S. Russell, M. Tipper and G.D. Ward,
'Recycling of Low-Grade Clothing Waste',
DEFRA Contract WRT152, Oakdene Hollins

Ltd, Salvation Army Trading Company Ltd, Nonwovens Innovation & Research Institute Ltd, September 2006

222 'In research': Ibid.

222 'around 10 per cent': Ibid.

223 'Wastesavers ... L.M. Barry': Author interviews and visits, 25 April 2009 and 16 March 2008

224 '300,000 tonnes': Morley, Slater et al., op. cit.

225 'a German documentary': B. Schwarz, *Second Hand: The Global Business*, Der Spiegel documentary, 2006

226 'vast free-trade warehouses': Ibid.

226 'For example, in sport': K. O'Connor, 'Mivumba – the Ugandan Way of Life', Monitor/All Africa Global Media, via COMTEX, 18 December 2006

227 'more than $1 billion': Baden and Barber, op. cit.

227 'One study showed': N. Reynolds, 'Goodwill May be Stunting African Growth', *Globe & Mail*, Canada, 24 December 2009

227 'Karen Transberg Hansen': Hansen, op. cit.

227 'Professor Garth Frazer': Garth Frazer, 'Used-Clothing Donations and Apparel Production in Africa', *Economic Journal*, Vol. 118, Issue 532, pp.1764–84, October 2008

228 'Neil Kearney': Ibid.

228 'Mali is the biggest': Ibid.

229 'almost 18,500 charity shops': N.J. Morley, C. Bartlett and I. McGill, *Maximising Reuse and Recycling of UK Clothing and Textiles: A Report to the Department for Environment, Food and Rural Affairs* (Oakdene Hollins Ltd, 2009)

229 'SATCOL': T. Holland, 'The Colour of Money: Why Textile Theft is on the Rise', *Materials Recycling Weekly*, 12 February 2010

230 'two million tonnes of textiles': Morley, Slater et al., op. cit.

231 'over one and a half million tonnes': DEFRA, 'Sustainable Clothing Action Plan', Queen's Printer & Controller of HMSO, 2008, updated February 2010

231 'a report on waste': House of Lords Science and Technology Committee, 'Waste Reduction, Volume 1: Report, 6th Report of Session 2007–2008', Published by the Authority of the House of Lords, 20 August 2008

232 'Cynthia Magnus': J. Dwyer, 'About New York', *New York Times*, 6 January 2010

233 'The *New York Times* claimed': Ibid.

233 'We are currently': J. Ayling, 'Sweden: H&M Reacts to Trashed Garments Report', Just-style. com, 11 January 2010

234 '2.4 billion pieces': '2.4 Billion Items of Unworn Clothes in British Wardrobes', Oxfam online report, 28 January 2008

234 'DEFRA has warned': Morley, Slater et al., op. cit.

Chapter 12: High-Street Thrills and Spills

237 '£21 billion a year': 'Value of Fashion', report prepared by Oxford Economics for the British Fashion Council, published September 2010

239 'Stella McCartney': 'Stella McCartney for H&M in 400 Selected Stores', H&M press release, 4 November 2005

239 'one in four women': Mintel survey quoted by S. Mesure and J. Owen, 'Organic Cotton Boom Hits the High Street', *Independent*, 31 July 2007

240 'I am not a plastic bag': R. Mendick, 'Exposed: "I'm Not an Ethical Bag"', *Evening Standard*, 27 April 2007

240 'If this dress were': R. Bruntse-Dahl, review of H&M organic cotton, Smartplanet website, 2008

241 'Hamnett terminated the deal': R. Fletcher, 'Hamnett Pulls out of Tesco Range', *Daily Telegraph*, 28 September 2007

241 'Jeffrey Hollender and Bill Breen': Hollender and Breen, op. cit.

241 'Milton Friedman': M. Friedman, 'The Social Responsibility of Business is to Increase its Profits', *New York Times Magazine*, 13 September 1970

241 'the global Eco Index': J. Bauser, 'Eco Index: How Green are Your clothes?', Ethics Corporation online, 15 October 2009

243 '1.36 million tonnes': R. Henderson, R.M. Locke, C. Lyddy, C. Reavis, *Nike Considered: Getting Traction on Sustainability*, MIT Sloan Management publication, 21 January 2009

243 '$800 million a year': Hollender and Breen, op. cit.

243 'the world's most sustainable': 'How we do Business', M&S report, online M&S, 2010

244 'Sir Stuart Rose flew': 'Sri Lanka: M&S Opens First Green Garment Plants', Just-style.com, 25 April 2008

244 'A sister plant': J. Ayling, 'SLDF 2010: A Visit to the M&S Eco-Factory', Just-style.com, 11 November 2010

245 '101 stages': Birnbaum, op. cit.

246 'Truth in Fur Labeling Act': Hollender and Breen, op. cit.

246 'one of the fifty largest': 'Timberland Environmental Stewardship', Timberland press release, 2009

247 'Yves Béhar': Profile, TED speakers, http://www.ted.com/speakers/yves_behar.html

249 '800,000 workers': Hollender and Breen, op. cit.

249 'Code of Conduct': R. Stengel, 'For American Consumers a Responsibility Revolution', *Time*, 10 September 2010

250 '$19.5 billion': Hollender and Breen, op. cit.

250 'We're not for one minute': Author interview

252 'sweatshop conditions': *Fashion's Dirty Secret*, Channel 4 *Dispatches*, 8 November 2010

252 'Our Core Business Practices Programme':

'Statement re: *Fashion's Dirty Secret*, Channel 4 *Dispatches*', Ethicaltrade.org, ETI news website

254 'downloads are available online': http://www.labourbehindthelabel.org/campaigns/item/593-lets-clean-up-fashion-2009

254 'has been campaigning': S. Maher, 'Taking Liberties: The Story Behind the UK High Street', Labour Behind the Label report, Clean Clothes Campaign, War on Want, December 2010

254 'World Bank's Purchasing Power Parity': 'Asia Wage Renewal Put to Euro Retailers', Clean Clothes Campaign press release, 5 October 2009

255 'seven hundred million tonnes': Distribution, http://www.levistrauss.com/sustainability/product/distribution, Levi Strauss CSR report, online

255 'In September 2010': D. Love, 'It's Time to Ban Sandblasting', Levi Strauss, 7 September 2010

256 'Water-Less technique': E. Grady, 'New Water-Less Levi's Jeans', *Treehugger*, April 2010

256 'Michael Kobori': Author interview, 23 February 2010

256 '*Time Out*': *Time Out*, 3 November 2010

256 'Two years ago': L. Weir and A. Sant, 'Reiss Sets its Sights on High Street Fast-Fashion', *Retail Week*, 26 November 2010

Chapter 13: Change Your Knicker Drawer, Save the World?

262 'a BBC *Newsnight* report': '*Newsnight* Investigates: Cotton Picked by Children Appears in UK High St Clothes', BBC Press Office, 30 October 2007

262 'Walmart joined a boycott': J. Birchell, 'Walmart Boycotts Uzbek Cotton', *Financial Times*, 1 October 2008

262 'forty international retailers': Author interview with EJF spokesperson via email, 11 February 2010

263 'If we cannot import': 'Bangladesh Textiles Face Boycott Over Uzbek Cotton', Reuters Dhaka Bureau, 18 October 2008

263 'The EJF considers': Author interview with EJF spokesperson via email, 11 February 2010

264 'the top twelve brand': 'Organic Cotton Market Report 2009', Executive summary, published by Organic Exchange, Texas, 2010

264 'It delivers': K. Hamnett, 'My Battle to Green the Clothing Industry', *Ecologist*, April 2005

265 'twelve million pounds': 'Walmart to Boost Supply of Organic Cotton', Reuters New York Bureau, 7 April 2008

265 'ITOCHU': ITOCHU company report, 2009

266 'Better Cotton Initiative': Better Cotton timeline, bettercotton.org

266 'Cotton Made in Africa': http://www.cotton-made-in-africa.com/Article/en/13

266 'three cotton pests': 'Pest May Beat GM Insecticide', BBC News, 5 August 1999

266 'the sixteenth nation': S. Ali Bhambhr, 'Proliferation of Illegal BT Cotton', *Business Recorder*, 27 February 2006

266 'over 80 per cent': 'India's GM Cotton Plantation Seen Rising', Reuters New Delhi Bureau, 18 February 2009

267 'fifteen million hectares': GMO Compass, http://www.gmo-compass.org/eng/grocery_shopping/crops/161.genetically_modified_cotton.html

267 'Ron Herring': R. Herring, 'Is There a Case for Growing Cotton in India?', Cornell University, April 2005

267 'a Monsanto-sponsored study': 'Nationwide Survey by AC Nielsen ORG-MARG Underscores Benefits of Bollgard™ Cotton', AC Nielsen/Mahyco Monsanto press release, 26 March 2004

267 'it was six hundred': G.P. Gruere, 'BT Cotton and Farmer Suicides in India: Reviewing the Evidence', IFPRI Discussions Paper 00808, October 2008

268 'Standards for cotton': Fairtrade cotton facts, fairtrade.org.uk

270 'a plant or animal source': K. Fletcher, *Sustainable Fashion and Textiles* (Earthscan, London, 2008)

271 'just 10 per cent': 'Consultation on Natural Fibres', ESC-Fibres Consultation no. 04/4, Rome, 15–16 December 2004, citing original study IGG on jute, kenaf and allied fibres, 1989

271 'Estimates suggest': D.B. Turley, J.E.Copeland, M. Horne, R.S. Blackburn, E. Stott, S.R. Laybourn, J. Harwood and J.K. Hughes, 'The Role and Business Case for Existing and Emerging Fibres in Sustainable Clothing: Final Report to the Department for Environment, Food and Rural Affairs (Defra), London, UK', Discover Natural Fibres, Year of the Natural Fibre, 2009, FAO

272 'indistinguishable from rayon': L. Barrie, 'Comment: Bamboo Ban Hints at Crackdown on Green Claims', Just-style.com, 9 February 2010

272 'usually eucalyptus': Fletcher, op. cit.

Chapter 14: Buying Better Clothes

275 'Vanessa Friedman': V. Friedman, 'Sustainable Fashion: What Does Green Mean?' *Financial Times*, 5 February 2010

277 'only sustainable designer': A. DuFault, '*Project Runway*'s Lone Sustainable Designer, Gretchen Jones', *Ecosalon*, 26 July 2010

277 'Julie Gilhart': S.R. Oakes, *Style, Naturally* (Chronical Books, 2010)

279 'biomimicry': For the definitive word on biomimicry, see J.M. Benyus, *Biomimicry* (William Morrow, 1997)

281 'a fairtrade fashion pioneer': S. Minney, *By Hand* (People Tree, 2008)

281 'seventy fairtrade groups': People Tree online
281 'We don't just want': Author interview, September 2010
282 'an extra 1.5 tonnes per acre': Miney, op. cit.
283 'It is a totally different situation': Author interview, July 2010
284 'ISA Tan': 'ISA to Set up New Ecological Tannery with LITE', vip-fashion blog, 19 January 2009
285 'Laura Bailey's *Vogue* blog': L. Bailey, '*Vogue* Christmas List', Vogue.com, December 2010
289 'Rogan Gregory': Rogan Gregory biography, fashionpedia, My closet.com
289 'How can you be': A. Block, 'Pure Bono', *Mother Jones Magazine*, May 1989
289 'Craig McLean': C. McLean, 'Edun Regained', *Independent*, 30 May 2010
289 'the Slow Food movement': C. Petrini and B. Watson, *Slow Food* (Chelsea Green Publishing, 2001)
290 'Carl Honoré': C. Honore, *In Praise of Slow* (Knopf, Canada, 2004)
297 'Julia Roberts': A. Singh, 'Valentino Pays Tribute to Julia Roberts at Venice Film Festival', *Daily Telegraph*, 28 August 2008
298 '370 million gallons': (Evergreen) http://www.ebcltd.org.uk/documents/Textilesrecyclininginfo.pdf, Wastewatch, n.d.
299 'Sanjay Kumar': Author interview, January 2010

Chapter 15: How Not to Buy
301 'environmentalist's hat': L. Milligan, 'Vivienne Westwood Says "Stop Shopping"', Vogue.com, 9 February 2010
302 'This morning': J. Brown, 'Vivienne Westwood in "Stop Shopping" Shocker', *Drapers* online, 9 February 2010
303 'an advertising campaign': J. Donaghy, 'The Hard Sell: Ariel', *Guardian*, 15 September 2007
303 'Wash Low, Spin Fast': Plan A press release, Marks & Spencer internal press office

303 'Nearly 70,000 tonnes': Scottish Power, *Green Magazine*, Issue 1, Winter 2006
304 'other ecological issues': Trash Fash: Designing Out Waste, Science Museum exhibition, January 2011
304 'Isabella Blow': Author interview, May 2005
305 'neurotoxic and carcinogenic': J. Schoff, 'Green up Your Cleanup', *House and Home*, 2008
305 'leukaemia and tumours': M.C. Perrin et al., 'Tetrachloroethylene Exposure and Risk of Schizophrenia: Offspring of Dry Cleaners in a Population Birth Cohort, Preliminary Findings', *Schizophrenia Research*, November 2006
305 'concentration of perc': M.M. Verberk and T.M.L. Scheffers, 'Tetrachloroethylene in Exhaled Air of Residents Near Dry-Cleaning Shops', University of Amsterdam, 1979, available online
305 '150 GreenEarth cleaners': Author interview, 2009
307 'the Society of Master Shoe Repairers': Author interview, 2009
307 'The service was reinstated': O. Horton, 'Mending Habits', New York Times, 17 September 2008
310 'four minutes a year': L. Siegle, 'Is it Better to Buy, Lease or Borrow?', *Observer*, 7 September 2008
312 'Lizzie Harrison': Author interview
312 'John-Paul Flintoff': J.-P. Flintoff, *Through the Eye of the Needle* (Permanent Publications, 2009)
313 'up by 46 per cent': R. Silverman, 'Sewing Machines Make a Comeback', *Independent*, 21 April 2008
316 'twenty-six pieces': Trash Fash: Designing Out Waste, Science Museum exhibition, January 2011

INDEX